The Polity of the School

Lexington Books Politics of Education Series
Frederick M. Wirt, Editor

Michael W. Kirst, ed., *State, School, and Politics: Research Directions*

Joel S. Berke, Michael W. Kirst, *Federal Aid to Education: Who Benefits? Who Governs?*

Al J. Smith, Anthony Downs, M. Leanne Lachman, *Achieving Effective Desegregation*

Kern Alexander, K. Forbis Jordan, *Constitutional Reform of School Finance*

George R. LaNoue, Bruce L. R. Smith, *The Politics of School Decentralization*

David J. Kirby, T. Robert Harris, Robert L. Crain, Christine H. Rossell, *Political Strategies in Northern School Desegregation*

Philip K. Piele, John Stuart Hall, *Budgets, Bonds, and Ballots: Voting Behavior in School Financial Elections*

John C. Hogan, *The Schools, the Courts, and the Public Interest*

Jerome T. Murphy, *State Education Agencies and Discretionary Funds: Grease the Squeaky Wheel*

Howard Hamilton, Sylvan Cohen, *Policy Making by Plebiscite: School Referenda*

Daniel J. Sullivan, *Public Aid to Nonpublic Schools*

James Hottois, Neal A. Milner, *The Sex Education Controversy: A Study of Politics, Education, and Morality*

Lauriston R. King, *The Washington Lobbyists for Higher Education*

Frederick M. Wirt, ed., *The Polity of the School: New Research in Educational Politics*

The Polity of the School

New Research in Educational Politics

Edited by
Frederick M. Wirt
University of Illinois at
Champaign-Urbana

Lexington Books
D. C. Heath and Company
Lexington, Massachusetts
Toronto   London

Library of Congress Cataloging in Publication Data

Main entry under title:

The Polity of the school.

    Includes bibliographical references.
    1. School management and organization—Addresses, essays, lectures. 2. Education and state—Addresses, essays, lectures. I. Wirt, Frederick M.
LB2805.P7   379′.15   74-26311
ISBN 0-669-97618-0

Published simultaneously in Canada

Printed in the United States of America

International Standard Book Number: 0-669-97618-0

Library of Congress Catalog Card Number: 74-26311

To David W. Minar

"He was a Scholar, and a ripe and good one; Exceeding wise, fair-spoken, and persuading."

Shakespeare

Contents

List of Figures

List of Tables

Introduction

The scholarship reported in this book testifies to the renewed interest of students of politics and policy making in the schools as an appropriate focus for their inquiry. That interest has organized itself during the last few years in a Special Interest Group on the Politics of Education within the American Educational Research Association. In addition, special panels of recent conventions of sociologists and political scientists have centered on this interest. After the call by Thomas H. Eliot in 1959, the next decade saw a slow but accelerating research by political scientists and educational administration scholars.[1] By the early 1970s, there had developed a substantial research base which viewed the school as a political institution,[2] there were conferences dedicated to furthering research in this topic,[3] and all the signs were evident of a brisk scholarly endeavor. This book presents some of the most current of that research, selections which the editor finds most appealing in their use of traditional categories of political science and in their robustness of design and breadth of data. Another editor might well select other pieces, of course, but it is likely that those too would testify to the growth in vigor which the concept of "politics of education" has known in a brief time.

The Concept of "Political"

For those new to this sub- (or inter-) discipline, it might be well to make clear the meaning of "political" as it is used in these selections. This concept suggests that schools are miniature political systems which share major characteristics with more obvious and familiar political systems.[4] In at least two major respects, the about 16,000 local and 50 state school systems take on a political cast.

First, they are a major agent of political socialization, which means they are a major—but not exclusive—training ground for the approved beliefs and behaviors appropriate for novice citizens. No one disputes this as a school function, for it is observed in democratic or authoritarian polities. What instruments are employed—teacher, curriculum, texts—what values are taught—capitalism or communism, democracy or democratic socialism —and how well the teaching is done—little or much cognitive material— are all subjects of considerable differences of view. But at least from the time of the Greek belief in the need for all social institutions to reinforce their concept of community, termed the *polis* or polity, the school's function in political socialization has been a familiar aspect of education in Western Civilization.

xiii

There is a second manner in which schools can be seen as political, though this phenomenon is less well manifested than the first. This is the fact that schools, like any political system, distribute particular kinds of resources to their clients in a manner legitimated by the larger political system in which they operate. These resources may go to children or to adults, and, they may most visibly take the form of material resources—as in contracts for construction, bus purchase, or textbook selection. Furthermore, schools distribute social resources by performing for the larger society a "sifting and sorting" of the population to place individuals in social and economic structures. In the fifth century B.C., Plato urged this function on schools in order to prepare the "gold, silver and brass" citizens for their differing roles in society. Sociologists Warner and Havighurst were finding a similar shunting in smalltown America 25 centuries later.[5]

Both these supportive and allocative functions have been conceived as important aspects of the systems analysis framework for understanding the political process. In this model of the political system pioneered by David Easton, there has developed a widely used paradigm—or "prevailing metaphor"—which incorporates diverse differences in modes and institutions of politics. To find a political system, then, one does not simply look at kings and presidents, parties and cliques, elections and revolutions, or the other manifest signs of political activity in the human experience. Rather, the political system is understood to be that organization, found in every society, which is legitimized to engage in "authoritative allocation of resources and values." There is no need for the readers of this book to have that concept developed further. But we can suggest, and the research of this book demonstrates, that schools are themselves the mechanism for just such allocation, as well as a source of support for the larger political system through political socialization.

The selections that follow demonstrate in different ways the applicability of traditional, political analysis categories to schools. Because schools can grant boons of resources and values, what they do and teach can become matters of significant but differing preferences among citizens, thereby setting the scene for political conflict focused upon school authorities. This conflict matrix of the schools is no different conceptually than that found around legislatures, courts, or executives. How authorities use their powers, to whom they feel responsible, to what segments of society they respond, what differences eventuate from the use of different structures and procedures of power, how conflict may be successfully managed—all are continuing problems in educational administration and sociology, as well as in political science. On each of these matters, and more, the research here reported has something to say that is rooted in broadly based data and careful methodology.

The Re-Marriage of Politics and Schools

Not all the domains common to education and politics are treated here. One not touched upon is the historical relationship between the discipline of political science and the study of education. Classical political philosophy, which provided such a rich intellectual basis to the discipline's development, gave considerable attention to the nexus of polity and school. We need a fuller disquisition on the lines of thought that emerged from that tradition, which treated the role of the citizen and his training; much has been said since Plato took stylus in hand, but little of it is assembled in terms of this discipline's development.

When the relationship between political science and education is analyzed, however, it may well be organized on the principle that Heinz Eulau noted recently.[6] This principle is concerned with whether the school or the political system is to be regarded as the independent variable. One stream of thought will emphasize the school's independent influence upon the political system, as that school properly stands free from political influences in reinforcing, if not shaping, the values of citizens. Another stream of thought reverses this interaction, urging that the proper relationship should have the political system influencing the structure, process, and content of education. It may be that this distinction also draws the line between democratic and authoritarian philosophies, for it is the independence of the educational from the political system that is a necessary, but not sufficient, condition of modern liberal democracies. Many democracies do have schools dominated by their political systems—France and Sweden, for example—but these should be regarded as authoritarian strains in the systems, for no system is ever pure. Authoritarian philosophy, according to its own basic principle, must make the political system dominate all social institutions, including the schools.

While the study of politics did pay attention to the schools and their functions in this normative stream of ideas over a long period, the connection was severed in this century. The history of that change has not been traced yet, but some visible factors seem of likely significance. Political science was too new—maybe too irrelevant—to be an identifiable contributor to the reformation of the American schools in the last part of the Nineteenth Century. While this reformation was thoroughly prescriptive, it rested on normative notions of the desirable relationship between the corrupt, boss-controlled political system and the schools which were embedded therein. Political science in the first half of this century continued its normative focus while restricting empirical interest to the formal analysis of institutions and laws. Students of the latter, interested only in large-scale political institutions and laws of broadest scope emanating from national capitals, found the numerous low-population school districts too insignificant for that generation of scholars. The behavioral revolution in political science which began after World War II rearranged the landscape in that discipline. Yet until quite recently, as noted earlier, this change in concepts and methods ignored the school as a unit of analysis. Only in the 1960s and since have some scholars in that discipline joined others in educational administration and sociology to produce the kind of research that this book illustrates.

So it is that these selections are characterized by their newness, for none was published before 1971, and some were prepared especially for this volume. Also, they illustrate and illuminate major concepts rooted in political science, but in which the two other disciplines have an interest. Moreover, all demonstrate the behavioral model of analysis rather than the normative or prescriptive. This emphasis is justified, for this collection at any rate, because of the editor's concern that too much writing about education policy has been either excessively prescriptive (Why Johnny can't read) or heavily descriptive (How I mounted a successful curriculum in communication skills and went on to become a principal in Cut and Shoot, Texas). If there is one lesson learned from the social reform laws of the 1960s, it is that before policy prescriptions are offered there is the need to develop a research base, grounded in widespread data and analyzed by sophisticated concepts and methods.

Other criteria have been used for selection here. None is a case study, in the sense of examining only one portion of behavior in one place; one or so do limit the analysis to one school district, but within that parameter they examine and seek to explain different phenomena. However, all of these selections have a large data base and broad theoretical purpose, thereby increasing the power of generalization of the findings. Too, they are clearly written, no small feat for social scientists. Each is almost complete in text from the original source, although in all except one case, all footnotes but a vital few have been omitted from the original; in each case, readers are reminded of this fact and directed to the original.

Finally, this book is dedicated to a scholar and gentleman, David W. Minar. He was among that "happy band" who first began rethinking the political aspects of school policy in the early 1960s. Some of the material selected here rests upon his ideas about conflict management, and many more knew him and were glad to do so. There is always a hint of our own mortality when a companion is abruptly removed from us, but in this case over that feeling there is laid the personal regret that a special person has left us. While the person is gone, the memory remains, and with it the model of scholar and human being to which we all can aspire.

Frederick M. Wirt
Columbia, Maryland
November 1974

Notes

1. Thomas H. Eliot, "Toward an Understanding of Public School Politics," *American Political Science Review,* 53 (1959), 1032-51. For a review of the subsequent research, see Frederick M. Wirt, "American Schools as a Political System: A Bibliographic Essay," in Michael W. Kirst, ed., *State, School, and Politics: Research Directions* (Lexington, Mass.: Lexington Books, D. C. Heath, 1972), 247-81.

2. The most recent reviews of this research are found in: Laurence Iannaccone and Peter Cistone, *The Politics of Education* (Eugene, Ore.: Eric Clearinghouse on Educational Management, 1974); and Paul Peterson, "The Politics of American Education," in Fred Kerlinger and John Carroll, eds., *Review of Research in Education II* (Itasca, Ill.: Peacock, 1974), 348-89.

3. The results of a conference on the subject, sponsored by the National Academy of Sciences, are found in Kirst, *loc. cit.*

4. This thesis is fully developed in Frederick M. Wirt and Michael W. Kirst, *The Political Web of American Schools* (Boston: Little, Brown and Co., 1972).

5. W. Lloyd Warner, *et al., Democracy in Jonesville: A Study in Quality and Inequality* (New York: Harper & Row Publishers, 1949), chapters 5, 12 and August de Belmont Hollingshead, *Elmstown's Youth: The Impact of Social Classes on Adolescence* (New York: Science Edition, 1949).

6. This distinction is developed in Heinze Eulau, "Political Science and Education: The Long View and the Short," in Kirst, *op. cit.,* 1-9.

Part I
Input Channels of Activities

Introduction to Part I

Popular Inputs to School Policy

In the last part of the nineteenth century, American schools underwent a transformation in structure, process, and content. One of these changes was the centralization of school administration. Where characteristically there had been many neighborhood school boards and hordes of board members within a city, there emerged one board of few members responsive to all, not just a section, of the city. This triumph of Progressivism introduced to schools the "professional" model of not merely what was taught but how decisions should be made. Compare the differing context of policy making inherent in this centralized model with that in the Philadelphia of 1905 with its 43 district school boards consisting of 559 members.

The intervening years have shown that this model made possible the professionals' success in altering school policy in highly controversial, often fiercely opposed, matters, ranging from rural school consolidation to sex education. In the process, school authorities were given considerable latitude over innovation and absolute control over system maintenance. Only in the matter of tax levies, where the voters had to be faced regularly on a vital matter for this system, has popular control been extensive, significant, and usually restrictive. Yet, the linkages between these authorities and their constituencies could not be encompassed within any simple model of policy making in a democracy. Some of that complexity is addressed in this section, where we find scholars uncovering the kinds of forces that both expand and limit popular control of professional educational service.

Dale Mann summarizes the existing literature about voting behavior in school board or tax levy elections. The finding that citizens are usually uninformed and uninterested rests on extensive research and cannot be ignored. Mann's development of the normative theories that shape our thinking about the relationship of the citizens to his schools clarifies often implicit models of democracy. Too, he displays and applies the empirical data which test these models.

Some of the complexity of the linkages is further brought forth in the work of Brett Hawkins and his associates. Their study of the structural ties between political and school systems in 60 cities explores, among other subjects, the widely held belief of school authorities that they are "apolitical," somehow unattached to the political structures and processes of the community. As these scholars show, however, the two institutions display a relatedness that reflects distinctive status configurations from place to place.

3

It is this linkage between the social system of a community and its school policy making which directly concerns the contribution by Howard Hamilton. He explores a little used data base, survey attitudes about school referenda voting, to test a debated conceptualization about society and policy in urban systems. This is that a distinctive "ethos"—or pre-disposition about the relationship between self and society as mediated by the political system—motivates different policy attitudes. This contribution finds that the frequency and direction of voting in referenda reflect occupation more than any other status measure. By breaking through the ecological fallacy that afflicted much of the "ethos" debate until quite recently, Hamilton draws us closer into the reality of the subtle relationships between leaders and citizens in the polity of the school.

But there are some school politics which episodically generate enormous uproar. These turbulent issues turn the usual dry arroyos of school electoral channels into a flash flood, with the careers of authorities strewn all over the bank after it passes if they are not sufficiently resilient. School desegregation is such an issue, which is why it is featured regularly throughout this book. Christine Rossell has specially prepared for this volume a study of the course of desegregation in over 90 Northern cities during the 1960s. Here we see the flash-flood consequences for elected officials. But the phenomenon is complicated, reflecting no simple model of "throwing the rascals out." Rossell demonstrates that voter turnout did increase in the course of this conflict, but only somewhat. More significant for incumbent board members was whether the desegregation was court-ordered or not; if under court mandate, the board incumbents regularly were defeated, especially in higher status districts.

In short, we see here no model of a citizenry and their officials which fits the numerous—even naive—components of the rationalist version of democracy. By and large, voters participate very little in the opportunity to vote on either officials or policy matters; whether this reflects satisfaction with what they have, alienated indifference, or massive ignorance is not fully clear. However, when issues of school policy arise which directly affect them, two things can occur. They can either enter these decisional channels in larger than usual numbers, or those who have regularly participated can change their signals to officials. The result in these episodic events is not too dissimilar from what the rational model has as its ultimate purpose—the responsiveness and responsibility of political authorities. Indeed, these contributions suggest the reality of what Hawkins and associates found, that "the more politicized the schools the more the educational spending, support, and effort." That reality has consequences for those responsible for administering schools, as the succeeding section will demonstrate.

1

Democratic Theory and Public Participation in Educational Policy Decision Making
Dale Mann *

The desirability of participation by an informed public in educational governance is a traditional value in education. Understanding, which is measured here in terms of levels of factual information about school policy, is usually regarded as a prerequisite to involvement. This article examines some evidence about public understanding of education policy especially in urban situations, compares it to similar understandings of more general policy fields, and discusses some of the ways that educational understanding may be improved.

Two premises recur throughout this discussion of the understanding of public education. The first is that governance problems in public education are a particularly vivid case of a more general social tension between norms of merit and norms of democracy. We expect education to be decided by and responsive to people in general, but also, and simultaneously, to be technically advanced and thus determined by standards of excellence. Despite fervent wishes to the contrary, the two expectations do not always coincide. The meritocratic/democratic schism underlies the opposition between bureaucrats and lay people, between professionals and amateurs, between civil servants and politicians, between centralization and decentralization, between representation and direct participation. It is dividing every professionally run institution including hospitals, social casework agencies, and redevelopment agencies from the clientele served, especially in big cities. The tension between democratic and meritocratic norms is like a great social fault line, education is its San Andreas, and the big cities are its most likely epicenters. Where the fault has cracked, the distance across the chasm may be measured in terms of the difference in understanding that separates the two groups.

The second premise is that increases in understanding and involvement on the part of the public have a paramount goal—more direct control over institutions which affect their lives. In the past, educators have sought increases in the public's understanding of education so that the public

Reprinted with permission of the University Council for Educational Administration from Dale Mann, "Public Understanding and Education Decision Making," *Educational Administration Quarterly* 10, no. 2, Spring, 1974, pp. 1-18. See original for footnotes omitted here.

* Teachers College, Columbia University

would more easily and generously pay for what educators believed necessary. Efforts to increase community understanding have resembled advertising and public relations while product determination remained in the hands of professionals. The scope and intensity of the crisis of participation which many cities have experienced can only be explained by widespread desire to control the output of the school as a crucial social institution. Traditionally, the goal of public understanding has been to support the school. In this articles, the goal of understanding for the public is to increase the control which they may exercise over the school. Thus, the phenomenon of understanding is viewed here not as an output of public relations on the part of school officials but as an input to political participation on the part of communities. The distinction is critical to an appreciation of school/community interaction. The distinction may be regarded as the difference between being asked to support what has been decided and being asked to help decide what is to be supported.

In many respects education is like most other social services to which citizens must relate. There is superficial consensus that it is desirable for democratic citizens to take part in institutional, as well as societal, governance. We want people to be aware of problems and alternative solutions, and to make decisions that maximize their own and especially the public's interest. This model of citizenship is essentially one of reasonable and well-intentioned action; since it places great emphasis on understanding as precursor to action it can be called a model of rational citizenship.

The theoretical desirability of an informed citizenry as a prerequisite to rational social action has a long tradition. The immediate question is—to what extent do actual levels of public understanding approximate the rational model? What is the depth and scope of the information which people have about the public schools?

Levels of Factual Knowledge about Education

The most extensive studies of school/community communications to date is the series conducted in the late 1950s and early 1960s by the Institute for Communication Research at Stanford University. In one of the studies, *Voters and their Schools,* Richard Carter concluded that the extent of knowledge about the schools was "only slight." For example, respondents were asked to name the "superintendents of the local elementary and high school districts and two board members for each district." 58% could not name a single official, another 19% could name only one person. Respondents were also asked questions about six current issues of local education policy (overcrowding, taxes, etc.). In addition to recording responses to the particular questions, the researchers also noted whether or not the respondents volunteered any items of information in addition to that provided by the content of the question. Such additional responses are a rough indication of the retrievable or manipulable information base of the respondents. Even though there were six different items of current interest to stimulate such retrieval, 42% of the sample volunteered no additional information.

The last volume of the Stanford studies reflects data collected in the middle Sixties. A more recent study sought to measure information levels more directly. Paul Kleine, Raphael Nystrand, and Edwin Bridges surveyed a roughly random sample of residents of Cincinnati and Columbus. Parents and non-parents were asked nine questions about school affairs (the name of the superintendent, teacher salaries, per pupil expenditures, etc.). More than half the respondents were able to answer only two of the nine questions correctly. No one in the sample answered all nine correctly, but 11% answered all nine *incorrectly*. In one city, 86% of the sample was unable to identify a single member of the board of education. Questions like these deal with system-wide attributes and not with matters about neighborhood schools about which we might expect people to be more familiar. But Kleine et al., found that "citizens appeared to have little, if any, more understanding of school affairs at the neighborhood level than at the system level."

In national samplings beginning in 1969, Gallup sought to measure directly the state of information about local schools and education. The first study concluded that, "the public is only fairly well informed about the local schools and very poorly informed about education itself." In contrast to the situation in the urban places which Kleine, et al., studied, Gallup found that 56% of all adults could name their superintendent of schools, 47% could name the local elementary school principal, and 40% could name the local high school principal. On these questions people were somewhat informed but questions related to the educational process itself did not fare as well.

"For example, when those in the survey were asked to tell how they would judge a school—the things that would make them decide that a school is a good school—their answers reveal a very low level of sophistication. The criterion most often cited is 'qualified teachers', but the replies reveal that there is little understanding of what is meant by a 'qualified teacher'." The second and third most frequently chosen criteria of school quality were discipline and physical equipment! Gallup found that when asked questions about the percentage of local high school graduates who went on to college, and the per pupil expenditure in the local schools, 33% and 75% respectively of all the respondents were not even willing to make guesses. In a study conducted by Jeffrey Raffel of the University of Delaware, the indicator of elementary school quality most frequently chosen by urban parents was class size despite the failure of years of research to uncover a conclusive relation between class size and student achievement.

Sometimes even very dramatic events have difficulty stimulating people's awareness of education. A Harris poll of elementary and secondary school parents in New York City, taken less than a month after the end of the protracted 1969 teachers strikes found that one-third of the respondents could not choose between supporting the local Governing Board and the United Federation of Teachers. During the strike itself, 9% of the *parents* in the most involved district were unaware of the strike. In another study in the Stanford series cited earlier, Carter et al., sought to understand the school-related communications process during the ten days before finance elections in five school districts. They reasoned that because of the imminence of the elections and the obligation to make one's vote on an informed basis, levels of public understanding would be at their peak. But when they content analyzed 2,000 reconstructed conversations, they discovered that 70% to 80% of the content was not even potentially verifiable, that is, it could not be believed to be grounded in fact. Similarly, when they analyzed the sources to which content statements were attributed, 84% of all statements had no source or basis except that of the speaker.

Personal Interests versus Policy Knowledge

The same study made an important distinction about the knowledge base of people's participation in education decisions. While matters of school policy are by definition general and somewhat abstract, most of what people are concerned with about the schools is intensely personal and therefore somewhat idiosyncratic. The concentration on personal issues robs much citizen interaction of its relevance to education at a policy level. Again citing the Carter findings, "There is a lack of formality in communication because of its separation from the formal decision processes in educational policy-making. Personal interests dictate the focus of conversation, not the particular issues of concern to policy making." Thus, much of what is understood, is not relevant to decisional participation. It is one thing to have a generalized awareness of the schooling enterprise and quite another to have a stock of specific information about the education process that can be used to arm one's participation in policy decisions. Eugene Litwak and Henry J. Meyer have inquired into how knowledgeable urban parents are about educational systems by asking mothers, "If a student has a lot of 'C' grades in high school, what are his chances of getting into college?" 90% correctly estimated that 'C' grades decreased their child's chances of college entrance, but it would be wrong to conclude from such evidence that those parents would therefore be equipped to convince their local school administrators of the prejudices implicit in 'standardized' tests or the advantages inherent in criterion-referenced instruction. Knowledge specific to one child does not necessarily aggregate to knowledge specific to the system and it is that latter sort of policy-relevant knowledge that concerns us here.

We need also recognize a second distinction—that between knowledge about, and attitudes toward the public schools. Assuredly, a great many people have attitudes about the public schools but those attitudes or opinions are based on widely varying amounts of information. Thus, the Gallup organization's annual survey of public attitudes toward the public schools records what respondents feel are the major problems faced by education. While the surveys are extremely useful for other purposes, with the exception of the first in the series they have not addressed the question of understanding. (Interview items are carefully designed so that the question content itself provides an information base for the attitude solicited.) Kleine et al., refer to the distinction between knowledge and attitudes when they observe, "the knowledge deficiencies were most glaring when citizens were asked about the basis for their opinions about the local schools. Few could support their opinions with facts."

That public understanding is characterized by low levels of factual information about the educational process will not surprise very many school administrators. In fact, a good deal of their antipathy toward community involvement in educational decision making stems exactly from that cause. In some recent research, Mann asked a sample of urban school administrators whether or not there were areas of educational policy decision-making in which it was appropriate for lay people to participate. While only 7% denied absolutely that there were such areas, the majority of respondents hedged their "yes" answers. The lack of knowledge and understanding on the part of lay people was the most frequent qualification. The same research demonstrated that there is a high negative correlation between an administrator's self-assessment of his own expertise and his willingness to acknowledge any sort of binding relationship between the community's needs and interests and his own actions; i.e., the more expert administrators feel themselves to be, the less likely it is that they will accept a representational role. Thus administrators feel that their greater store of knowledge franchises and legitimates their decisions just as surely as it disfranchises and makes illegitimate the decisional participation of the lay person. The professional litany reinforces such attitudes by teaching that people who are not professionals are ipso facto not competent to participate in "professional" education decisions. In his *A*

Citizen's Manual for Public Schools, Mortimer Smith says, "Perhaps the first step any layman who is interested in the betterment of the schools should take is to attempt to enlarge his knowledge of educational history, philosophy, and theory in general." Thus the level of the public's understanding of education (and also the public's capacity to become informed) is already "known" and needs no further attention.

The traditional method of dealing with the public's lack of understanding has been to reduce their role in education decisions until that role could be supported by, justified by, or legitimated by their stock of available knowledge. Since the amount of participation is to be justified by the amount of knowledge, the role of the public has been suppressed far below a level of active involvement to the level of passive support. Thus, for most districts the role of the community becomes a problem in public relations, not an exercise in political participation. In public relations, attitudes are more important than information. School people are indeed concerned about the consumer's attitude toward the product, especially their support for it. But that concern focuses on the attitude itself and not on the information on which it is (or is not) based. As long as people were generally supportive of the schools, the reasons for that support were less important than the fact of its existence.

Explanations for the Existing Levels of Knowledge

To this point the evidence suggests that the public has very low levels of knowledge about education and that the gap between the knowledge bases of the public and the professional educator has been used by educators to exclude the public from participation in education decisions. The most widely held explanations for this gap are that the public (1) has little access to information; (2) little ability to interpret what information is available; (3) little motivation to make use of information; and (4) insufficient leisure time to devote to educational affairs.

Survey documentation of the inadequacy of people's store of factual information may be misleading if an otherwise uninformed public has quick and reliable access to relevant data. Unfortunately, this is not the case in education. Even in local newspapers, subjects other than education are stressed, and education coverage deals mainly with disjointed happenings rather than with the context or process of education which might relate such events to policy questions. Much of the stock of information which is held by parents deals with very particular school-related incidents. M. Kent Jennings has documented that, "The parents' basis clues inevitably come from their offspring." Much of the most policy-relevant information about education is to be found in books and journals not encountered by the average citizen, or for that matter by the average school administrator. The fact that the material in these specialized and fugitive sources, as well as in the official publications of most Boards of Education is not presented in layman's terms, blocks its use. Finally, overt and covert restrictions on public access to such relevant data as achievement records, teacher evaluations, and expenditure figures further impedes understanding.

Besides the arcane and inaccessible nature of the information, it has been argued that many people, especially those of low socio-economic status are unable to make use of even that information which is available. For example, in discussing the difficulty of involving poor people in the planning process for urban redevelopment, Harold Edelstone and Ferne Kolodner say: "Another kind of restriction is inherent in the inability of the poor to comprehend theoretical formulations and to conceptualize well enough to gain a complete understanding of causative factors to which a program should be directed." Herbert McClosky found in his research that while a person of low socio-economic status can identify abstract political and social principles he has difficulty applying them to specific situations. In addition, he is more likely to have conflicted political views, with a stance on a particular issue which contradicts his avowed political values. These contradictions and inconsistencies make it even more difficult to exploit an already limited information base.

Perhaps more important than the availability of information and the (putative) inability of poor people to interpret it, is the motivation to make use of what is already known. There are a lot of reasons why people in general and poor people in particular are not much motivated to learn about the operation of the schools in order to make their participation more informed. If the schools won't listen, won't change, can't help, or aren't the main problem, then why bother to learn about them? Where professionals refuse to listen to people and where, if they do listen, they fail to take action, then having become informed was a waste of the citizen's time. Similarly, to the extent that the poor perceive that schools can't significantly increase their life chances, and to the extent that the major problems of the poor come from discrimination and inequity in the non-educational parts of society (business, housing, etc.), then why indeed should they bother to become informed about schools?

The foregoing disincentives to informed participation stem from institutional sources, but self-deprecation is also an important depressant to informed participation. Carter found that 43% of his sample felt that education policy was too complicated for them to understand. A survey sponsored by the Office of Economic Opportunity of three possible sites for voucher plan experiments showed that while between 75% and 82% of the respondents felt that parents should have the right to choose schools for their children only between 25-40% felt that parents were well enough informed to make that choice.

The final explanation put forward for low levels of understanding has to do with the competition for people's attention. A lack of information about a given policy area among middle class people is often justified by referring to the number of issues that clamor for attention. Faced with problems of inflation, pollution, race, law and order, and education—specialization in one area and relative ignorance of the others is an acceptable response for the middle class. But, in addition to that sort of issue competition, the lower classes face a struggle for material existence that ordinarily pre-empts attention to civic affairs. The leisure and other resources necessary to civic understanding of public affairs are simply not available until private wants for survival and comfort have been satisfied.

With the partial exception of the purported inability of the poor to utilize information, the reasons put forward to explain the low information levels about education policy seem persuasive. The putative deficiency of the poor in calculating and interpreting information is however extremely questionable given the dominance of low motivation and scarce resources in suppressing levels of information. Until these latter barriers can be removed and information levels raised, it is impossible to evaluate calculating ability, and once those barriers are removed, we know of no reason to believe that such an "inability" will persist. On the other hand, educational policy is an extremely complicated field and decision making there is an intensely uncertain business. The inability (to use Edelstone and Kolodner's phrase) "to gain a complete understanding of causative factors" is shared by all social classes including, we might add, by policy-making elites in education.

Levels of Factual Knowledge about
Other Public Policy Areas

From another point of view, the evidence documenting the low levels of people's information about education does not seem surprising. In fact, it largely parallels the low levels found in other areas of public policy. In discussing the results compiled from 95 of the most reputable survey measures dealing with public understanding of a wide variety of public issues, J. P. Robinson, J. G. Rusk, and K. B. Head conclude:

Data from various polling organizations clearly show that the majority of Americans have paid relatively little or no attention to most international and national issues, and only relatively small minorities have possessed rudimentary information about these issues . . . Accurately informed persons are few—about 5 per cent of the population—whereas the chronic 'know-nothings' . . . (constitute) 5-20 per cent in the late 1960s. On most of the questions discussed here, however, a third to as much as two-thirds of the sample may be typed as ignorant, apathetic, or both.[a]

An idea of the flavor of much of this research can be had by considering the classic study, *The American Voter*. With a random sample that represented the 60% of the American people who voted in the 1956 Presidential election, Angus Campbell, Philip Converse, Warren Miller, and Donald Stokes, sought to discover what proportion of the voters had determined their vote by a calculation of something more than self or group interest. They could classify only 2½% of the voters as having made any sort of even grossly conceived link between the party of their choice and their own preferences about issues. On the other hand 22.5% of the electorate had determined their votes with no reference whatsoever to issue content! Converse refers to these people as "respondents whose evaluations of the political scene had no shred of policy significance whatever." These voting statistics refer to those people who are politically active enough to cast a ballot: the information levels of the roughly 40% of the electorate who do not vote even in Presidential elections is even lower. Thomas Dye and Harmon Zeigler write:

Some years ago, public opinion analysts reported what is now a typical finding about the low level of political information among adult Americans . . . Only about one half of the public knew the elementary fact that each state has two United States senators; fewer still knew the length of the terms of congressmen or the number of Supreme Court Justices.[a]

In summarizing this and other evidence, Lester Milbrath concludes, if it is "a duty for all citizens to be interested, informed, and active . . . then it should be obvious . . . that very few United States citizens measure up to that prescription."

Now what? Levels of public understanding about education may be low,

---

[a] From Alfred Hero, "Public Reaction to Government Policy," chapter 2 in J. P. Robinson, J. G. Rusk, and K. B. Head (eds.), *Measures of Political Attitudes* (Ann Arbor, Mich.: Institute for Social Research, The University of Michigan, 1969), p. 24. Reprinted by permission.

[a] From *The Irony of Democracy: An Uncommon Introduction to American Politics* by Thomas R. Dye and L. Harmon Zeigler. © 1970 by Wadsworth Publishing Company, Inc., Belmont, California 94002. Reprinted by permission of the publisher, Duxbury Press.

but they are also depressingly low with respect to all other areas of public policy. The fact that people know very little about the process of education is just one example of a much more general pattern of vivid lack of information about practically everything in the public sphere. (It should be noted that these are objective, not pejorative statements. Most citizens prefer to exercise their right to invest themselves in private concerns like jobs and families; their lack of knowledge is in some sense consistent with their values, and perhaps with their situations.) Regardless of how generous we may be in selecting the operational features of the rational model of democracy or in interpreting the evidence, it is hard to believe that people are, as a whole, informed about the operations of the schools, aware of alternatives, cognizant of probable outcomes form the alternatives, and in possession of a consistent set of values by which to guide their choices. Although there are fragments of these features distributed through the population, the distribution hardly seems broad enough and deep enough to encourage optimism about the prospects for widespread public involvement in the policy-determination process. Under these circumstances the rational model of informed action seems wildly optimistic.

Political Consequences of Rationalist Expectations

Rational democratic man was a creature who based his actions on reasoned consideration of information. Does his disappearance mean that he was made from straw? The answer to that question is both yes and no. Yes, social scientists might have warned us against a protracted search. But no, he is not at all a straw man, because the conception and concomitant expectations about such behavior are widely held by educators and especially by critics of lay participation. The politics of urban education is in large part a confrontation between masses and elites distinguished among other things by their vastly differing information bases. Since education is in part a technical subject, a great deal of the struggle for policy domination is conducted through the partisan uses of information and analysis. The situation gives the role of understanding its special importance as a political resource.

The conclusion based on the failure of the public to live up to the model of democratic rationality is that the public should therefore be excluded from participation. It is ironic that administrators should seek to deny citizens access to the decision-making process of schools on the grounds that the citizens' failure to live up to the informational tenets of the rational model disqualifies them for participation. The irony stems from the fact that the burden of research done in the last twenty years on the behavior of firms in the market place and of decision-makers in the public sector has been to exempt both entrepreneurs and administrators from evaluation according to the rational model. The reason for this exemption is quite simple; the real-world behavior of entrepreneurs and administrators was found to differ so radically from the rational model, that very little behavior could be explained by it. Entrepreneurial decisions were not governed by a goal of profit maximization, firms did not take indicated risks, they did not respond sensitively to competition. Administrators were found to be making decisions before they had searched for alternatives, their preference rankings were incomplete or inconsistent, their understanding of outcomes was found to be practically nonexistent. Administrative decisions turn out to be visceral as well as cerebral. They turn out to fall so short of the tenets of rational decision that a new term, "satisficing" had to be invented to describe the use of aspiration levels (instead of optimal goal-seeking) as a guide to real world decision making. Yet somehow administrators manage to muddle through even though their performance like the citizens' dramatically departs from the tenets of the rational model.

This no longer bothers students of administration who are replacing the rational model with new ones, more suited to the demonstrated limits of corporate and public decision-makers. Nonetheless, educators persist in disbarring citizens on the grounds of their low levels of understanding. The irony is compounded when we consider that educators bear a far greater responsibility for institutional teaching and learning than do lay people. The community's involvement at its most intense, can never equal that of the professionals, yet the professional has been exempted from the rational model while the citizen has not!

There are important political consequences to continuing to hold such high expectations of citizen knowledge as a prerequisite to involvement. The gap between the ideal and the real is a convenient way to discredit new participants. Policy decision-making thus remains concentrated in the hands of the more knowledgeable professionals, and the status quo of education, especially urban education, is maintained. Because of that, there is a clear need for new expectations for citizen performance, and then, built on those expectations, new ways to buttress and augment the citizen role.

This is hardly an argument for irrationality. Because citizens lack the information base necessary to support fully rational decisions (in any area) and because administrators fail to use what they do possess does not mean that we should sanction poor preparation or inadequate performance. What it does suggest is that we need to reexamine the models, and the concomitant expectations which we have been using to judge public understanding and its relation to policy decision in education. As long as we apply the wrong models, we also risk making the wrong prescriptions for improvements.

Political Mechanisms and Public Understanding

One way to reexamine this area is to recognize that involvement on the part of the public, especially the urban public, has a paramount goal—more direct control over institutions which affect their lives. If that is the case, then the goal of understanding on the part of the public is to increase the control which it exercises over schools.

The difficulty in education of incorporating the decisional involvement of citizens premised on a highly imperfect information base is not unlike the difficulties of incorporating the same sort of involvement in the polity as a whole. The seemingly unavoidable and reinforcing impacts of the size of constituencies and the complexity of public issues have forced most political scientists to the conclusion that participatory, or direct democracy, is even more impossible now than it has been in the past. Consider, for example, how big a meeting would have to be, and how long it would have to last, if everyone affected by a proposed rapid transit route were to participate in its determination. A permanently assembled committee of the whole for any urban area, even with the most sophisti- cated technical and media assistance, would never cope with even its metropolitan problems. To the extent that it could be determined at all, transit policy could be decided only at the expense of urban policy like welfare, housing, law enforcement, education, and health. But then what of that city's role in similar policy determinations at the state and federal levels? (The factors of size and complexity have obvious application to the politics of education. Decentralization tries to cope with size but we have yet to come up with anything except rabid ideology to cope with complexity.) Yet, since people seem to believe themselves to be demo- cratically governed and since, for the most part, they are reasonably satisfied with their form of government, political scientists have turned to a search for the "real" as opposed to ideal mechanisms of democratic government.

Most observers now agree that we have a "polyarchal," rather than a "direct" democracy. The basic tenets of polyarchy are that (1) elites decide issues but (2) followers have periodic opportunities through elec- tions to replace one set of elites with another. Because elites would rather not be replaced, competition between them for the support of followers keeps the system's outputs somewhat in line with the interests of non-elite participation. Under polyarchy, low levels of mass understand- ing are acceptable because the choices that the mass makes are very infrequent and confined to the endorsement of either one set of (informed) leaders and their policies or another set of (informed) leaders and their policies. This elite competition model of polyarchy deals with size and complexity by locating most decisions in the hands of a small group which makes the unwieldy mass of people "irrelevant" most of the time. Thus under polyarchy, the low levels of public understanding are not necessarily damaging since they are linked with low levels of involvement.

While no one questions very seriously the explanatory adequacy of the polyarchal model, there has been a great deal of debate about the normative consequences which flow from it. The main contentions are that elites benefit far more than do masses, that access to the ranks of the elites is unfairly restricted, and that the de-emphasis of citizenship atrophies those civic muscles that masses need to guard their interests. For example, consider the question of popular control over education in New York City. Clearly, a professional cadre ("elites") had historically decided the issues; the controversies turned around whether or not the "followers" could change the elites. It is also clear that the elites came eventually to benefit disproportionately from the City's educational system, that the elites fiercely guarded access to their ranks, and that the City as a whole paid a heavy price for its accumulated lack of experience in this area of self-government.

Polyarchy and Education Governance

Some even more serious difficulties attend the use of polyarchy to compensate for levels of citizen understanding in education. In the larger political sphere citizen understanding is augmented, or its absence is compensated for by five forces, none of which is very vigorously present in education. (These features have been selctively not empirically abstracted from dozens of such features which political scientists might adduce. They are presented here to provoke attention to improvement in the constitutional design of decision-making structures.)

The first of these is personnel competition between sets of alternative elites who are in and out of office. In theory, and to a considerable extent in practice, the competing elite groups of "ins" and "outs" can be expected to keep an eye on each other. The "outs" educate the public about the foibles and misdeeds of the "ins" and about their own accomplishments. But in education, credentialling requirements, state certification, homogenization by graduate schools of education, professional socialization, and professional domination of the recruitment and promotion processes all operate to assure that there are no alternative elites waiting in the wings. Instead, there is only more of the same.

Second, in the larger polity, a certain degree of institutional competition helps inform the public. Congressional committees read the *Pentagon Papers* into the public record, the Courts oversee Executive action, the Executive points with horror (and statistics) at the Congress, state agencies investigate local agencies (and vice versa) and out of it all there is more available and relevant information on political system performance than we have ever had on school system performance. At least part of the justification for the voucher plan is the nation that, if schools must compete for their clients, they will make more information available to the public, and parents, in order to choose schools wisely, will have to become informed about educational matters. But at the present the public schools simply do not have any effective competition.

Third, although most people fail to make effective use of it, the communications media assists public understanding. But, outside of a few major cities, there is no regular reporting of educational news by any popular media, most of what occurs is due to the public relations efforts of the schools themselves. Thus, even if they had a will toward greater understanding, most citizens would be hard pressed to keep informed of educational policy.

The fourth factor assisting polyarchy generally is that of political parties. While, inter alia, centripetal tendencies diminish ideological clarity, the parties nonetheless provide some issue continuity and especially a mobilizing basis that is lacking in education. (That is of course related to the lack of personnel competition mentioned above.)

The fifth and last factor which compensates for the citizen's lack of understanding in electoral politics but not in educational politics is that of groups. The group basis of politics has been promoted to near exhaustion, but groups undeniably perform an enormous service in stimulating, aggregating, amplifying, reducing, presenting, and pursuing demands to the political decision makers that would otherwise be atomized and unfulfilled. Mann has shown the presence of organized groups in communities to be associated with the responsiveness of school administrators to community needs and interests. Yet, in education, Carter found "in general, citizens know little about mediating agency usefulness, make little use of them and only occasionally have anything specific to say about functions of the more important agencies: school boards and parent organizations . . . Citizens committees are nearly unknown." Except around extraordinary (and for that reason transitory) issues there are very few effective, independent groups for local education, and thus most demands that arise in the community remain isolated, idiosyncratic, short-lived, and ineffectual.

The efficacy of any single one of these factors is open to considerable question. With respect to issue competition among party elites for example, Dye and Zeigler conclude, "it is probable that two thirds of the electorate make a choice unrelated to the issues raised by the competing candidates." [b] The argument about the efficacy of groups representing the interests of poor people is well summarized by E. E. Schattschneider's remark, "The flaw in the pluralist heaven is that the heavenly chorus sings with a strong upper-class accent. Probably about 90 percent of the people cannot get into the pressure system."

One purpose in introducing these features was to point out that none of the more or less meliorating aspects of the larger political sphere are very readily available to buttress the low levels of citizen understanding about educational policy. Yet, regardless of their preparation, the participation of lay people in educational decisions seems likely to be increased by several forces. Administrative decentralization has broken the school establishment into smaller and therefore at least theoretically more accessible units. Declining birth rates will also help reduce the foreboding bulk of schools. The increasing credentials level of the society removes some of the status apprehensions that formerly placed educators beyond reproach and the de-mythologizing of the accomplishments of the schools is also contributing to their vulnerability. Our growing appreciation of the educational contributions of non-school entities (families, peers, the media, etc.) further erodes the school man's monopoly and makes them more accessible to the sorts of pressures and dilemmas inherent in shared decision-making. Such overriding issues in education as race and finance cannot be solved without participation of the public. If that participation is to increase, then it behooves us to attend to the levels of understanding which will inform it.

One part might be through the frankly political mechanisms of the sort described above. But accepting them would imply an admission of the appropriateness of political concerns in educational decision making that is certain to trouble many school people. Extending participation to lay people—that is, to the school's democratic base—will inevitably move educational decisions away from the meritocratic, "objective" criteria and processes through which they are now supposedly made. Such a development would require the public admission of what is now a private reality: education decisions are made at least in part by calculations of: pressure group strength, the needs of special interests, bargaining, compromise, and especially conflict. Wider participation, more akin to general political participation seems likely to increase the amount of conflict in the system. In discussing school bond campaigns, Philip Piele and John

[b] From *The Irony of Democracy: An Uncommon Introduction to American Politics* by Thomas R. Dye and L. Harmon Zeigler. © 1970 by Wadsworth Publishing Company, Inc., Belmont, California 94002. Reprinted by permission of the publisher, Duxbury Press.

Hall point out that, "new publicity and increased campaign activity almost always increase the polarization of public opinion and escalate the intensity of community conflict."

A second and related change may be more congenial to educators. The salience of issues in educational controversies may increase. There is some evidence about the growing ability of the electorate to pursue its interests. Specifically within education, Robert Agger and Marshall Goldstein have shown that "lower class cultural groupings are not anti-education. Rather, the degree of approval which they exhibit is greater for programs perceived to be of benefit to them than for programs for the few others, the so-called academically able or the presumably underpaid teacher or administrator."

Undoubtedly it will be a difficult task to simultaneously increase the levels of participation and the level of public support for education. Over recent decades, the school establishment has dribbled away an enormous reservoir of diffuse support (i.e., a generalized feeling of good will which can be applied to a wide variety of needs). Rebuilding that diffuse support may require the development of political party-like mechanisms whose adherents would be organized around distinctive and roughly alternate pedagogies (and philosophies of social justice) and whose rotation through school posts might increase accountability and responsiveness. Some of the faint outlines of such a system are already visible at the level of the superintendency, but moving beyond that to the delivery level of the schooling system—to building principals, at least—will require profound changes. In any case, increasing the polyarchal features of educational decision making will still suffer from the shortcomings associated with that model which have already been identified. In addition, education as a field of decision making retains many undeniably and unobjectionably technocratic features (the role of expertise, for example) which will continue to vitiate most models of accountability until they are better understood.

In fact, the most likely reaction of educators to the pressure for increased lay participation is a new defense of their autonomy employing (ironically) education as a political weapon. Thus, we are likely to follow the long tradition in this country of resolving political problems by supposedly "non-political" means and institute educational campaigns to increase people's information level so that they can take part in educational decision making. In 1969, 65% of the people in the country said they would like to know more about the schools in their communities. In 1971, 81% of the people said they thought it would be a good idea for parents to attend a monthly class in order to find out more about education.

2

Good Government Reformism and School Spending in Cities

Brett W. Hawkins, Paul K. Villar, and Linda L. Knuth*

In the literature of urban policy analysis, a few comparative studies examine the impact of good government reformism on total city expenditures. Nonexpenditure correlates of reformism have also been probed, notably urban renewal achievement and the adoption of political integration proposals. In comparative studies of education expenditures, however, there is no explicit attention to the policy impact of good government reformism. Some comparative studies of school spending do not consider any political influences at all. Some look at the consequences of intergovernmental aids. Two studies do include reformist variables; but they do so only within a hodgepodge of political variables labeled "governmental arrangements" and "structural characteristics of school systems."

We think it worthwhile to remedy this omission in the comparative study of urban education policy. We undertake the remedy by investigating separately the expenditure consequences of general government (municipal) reformism and school government reformism. This refinement in the analysis of reformism's policy impact is imperative because, historically, the good government movement has affected schools as well as other municipal institutions. Our question is, do either or both phenomena in the formal decision process affect expenditures for public schools?

The conclusion of this study is that both reformist phenomena have a negative impact on education spending—school reformism more so than general. That negative impact, moreover, is independent of the socioeconomic environment. No previous study has found reformism to have an important effect on education expenditures.

Reformism as an Explanatory Concept

The fact that other scholars have not investigated reformism's impact on school expenditures is by no means the only reason for our doing so. We

---

Prepared for original publication in this book from a paper presented to the annual convention of the American Political Sciences Association, September 1973. Write senior author for footnotes omitted here.
We wish to thank Peter Lupsha for his comments on an earlier draft.

* University of Wisconsin—Milwaukee

do so for the further reason that it is reasonable to suppose, from theory and research, that reformism might affect education expenditures. The following section elaborates on this.

General Government Reformism and Urban
School Expenditures

The objective of the municipal reform movement was to depoliticize city government in order to make it more efficient in providing services. Reformed institutions were designed to remove politics as a basis of policy choice in order to stress managerial and technical standards. More than partisanship was attacked; so was access to decision making by unqualified persons and "partial," "factional," or "particularistic" community interests. Reformers sought specific changes in general government structure —notably nonpartisan elections, city-wide electoral districts, a trained manager as chief administrator, civil service, and a shortened ballot. Each change envisioned less political and more professional governmental management.

In contrast to these reformed institutions, unreformed ones presumably encourage political bargaining and popular access by groups that are residentially segregated, of lower class standing, or that constitute identifiable voting blocs. Reformers excoriated unreformed institutions precisely because of their accommodation of community factions.

Reformers wanted institutions less responsive to "factions;" and there is some evidence that they succeeded. Reformed institutions are associated with less policy responsiveness to lower class and ethnic-religious minorities. Communities with less diversity, in addition, are more likely to have adopted reformed institutions in the first place. Also, voter turnout is lower where reformed institutions exist, suggesting thereby a disproportionately middle class electorate in reformed cities. In community conflicts over governmental forms, moreover, there is more middle than working class support of reformed institutions.

To sum up, a considerable literature, some of it offering quite indirect evidence and some dealing only with goals, suggests that (1) reformed institutions expedite middle class inputs to government but impede the input of lower class or minority citizens (2) minority and lower class citizens support the retention of unreformed institutions, possibly because of (1). What does this imply for public school spending? For one thing, cities with reformed institutions may respond more in their education policy choices to the preferences of middle and upper class citizens. The latter may dislike government spending in general (as Lineberry and Fowler's negative correlations between policy and middle class variables suggest), but they often support generous local expenditures for education. One might therefore expect reformed general government to correlate positively with public school expenditures. (In fifty cities a reformed government index does correlate positively with general city expenditures, even when other possible influences on spending are taken into account. Also, manager cities spend more in total than non-manager cities.)

Additional credence is lent to this expectation by the "ethos theory," which suggests that reformist middle and upper class groups, in their "public-regarding" desire to advance the good of the whole community, may logically have supported both reformed institutions and generous spending for free, public education. A related line of ethos-like reasoning is as follows. Middle and upper class people may be *for* government spending generally, not against it, because they hope thereby to promote the good of the whole community. In addition to their support of reformed institutions, they would then support educational expenditures among other categories of spending.

On the other hand, the greater public access afforded by unreformed institutions might also lead to generous educational spending if people in unreformed cities wanted it. That depends entirely on public preferences; and aggregate data studies include no measures of preference. However, aggregate data studies can seek to determine if municipal reformism correlates with expenditures for public education, and if so in what direction.

Still another possible connection between reformism and educational spending derives from a straightforward application of Lineberry and Fowler's 1967 study. One might expect a higher correlation between ethnic percentage and educational outputs—whatever the direction, depending on popular values—in unreformed than reformed cities. In contrast, one might expect a higher correlation between upper-middle class variables and educational expenditures in reformed cities.

School Government Reformism and Urban
School Expenditures

Historically, the schools underwent a series of structural changes similar to those that took place in cities; and school reforms were similarly intended to remove other than professional influences on authoritative decisions. Changes included a switch from partisan to nonpartisan school board elections, from ward to at-large election districts, from school board (and bond) elections concurrent with other elections to separate school elections, and from another agency exercising authority over the school board's budget ("dependent fiscal powers") to the board being free of outside control ("independent fiscal powers"). Also consistent with reformist goals was the placing of property restrictions on voter eligibility in bond referenda, the use of a "superintendent" as board executive officer, the lengthening of the terms of board members, and a decrease in the size of the school board. The effect of the municipal reform movement on schools is perhaps represented by the strong trend toward at-large election districts. Of 30 boards elected in the 1890s by ward, only one was still elected by wards in 1972.

There is, unfortunately, no literature on school reformism's policy impact comparable to that on general government reformism. Hence we must call on logic, or extrapolate from the general literature, to discuss the possible effect of these reforms on education expenditures. Clearly reformed structures augment the historically self-promoted independence of the schools. They strengthen the decision-making autonomy of schoolmen who have generally claimed that their expertise in the uniquely important field of education justifies an extraordinary degree of autonomy. The less reformed and more political the schools, the less the schoolmen's decisional autonomy and the more the decisional access of nonschool people; among them lower class citizens, minority groups, officials of general government, and inexpert individuals.

In what specific ways do unreformed institutions lessen school officials' autonomy and inject nonschool political influences? Partisan elections are political because they connect the schools to an important base of general political mobilization and to conflict involving other governmental bodies. Ward districts are political because they facilitate the representation of minority or lower class elements that geographically segregated (a common phenomenon of urbanism, of course). At-large districts, on the other hand, reduce neighborhood identification as a basis of conflict over the schools. Holding school elections at the same time as general elections enhances the lower class voter's opportunity to select school officials and make budgetary decisions. So does the absence of property restrictions on bond voting. "Dependent fiscal powers" connect schools to the general political process, while independence means less accountability to the political interests represented by the major and his coalition. The independent school district is perhaps an extreme manifestation of the claim of educators that education should stand alone as a distinct and "non-political" program of government.

The question is, what are the possible expenditure consequences of school systems varying along a continuum from more political to more reformed? One line of thinking is that more reformed schools will spend more because their reformed character is a manifestation of successful middle-upper class inputs concerning schools—inputs that should also lead to the generous educational expenditures that those classes generally want. In addition, reformed structures may expedite the budgetary influence of schoolmen who are experts and thus presumably more potent under expert-accommodating (reformed) institutions. Like all of us, school officials prefer more investment in their product to less. Relatedly, reformed structures may lessen the impact of values (working class values, for example) that are not reinforcing of formal education.

One could also argue, however, that politicized school structures lead to higher expenditures. Indeed, former Philadelphia Superintendent, Mark Shedd, advocates placing control of the schools in the office of mayor because, situated in the mayor's cabinet, the superintendent would be in a better position to fight for a large share of the tax dollar. Political scientist Robert Salisbury also proposes that the school superintendent be a member of the mayor's cabinet. He suggests that under this arrangement the schools could compete more effectively with other city programs for available money.

In addition, institutions facilitative of lower class and minority inputs could lead to *more* spending if these groups, *or* their potent supporters, wished it. Less reformed structures might mean successful interventions in school decisions by city administrators who owe their incumbency to minority and lower class voters. Politicized institutions may thus reflect a generally politicized setting where, even if lower class and minority voters do not prize formal education, city administrations and community organizations successfully fight for generous spending on public schools.

Parallel to Lineberry and Fowler, finally, one might expect a higher correlation between ethnic percentage and educational expenditures— whatever the direction—in *unreformed* than reformed cities. One might also expect a higher correlation between middle-upper class variables and educational expenditures in *reformed* cities.

Main Questions for Analysis

No previous study finds reformism to have an important impact on education expenditures. Hence, the first question to which we address ourselves is, what is the magnitude of reformism's independent impact on spending? We are interested in the combined effect of school and municipal reformism (the reform movement's total contemporary effect) and in the independent effect of each. Because political scientists want to know whether the formal organization of a political system affects its policy output, we ask about the effect on educational spending of *municipal* government variation in reformism. This question has not yet been pursued systematically. In addition, because a considerable literature on education suggests that school independence has important consequences, we ask what is the effect on educational spending of variation in the degree of *school* government reformism? In other words, how important to higher spending is the independence traditionally demanded by schoolmen? Are "independent, nonpolitical" schools likely to get more of the tax dollar?

The second major question deals with direction. One could readily set forth directionally conflicting hypotheses about the relationship of municipal and school reformism to education expenditures. But that complexity does not eliminate the need to understand more about the political conditions under which cities are likely to spend more on public education; it just tangles hypothesis-making. At this stage it is simpler to ask: what is the direction of reformism's impact on school spending?

Finally, we ask what support there is in our data for expectations derived from Lineberry and Fowler's analysis of reformism and city government responsiveness to urban subpopulations.

Data and Indicators

Dye's sixty-seven city study already contains variables pertinent to these questions. In the absence of earlier studies expressly investigating reformism's impact on school expenditures, it is appropriate to begin with available data that are germane and add other indicators as needed. Hence we make use of Dye's data. Of course, our units of analysis are in no sense a probability sample: Dye selected them because of the availability of requisite variables from published sources (reported below). However, since our interest here is in explanatory questions about classes of variables, not in descriptively generalizing to some universe, the sample is not an obstacle.

The two studies most like this one are those of Garms and Dye. Garms found it "most difficult to devise measures of governmental arrangements," and Dye said that "the problem is to guess what governmental arrangements will have an independent effect on educational policy if any." In actual analysis neither Garms nor Dye expressly conceptualizes his political variables as measures of reformism. Also, they merge variables that describe the structure of general government with variables that describe the structure of school government. Their manner of merging the two phenomena differs, however. Dye notes that he has indicators of the structure of city government and also the structure of school government, but he then combines the two in an undifferentiated manner under "structural characteristics of school systems," "system variables," and "structural variables." Under "governmental arrangements" Garms combines (1) whether the board of education is appointed or elected, (2) whether board election districts are at-large or ward, (3) whether the tax assessor is elected or appointed, (4) whether another governmental agency has authority to reduce the board's education budget, (5) whether the business manager reports directly to the board, (6) whether there exists an effective state maximum tax rate, (7) the percent of full time teachers not on regular salary, and (8) the logarithm of the actual ADA of the school district. Not only does Garms unite school and general government attributes, he also appears to include an indicator of the quality of the schools—namely, the proportion of long-term substitute teachers who are not paid on the regular salary schedule because they do not meet certification qualifications.

Our indicators of general government reformism (most from Dye's data) with their rationales are:

1. —manager form, a basic item in the reformist agenda intended to provide expert administrative direction separated from mayoral politics;
2. —nonpartisan general elections, also a basic reform item, intended to separate municipal decisions from considerations of party politics;
3. —an appointed tax assessor, included because consistent with short ballot principles stressing better informed voter choices and the leaving of technical decisions to experts.

Our indicators of school government reformism are:

1.[a] —special elections for school board, included because concurrent elections facilitate the turnout of lower class elements and tie education to issues and organizations involving other public programs;
2.[a] —property restrictions on voter eligibility in bond referenda, included because the absence of such restrictions facilitate public, nonexpert, and especially lower class participation in budget decisions;
3. —no city oversight of school board's education budget, included because oversight means less budgetary independence for education officials;
4. —at-large school board election districts, a basic reform item, intended to minimize the representation of factional interests;
5. —nonpartisan school board elections, also a basic reform item, intended to separate education decisions from considerations of party politics.

Since most studies comparing political and socio-economic variables for their influence on education policy find the former to contribute more

---

[a] Indicator a supplement to Dye's data. Sources—Education Research Service Circular, No. 6 (November, 1967) and Office of Education," Public School Finance Problems 1958-1969" (Washington, D.C.: Government Printing Office, 1969).

to statistical explanation, we must consider indicators of the socio-economic environment. Community size, resource capacity, race, and class are the attributes of environment represented by our indicators. The indicators are total population, median family income, percent nonwhite, percent white collar workers, and median school years completed by adults 25 years of age or older.

Our dependent variables are common financial indicators used by Dye and others, or similar thereto. They are per pupil expenditures, local school support (proportion of school expenditures from locally raised money), and educational effort (per pupil expenditures over median family income and per pupil expenditures over property value per pupil). The last variable is not among Dye's measures of educational spending.

Because the idea of "ability to spend" is reflected in one measure of environment (median family income) *and* in several measures of policy, the reader might expect, on that basis alone, to find a sizable correlation between environment and educational spending. (More generally, it should not surprise anyone to find the capacity to consume associated with the fact of consumption—in this case of a governmental service all but universally extolled in American society.) Our measures of educational effort are intended to take into account an expected correlation between environment and policy simply because capacity is reflected in both. Each measure of effort expresses per pupil expenditures as a ratio of an indicator of capacity. Hence, each controls for capacity in the sense that each expresses spending in terms of whatever capacity is present.

Findings

We start with the question of magnitude, then go to the question of directionality, and finally take up the question of responsiveness to urban subpopulations under different degrees of reformism (the Lineberry and Fowler question).

In order to ascertain the magnitude of reformism's impact on school expenditures, we first compare the effect of both types of reformism together with the effect of socio-economic environment. Interest here is in detecting whatever effect there might be through the reform movement's impact on all urban governmental institutions, general and school. The effect of reformism on school spending is thus measured by the combination of general government and school indicators. Hence Table 2-1 answers questions about which of *two* factors—reformism or environment—has the greater explanatory power.

Of course, it would violate the logic of comparability to liken the effect of five environmental variables to that of eight reformism variables. We therefore selected five of the latter eight in the following manner. First, we ranked all school reformism variables according to their mean, zero-order correlations with our dependent variables. We then picked out the highest three correlators. These we combined with the three indicators of general government reformism and, using the same criterion of average correlation with our dependent variables, selected the highest five correlators without regard to category.

When we compare the total explanatory power of the five reformism variables with that of the five environmental variables (each indicator set in a separate equation), we discover (Table 2-1, columns 1 and 2) that reformism correlates moderately with spending, and not far behind the environmental variables found so important in earlier studies. Indeed, reformism is more strongly correlated with local support than is environment. When the independent effect of reformism is considered (each indicator set in the same equation), the results (Table 2-1, columns 3 and 4) show that reformism has a moderately strong correlation with educational spending over and above environmental influences. Reformism's net effect on spending is sizable.

Table 2-1

Total Effect (Multiple Correlation Coefficients) and Independent Effect (Multiple-Partial Correlation Coefficients) of Reformism and Environment on City Educational Spending

	Multiples		Multiple-Partials	
	Reformism [d]	Environment [e]	Reformism [d]	Environment [e]
Per Pupil Expenditures	.38	.62	.31	.59
Local School Support [a]	.48	.38	.37	.18
Educational Effort [b]	.33	.51	.30	.50
Educational Effort [c]	.36	.43	.32	.41
	(mean = .39)	(mean = .49)	(mean = .33)	(mean = .42)

[a] Proportion of school expenditures from locally raised revenue.
[b] Per pupil expenditures/median family income.
[c] Per pupil expenditures/property value per pupil.
[d,e] Five indicators of each concept were used in this multivariate analysis, to insure comparability. We therefore picked five of the available eight indicators of reformism according to mean, zero-order correlation with our dependent variables. Using this criterion we chose the three best school reformism variables (out of five), combined them with the three general government reformism measures and, using the same criterion, picked the best five out of these six. They were form of city government, partisan character of city election, independent fiscal powers for schools, property restrictions for school bond voting, and separate school board elections.

Table 2-2 answers questions about which of *three* factors—general government reformism, school reformism, or environment—has the greatest effect on school spending. The combined explanatory power of three measures of each factor (each indicator set in a separate equation) is reported in the first three columns, with the five original measures of environment and school reformism reduced to three by the same procedure as in Table 2-1. Environment emerges first in statistical explanation, with a mean multiple correlation of .43. But school reformism also has a moderate effect on spending: the mean multiple correlation is .33. School reformism again emerges first in the explanation of local school support.

Table 2-2

Total Effect (Multiple Correlation Coefficients) and Independent Effect (Multiple Partial Correlation Coefficients) of General Government Reformism, School Reformism and Environment on City Educational Spending

	Multiples		
	General Government Reformism [d]	School Reformism [e]	Environment [f]
Per Pupil Expenditures	.16	.37	.57
Local School Support [a]	.30	.42	.32
Educational Effort [b]	.22	.29	.42
Educational Effort [c]	.30	.22	.39
	(mean = .25)	(mean = .33)	(mean = .43)

	Multiple-Partials		
	General Government Reformism [d]	School Reformism [e]	Environment [f]
Per Pupil Expenditures	.16	.33	.57
Local School Support [a]	.26	.33	.18
Educational Effort [b]	.16	.34	.46
Educational Effort [c]	.31	.21	.35
	(mean = .22)	(mean = .30)	(mean = .39)

[a] Proportion of school expenditures from locally-raised revenue.
[b] Per pupil expenditures/median family income.
[c] Per pupil expenditures/property value per pupil.
[d,e,f] Three indicators of each concept were used in this multivariate analysis, to insure comparability. We therefore picked three of the five available indicators of environment and school reformism. The criterion for doing so was according to mean, zero-order correlation with our dependent variables. We ranked the mean correlations, separating each set of five, and used the top three of each five in the multivariate analysis.
The selected set of environmental measures includes median family income, percent nonwhite, and population size.
The selected set of school reformism measures include separate school board elections, property restrictions for school bond voting, and independent fiscal powers.

With general government reformism the mean correlation—.25—falls somewhat below generally-accepted criteria of moderate size.

The results are similar when we compute multiple-partial correlations (last three columns) to determine the effect of each set of explanatory variables independent of the other sets (all three indicator sets in a single equation). Again, the set representing environment emerges first, but not overwhelmingly so. Again, school reformism is the strongest correlate of local school support and displays overall a moderate correlation with school spending. General government reformism brings up the rear, independently explaining about 5 percent, on the average, of the variance in school spending.

This analysis of the magnitude of reformism's effect suggests that school and municipal reformism do play a part, and independent ones, in shaping city school spending. Since reformism thus manifests noteworthy expenditure consequences, additional analysis inquiring into the nature of those consequences is in order.

One important question about the nature of reformism's impact on school expenditures is the directional one. Table 2-3 answers that question in consistent fashion; both general government and school reformism are negatively related to expenditures. Strong negativity manifests itself both when all five indicators of school reformism are examined, and when three indicators (selected according to the criterion of highest mean correlation with our dependent variables) are examined. The implication of this directional finding, of course, is that the more open schools are to policy participation by nonschool, minority, and lower class people, and the more politicized the general government, the greater the city's per pupil expendi-

Table 2-3

Direction of the Relationship between General Government Reformism, School Reformism, and City Educational Spending: Percent Negative Zero-Order Correlations

	With All Three Indicators of General Govt. Reformism	With All Five Indicators Of School Reformism	With Three Indicators Of School Reformism [d]
Per Pupil Expenditures	100	80	100
Local School Support [a]	100	80	100
Educational Effort [b]	100	60	100
Educational Effort [c]	67	20	67

[a] Proportion of school expenditures from locally-raised revenue.
[b] Per pupil expenditures/median family income.
[c] Per pupil expenditures/property value per pupil.
[d] The three used in the multivariate analyses, selected according to the criterion of highest mean correlation with our dependent variables.

tures, local school support, and (less so) educational effort. Politicization, not reformism, leads to more spending.

Our final question deals with cities' responsiveness (in the Lineberry and Fowler sense) to their subpopulations as affected by the degree of reformism in municipal and school governments. Consistent with Lineberry and Fowler, one might expect variables like income, education, and occupation to correlate more strongly with school spending—suggesting greater responsiveness to the middle class—where municipal and school institutions are reformed than where they are unreformed. One might expect the opposite of ethnic or racial minority variables like percent non-white. In fact, no meaningful relationship concerning such responsiveness emerges in these data, either with municipal or school reformism.

We divided all cities into three categories of general government reformism according to total number of reformed attributes present: high ($N = 28$), medium ($N = 15$), and low ($N = 24$). In doing so we followed obvious cutting points in the data. Then we correlated education, income, and occupation with each dependent variable under these categories of general government reformism. Mean zero-order correlations revealed no pattern. For example, for two of the dependent variables, the strongest correlation (middle class and educational spending) is in the *medium* reformism category, not in the high category. For the remaining two dependent variables, the strongest correlation (between spending and middle class variables) is evenly split between the low and high reformism categories. Also, about half of the correlations are negative (56 percent) and half positive. When categories of school reformism are considered, the picture is similarly unpatterned. No theoretically meaningful results emerge from this effort. In our data neither reformed nor unreformed institutions, municipal or school, are more responsive in the Lineberry and Fowler sense.

Discussion

Political scientists are naturally interested in the political conditions of public policy, and urban political scientists seem particularly interested in good government reformism as a possible political influence on policy. However, previous studies have not uncovered any reformist influence on city educational expenditures, although other policy consequences of reformism have been detected. Of course, previous studies of educational policy have not directly investigated reformism's impact. This study does, and it reveals reformism to have a sizable, negative impact on city educational spending.

Particularly noteworthy for its negative impact is school reformism.

Questions about the possible financial consequences of school institutions varying along a nonpolitical-political continuum are clearly answered here. More reformism (less politicization) is associated with less per pupil spending, local tax support of education, and educational effort. Evidently, more politicized institutions—those manifesting greater departures from the schools' historically self-promoted autonomy and permitting greater access by lower class and minority citizens—lead to more spending, support, and effort. At least this is the statistical relationship.

It is more than a little ironic that the more politicized the schools the more the educational spending, support, and effort. Good government school reformers, many of them upper class in background, wanted to limit politicization of the schools, including the input of nonschool forces like inexpert citizens of lower class or minority background. Often uneasy with conflict, and especially with conflict based on the "partial" or "manipulated" interests of minorities and the working class, they doubtless wanted to reduce class and ethnic conflict over that much-valued commodity, education. But surely they did not want this depoliticization to bring less per pupil spending, educational effort, and educational support. Yet that is what our data suggest was the consequence of their reformism. If middle and upper class reformers really wanted more educational spending, effort, and support they should perhaps have championed institutional arrangements facilitating class and ethnic differences as inputs to school policy.

The fact that they did not do so is due in part to the absence of empirical research relevant to their reformist doctrines. Without evidence, those doctrines are most plausible; and yet recent research shows reformism to have had consequences markedly at variance with reformist intent. For example, there is evidence that in nonpartisan elections the voter's choice is heavily influenced by considerations of national origin, which is a far cry from the voter performing some rational calculus with his interests and the policy stance of candidates. Also, expenditures by metropolitan area governments do not correlate with the number of SMSA governments, total or per capita, even though reformers have for years bemoaned the harmful expenditure consequences of fragmentation.

The present study adds to the accumulating body of evidence about the consequences of good government reformism—in this case for school expenditures—and, while we lay no claim to the final word, we do believe that our research is a better basis than doctrine for generalizations about reformism's educational impact.

There remains the question of why reformism should be negatively correlated with school expenditures. Our data show reformism to have a negative statistical impact: they do not show the how of this. But two bits of evidence contained in the data do suggest a plausible explanation. (1) General government reformism also correlates negatively with school expenditures; and it does so independently of both school reformism and socio-economic environment. (2) Pluralist, competitive power structures (we have measures only on 17 of our 67 cities) correlate positively with educational expenditures.[b] Thus, politicized municipal institutions, politicized schools, and competitive community power structures all correlate with more school spending, effort, and support. This suggests that more politicized urban settings may bring more education inputs to which school decision makers respond. According to this line of thinking, unreformed schools would be positively related to school spending (and reformed ones negatively related, as in this study) because such schools are a component of this politicized general setting as it affects policy action in the education area. Nor need the masses be involved in policy action. Education-relevant inputs may be transmitted by leaders of diverse community organizations, such as we would expect to find in "pluralist" cities, or by elected and appointed officials who owe their offices to working class and minority voters, such as we would expect to find in unreformed cities with more machine-like politics. To fully verify this explanation, of course, would require different data than we have here, but our data and the literature on unreformed institutions are consistent with this explanation.

Another possibility, of course, is that variables not introduced into our analysis, and therefore not examined, account for the negative relationship between reformism and expenditures. One possibility is the role of state aid, which is proportionately larger in large cities than small. Another is the use of the popular referendum. The relevance of such factors to the relationship that we have discovered should be considered in any further analysis along present lines.

---

[b] Using measures of decentralized (pluralist) community decision structure from Clark, 1971. All our spending measures manifest positive zero-order correlations with the Clark index. As a further check, we computed factor scores (using the principal component solution) on the original indicators of our three main explanatory factors (general government reformism, school reformism, and environment). Then we obtained highest order partials of these three scores and the Clark index. The Clark index of pluralism was still positively related to spending.

3

Political Ethos: The Evidence in Referenda Survey Data
*Howard D. Hamilton**

The political ethos theory has been the subject of considerable interest and controversy since it was propounded by Wilson and Banfield. They asserted that two distinct and opposing orientations toward politics "have decisively influenced attitudes toward both issues and governmental structures," an Anglo-Saxon Protestant public-regarding ethos and an immigrant private-regarding ethos. Subsequently, apparently in response to criticism of the validity and invidious appearance of those terms, they have relabeled those syndromes as the unitary ethos and the individualist ethos, which they describe thusly:

> The middle-class Anglo-Saxon Protestant ethos, we said, conceived politics as a cooperative search for the implications of an "interest of the whole"; accordingly it stressed the obligation of the individual to participate disinterested in public affairs, the desirability of rule by the "best qualified" (meaning "experts" or those otherwise specially equipped by training or character to perform the essentially technical operation of discovering the interest of the whole), and the ideal of "good government" (meaning especially honesty, impartiality, and efficiency). The logically implied (but not always achieved) institutional expressions of this ethos were at-large representation, nonpartisanship, a strong executive (especially the council-manager form), master planning, and strict and impartial enforcement of laws. The other ethos, we said, was characteristic of the immigrant—and, therefore of the lower- and working-class—life; it emphasized family needs and personal loyalties and took no account of the larger community; it conceived of politics as competition among individual (that is, family or parochial) interests. The institutional forms that expressed it were ward politics, the boss, and the machine.[a]

Reprinted with permission of Academic Press, Inc. from Howard D. Hamilton, "Political Ethos: The Evidence in Referenda Survey Data," *Ethnicity* (forthcoming). See original for footnotes omitted here.
* Kent State University

[a] James Q. Wilson and Edward C. Banfield, "Political Ethos Revisited," *American Political Science Review* 65 (December 1971), 1048. Reprinted by permission.

The validity of those syndromes has been investigated by ecological analysis of the hypothesized association of forms of city government and the proportions of persons with the census attributes associated with each ethos. The findings have been mixed: Two studies report little or no association between ethnic variables and the incidence of reformed political structures in cities of over 50,000 population in 1960; another found some association, and still another, based on the 1930 census, reports a strong association of the percentage foreign born and the incidence of unreformed institutions.

Substantial support for the ethos theory, however, is furnished by the studies of voting on metropolitan government proposals. They consistently find a strong association between support for metropolitan government schemes and the social rank of areas, education, income, and the value of residential property. Similar findings are reported in a survey of voting on a reform county charter which was widely perceived as a step toward metropolitan government. (See Table 3-2.)

Wilson and Banfield say that ecological studies which correlate forms of government with ethnicity and other census data have methodological weaknesses. That method does not take into account intervening variables and "the temporal sequence by which electoral attitudes at one period are converted into institutional forms which endure in later periods." They are confident that ethos has had great historical importance. At the turn of the century, they argue, each ethos was more widespread and more intensely held, particularly by rival leadership cliques of Yankee businessmen and working class politicians of immigrant origins.

Subsequent assimilation processes, Wilson and Banfield hold, have eroded but not eradicated the ethos factor. To verify its continued existence and importance, they have employed two methods of investigation. An ecological analysis of fiscal referenda disclosed voting patterns which match their theory impressively. Property taxpayers in some wards and precincts voted for various public expenditures that would not benefit them directly. Such public-regarding voting was greatest in high income areas and those with Anglo-Saxon, Jewish, and Negro concentrations. Support for those expenditures was distinctly less in European ethnic precincts.

Subsequently, attitudinal scaling was used to ascertain the attributes of persons with the unitary or individualist ethos, each ethos being defined in terms of three attitudinal components. The results were not clear cut. There was no association between one component and the other two, some results did not fit the theory, and they found only 97 pure "unitarists" and 26 pure "individualists" in a sample of over 1000 Boston homeowners. Overall, there was some support for the theory. Each ethos was associated independently with income, schooling, and ethnicity. Unitarists were disproportionately persons with the most schooling and income, and overwhelmingly Yankee or Jewish.

Referenda Surveys

Manifestly there is another untapped method for investigating the ethos theory: surveys of voters in local referenda. Voting on property tax levies and bond issues afford the most distinct opportunity for acting on the basis of either public- or private-regarding attitudes. Furthermore in some referenda, notably school taxes and bonds, public-regarding votes are patent and numerous private-regarding votes are identifiable. Frequently there is an assortment of simultaneous propositions, which may illuminate the extent that voting decisions are products of general attitudes. The findings of Wilson and Banfield's analysis of aggregate data are unambiguous, but they are principally from two areas (Chicago and Cleveland) and are subject to the hazards of the ecological fallacy. Hence it is appropriate to check their results with survey data, which also may indicate something about the conditions in which ethos is a potent or weak influence.

We have located surveys of fiscal referenda in eleven communities situated in four states and of one charter plebiscite with relevant data; three of the surveys explicitly investigated the ethos theory. All but three involved school issues, which are the most numerous, the most controverted, and the most studied; the catalyst for most of the referenda surveys has been a local school crisis. Three studies were of elections involving an assortment of propositions: one with four competing programs, a cafeteria of public works projects in one county, and a reform charter and several tax measures in another county.[1]

The data have some distinct limitations. Independent studies undertaken for different purposes pose the familiar problem that the data are classified in various ways, but that is not an insurmountable obstacle in this instance. Moreover, any liabilities are more than offset by the novel elements in several of the studies. Most of the samples are small, which bars refined categories and handicaps the application of controls in analysis. The most serious limitation for our purpose is the paucity of ethnic data. Only four of the studies were in large cities; most referenda occur in smaller communities. However, the absence of an ethnic classification of referenda voters does not render the data useless for investigation of the ethos theory. Public- and private-regarding attitudes surely exist in communities without much ethnicity, as the survey data confirm. Although Wilson and Banfield hold that historically one ethos derived from immigrant life and the other from upper-class Anglo-Saxon Protestant life, they explicitly say that neither ethos is restricted to the respective ethnic groups, and, because of assimilation and social mobility, today may be largely a function of social status. Indeed the data of their Boston sample indicates that status variables are stronger determinants of political ethos than ethnicity.

Voting Patterns in Fiscal Referenda

Wilson and Banfield's aggregate data analysis of referenda in Chicago and Cleveland (and limited data elsewhere) displayed sharp patterns in fiscal referenda voting, those shown by the Table 3-1 extract. Support for local public expenditures financed from property taxes was positively associated with income and negatively associated with ownership and European ethnicity. With income and ownership controlled, support voting correlated negatively with percent foreign stock in Cleveland wards on seven of ten measures, and negatively with percent Polish-Czech in all cases. Negroes were overwhelmingly favorable to expenditures, although the correlation vanished with income and homeownership controlled. Upper-income homeowners were generally more favorable to expenditures than middle- and low-income homeowners. The most favorable groups, exclusive of Negroes, were upper-income Anglo-Saxon and Jewish homeowners, the foremost possessors, say Wilson and Banfield, of the public-regarding or unitarist ethos. Additional support for the theory is furnished by the contrasts in voting between proposals of selective benefits and those for public institutions and other indivisible public goods. Ethnics gave much more support for a veterans bonus, but the Anglo-Saxon and Jewish unitarists gave less support to it than to collective public goods.

Are the voting patterns indicated by ecological analysis corroborated

Table 3-1

Ethnicity, Income, and Ownership—Percent Voting "Yes" in Selected Precincts, Referenda in Cleveland and Cuyahoga County *

Character of Precincts	Veteran's Bonus	Other Issues
Low-Income Renters		
Negro	90	71
Italian	75	54
Polish	72	39
Middle-Income Homeowners		
Negro	79	59
Italian	67	52
Polish	62	42
Upper-Income Homeowners		
Anglo-Saxon	54	61
Jewish	57	58

* Bonus in 1956 and means of votes in 1959-1960 for a hospital, courthouse, parks, and welfare.
Derived from data in Wilson and Banfield, "Public Regardingness," *American Political Science Review*, 58(1964), 884.

by the survey data? The paramount observation that can be made about the survey studies is the consistency of the findings. There definitely are distinct and stable patterns in fiscal referenda voting behavior, in part because most of them concern school issues, and the patterns in the survey data generally are consistent with those indicated by ecological analysis. There are, however, additional patterns and some basis for additional evaluation of the ethos theory.

A *sine qua non* for the validity of the ethos theory is that a substantial portion of voting in referenda is based on stable predispositions; there must be evidence of some stable attitudes. Casual observation might suggest that such stability is absent, because of the not infrequent gyrations in referenda results. Thus a levy or bond issue may lose in May and pass overwhelmingly in November. But that phenomenon is principally because of instability in the composition of the electorate, ensuing from extreme changes in turnout, rather than because of instability of voter attitudes. The survey data demonstrate that most referenda voting decisions are rooted in stable attitudes about the public interest and property taxes. In one election with an assortment of four propositions, half of the sampled voters stated that they voted a "straight ticket." Observe the consistency of the Summit County electorate in passing judgment on a proposed charter and four tax measures (Table 3-2).

The Summit County (Akron, Ohio) study is a noteworthy test of the full scope of the ethos theory, of attitudes toward political structures as well as public expenditures. The proposed charter, a reform model to supplant the Jacksonian county government structure, was drafted by municipal reformer archetypes and promoted by appeals for good government, honesty, impartiality, professionalism, efficiency, and the commonweal. The voting corresponded consistently to social status variables, and the charter received majority support from only businessmen (modestly) and professionals (markedly). The bourgeois charter was supported by the bourgeoisie. The pro-charter voters almost unanimously endorsed the simultaneous tax levies and a homestead exemption for the elderly, but a substantial portion of the anti-charter voters opposed the homestead exemption and the picayune public health levies. Where could one find a clearer and more extensive enactment of both sides of the ethos theory coin?

There are three other implications of this case. The five referenda had a common thread; all were, in Lowi's typology, redistributive policy issues. (The charter was viewed as redistributive by the protagonists on each side and by a substantial share of the electorate.) "The tendency of a voter to take a public-regarding view and the content of that view," say Wilson and Banfield, "are largely functions of his participation in a subculture that is definable in ethnic and income terms." In this instance, the respec-

Table 3-2

Public-Regarding Voting in Referenda on Summit County Charter and Tax Issues, 1970

Correlates of Vote on Charter	Percent Yes		Percent Yes
Income		Occupation	
Less than 10000	35	Workers	33
10000 to 14999	46	Executives	55
15000 and up	56	Professionals	73

Percent Yes Vote on Tax Issues of:	Pro-Charter Voters	Anti-Charter Voters
Mental Health Renewal Levy	95	71
New Mental Health Levy	95	68
New Hospital Levy	86	52
Homestead Exemption for Persons over Age 65	88	74

Source: Bowden, *op. cit.* in f. 1.

tive subcultures were not distinctly defined in ethnic terms, and they were defined more by occupation than by income. Among high-income voters, unitary ethos behavior was displayed most by professionals, who, Lane has noted, are also the principal bearers of the democratic creed.

That there is a reservoir of public-regardingness is manifest in the studies of school referenda. Even when school proposals are defeated, as in three of the cases of Table 3-3, a fourth or more of the voters without children in the school system vote affirmatively. (The ratio evidently is higher when there is less opposition, but such cases are rarely studied.) Very fortunately, school referenda are not purely a parents v. "taxpayers" contest. Indeed if they were, few school measures would prevail, because the parents are a minority in most districts. There also may be considerable private-regarding behavior. Thus in the Bowling Green case, 51% of the voters did not display public-regardingness, and at least 76% of the ballots were consistent with the voter's self-interest.

The hypothesis that some categorical groups are more public-regarding than others has been challenged vigorously. "Such upper status people may not be more public-regarding; they only appear to be, because they can afford to vote for public expenditures." Occasionally the diminishing utility of money also is mentioned. One referendum study shows that there is some basis for this challenge, deriving from the incidence of the general property tax. Voters were grouped in five income intervals and five prop-

Table 3-3

Public- and Private-Regarding Voting in School Referenda (Percent voting Yes)

	Austin-town	Birming-ham	Bowling Green	Detroit	Okemos
* Parents	52	80	60	76	59
(N)	(176)	(143)	(135)	(?)	(63)
Others	35	40	41	56	26
(N)	(182)	(131)	(187)	(?)	(41)

* Of children in the school system.
Sources cited in f. 1.

erty tax payment intervals to produce the five categories of tax/income relationship of Table 3-4. The association of voting and tax/income ratio was dramatic, far stronger than the association with either income or tax payments. Most of the upper status other-regarding voters, particularly

Table 3-4

Vote by Tax/Income Ratio Bowling Green School Levy (November 1966), Percent Voting Yes

	Parents	Others
I level below T:		
Two intervals	26	17
One interval	47	23
Same I and T level	51	24
I level above T:		
One interval	51	45
Two intervals	73	67
Renters	68	69

Source: Marlowe and Hamilton, *op. cit.* in f. 1.

those without school-children, had a favorable or very favorable tax/income ratio. This analysis does not negate the ethos theory at all, but it demonstrates that acting out their unitary ethos by generous support of public expenditures entails little strain for most upper status voters.

The Importance of Occupation

Occupation is the neglected variable in the political ethos research. Wilson and Banfield's correlations of referenda voting treated income, home own-

Table 3-5

Voting in Referenda by Occupation (Percent voting Yes)

Subject (N)	Austin-town school levy (351)	Bowling Green school, welfare (322)	Corning school bonds (189)	DeKalb County public works (163)	Ithaca school bonds (158)	Summit County charter, health (112)	Toledo Open Housing (374)
Farmer	—	26	⎫	—	⎫	—	—
Manual worker	33	37	⎬ 27	46	⎬ 37	30	24
White collar	33	71	43	67	59	38	16
Managerial	50	61	⎫	66	⎫	55	21
Professional	85	84	⎬ 49	84	⎬ 72	73	45

Sources: *Op. cit.* in f. 1 and Hamilton, "Voting Behavior in Open Housing Referenda," *Social Science Quarterly*, 51 (Dec., 1970), 717.

ership, and ethnicity; their subsequent study adds schooling and religion, but again omits occupation. It also is neglected in the other studies, perhaps because it is less amenable to the ecological method. The surveys of referenda furnish occupational data, and that may be their principal contribution.

How important is occupation for defining the subcultures of the unitary or individualist ethos? We have observed that voting on a reform charter was more strongly associated with occupation than income. That appears to be true of referenda on other subjects (Table 3-5). Indeed one of the most prominent aspects of the referenda surveys is the strength and consistency of the association of occupation and voting in strongly contested referenda. (All variables fade in consensual ones.) Almost invariably the highest correlation is with occupation, and sometimes it is even stronger than parentage in school referenda!

The Austintown data afford the best test of the relative importance of

Table 3-6

Voting by Occupation and Income on Austintown School Levy (Percent voting Yes)

	Below 10000 (N)		10-14999		15000 up		Total (N)	
Manual	35	(112)	27	(52)	56	(18)	33	(182)
Clerical	18	(34)	60	(15)	67	(3)	33	(52)
Managerial	47	(19)	54	(28)	48	(23)	50	(70)
Professional	83	(12)	92	(24)	73	(11)	85	(47)
Total	36	(177)	50	(119)	56	(55)	44	(351)
	$p < .05$		$p < .001$		ns		$p < .001$	

occupation and income. Cross-tabulation of those variables (Table 3-6) demonstrates that occupation is far more significant. The range between occupational categories within income classes is substantially greater than the range between income intervals. Income had only a modest effect on professionals and businessmen, but it did affect the decisions of clerical and manual workers. The least enthusiasm for expenditures and taxes was among low-income white collar and middle-income blue collar workers. Middle-income clerical workers displayed public-regardingness, but that was manifested by only those manual workers with high family incomes.

Table 3-7

Strength of Demographic Variables Bowling Green Tax Levies (November 1966)

	Coefficients of Correlation	
	Simple	Partial
Urban residence	.35	.26
Occupational rank	.43	.23
Education	.26	.50
Age	−.23	−.03
Parentage	.18	.13
Income	.24	.03
Property tax pay't	−.18	−.18
Tax/income ratio	.33	.12

To confirm the primacy of occupation, another method and another case were used, partial correlation of eight demographic variables in the Bowling Green referenda. When all the variables were controlled but one, both income and education faded and occupation remained as the strongest correlate except urban residence, even stronger than parentage and property tax payments. Evidently political ethos not only is more accurately defined by occupation than income, but occupation also is the principal generator, which would not surprise sociologists.

The subcultures of each ethos are "definable in ethnic and income terms," said Wilson and Banfield. The latter defining characteristic appears to be erroneous and the former is not very relevant to numerous or most communities. European ethnicity was of some consequence in only three of these eleven fiscal referenda cases. If the political ethos theory currently has much significance throughout America, political ethos must be an element of class subcultures. The referenda studies unanimously attest that it is—and substantially so. Hence occupation, because of its contribution to the class structure, is of singular importance as a conduit of both the unitary and the individualist ethos. European ethnicity, however, remains prominent in some places outside Boston, and we now turn to it.

Ethnicity

The survey data are inconclusive about the public-regardingness of Negroes, because only four of the studies were in communities with a substantial Negro population. In Chicago and Cleveland, Wilson and Banfield found that Negroes were consistently and substantially more supportive of expenditure proposals than whites among both renters and middle-income homeowners. All that can be deduced from the few surveys that treat this variable is that there are occasions when Negroes do not display an exceptional volume of public-regardingness. The Negro affirmative vote was higher than the white on the Detroit and Youngstown school levies, but less than the white on the Atlanta transit bonds, even when controlled for education level, and only slightly higher than the white working-class vote on the Summit charter.

It is European ethnicity that is important for the ethos theory; the syndromes are ascribed respectively to Anglo-Saxon Protestants and European Catholics, specifically the Irish, Italians, and Slavs. Do survey data confirm the voting behavior differences which ecological analysis indicates? If so, what are the quantitative differences, and is the association authentic or only epiphenomenal? Unfortunately few surveys have been conducted in suitable communities, and even three of the big-city studies report only black-white voting. The Youngstown study found the least support for the school levy among European ethnic voters, but the data are fragmentary. The most comprehensive ethnic data are in the Austintown study, a remarkably accurate study of two referenda in a suburb of Youngstown. We have done some secondary analysis of those data.

The voting of ethnic groups in Austintown (Table 3-8) matches the Chicago and Cleveland gross data patterns and the ethos theory in every respect. The affirmative vote of the British was 58% compared to 36% by the European ethnic groups, and the Slavs voted overwhelmingly against the levies—even the parents of children in the public schools. The correlation is not spurious. When controlled by each of the other two most potent influences on the voting, social class and parentage, the association is undiminished; the distributions are much the same in all columns of Table 3-8. Ethnicity was distinctly more potent than social class or parentage.

A significant aspect of this case is the voting of the German segment. The Germans and Scandanavians are never mentioned by Wilson and Banfield, perhaps because they are not Catholic (or do not reside in Boston). The voting of the Germans also fits; their support rate should be, and was, between the Anglos and the Catholic Europeans, but closer to the "immigrant ethos" than the Anglo-Saxon. In an open housing plebiscite, however, the German affirmative vote was equal the British rate and double the Polish.

Table 3-8

Voting on Austintown School Levy (November 1971, Percent voting Yes)

| | By Ethnicity and Social Class [a] | | By Ethnicity and Parentage | | |
	Working Class	Middle Class	Parents [b]	Others	Total (N)
British	49 (35)	66 (44)	64 (42)	51 (37)	58 (79)
German	26 (27)	52 (44)	54 (37)	29 (34)	42 (71)
Italian	47 (34)	30 (27)	50 (24)	32 (37)	39 (61)
Slavic	17 (34)	37 (32)	29 (31)	26 (35)	27 (66)
Total	32 (130)	49 (147)	51 (134)	35 (143)	43 (277)
	$p < .03$	$p < .02$	$p < .03$	$p < .10$	$p < .01$
British	49 (35)	66 (44)	64 (42)	51 (37)	58 (79)
Others	31 (95)	42 (103)	45 (92)	29 (106)	36 (198)
	$p < .06$	$p < .01$	$p < .05$	$p < .02$	$p < .001$

[a] Self classification
[b] Of children in public schools.

Political Alienation

More attention has been given to identifying the holders of the other-regarding ethos than those with the private-regarding ethos. The fiscal referenda surveys show clearly one hitherto unmentioned characteristic. There is a high incidence of political alienation among private-regarding voters. A high volume of alienation among convoters was reported by six of the surveys, and also has been observed in open housing and fluoridation referenda. In the Austintown case, 30% of the convoters scored high on an alienation scale compared to 8% of the provoters.

The explanation for the coincidence is not obscure; both are located preponderantly in the lower social strata. Half of the alienated in Austintown were manual workers and 30% were white collar workers. This raises the question: is this an instance of mistaken identity? No, even in Austintown, where the scenario catalyzed an extraordinary volume of alienation, 70% of the anti-voters were not alienates. Furthermore, as noted in the Bowling Green case, frequently political alienation merely furnishes reinforcement for private-regarding voting.

Conclusion

Three fundamental arguments have been advanced against the political ethos theory. One is that upper-class people really are not more public-regarding; they merely are affluent. The preceding data show that many upper strata voters do not display public-regardingness, and that the burden is light for many of those that do, but the survey data also confirm that the syndrome is associated with class. E.g., in Austintown, the support for school taxes by middle-income manual workers was far below the other occupational groups in the same income interval; and professionals, irrespective of income, vote for public services and taxes. Indeed, we have seen no survey data which did not display distinct class differentials.

Another argument is that political ethos is an invalid blunderbuss, that there is no basis for the proposition that preferences about public expenditures, governmental structures, and "good government" values are bound together in two polar syndromes. Those may be disparate attitudes rather than dimensions of an ethos. That is the implication of the studies which found no contemporary association of political structures with ethnicity and status variables, but, for this subject, correlation analysis using whole cities as units is hardly an efficacious method and there is the additional temporal complication. The survey data furnish evidence in rebuttal of this criticism. Two surveys of metropolitan charters found that the loci of support and opposition by status variables correspond to the voting patterns in fiscal referenda and on open housing. In that fortuitous, quasi-laboratory test of the amount of coincidence of the hypothesized elements in the ethos theory, the Summit County referenda set, there was a remarkable display of congruence.

The other challenge has been put succinctly by Ippolito and Levin:

> It is also questionable whether or not white middle class support for various "good government" or community interest proposals not tied directly to self-interest constitutes "public-regardingness." These types of proposals do serve the white community. Political and social stability, governmental efficiency, and the like are, after all, quite important to the white middle class community.[b]

To this argument, one may demur. The fact that "middle class" people may perceive a stake in social stability or the city beautiful and think that such is fostered by voting for hospitals, schools, public works, or metros, does not of itself annihilate the theory. Public regardingness initially was defined not as philanthropy, but as voting against "self-interest narrowly conceived," and the voter is not an economic man because his frame of reference is some concern for the welfare of the community. That he may perceive some congruence of his notion of the community interest and a personal stake in social stability is irrelevant. The survey data measure the volume of voting inconsistent with economic self-interest, and who

---

[b] Reprinted with the permission of *Social Science Quarterly* from Dennis S. Ippolito and Martin L. Levin, "Public-Regardingness, Race, and Social Class," *Social Science Quarterly*, 51 (December, 1970), p. 633.

does it, but of course do not document that community is a benchmark of the voting decisions. How else would one explain a favorable vote for a county home or a courthouse, the voting pattern of professionals, or the straight ticket voting? That community interest is a benchmark is quite visible to anyone doing interviewing in a referendum survey.

The survey data furnish impressive support for the ethos theory; indeed we have observed no contradictory evidence in any of the eleven studies. They certainly confirm that the voting patterns indicated by previous ecological analysis are correct, and they furnish proof that voting on charters, public expenditure proposals of all sorts, and open housing is preponderantly the enactment of general and stable attitudes held by the voter. It could hardly be otherwise, because the voter rarely has sufficient information for a decision on any other basis. While they do not speak to the historical origin of the syndromes, the (limited) data sustain the asserted association of ethnicity and ethos, and confirm that it is authentic as well as strong. The data furnish abundant evidence for the initial supposition that those syndromes are not confined geographically to those cities with European ethnics, but exist elsewhere as components of class subcultures. The survey data demonstrate conclusively that the subcultures of each ethos are defined more by occupation than income, and analysis indicates that occupation also is the principal molder. These data incidentally suggest that there are more class dimensions of American politics than the national voting studies reveal, some dimensions which have been little noticed.

Notes

1. The studies are: Dennis Ippolito and Martin L. Levin, "Public Regardingness, Race, and Social Class: The Case of a Rapid Transit Referendum," *Social Science Quarterly,* 51 (Dec., 1970), 628-633; Sylvan H. Cohen, *Voting Behavior in School Referenda: An Investigation of Attitudes and Other Determinants by Q Technique and Survey Research* (dissertation, Kent State University, 1971); R. V. Smith *et al., Community Organization and Support of Schools* (Institute for Community Research, Eastern Michigan University, 1964); Byron Marlowe and Howard D. Hamilton, *Survey of Voting on Tax Levies in Bowling Green* (unpublished); John E. Horton and Wayne E. Thompson, "Powerlessness and Political Negativism: A Study of Defeated Referendums," *American Journal of Sociology,* 67 (1972), 485-593; Alvin Boskoff and Harmon Ziegler, *Voting Patterns in a Local Election* (Philadelphia: Lippincott, 1964); Roberta Sigel, *Election With an Issue: Voting Behavior of a Metropolitan Community in a School Fund Election* (unpublished); Wayne E. Thomp-

48

son and John E. Horton, "Political Alienation as a Force in Political Action" *Social Forces,* 38 (1960), 190-195; Gary W. King *et al., Conflict Over Schools* (Institute for Community Research, Michigan State University, 1963); John W. Bowden, *The Summit County Charter Debacle* (thesis, Kent State University, 1971); J. Kiriazis and S. Hotchkiss, *Community Attitudinal Survey of Youngstown Voters on School Tax Levies* (unpublished).

4

School Desegregation and Electoral Conflict
Christine H. Rossell*

Introduction

To many observers, it appears that in the last decade American schools have become embroiled in a "new politicization" of education. This is not necessarily a change in magnitude, for education has long been the hottest local issue. The uniqueness of the new politicization lies in the major common demand made by community groups—the demand for "equality of education." Equality of education may mean a major redistribution of school resources, an end to de facto segregation, the adoption of remedial programs, the enrichment of ghetto curriculum, decentralization of the school administration so that "black schools are run by black people," or the abolition of the local property tax as the major source of funding for school districts. Whatever the particular local variation, these demands appear to many white citizens to offer advantages for lower class and minority students at the expense of higher social status families. None seems to be more threatening than the demand for an end to de facto segregation.

The demand for an end to de facto school segregation was front page news from 1963 to 1970 in most northern U.S. cities, one decade after the 1954 Supreme Court decision, *Brown v. Board of Education,* declaring all legal provisions for maintaining segregated schools to be unconstitutional. Typically the focus of this demand and the school administration's response varied from community to community. The desegregation controversy began as a bitter conflict over principle since most school administrators believed that desegregation was not a proper function of the schools. The professional school administration, whose expertise was generally unsuited for resolving value conflicts, usually handed the issue back

Prepared for original publication in this book. The research for this study was made possible by the generosity of Robert L. Crain, formerly at Johns Hopkins University and now at the Rand Corporation. Data were relinquished from a 1968 NORC study funded by the Carnegie Corporation, and funds were obtained from a National Institute of Mental Health grant awarded to Professor Crain for establishing the Permanent Community Sample Archive, now at the University of Michigan, ICPR.

* Bureau of Governmental Research, University of Maryland

to the school board without any specific policy recommendations. Therefore the issue of school desegregation has become one of the few important
policy issues in which the school board is the central decision maker.
School board responses range from ignoring the demand all the way to
radical actions such as totally desegregating the school system or busing
white students to black schools.

The research reported here is an attempt to measure community conflict as a result of school desegregation by analyzing school board elections.
Because the school board rapidly becomes the center of the controversy
and is responsible for the decision to desegregate, community reaction can
be measured by looking at how the community votes on school board incumbents who have made such a decision.

The Unit of Analysis

It is important that the unit of analysis be clearly defined. In this study it
is the school district. All but two of the school districts have the same
name as the city whose boundaries coincide or nearly coincide with those
of the school district. Thus the city and the school district have much the
same spatial boundaries. They also have the same interactional boundaries,
particularly during a school desegregation controversy, since the decision
to desegregate is the result of the interaction between civil rights leaders,
school board members, school administrators, civic leaders, elected city
officials, and in some cases, local courts.

It is also important to emphasize that this is an aggregate level analysis
of community phenomena. This kind of analysis, often called macro or
ecological analysis, deals with the behavior or properties of communities.
Probably the most important principle to be followed when studying community politics at the aggregate level is that individual level phenomena
cannot be explained solely by community level data, and vice versa. Although high status individuals may vote more than lower status individuals,
that does not necessarily mean that higher status communities have higher
turnout than lower status communities. Because research has shown that
public sentiments are not spawned in isolation and that the environment
imposes powerful constraints on the behavior of individuals, it can be useful to examine voting patterns at this level. However, the reader must remember these findings are not automatically applicable to individuals of
the same characteristics.

Sample and Data Collection

The data examined in this paper are from the latter part of a study of de
facto school segregation controversies in 91 northern cities.[1] Because the

research reported here is a study of community conflict as it is reflected in school board elections, 33 cities that did not have elected school boards, or that had data collection problems, were eliminated from the 91 city sample.[2] The resulting sample of 58 cities with elected school boards comprises 28 percent of all northern cities and 45 percent of the population in the North.[3] Within each of these cities, NORC trained interviewers administered a series of 18 interviews with selected school system personnel, politicians, civil rights leaders, civic leaders, city officials, and the education reporter of the local newspaper.

An attempt was made to resolve several problems of local election data (collected separately from the NORC data). The first problem is that school board elections are not always held concurrently with the same elections even within the same city. Although Martin states that a general characteristic of board elections is that they are held separately from other elections,[4] in the sample used in this study only 10 school systems held special elections (where only school offices and issues are on the ballot) consistently during the entire period. The vast majority held them on the same ballot as city primaries or city general elections, although this varies from year to year. Thus most of our school systems are not isolated from city politics as the early educational administration literature would have us believe. Had the sample been divided into those with like elections, or special elections, it would have been reduced to an unacceptable size.

This problem was partly solved by turning each of the following types of elections into dummy variables. The variables are: a special board election with no other offices on the ballot; a board election in which a bond or tax referenda was also on the ballot; one concurrent with a city primary; one concurrent with a city general election or county election; and one concurrent with a state election or national election. The data bank for the nine-and-one-half-year period represents 459 school board elections in 58 school systems in the North. Sixty-five percent of the school systems in our sample held elections every two years, while another 49 percent held elections every year.

School Desegregation and Electoral Politicization

The first questions to be dealt with in this paper are whether school desegregation causes electoral politicization and whether this politicization, as measured by high turnout, is an indicator of conflict. School board elections typically have had low turnout and low levels of competition compared with other elections. Jennings and Zeigler found that in the last election preceding the summer of 1968, about 23 percent of the school districts in the United States had no ballot opposition at all. Similarly, in 44 percent of the districts, no incumbents had been defeated over the past several elections. In more than a third of the boards over 25 percent of their incumbents had first been appointed to office, and in more than one-half over 25 percent had been asked to run by a board member.[5]

It is anticipated that school desegregation will be a politicizing factor (both as a demand and as a policy decision) in school elections. Politicization is defined here as political socialization—one type of socialization distinguished primarily by the fact that political groups are the ones active as socializing agents. Here the proponents and opponents of school desegregation perform the socialization, although it is interpreted through the mass media. Opposing group leaders will often appear on local television to argue their case, and the local newspaper usually accords the issue front page status. Thus in many communities school desegregation is the most well known and important policy decision ever considered by the school system, or any local agency for that matter. It is hypothesized that the effect of this public controversy will be to increase markedly electoral participation in school board elections—in short, to politicize the electorate. Elections that once went almost unnoticed should become the most well attended in the community.

In addition to the effect that school desegregation might have on electoral politicization, it is hypothesized that certain social background characteristics and intervening political structures will also have an independent effect on turnout in school board elections. Undoubtedly school desegregation (or any other controversy) will not be the only reason why a community would have high levels of electoral turnout. It is important in understanding the causes of electoral conflict to identify other social and political causes of electoral politicization.

Degree of school desegregation is measured by the percentage of black students reassigned to predominantly white schools within a school district from September 1964 through the school year ending in August 1972.[6] The school board election variables for the period 1963 to 1972 are: (1) a measure of *turnout* computed by summing the votes of each candidate, dividing by the number of positions to be filled and then standardized by dividing by the number of registered voters; and (2) three measures of *dissent*: percentage of incumbents running who are defeated, the number of recalls, and the percentage of the school board recalled.

After some preliminary correlational analysis, important variables were entered into a multiple regression program in a stepwise fashion predicting electoral participation. When the whole period was analyzed by using multiple regression, school desegregation had no effect. However, it was felt that school desegregation as an issue would be increasing in its ability to politicize as more and more school systems initiated extensive school desegregation, many of them under court order, and as busing became a national political issue. Thus a school desegregation action in the later years would have more of an effect on school electoral participation because most citizens would be more "sensitized" to the pros and cons of the decision. Accordingly, election data and school desegregation data were recomputed for the period from the Fall of 1968 through August 1972.

The result, shown in Table 4-1, is that a local school desegregation action does have an impact on electoral participation in the later years of this study. It is, however, a small impact and it is not evident until the stimulus of concurrent elections is controlled for. School systems that hold

Table 4-1

The Relationship of School System Characteristics to School Board Electoral Participation, 1968, 1972

Variable	Relationship to Voting Turnout (r)	Relationship Controlling for Other Variables (Beta)
Special Board Elections [a]	−.53	−.74
Board Election Held Concurrently with School Tax or Bond Referenda [a]	−.30	−.60
Board Election Held Concurrently with City Primary [a]	−.18	−.39
Board Election Held Concurrently with City General Election [a]	.50	.03
Socio-economic Status [b]	.23	.26
Racial Liberalism of the 1968 School Board	−.17	−.46
Controversy Over Education	.08	.34
School Desegregation	.12	.31
	($r^2 = .86$)	

[a] Variable is a dummy variable.
[b] Socioeconomic status is an index created by multiplying the median income of a school district by its median educational level.

their board elections concurrent with higher stimulus city, state, or national elections tend to be low on school desegregation impact. Thus in order for the effect of desegregation on electoral participation to be detected, the "structural" effect of concurrent elections on participation had to be controlled for.

No other school policy, such as the school tax rate or assessment ratio, or specific school controversies, like teacher strikes and civil rights activity on behalf of school desegregation, has an effect on turnout. In short, the effect is that of the controversy surrounding the *implementation* of desegregation rather than simply controversy surrounding the demand for desegregation.

The relationship of less liberal school boards and high levels of electoral participation is difficult to explain. Perhaps more conservative school boards take more decisive stands on issues and thus electoral participation is stimulated. Although no specific controversy has an effect on turnout, school systems that are rated by their leaders as being high on controversy over education, tend to be high on electoral participation. This makes sense since citizens would be more aware of and more likely to participate in elections in which the school system is embroiled in publicized issue conflicts.

Because there have been contradictory findings in earlier research, it is interesting that school systems of high socio-economic status tend to be more participative. This relationship is the same as that commonly found at the individual level. Minar's study of 48 suburban elementary school districts in Cook County, Illinois found that higher status districts tend to have lower rates of participation.[7] There may be two reasons for the difference between this study and his. First, Minar's study is of one small, fairly homogeneous region, Cook County, and secondly, the time period of his study is almost a decade earlier. The advent of redistributive politics may have a lot to do with reversing a negative relationship between status and participation found in earlier studies. When school board elections represented no threat to upper status communities, the turnout was lower. As Almy and Hahn point out, increasingly upper status groups have begun to vote in large numbers in defense of their position in what were once low salience "controlled" elections.[8] The same trend may be perceived in upper status communities.

We can conclude at this point that school desegregation has a politicizing effect on school board elections, but that other social and political characteristics of a school system are more important in producing this effect. The combination of variables listed in Table 4-1 explain 86 percent of the variance in school board election participation.

School Desegregation and Electoral Dissent

In this section the relationship of school desegregation and electoral dissent will be analyzed—first as the percentage of incumbents defeated in regular elections and then as the number of recalls and percentage of board members recalled. The percentage of incumbents running who are defeated is a variable that represents a "referendum" on school desegregation. The voters are in a sense voting "yes" or "no" on school desegregation, although ostensibly making a choice of one candidate over another.

When a number of important political and social variables are entered into a multiple regression program predicting the percentage of incumbents defeated, the best explanatory variable is court ordered school desegregation.[9] As Table 4-2 indicates, cities that desegregate under court order have a larger percentage of incumbents defeated.[10] This is not true, however, of school desegregation per se. When all school systems, court ordered and non-court ordered are considered, the higher the amount of school desegregation (e.g., the percentage of black and white students reassigned), the lower the percentage of incumbents defeated. Although the zero order correlation (r) is next to nothing, the standardized regression coefficient (Beta) is strengthened to $-.31$ when court order, number of

Table 4-2

The Relationship of School System Characteristics to Electoral Dissent in School Board Elections

Variable	Relationship to Electoral Dissent (r)	Relationship Controlling for Other Variables (Beta)
Desegregation Under Court Order	.26	.53
Number of Tax and Bond Referenda Held	−.28	−.36
Socio-economic Status [a]	.13	.32
Degree of School Desegregation	−.04	−.31
Being in the Pacific Coast Region [b]	−.30	−.29
Holding Run-off Elections [c]	−.17	−.16
	$(r^2 = .41)$	

[a] This is an index composed of median income times median education in a school district.
[b] This is a dummy variable.
[c] School boards which hold run-off elections do so because they require candidates to get a majority vote in order to be elected.

bond and tax referenda, and the socio-economic status of a community are controlled for. There is little negative effect in terms of *degree* of school desegregation (e.g., the percentage of black and white students reassigned). In other words, an incumbent is no more likely to get defeated if the school board desegregates 50 percent of its black and white students than if it desegregates 5 percent. Indeed, once having controlled for socio-economic status and court order, one finds that an incumbent is *more* likely to get defeated with less school desegregation.

Does this mean that voters want more school desegregation? This is unlikely—these findings probably reflect the fact that low status, heterogeneous school districts tend to be unable or unwilling to initiate much school desegregation, but have a good deal of conflict, some of which is reflected in elections.

The policy implications of this are interesting. For school board members this means that school system support is not dependent on how *much* the school system is desegregated (e.g., the percentage of black students reassigned). Voters are apparently angry at what they consider to be the outside interference of the courts and the "forced busing" aspect of court ordered school desegregation. It might seem strange that school board members would get the blame for court ordered desegregation, but the case data indicates that many white voters feel that the decent and honorable action for the court ordered school board is to fight the "outside interference" in their community. In short, it would seem that a significant portion of the community is furious if the school board does not appeal, and keep on appealing, the court's decision. The most publicized and violent school desegregation controversies in recent years have been in court ordered school systems such as Pontiac, San Francisco, and Denver, to name only a few.

Table 4-2 also shows that cities outside the Pacific Coast region have more incumbents defeated than those in the Pacific Coast. This relationship holds true even for those school districts in California that desegregated under court order (San Francisco and Pasadena) and the one school district that underwent a recall election (Berkeley) during the period of our study. Part of the reason may be that California school districts hold their elections concurrently with city elections, thus in some sense isolating the school office from the critical scrutiny of the voters. In addition, in desegregated school systems some of the heat may be taken off the school board members by the fact that the California State Department of Education has ordered all school districts to maintain racial balance in their schools. No school, according to the guidelines, may deviate more than 15 percent from the percentage of minorities in the whole school district. It appears that for many school districts, community conflict and cleavages resulting from desegregation tend to be reduced in the face of this kind of state pressure and specific policy guidelines, unless they are court ordered.

One of the interesting findings of aggregate voting studies has been that institutional rules can influence the outcome of elections. For example, a common finding is that cities with partisan elections, all other things being equal, will have higher turnout than cities with nonpartisan elections. Here, an institutional rule also proves to be important: where school boards have run-off elections, a smaller percentage of incumbents are defeated. Incumbents that manage to survive a primary, can often win in the run-off because the fact of incumbency (and thus the benefit) is clearer to voters when there are only two candidates.

The number of tax and bond referenda held is negatively related to electoral dissent because they seem to distract attention from school board elections. School districts that hold a lot of financial referenda tend to find that voters defeat referenda, rather than candidates, as a way of voicing disapproval of school policy or controversy. As was found in a related study, these tend to be lower status school districts—the opposite of the type of school districts that are high on school board election dissent.[11]

The lack of relationship between electoral participation and the percentage of incumbents defeated is evidence of a more complex political process than the early community conflict and voting studies would have us believe. Most aggregate voting studies have shown a positive relationship between turnout and negative voting. This is because a small vote consists mainly of votes cast by the non-alienated—those most involved in community affairs. A large turnout, indicative of increased tension in the political system, presumably means that the alienated, often non-participants, have been attracted to the political arena to register a protest. Therefore, voting turnout is generally higher for defeated than for passed referenda. In addition, "no" voting has been found to be greatest among the lower social status groups, because they tend to have the strongest feelings of helplessness and political inefficacy.

In this study, high social status communities tend to have higher levels of school board dissent (even controlling for level of school desegregation) than lower status communities. In addition, desegregated school systems often have low turnout elections where the people most involved in community affairs vote out of office those officials responsible for the controversial policy. This may be a recent development in local politics.

Rochester, New York, is an example of this phenomena. It is a lower middle class city that reassigned a total of 5.16 percent of its black students for the purpose of integrating the school system. A small percent were moved in the fall of 1970 (.86) and a larger percent (4.30) in the fall of 1971. The board election in the following November was the most issue oriented in that decade. Gordon DeHond, an employee of the Monroe County personnel and civil service office, organized a slate to run for the five school board vacancies to be filled in that city general election. He was supported by a coalition of whites in middle class neighborhoods who seemed to be afraid of blacks, experimental education, and rising taxes. The platform of the DeHond slate condemned lack of discipline, sex education, and teacher tenure, but carefully avoided the negatives that would have opened them to attack as bigots and reactionaries; they were *for* "neighborhood schools," "parental control," and "fiscal responsibility." DeHond took credit for the low key approach—the word "busing" was not used, nor did the candidates explicitly state they would rescind the school desegregation plan.

The DeHond slate won every seat, decisively defeating the pro-integration slate that included two incumbents who had voted for the plan earlier that year. DeHond is now president of an all-white school board in a school district that is almost 50 percent black. The day after election, DeHond instructed the superintendent to rescind the desegregation and reorganization plan. Rochester still has voluntary open enrollment, but it is a policy that has not prevented the increasing segregation in Rochester schools.

In short, the voters of Rochester chose the policy of segregation in preference to the policy of compulsory desegregation advocated by the incumbent board members. The one incumbent school board member who was re-elected was someone who had previously voted against the school desegregation plan. Furthermore, the highest electoral dissent in the history of the school district (and city) is associated with the lowest turnout. The campaign was low-keyed, controlled, and issue-oriented—the effect was to draw out those people most involved in community affairs and, one suspects, these are probably the people most threatened by school desegregation.

In the Table 4-3, the election figures for Rochester are presented. The bottom row presents Minar's dissent variable, the percentage of votes cast for the losing candidate. As can be seen by comparison with a measure of dissent that uses the percentage of incumbents defeated, there is not a highly significant relationship. The problem with Minar's variable is that, while closely contested elections may indeed be indicative of dissent, it is not at all apparent that elections that are *not* close are *low* in dissent. It is difficult to interpret an election in which two-thirds of the incumbents are defeated as a low dissent election; yet this is what Minar's variable seems to indicate.

Thus Minar's study not only suffers from a poor sample of school districts, but his variable is rather questionable. It could be argued that while he claims that high status communities have lower levels of dissent, he may just be saying that they have less closely contested elections. As we have seen in Rochester and will see again in the next section on recall elections, closely contested elections are quite likely to be unrelated to dissent and dissent unrelated to turnout. Thus his argument turns on a poor measure. In addition, his characterization of upper social status communities may be, at the least, out of date. He claims that high status

Table 4-3

Electoral Participation and Dissent Voting in Rochester, New York, 1963-1971

School Board Election Variables	1963	1965	1967	1968	1969	1971
Participation	82.7	76.6	80.5	84.0	76.2	53.4
Dissent (percent defeated)	0	a	50.0	0	0	66.6
(number defeated)			(1)			(2)
Minar's variable/dissent [b]	49.2	46.9	49.1	47.4	40.9	39.2

[a] No incumbents ran.
[b] Minar, "The Community Basis of Conflict."

communities have low conflict because they possess the conflict management skills necessary to control conflict. Yet his study took place during a period when there was no controversy to match the demands for redistribution of resources being made today by dissident groups. Furthermore, it is even questionable whether high status communities were ever blessed with superior conflict management skills, if this conflict management means a lack of dissent.

For example, although Crain, Katz, and Rosenthal's study of fluoridation referenda only covers a slightly later period, they found that middle class communities had *higher* levels of dissent. In an article based on the same data, Crain and Rosenthal argue that high status communities are more participative, and that this high level of citizen participation results in (1) a more easily mobilized opposition to the existing government and its policies; (2) political campaigns being more issue oriented; and (3) more likelihood of the presence of the kinds of political structures which break down the barriers that insulate government from the citizens. Thus middle class cities will have less stable government, and they will be less willing to embark on controversial programs. When they do attempt to innovate, there will be higher levels of community debate, hence higher levels of controversy and a greater possibility of stalemate.[12]

Although the first part of this thesis is applicable to this study, the last part is not true with regard to school desegregation policy. Middle class communities are more likely to desegregate mainly because they tend to possess highly educated black communities and civil rights groups whose primary concern is school desegregation, rather than some other political issue such as black power or decentralization. Because communities with highly educated black populations tend to possess school boards and civic leaders who are somewhat more racially liberal, black pressure to desegregate lands on fertile field—in communities where it is at least possible demographically and less politically unacceptable than in other communities. This is also true of court ordered school desegregation.[13] However, the rest of the Crain and Rosenthal thesis is valid. Defeat of incumbents in both high status cities and court ordered school districts is due to the fact that middle class communities tend to have very issue-oriented elections in which each candidate's position is clearly delineated and hotly debated. But in many communities, this can be controlled so that only the white voters turn out and the pro-integration black voters stay at home unaware of the importance of the election.

A school board recall election is even more like a referendum on school desegregation. Recall elections are, however, regionally differentiated in two ways that make them an insufficient measure of dissent in the study. First, they are only legal in 52 percent of the school districts in the sample. Secondly, recall elections have clear regional differences in the degree to which these kinds of progressive movement reforms (e.g., non-partisan-ship, recall, initiative, and referendum) actually are used even where they are legal. The farther west one goes, the more likely they will be used.

Among the minority of school districts in which it is legal to hold recall elections, only three have done so within the time span of this study (up through August, 1972). The three school districts in two, non-eastern states are Detroit, Michigan; Berkeley, California; and Pasadena, California.

All three have had recall elections because of a school desegregation decision by the school board.[14] This does not mean that all school boards that desegregate will be named in a recall where it is legal, but that all board members named in a recall election have been on a board that made a school desegregation decision. The recall elections were held in 1964 in Berkeley, and 1970 in Pasadena and Detroit. However, in the case of Detroit, the school desegregation-decentralization plan had not yet been implemented when four out of seven of the board members who voted for the plan were recalled one month before the plan was to go into effect. (The new board rescinded the plan.) Pasadena and Berkeley had already initiated school desegregation by the time their unsuccessful recall elections were held.

There does not seem to be anything unusual about these three cities that would explain why they had recall elections and other cities that desegre-gated, did not. Of the 47 school districts in the original sample of 67 school districts, 25 could have been involved in a recall election, although only three were. Of the top five desegregated school systems (all above 38 percent black students reassigned), all had legal provisions for school board recall elections. Yet only two, Berkeley and Pasadena, actually had such an election and neither of these had any board members recalled.

The outcome of these elections seems to be due in part to their timing. The successful Detroit recall election was held *before* school desegregation was actually implemented. In Berkeley and Pasadena, school desegrega-tion had already been implemented, and most citizens probably decided to support the board because they felt it was too late to do anything about it. As mentioned earlier, the fact that Pasadena had been ordered by a court to desegregate did not prevent the school board from being held responsible for not appealing the decision.

As we saw with regular school board elections, turnout is not related to dissent. Detroit with 35.1 percent turnout had the lowest of the three school districts. (Berkeley had 59.5 percent and Pasadena had 51.6 per-cent turnout.) However, Detroit had the highest level of dissent, 59.3 percent for recall, while Berkeley only had 39.3 percent and Pasadena only had 48.8 percent for recall. All of the Detroit board members up for recall were indeed recalled, and this represents more than half of the school board at that time. One of the reasons why turnout is not correlated with dissent is that primaries and recall elections tend to favor organized groups. If a dissenting interest group can organize a low keyed campaign in which those citizens most likely to vote "no" are encouraged to turn out for the election, then a low turnout will favor a high dissent.

Hamilton's recent analysis of fair housing referenda in Toledo found results similar to this study. There are several reasons why alienation could not be blamed for the defeat of integrated housing in Toledo. For one thing, a large portion of the "alienates" are blacks who, if they voted, would engage in positive voting on the issue of fair housing. Furthermore, the alienation model equates high turnout with voluminous negative voting, yet the turnout was low in the Toledo referendum that was defeated.[15] Similarly, in Detroit, a high turnout would have meant the infusion of large numbers of blacks, who while "alienates" would have surely voted against recall of the board members who had supported the desegregation-decentralization plan.

Conclusion

There is no doubt that the controversy over the implementation of school desegregation has caused electoral conflict in school districts experiencing it. In many of these communities, school board elections have become bitter ideological contests for control of the ultimate fate of a community.

Electoral politicization was the first indicator of conflict that was examined. High turnout, however, is an inadequate measure of electoral politicization. The issue of school desegregation has had the effect of politicizing anti-integration groups so that in many communities they run highly organized election campaigns that succeed in turning out the negative white vote while keeping overall turnout low. The "alienates" are blacks who, if they bothered to vote, would vote in favor of a desegregating board. Most important predictors of that aspect of politicization measured by turnout are institutional rules, like the concurrence of the election with social and political characteristics like a racially conservative school board, general controversy over education, and high community social status.

Electoral dissent as defeat of incumbents is probably a better measure of conflict than either turnout or the closeness of elections (used by Minar). The defeat of incumbents almost always occurs amidst a serious controversy such as that surrounding a court ordered school desegregation plan. Furthermore, competing elections like tax and bond referenda, concurrent elections on the same ballot, and run-off elections make incumbents less vulnerable to defeat.

The positive relationship between high social status and high electoral dissent does not conform to what we know about individual relationships. Generally, individuals of high social status tend to be more supportive of school leaders and policy, as well as more racially liberal. However, the effect at the aggregate level is the opposite due to the intervening mechanism of campaign style. As Crain, Katz, and Rosenthal discovered in their study of fluoridation campaigns, because high social status communities had more heated debates, more published literature, and more discussion of the pros and cons of the issue, fluoridation was usually defeated in referendum. Low social status communities tend to have low stimulus, non-issue oriented elections that virtually guarantee re-election of incumbents. However, an interesting sidelight of this study is that for all school districts, defeat of incumbents is on the increase. School board offices are no longer the safe positions they once were.

These findings do not show an unequivocally bright future for school desegregation, but they are by no means a death sentence. The fact that there is less support for the school board that desegregates can have serious consequences as in Detroit and Rochester where school desegregation plans were rescinded when the pro-integration board members were voted out of office. On the other hand, Wichita, Kansas; Berkeley, California; and Riverside, California, have all implemented a great deal of school desegregation (voluntarily) with no apparent decrease in support. The school board that reassigns fifty percent of its students for the purposes of desegregation is not necessarily more likely to get defeated than one that reassigns 5 percent, unless it is court ordered.

Five propositions are presented below as an attempt to generalize the findings of this study beyond the issue of school desegregation and school board elections.

Proposition 1: High turnout is not a consistent measure of electoral conflict in local, issue-limited elections, such as school board elections. Whereas high turnout may mean electoral conflict, low turnout does not necessarily mean an absence of conflict.

Proposition 2: High social status communities have high turnout and high dissent because campaigns tend to be more issue oriented and more publicized. Although those high status communities that have high turnout are not necessarily the same communities that have high dissent, similar characteristics cause both phenomena.

Proposition 3: General controversy increases turnout more than the implementation of a specific controversial racial policy. In the latter case, organized groups often conspire to keep turnout low.

Proposition 4: The implementation of a specific controversial policy causes more electoral dissent if the local decision makers implement a decision "forced" on them by an outside authority than if they "voluntarily" come to the decision themselves.

Proposition 5: The implementation of a specific controversial policy causes more electoral dissent than the controversy surrounding the demand. Citizens do not defeat incumbents because of controversy over policy demands until the decision making body actually acquiesces and agrees to implement the demand.

These propositions are, of course, tentative until similar research is conducted on other issues and other types of local elections. The next step in research on the electoral impact of school desegregation should probably be to develop typologies of "successful" and "unsuccessful" school desegregation—that is, where, when, and how school desegregation causes high conflict in one community and low conflict in another.

Notes

1. David Kirby, Robert Harris, and Robert Crain, *Political Strategies in Northern School Desegregation* (Lexington, Mass: Lexington Books, D. C. Heath and Company, 1973).

2. School desegregation data were collected for the 91 cities described above (reduced to 90 due to non-response) and the results are presented in chapter 12 (by Christine H. Rossell) "Measuring School Desegregation," in Kirby, Harris, and Crain, *Political Strategies in Northern School Desegregation.* School bond and tax referenda data was collected for 48 of these cities and the results are presented in Christine H. Rossell, *The Electoral Impact of School Desegregation in 67 Northern Cities* (unpublished Ph.D. dissertation, the University of Southern California, 1974).

3. For a breakdown by city size, see Rossell, *The Electoral Impact of School Desegregation in 67 Northern Cities,* p. 301.

4. Roscoe Martin, *Government and the Suburban Schools* (Syracuse: Syracuse University Press, 1962).

5. M. Kent Jennings and Harmon Zeigler, "Response Styles and Politics: the Case of School Boards," *Midwest Journal of Political Science,* 15 (May 1971), 290-321.

6. The computation of this index is explained in more detail in "Measuring School Desegregation," by Christine H. Rossell, chapter 12 in Kirby, Harris, and Crain, *Political Strategies in Northern School Desegregation.*

7. David W. Minar, "The Community Basis of Conflict in School System Politics," *American Sociological Review,* 31 (December 1966), 822-835.

8. Tomothy A. Almy and Harlan Hahn, "Perceptions of Educational Conflict," *Education and Urban Society,* III (August 1971), 440-452.

9. This is a dichotomous variable with 0 = not desegregating under court order and 1 = desegregating under court order. It is a measure of both the likelihood of a court order and the likelihood that a school board will obey the court order rather than endlessly appealing.

10. Analysis of the 1968-1972 period showed little difference in the standardized regression coefficients, although there was a reduction in explained variance.

11. Rossell, *The Electoral Impact of School Desegregation in 67 Northern Cities.*

12. Robert L. Crain, Elihu Katz, and Donald B. Rosenthal, *The Politics of Community Conflict* (Indianapolis: Bobbs-Merrill Company, 1969); Robert L. Crain and Donald B. Rosenthal, "Community Status as a Dimension of Local Decision-Making," *American Sociological Review,* 32 (December 1967), pp. 971-972.

13. Rossell, *The Electoral Impact of School Desegregation in 67 Northern Cities.*

14. Three more school districts—Lansing, Michigan; Seattle, Washington; and San Bernadino, California—have held recall elections over school desegregation since August 1972 and they also are non-eastern.

15. Howard Hamilton, "Voting Behavior in Open Housing Referenda," in *Political Attitudes and Public Opinion,* Dan Nimmo and Charles M. Bonjean, eds. (New York: David McKay Company, 1972).

Part II
Representatives and Representative Theory

Introduction to Part II

Representatives and Representative Theory

The preceding research directly infers the need for a more complex model of the school as democratic polity, particularly in the representational possibilities between leaders and citizens. Role theory, the *lingua franca* concept of social sciences, has been used in political science to explain some aspects of actors' behavior. This concept has been fully mined during the last two decades in examining legislators in Congress, state house, and city hall. In the context of classical representation theories, there now exists a full and rich empirical literature about such legislators. But the discipline has ignored the far more numerous unit of school boards (currently about 16,000) and their members, the most typical elected official in this country. In this section, contributors transfer some of these theories of representation to school authorities, both elected and appointed.

Leigh Stelzer analyzes a national sample of almost 500 board members in 82 districts to explain their perception of their role behavior toward citizens, especially when official and citizen are in conflict. Under the latter conditions, the elected officials adopt a strategy of "receptivity," which channels the conflict into opposition to the superintendent, a process undergirded by the phenomenon of competitive elections. In these data is a picture of the elected bowing before the wind of popular pressure—when it exists.

Dale Mann's contribution focuses upon the administrator, however, whereupon a different picture emerges. One theme of recent administration literature has been the possibility of the bureaucrat being representative of certain constituents. This theme, applied to 165 administrators in New York (and more fully developed in his forthcoming book), is an impressive demonstration of something else. Namely, it shows the degree to which professional norms engender a sense of these administrators' autonomy, which resists popular or participatory judgments about the quality of services received. This author's contribution, contrasted with that from Stelzer, strongly makes the point of the crucial difference in receptivity made by the electoral process. As Mann concludes about the citizen's role with and without this process, "The difference is the difference between being asked to help decide what is to be supported and being asked to support what has been decided." That difference, not a minor one, illuminates crucial differences in representational theory—and in kinds of polities.

5

Institutionalizing Conflict Response: The Case of Schoolboards [1]
Leigh Stelzer *

Introduction

A major problem for the polity is harmonizing diverse interests and substituting peaceful forms of conflict resolution for physical force. Authoritative institutions, governments, intervene in the decision process. Intervention may reduce conflict or exacerbate conflict. James Coleman's [2] concern in the monograph *Community Conflict* and the concern of others who wish to forestall the destructive consequences of intense conflict is the identification of institutional mechanisms for holding conflict within bounds of normal decision making.

Coleman argues that authoritative institutions that provide built-in procedures for the expression of dissent can avoid destructive aspects of rancorous community conflict. One procedure is formal channels which groups outside the institution use to express disagreement with policy makers. A second procedure is cooptation, the inclusion of representatives of divergent interests within the governing body.

By building-in dissent, the institution can forestall the intensification of conflict in two ways. First, the "system can drain off in small, everyday disputes the hostilities and dissatisfactions which otherwise accumulate and break out in intense controversy." Second, disagreement is not expressed against the institution but against specific officials. In other words, machinery which builds in dissent helps the institution avoid constitutional crisis.

A failure to build in mechanisms of dissent, Coleman argues, can result in popular quiescence or undesirable behaviors including organized anomic outbursts and organization outside the institution. Coleman observes that disaffected people organize when they think they can exercise influence through public controversy and possibly overturn an administration. The strategy calls for "sniping" or "full-scale battle."

Coleman provides two examples, one legislative and one administrative,

Reprinted with permission of the *Social Science Quarterly* from Leigh Stelzer, "Institutionalizing Conflict Response: The Case of Schoolboards," *Social Science Quarterly,* 55, No. 2, September, 1974.

* Graduate School of Public Affairs, State University of New York at Albany

of authoritative institutions with conflict containing mechanisms. The "two-party system" in the legislative setting is one mechanism. Although Coleman does not discuss the two-party system thoroughly, it is clear that what it provides is a political infrastructure that seeks to mobilize the opposition to the majority government and to be available to dissenters as a vehicle for their protest.

Cooptation in an administrative setting is the second example of the institutionalization of conflict. Cooptation is the process by which an administrator brings potential opposition into the decision process. Conflict thus takes place within the decision-making body.

Coleman's examples of built-in systems of dissent have two things in common. First organization of the constituency is substituted for lack of organization. The agents of the institution mobilize the community around available cleavages or divisions. Second, diversity of membership is substituted for homogeneity. The institution represents the community by including representatives from diverse constituencies.

School systems traditionally lack formal institutional mechanisms to channel dissent. Yet clearly this is not for want of intense, varied, and conflicting demands upon school systems. Minority groups seek equality of opportunity and representation. Teachers want increased salaries and professional recognition. Taxpayers seek respite from rising tax rates. Numerous research reports [3] have related these and other demands to rancorous conflict.

When confronted with conflict, school governments have, for the most part, lacked institutional mechanisms for channeling. Historically, the lack of channeling mechanisms is the result of the impact of the municipal reform movement on school boards. School boards underwent a set of structural reforms similar to those which took place in towns and cities. The reforms were designed to assure the political independence of school boards, to remove partisan politics and to substitute a bureaucratic model of governance for a legislative model. In effect reform fostered an unstructured or disorganized community and a homogeneous governing body.

School governments were radically reorganized at the turn of the century. Institutional changes included a switch from partisan to nonpartisan elections, a switch from ward level to at-large election of members, the scheduling of elections to occur independently of other elections, a lengthening of individual terms of board members and a decrease in the size of the school board. These changes constituted a package of reforms. Although appointive membership on boards of education was often part of the articulated package, there were very few changes from elective to appointive boards. Concurrent with these institutional changes, the office of superintendent of schools was developed and widely adopted.

An examination of medium and large sized cities at two time points, the 1890s and 1927, illustrates these changes. In 1890, data for sixty-nine school boards show twenty-two elected at large and thirty elected by ward. In 1927 twenty-six of the latter boards were elected at large and only one remained elected by ward. There was no movement in the opposite direction.

Changes in the selection procedure were accompanied by other reforms. The number of members per board was decreased and the length of their terms was increased. Of seventy-two boards for which data are available, twelve remained the same size, twelve increased in size, and forty-eight decreased in size. Similarly, a majority of the boards adopted longer terms of membership. Of sixty-nine boards for which data are available, fifteen remained unchanged, seven decreased the length of a term and forty-seven increased the length of the term.

The position of superintendent of schools was developed and widely adopted during this same period. Population growth and advances in pedagogy in the mid 1800s encouraged boards of education in large cities to turn over their instruction supervisory tasks to full-time employees. By 1883 all large cities had superintendents of instruction. Gradually superintendents were entrusted with greater administrative responsibility and came to function as executive officers for the boards.

Although there is no way to know what effect these reforms had on the course of community conflict, it can be argued that if they had any effect it was to deny dissenters the common bases of organization, to close off channels for the expression of dissent and to exclude representatives of divergent viewpoints. One way to view the reforms is as an effort to make the school system independent of any other cleavage basis in the society. Thus on-going organizations and loyalties not directly focused upon the school system were unavailable to those who wished to dissent. A second way to view the reforms is as an attempt to substitute for a legislative model of governing a bureaucratic model. Thus the school board was no longer a body of representing legislators, but, rather, a board of directors overseeing the work of the superintendent.

The reform package was designed to set the school system free of any outside basis of loyalty or organization. Non-partisanship set the school free from the primary cleavage of other governmental bodies and a major basis of mobilization in the nineteenth century. At-large elections removed neighborhood identification and organization as a viable basis for contesting board elections. Separate elections cut school board contests off from the effects of organizations and issues involving other governments. Thus reform eliminated some of the bases upon which a two-party system could be built.

The small board and the long term were advocated by reformers on the grounds that they would increase the efficiency of board operations. Reformers argued that these changes would increase control and continuity, and make the board more businesslike. Actually, the two changes were designed to fit a new model of school board government. In the past, boards had acted as legislative bodies. Large boards and short terms were designed to meet the demands for representation. Committees and subcommittees of the board administered the system. The new board was designed to be a board of directors and to meet the demands for efficiency and professional administration.

Rather than administer the school system directly through committees, the new board was designed to supervise the superintendent. The reduction in size decreased the propensity for factions on the board. It also decreased the likelihood of the creation of substantive committees that might develop sufficient expertise to challenge the authority of the superintendent. Longer terms facilitated the identification of the member with the superintendent and reduced the member's reliance on his constituents.

The reduced size of the board necessarily decreased the number of different views and backgrounds of board members. There is reason to believe that in fact the reduced size increased the prestige of membership and thus led to more homogeneous upper-class school boards. George Counts found that boards with three members were more selective in terms of occupational class than were boards with from four to seven members. He reported "The large board exhibits a considerably smaller degree of social selection than does the three man board."

To summarize, the reforms worked in the directions of disorganization of the community and exclusion of diversity. The reforms reduced the availability to dissenters of on-going divisions and organization in the community. Party and neighborhood were no longer viable bases of organization in non-partisan city-wide independent elections. The reforms increased the electoral independence of board members and encouraged them to take on a fiduciary role rather than a representation role. Coleman argues for the importance of institutionalized procedures of dissent to inhibit the cycle of polarization of community conflict. Reform denied school governments mechanisms that would have fostered the organization and representation of dissent. Thus school boards have had to develop their own mechanisms for coping with community conflict.

In the 1970s, the issue is no longer specific reform institutions but the pervasiveness of the culture which spawned reform. Several scholars have noted the failure of school governments to develop mechanisms for articulating and aggregating citizen demands.[4] School governments have chosen to frustrate articulation and deny the legitimacy of aggregation, especially partisan aggregation.

In eschewing partisan solidarities as bases for mobilization, the schoolmen have not been entirely lax in finding substitutes. They have focused on parents and their concern for education. Furthermore, they have fostered the creation of groups such as the PTA to provide on-going support.

The PTA, a mainstay of support for many boards, has several obvious drawbacks. The PTA is a creation of school administrations for passing on information—not for articulating demands—and its members are justifiably perceived as boosters. Furthermore, the PTA appeals to a narrow segment of the constituency. Few members, much less outsiders, would seek or expect its support in articulating grievances.

Citizen committees, ostensibly designed to facilitate two way communication are typically *ad hoc* and narrowly focused on a specific issue. Most do not perform a mobilization or channeling function. "Caucuses," by contrast, have been created in a relatively few districts to recruit and elect board members. However, instead of aggregating demands and involving greater numbers the caucus is often used to preclude debate and opposition.

School governments could not survive in the face of conflict without developing some kind of coping mechanism. The sensitivity of so many school-related issues is a natural foundation for conflict. The widespread requirement that school governments submit budgets, tax levies, and bond proposals to public referenda assures conflict sooner or later.

The Study

Hypothesis

I offer the following hypotheses.

School boards employ a strategy of receptivity when faced with community conflict: Receptivity, as I define it, is the belief that the school system should be open to public participation and influence. A receptive board member is one who advocates increased participation of the public in board decision processes. When confronted by conflict, boards respond by advocating additional openness for the board.

Receptivity is the mechanism by which the board channels community conflict into opposition to the superintendent: Receptivity is not simply a public relations ploy. It is a true response which provides a channel for the expression of popular opposition to the chief administrative offices of the school district. Thus the receptive board translates public disaffection into policy opposition.

Competitive elections are an institutional mechanism that support school board receptivity: Elections are institutional arrangements designed to keep the representative in touch with his constituents through the periodic need to mobilize plurality support. The election is an incentive to elected leaders to maintain contacts and a focal point for renewing contacts. Competitive elections are an institutional support for receptivity.

The Sample

An examination of receptivity, the conditions that create and maintain it, and the policies to which it leads is made possible by a national study of school board members and superintendents. Interviews were conducted with 492 board members and 81 superintendents from 82 school boards in 1968.

Boards were chosen for inclusion in the study on the basis of a prior national study of the political socialization of high school seniors. The socialization study used a probability sample of high schools stratified by size. The sample boards have jurisdiction over the public schools in the prior study. Thus, they represent boards in rather direct proportion to the number of secondary students in the school system. A straight probability sample would have yielded a preponderance of boards representing small school districts.

Eighteen of the boards are in the Northeast, 24 in the Midwest, 15 in the West, and 25 in the South. Different degrees of metropolitanism are reflected in the sample as well. Six of the boards are in the central cities of the 12 largest Standard Metropolitan Statistical Areas (SMSAs). Fourteen are in the suburbs of these metropolitan areas. An additional 29 boards are located in the central cities of the remaining SMSAs. Thirty-three boards are located outside SMSA central cities, not including the suburbs of the largest SMSAs.

Concepts

Receptivity

In the course of an extensive interview, board members were asked a series of directed and nondirected questions about popular participation and communication. They were asked generally about their satisfactions, dissatisfactions, and problems as board members and specifically about representation and interest group activities. In the coding process, board members received a single point for each response that favored public participation in board deliberations. The scores of the members ranged from zero to seven. Fourteen percent of the members scored zero, seventy percent scored one or two, and sixteen percent scored three or more. The interpretation of these scores is facilitated by examination of how scores on the index correlate with related activities.

The validity of the measure was established by comparing it to three board member activities. Board members received points on the receptivity index when they expressed support for greater public participation and communication. Thus, we expect the more receptive board member to be more involved in a board-community communications net. Furthermore, if receptive members have serious commitments to greater communication and participation, they will spend more time with the public.

We asked board members, (1) "When the schoolboard is about to make a policy decision, do you personally ever try to gain support for the policy from any community groups or organizations?" and (2) "Do any representatives of community groups or organizations ever contact you personally to seek your support for their position?" We also asked them to estimate the proportion of their time they spend on "requests or questions from the public." The gamma measures of association between receptivity and the three activities were .25, .25 and .22 respectively.

Community Conflict

I have created three measures of community conflict. The first is a dichotomous variable created from board member answers to the question, "Is there any tension or conflict among people in the district on questions having to do with school policies?"

The second variable is the system's ratio of success in passing financial proposals as reported by the superintendent. The question was applicable to only fifty school districts. The remainder either had no provisions for popular referenda or had not held one during the preceding three years. A third variable is created from answers to seven questions about general and specific conflict in the community. The questions include the question about tension and conflict used to create the first variable as well as questions about criticism of the board and teachers, racial problems, money problems, and pressures for change. The variable is an index of all positive responses to the questions.

These conflict variables are interrelated with gammas of .38, .41 and .91. The latter correlation is that between the single conflict question and the index. For further validation I have also correlated the three variables with an index of community arousal derived from the superintendents' interviews. The correlations between the superintendents' index scores and the other measures are .49, .51 and .64.

Electoral Competition

The first measure of electoral competition is derived from questions about the members' initial elections. We asked board members if they had faced competition, if an incumbent had been involved and if the respondents' ideas were different from those of other candidates. The assumption underlying the latter queries was that competition has more meaning if the competitor is an incumbent and if his ideas are different.

Eighty-two percent of the board members had nominal competition in their first race. Of this group, sixty-six percent ran against incumbents and fifty-nine percent faced incumbents whose ideas differed from their own. Positive responses to these questions were used to create an index of electoral competition. Board members received one point for each positive response. This yielded a four-point index ranging from zero to three.

A second measure of competitiveness is incumbent defeats in the election preceding the interviewing. The more defeats, the more competitive the election. This measure is based on district election figures and is not subject to distortion by board member perceptions or memory.

Board Opposition to the Superintendent

To identify opposition to the superintendent, we asked board members, "Does any person or group on the board often oppose the superintendent?" If the response was affirmative, the member was asked, "would you consider yourself one of these persons?" Answers to this question were used to form the measure of opposition to the superintendent.

Measurement at the Level of the Board

Because the focus of this research is on institutions and institutional mechanisms for channeling conflict, it is appropriate to use board-level measures of the variables. Some of the measures, such as incumbency reelection success and the financial success ratio, originate at the board level. Other measures require that the responses of individual board members be aggregated to produce a board score.

Findings

Conflict and Board Receptivity

Board members are inclined to express receptivity in the face of community conflict. There is a positive association between conflict and receptivity (Table 5-1). The more conflict perceived, the more receptive the board. Answers to the single tension and conflict question and receptivity are associated with a gamma of .29. The independently derived

Table 5-1

Board Index of Community Arousal and Board Receptivity

Index of Arousal	Receptivity Low	High	Total	Number of Boards
Low	63%	37%	100%	51.5
Medium	51	49	100	33.0
High	35	65	100	21.4
Total	54	46	100	105.9
		Gamma = .30		

non-perceptual financial success ratio and receptivity are associated with a gamma of .33.

Conflict, Receptivity and Opposition to the Superintendent

Coleman argues that community conflict is a result of the failure of authoritative structures to provide channels for the expression of dissent. Schoolboards, lacking institutional channeling mechanisms, have adopted receptivity as an informal means for channeling dissent. For the board to act as a channel, it must provide a connection between community arousal and the school administration represented by the superintendent of schools.

To test if receptivity channels conflict into opposition to the superintendent, we can look at the relationship between board receptivity and opposition controlling for community arousal. Under conditions of community arousal, receptive boards should express opposition to the superintendent. Under conditions of community quiescence, receptive boards should not voice opposition to the superintendent. Table 5-2 confirms these expectations. The same conclusions can be derived from Table 5-3

Table 5-2

Board Receptivity and Opposition to the Superintendent (Controlling for Community Conflict and Tension)

	Board Opposition				
	None Oppose	Mixed	All Oppose	Total	Number of Boards
Receptivity	A: Community Conflict; High Arousal				
Low	37%	39%	24%	100%	16.4
High	40	11	49	100	19.3
					Gamma = .26
Receptivity	B: Community Conflict; Low Arousal				
Low	28	41	31	100	20.5
High	54	37	9	100	11.8
					Gamma = −.51

which shows measures of association when the three measures of community conflict are used as controls.

These results suggest that receptive boards are "tuned in" to the public. They constitute an on-going channel. When there is public dissent and arousal, the receptive board translates it into opposition to the superintendent. When, however, the boards do not perceive popular arousal, the more receptive boards are less likely to oppose the superintendent.

Table 5-3

Board Receptivity and Opposition to the Superintendent (Controlling for Community Arousal)

A: Conflict and Tension		
Conflict and tension		The more receptive the board
Low arousal	−.51	the *less* the board opposes the superintendent
High arousal	+.26	the *more* the board opposes the superintendent

B: Finance Rejection		
Finance rejection		The more receptive the board
Low arousal	−.58	the *less* the board opposes the superintendent
High arousal	+.25	the *more* the board opposes the superintendent

C: Board Index of Community Arousal		
Board index		The more receptive the board
Low arousal	+.03	the *more* the board opposes the superintendent
Medium arousal	−.40	the *less* the board opposes the superintendent
High arousal	+.56	the *more* the board opposes the superintendent

Electoral Competition and Receptivity

The electoral mechanism is designed to foster communication between leaders and followers. Periodic mobilization of support is supposed to foster greater contact. Elections facilitate the replacement of representatives who fail to keep pace with voters.

Elections are a necessary condition but competitive elections are required to insure sustained contacts between leaders and followers. We often assume, as Seymour Lipset writes, that an election is "a social mechanism which permits the largest possible part of the population to influence major decisions by choosing among contenders for political office." Limits to this assumption are suggested by Kenneth Prewitt's study of California city councils in which he found low popular participation, few incumbent defeats, widespread use of appointment to circumvent elections and minimal political ambition among councilmen.

Our own data show similar patterns for school boards. Roughly one fourth of the board members in our sample were originally appointed to their seats. Eighteen percent of the board members did not face even nominal opposition in their first bids for election. In the most recent elections, all incumbents were reelected in two thirds of the cases where incumbents ran for reelection.

The index of electoral competition and receptivity are positively related, gamma = .37. Twenty percent of the boards scoring zero on the competition index have high receptivity; sixty percent of those scoring three on the competition index have high receptivity. Approximately thirty-five percent of the boards in the middle range of competition are high in receptivity. Similar results are achieved using the more objective election data. When all incumbents are reelected, twenty-eight percent of the boards have high receptivity. By contrast, when some or all incumbents are defeated about fifty-six percent of the boards exhibit high receptivity. The gamma association between incumbent defeats and receptivity is 0.5.

Political Ambition and Perceptivity

When a person runs for office, we assume he is ambitious. The theory of electoral responsibility assumes that the official cares about reelection or election to another office. As Joseph Schlesinger has written, "representative government, above all depends on a supply of men so driven; the desire for election, and, more important, for reelection, becomes the electorate's restraint upon its public officials . . . No more irresponsible government is imaginable than one of high-minded men unconcerned for their political futures."

The relationship between ambition and receptivity is logically related to the cycle of incumbency. Though a board member may be ambitious for another post, it is unlikely that his ambitions will greatly affect his behavior on the board until he has some hopes of fulfilling those ambitions. Such a moment is most likely to occur after he has proven himself on the board and been successfully reelected. Afterwards, any relationship between ambition and receptive behavior would likely decline. Either the board member is content to remain on the board or he wishes to give up office holding altogether.

The majority of board members are elected for three and four year terms. Since one-fourth of the members were initially appointed, their second election would come a bit later. For the aggregate, peak ambition would occur at four and five years of service. Table 5-4 shows that the

Table 5-4

Political Ambition and Member Receptivity (Controlling for Tenure, Individual Level)

Years of Tenure	Gamma	Table N
1 or fewer years	−.05	70
2-3 years	.24	109
4-5	.51	72
6-7 years	.15	50
8 or more years	−.02	133

relationship between ambition and receptivity is strongest for members with this number of years. Elections and personality combine to support receptivity.

Discussion

James Coleman has argued that institutions without built-in mechanisms for channeling dissent are unable to forestall the intensification of conflict. Although the literature on school politics is broad and varied, it appears to support Coleman. School systems lacking channeling mechanisms face rancorous conflict.

School politics as described in scholarly literature tends to fall into three categories. The first category may be described as "rule by a narrow elite." A traditional group in the community, sometimes referred to as a "power structure" controls the school board; the superintendent works for or with this group. The second category is the attempted takeover of the board by a small "anti-school" element. Generally, this group is emotionally charged and wishes to replace the superintendent. The third category is the "full-dress battle." This category is distinguished by the unusually large proportion of the citizens that participate frenetically in school-related activities.

These three types of politics may be described in terms of the numbers involved in the conflict and the skills of opposition groups (Table 5-5). Small numbers of people are generally involved in the first two types of politics, the traditional ruling group and the takeover group. The ruling group maintains itself in power when the opposition has low skills (Quadrant IV). The takeover group challenges the hegemony of the ruling group when the takeover group has the requisite organizational

Table 5-5

Styles of School Politics

Skills of Opposition	Numbers Involved in Conflict	
	High	Low
High	I Reform Ideal of Citizen Democracy	II Challenge by Takeover Group
Low	III All-out Battle	IV Continuity under Traditional Ruling Group

skills (Quadrant II). There is full-dress battle when the numbers involved are large and the opposition groups have few skills for manipulating school politics.

School controversies often pursue the following course: Traditional ruling groups are supplanted by takeover groups which in turn are replaced in high-involvement contests. Soon, interest wanes and one or another small group of activists becomes the ruling group. Thus, school politics is characterized by cycles of activity and quiescence.

Reform assumptions and institutions help to explain these styles of politics and the course of controversy. Reform was based on an image of democratic man as one who knowledgeably participates in politics. Citizens should make decisions based on the merits of particular cases and therefore they should be free from outside pressures. However, under normal conditions, large numbers of citizens lack sufficient motivation to participate in school politics. Thus much of school politics falls in Quadrant IV instead of Quadrant I.

Earlier, I described how reform institutions eliminated traditional bases for organization of the community and reduced the channels available to potential participants. Ironically, reform set up conditions for rancorous conflict by requiring high motivation as a condition of participation without providing the infrastructure to channel highly motivated dissent. Separate elections and separate registration rules make participation in school politics more difficult than it need be.

At-large elections and nonpartisanship reduce the information available upon which voters can make decisions. Separate elections reduce information further by denying opportunities to make comparisons among several different kinds of services at a single election. These institutions create barriers to participation.

High motivation enables prospective participants to overcome barriers imposed by reform. Those with low motivation find it difficult to acquire the information required to participate. This means that the school system depends on a small group of highly motivated people for support. Only intense opposition groups can surmount the usual barriers; thus, to surmount the barriers, groups must be intense. The lulls between rancorous conflicts then would not be periods of apathy, but rather periods of low-visibility frustration in the face of barriers to participation.

The high degree of activism and concern that are required to participate intelligently under normal conditions leave the school boards in the hands of leaders with a narrow base of support in the community. Reform institutions enable leaders to reign without creating an extensive infrastructure of supportive groups. Thus the ruling group does not attempt to create an infrastructure. This increases the isolation of the board and feeds the frustrations of aggrieved citizens.

Coleman argues that without an infrastructure of mobilization there are few institutions linking leaders and followers to articulate and aggregate citizen demands. Demands remain unarticulated and unaggregated. A second consequence is that the ruling group can be supplanted by fairly small groups with skills comparable to those of the ruling group (Quadrant II politics). The absence of institutions makes it likely that frustration will build among some segments of the community. A buildup of frustration will impel the expenditure of sufficient energy to threaten the hold of the ruling group.

Although quiescence is the normal state of school politics under reform conditions, the quiet is periodically broken. The issues of school politics touch too many too intimately for low involvement to persist indefinitely. An increase in the frustrations or fears of a small group will lead to organization and skill mobilization. Sometimes, the struggle between the ruling group and the takeover group will lead to large-scale participation. The struggle between the two small groups articulates the issues or ignites the fears of a broader public. The outstanding characteristics of these struggles is rancor.

In the absence of institutions for organizing the community and channeling dissent, school politics has taken on a plebiscitary character. The voters communicate their desire for changes in policy by electing new board members. Several studies show that incumbent defeats are followed by changes in policy and the involuntary resignations of superintendents.

The plebiscitary character of elections raises two problems. First, under conditions of low involvement, it is fairly easy for a small, narrowly focused group to defeat an incumbent. The changes that occur as a result may not be favored by the majority of the citizens. Second, even when large numbers of citizens participate in changing personnel, the change may be superficial. A change in personnel may not improve the quality of representation.

Receptivity

Very few board members are prepared to think in terms of developing an infrastructure to channel participation. At the very least, they would have to be willing to enter a relationship in which they sought support for their positions and were open to support the efforts of groups. Only twenty-two percent of the board members have sought support for their positions. Only forty-one percent were approached by groups with requests for support.

Though few members are willing to engage in political mobilization, a goodly number are committed to the concept of accessibility and public participation. They support the idea of a dialogue, a belief in the need for communication between themselves and citizens. I have called this set of beliefs in communication and participation "receptivity." Receptivity is a first step in the acceptance of the need to create permanent institutions to organize the constituency and channel dissent. As we have seen, it is the more receptive members who are creating permanent linkages to the public by engaging in mobilization and by being available to groups.

Receptivity is not dependent on personality quirks of the board members. Competitive elections provide an institutional spur for receptive behavior. Political ambition combined with an electoral system that rewards ambition likewise encourages board member receptivity.

Competition and candidate ambition are variables that are manipulable. Concerned citizens can arrange that no one gets elected to a board without a struggle. They can further see to it that the member will face a contest for reelection. Finally, concerned citizens can eschew those who are compelled to run by civic duty and embrace the ambitious. This is not an exact formula for receptivity, but it is a beginning.

84

Notes

1. This work is based on research which appeared originally in L. Stelzer, *The Receptivity of School Board Members: A Study of Reform and Representation* (Doctoral Dissertation, The University of Michigan, 1971). A complete discussion of the data collection instrument, analysis techniques, and sources of historical data and inspiration can be found there.
I would like to thank Joanna Banthin, Tom Baylis, Kent Jennings, and Fred Wirt for their generous assistance.

2. James S. Coleman, *Community Conflict* (New York: The Free Press of Glencoe, 1957).

3. R. E. Agger and M. N. Goldstein, *Who Will Rule the Schools: A Cultural Class Crisis* (Belmont, California: Wadsworth Publishing Company, 1971); R. L. Crain, *The Politics of School Desegregation* (Garden City, N.Y.: Doubleday and Company, 1969); R. G. Damerell, *Triumph in a White Suburb* (N.Y.: William Morrow & Company, 1968); Herbert Gans, *The Levittowners* (New York: Random House, 1967); M. Gittell, *Participants and Participation* (N.Y.: Frederick A. Praeger, 1968); K. Goldhammer and R. Pellegrin, *Jackson County Revisited* (Eugene, Oregon: Center for Advanced Study of Educational Administration, 1968); A. B. Hollingshead, *Elmtown's Youth,* Science Editions (New York: John Wiley and Sons, 1966); D. Hulbard, *It Happened in Pasadena* (New York: Macmillan Company, 1951); A. Vidich and J. Bensman, *Small Town in Mass Society* (Garden City, N.Y.: Doubleday and Company, 1958).

4. Coleman, *op. cit.;* Crain, *op. cit.;* L. Iannaccone, *Politics in Education* (N.Y.: Center for Applied Research in Education, 1967) R. Martin, *Government and the Suburban School System* (Syracuse, N.Y.: Syracuse University Press).

6

School Administrators as Political Representatives
Dale Mann *

Many of the problems faced by administrators of public schools are problems of political representation, that is, they deal with the way school
administrators take account of the needs and interests of the public. Take
for example the case of a school principal who has spent the early part of
her career as a specialist in reading research. When she takes over a new
school, she discovers that a particular early-reading curriculum which she
had discredited in one of her earliest studies is still being used in the
district; moreover, it is very popular among the parents. What should she
do? Replace it immediately with the best alternative available? Replace it
and explain to the parents what was wrong with it? Resolve to wait until
she is better established in the district before making such a major change?
Propose a cooperative re-evaluation committee on which parents are
represented? Keep it and try to improve on it? Or, put yourself in the
position of a high school principal faced with a large group of students
who want to hold a protest rally in the school's cafeteria. You are confident that the rally will be a peaceful way to vent grievances, but some
vocal community leaders are adamant about their fear that it will spill outside the school and cause widespread damage. Would you: Authorize it
and hope to demonstrate to the community the soundness of your judgment? Go ahead with plans but work with student leaders to ensure it does
not get out of hand? Delay the students and hope to change the community leaders' attitudes? Negotiate with the intent of stopping the rally?
Or would you prohibit it?

 Problems of administrative action such as these and many others re-
volve around ideas about the proper inclusion and weighing of community
wishes and interests in administrative action. The continuing dilemmas of

This revised, abridged version of "The Politics of Representation in Educational
Administration" by Dale Mann is reprinted from *Education & Urban Society*, vol. 6,
no. 3 (May 1974), pp. 297-317 by permission of the Publisher, Sage Publications,
Inc. This research was part of a project supported by a grant to the author from
the New York State Commission on the Quality, Cost and Financing of Elementary
and Secondary Education.

* Teachers College, Columbia University

representation also underlie demands for decentralization, community control, and accountability. In decentralization, for example, the Board of Education of the City of New York declared that:

> Decentralization should result in making all administrative and super-visory services more readily responsive to the needs of the children. . . . It is to be hoped therefore that as much authority as possible will be delegated by local school boards to the schools, so as to make it possible for them to operate more independently and thus more effectively and more responsively to local needs.

The community control movement sought to ensure particular styles of representation by giving laymen authority over the schools at the neighborhood level. But even under community control, school administrators must somehow decide how to enact the expressed desires and interests of the neighborhood in their own professional decisions.

Similarly, the new shibboleth of "accountability" requires representational decisions. The derivation of the goals to be achieved, the selection of the means to reach them, and the measures of their achievement must be done with reference to popular expectations. Additionally, accountability is generally understood to be related to popular control over the official's career. Educators have so far been able to keep the accountability tiger a toothless one by ignoring the ordinary and implicit career-affecting features that make the actor "accountable for" his performance.

In urban areas, the demand that administrative decisions be representative is often pressed by militant groups and expressed through confrontations; in the suburbs, similar demands are pushed by taxpayers and are expressed through defeated bond and budget proposals. Many suburbanites fled the city at least in part because its schools were perceived to be unresponsive to their demands and decreasingly representative of their interests.

The research reported here concentrates on the representational role orientations of school administrators. Representation is a political concept; as a group, administrators have often sought refuge in the supposedly "nonpolitical" nature of schools. Politics has been defined by David Easton as the "authoritative allocation of values for (the) society," [1] and to the extent that schools serve that purpose they are also political institutions. Schools and their administrators are responsible for the distribution of three major types of values: material goods and services (especially employment), political socialization, and social mobility.

Beginning at the level of the local building principal, administrators either make, participate in, or influence decisions about personnel, curriculum, teaching practices, and budget matters. They inculcate children with social norms such as individual over collective effort, cognitive over affective procedures, civic attitudes, and public values. And, although we have recently learned a more useful modesty about the school's ability to boost people up the ladder of socio-economic mobility, the school remains the society's only conscious agent of such mobility. Despite their smoke-screen complaints about too little authority and a lack of control, administrators have a great deal of latitude and influence in a wide range of operational matters, and those operational decisions translate directly into control over how these social values are, or are not delivered to students.

Because of that discretion, the old policy/implementation dichotomy, which places policy determination in the hands of formally representative bodies such as school boards, and policy implementation with administrators, has as little to recommend it in education as it does in other areas of public policy. Since policy is determined as much by implementation as by enunciation, administrators must share the burden of representation with the formal agencies created for that purpose.

Still, many school administrators try to contend that theirs is a world of value-free expertise, in which they are "above" politics, neutral and olympian, administering simultaneously to all the needs of all the children all of the time in a kind of curricular loaves-and-fishes act. In fact, no social institution has ever been, or will ever be, able to perform with such equity and moral certainty. The demands placed on schools always outstrip the available resources. The result is that administrators must choose which demands to satisfy at the expense of which others. Because of that unavoidable discrimination, and because of the other political functions the school is charged with fulfilling, school administrators are increasingly caught between the meritocratic and democratic horns of a representational dilemma.

The best general exploration of political representation is Hannah Fenichel Pitkin's *The Concept of Representation*.[2] In general, for the actions of public officials to be considered representative (1) the official must act with respect to (some version of) the wishes and interests of the public; (2) that public must have some control, however faint, over the official; such that (3) the official's acts may in some sense be attributed to the public. When school administrators make representational decisions, they face the same practical and ethical dilemmas that confront all political representatives. Essentially, they must choose a style of representation. The major choices of style and their rationalizations have been nicely expressed by Pitkin:

The majority of theorists argue that the representative must do what is best for those in his charge, but that he must do what he thinks is best, using his own judgment and wisdom, since he is chosen to make decisions for (that is, instead of) his constituents. But a vocal minority maintain that the representative's duty is to reflect accurately the wishes and opinions of those he represents. Anything else they consider a mockery of true representation.[3]

The roles described above are called "trustee" and "delegate." Briefly, a trustee is someone whose decisions are based on his own values (in the case of school administrators, usually "expertise"), even though those whom he represents may disagree. A delegate reverses this priority and is guided by expressed citizen preferences, even at the expense of his own best judgement. An intermediate position between the trustee and delegate decision-making styles is usually called "politico." A politico is simply someone who borrows from both trustee and delegate styles as dictated by situations but who has some internally consistent rationale for doing so.

The trustee/delegate/politico distinction is important to public policy because it captures the essence of people's expectations and of administrators' decisions in an area where there are no clear guides and where, consequently, a great deal of school-community dissension occurs.

Methodology

In order to explore the representational behavior of school administrators, a process was designed that had four stages: (1) an interview with 165 school administrators at all levels of administrative responsibility in all types of communities within New York State; (2) interview coding and preliminary analysis; (3) a series of case studies to verify the characterization of representational types from the interview data; and (4) final analysis and interpretation. Of the 165 people interviewed, 146 were principals, 11 were superintendents, and 8 were headquarters staff with community-related positions. Site selection and interview sampling rates within each site were weighted toward urban problems and toward a variety of pre-existing community/school situations that seemed likely to illuminate representational relations. Two of the ten districts were New York City "Community School Districts" (i.e., decentralized); one was a large city in upstate New York; one an industrial suburb of a Standard Metropolitan Statistical Area (SMSA); another was a mixed-income industrial and residential small city; two were SMSA-area bedroom communities; two were rural farming districts; and one was an industrial and farming district. Seventeen detailed case studies were made to verify the accuracy of the representational type assignment made on the basis of the interview evidence. Sixteen of the seventeen cases (93%) verified the interview-based assignment of representational roles. Each case study lasted about a week and contained aspects of reputational, issue career, and non-decision-making methodologies. To ensure factual accuracy, all case studies were returned in draft form to the principals for their comments. Although at times this procedure was as uncomfortable for the respondents as it was for the principal investigator, it generally resulted in a higher degree of validity than might otherwise have been expected.

Summary Representational Orientations and the Structure of Authority

The summary representational role orientations of the sample were as follows: 61% trustee; 30% delegate; and 9% politico (n = 161). Four individuals so completely lacked any orientation to their communities that they simply could not be described as representatives in any sense. This "insular" group, who were mostly headquarters staff, were not further analyzed (n = 161 plus 4 "insular" = 165).

For several reasons, this discussion is organized around trusteeness as the basic measure of representational role orientation. The first reason is of course that the trustee role is the one chosen most often by administrators. In the second place the trustee role is likely to be the most significant for public policy. By definition, trustees will choose to override the expressed needs and interests of their communities when they, the trustee administrators, disagree with that expression. It is true that some communities seek out and honor trustee orientations by their administrators; they prefer to let someone else decide. But, as people lose confidence in the conduct of public affairs and as they seek to expand their own participation, it becomes more likely that the trustee style will collide with the public's intentions. The trustee orientation is a latent source of friction. Finally, because administrators control so much of school/ community interaction, trusteeness can be interpreted as an indicator of citizen access to educational decisions and the general responsiveness of the school's administrators to the community.[a]

A number of variables dealt with differences in the structure and perception of authority. More public school administrators who were re-

---

[a] In order to reduce some statistical problems, the following discussion treats trustees and delegates in one group and politicos in a separate group. Thus, unless otherwise indicated, results reported as "percent trustee" indicate the percent taking trustee orientations of the group that took either trustee or delegate orientations. One hundred forty-seven individuals took either trustee or delegate representational role orientations, i.e., "trustee/delegate representational role orientations" (147 + 14 politicos + 4 "insulars" = total n of 165).

sponsible to appointed boards of education were willing to override expressed citizen preferences than were administrators who were responsible to elected boards. Seventy-four percent of those responsible to appointed boards were trustees, whereas only 61% of those responsible to elected boards were trustees.

We also looked at differences in the authoritativeness with which lay inputs were expressed. School administrators must determine their responses both to generalized, informal community preferences and to preferences expressed through boards of education. Sixty percent of the sample said that they would feel free to reject nonboard community preferences, even if those preferences were expressed with vigor and near unanimity. Only 37% of the administrators felt free to reject board preferences. The difference is one measure of the impact legitimacy has on school administrators.

Analysis of the interview schedules indicated three possible sources of representational cues: (1) the board, (2) "the community," or (3) both the board and the community. As the clarity with which an administrator perceived the sources increased (measured by familiarity and frequency of interaction with the various sources), and as the number and community-relatedness of the sources increased, the tendency to take trustee orientations declined.

The finding was similar to the relation between trusteeness and the level of administrative position. Headquarters administrators other than superintendents were most likely to be trustees (83%), building principals were next most likely (66%), and superintendents were the least likely of the three groups to be trustees (60%). The trusteeness of the headquarters staff is probably related to the facts that they rarely have contact with the public that is as direct as that of the other two groups, they are organizationally the furthest removed from popularly legitimated authorities, and they have the fewest sources of representational cues.

In general, then, with respect to the structure of authority, the evidence indicates that school administrators are most constrained by boards with direct electoral legitimation and direct oversight of their work. In addition, as the sources of representation are aggregated, and as they present clear cues, it becomes less likely that those cues (or expressed preferences) will be overridden.

Most institutional characteristics do not have strong impacts on representational orientations. Elementary, junior high or intermediate, and high school principals were about equally likely to be trustees. There were, however, three times as many politicos in junior and senior high schools as in elementary schools. The politico orientation, especially insofar as it fits representational style to particular situations, appears throughout the research to be a response to conflict; and the greater conflict at those higher grade levels probably explains the difference.

Neither the size of the school being administered nor the complexity of its program organization was related to the style of representation. The only exception was for those 23 administrators in charge of schools with enrollments of less than 500: three-fourths of these were trustees. Since smallness is generally supposed to be related to responsiveness to public interest, this is surprising. It also suggests that there is a lower limit on the size of decentralized units. When schools are very small, administrators are probably encouraged to believe that they already know the wishes and interests of their clientele and that reduces their motivation to search for additional representational cues.

Community Characteristics

Within the small sample of ten locations, suburban communities seemed to have a somewhat higher proportion of trustee administrators (81%) than did urban communities (64%) or rural communities (60%). Among large urban districts, the New York City Community School Districts were not more trustee than other similar districts. One suburban community with a rich history of almost every possible kind of educational controversy, including Supreme Court test cases, also had three times more politico administrators than its size would indicate. Again, the association between conflict and the politico style is clear.

The variations among urban districts seem to be related to the social class composition of those districts. We had hypothesized that the greater the range of social classes present and the more evenly balanced the class distribution, the more difficult it would be for administrators to know whose interests to represent about what; and thus, the greater the likelihood that a trustee orientation would ensue. That expectation was not borne out. Instead, there were more trustees where the schools were more homogeneous. Schools that were dominated by single groups from either end of the social class scale were especially likely to be administered by trustees. Thus 80% of the predominantly welfare-class schools and 75% of the predominantly upper-middle-class and above schools have trustee administrators. Many of the latter were boarding institutions, and it seems likely that those parents would encourage the administrators in their in loco parentis autonomy. The lowest-class schools, however, are probably run in a similar fashion but for very different reasons.

Interestingly, the addition of significant numbers of working-class parents seemed to decrease the tendency to take trustee orientations. That effect was especially noticeable where the school's attendance area was divided between welfare and working-class residents. It seems that the working-class parents, feeling threatened by their welfare-class neighbors and unable to escape to either private or suburban schools, then become actively involved in their own schools and that involvement provides clear representational signals, increasing the likelihood of delegate behavior by the administrator.

Personal Characteristics

One factor that is commonly supposed to be associated with responsiveness is that of virtual representation, the sharing of racial or ethnic characteristics between the public official and the community. Forty percent of the school administrators in New York State are virtually representative of their communities. In recent times we have come to expect that those who are virtually representative of the communities they serve will be much more responsive than administrators who are of a different racial or ethnic background. That expectation was not borne out by this research. The proportion of trustees in the virtually representative group was only slightly smaller than in the group who did not share racial and ethnic characteristics with their communities (64% and 69% respectively). Even at the most intimate level, that of the building principal, the sharing of presumably salient characteristics does not seem to contribute a great deal to the willingness to be bound by the community's expressed preferences (62% and 70% were trustees for the groups who were and were not virtually representative). The failure of virtual representation to effect a great reduction in the trustee orientation may be due to the effect of profssional socialization or the assumption by these administrators that, exactly because they are so much like those represented, it is permissible to make decisions instead of them or on their behalf.

Other characteristics of personal demography are more clearly related. There is a steady increase in the tendency to take trustee orientations as the age group being examined increases. There is a 24% increase in the tendency to be a trustee between the youngest and the oldest groups of administrators. But when administrators are grouped either by the amount of experience in their current positions, or by the length of time spent in a geographic locale, trusteeness is not related in any direction. It seems doubtful that the relation between increased age and increased trusteeness can be rationalized by greater job experience and greater familiarity with the community.

Proportionately fewer female than male administrators are trustees. Sixty percent of all women choosing either trustee or delegate roles chose trustee roles; 70% of the men did so. There were no women politicos, although their proportion of the sample indicates that there should have been three.

Table 6-1 shows the representational role distribution of the sample by administrators' minority/majority racial groups.

Since not even 10% of our sample was from the various minority groups, it is difficult to generalize about these results with much confidence. It is apparent that minority group administrators are seriously underrepresented in educational leadership positions in the state. Thus,

Table 6-1

Representational Role Orientation and Ethnicity of Administrator (in percentages)

Ethnicity (minority/majority groups)	Trustee	Delegate	Politico	Totals	(n)
Black and Spanish surnamed [a] (minority groups)	29	43	29	101 [b]	(144)
Other (majority groups)	65	30	5	101	(144)
n = 14 + 144 + 7 − 165					

Note: Seven individuals have been excluded from this table. They are the four insular non-representational decision makers, all of whom were white, two individuals whose racial background could not be determined, one of whom was a trustee and the other a politico; and one Oriental, who was a politico.
[a] Of these individuals, two were Spanish surnamed and both had delegate orientations.
[b] Error due to rounding.

they are a small but realistic proportion of the sample. When they are present, these results indicate that they go about the business of incorporating community interests and desires into their decisions in a fashion distinctly different from that of the majority group. Fewer than half as many take trustee orientations; many more are delegates; and a much greater proportion are politicos. The latter tendency probably reflects the practice of attempting to calm conflict-laden situations by appointing a principal from one of the minority groups.

A number of factors concerning administrative careers were investigated. Those administrators with tenure turned out to be much more trustee than those without, which demonstrates exactly the insulating effect for which tenure had been instituted, and the reason why, in 1971, the New York State Legislature abolished the granting of tenure to any individual who did not then have it. Curiously enough, more administrators expressed disapproval of tenure than approved it.

The fate of one's predecessor and the role played by the community in that disposition were also associated with the choice of representational style. If the predecessor's fate was an unhappy or involuntary one, the next incumbent was 20% less likely to be a trustee than otherwise. Similarly, if the community had a strong part in determining the career fate of the predecessor, there was a 20% decline in the tendency of the next incumbent to take trustee orientations toward that community. Almost half the politico group had assumed their positions in the wake of someone who had been involuntarily removed. Again, this reinforces the pattern of the politico orientation as a response to stress.

The relationship between the administrator's ambitions and responsiveness to the public is similar to that found in other areas of public life. As ambition decreases, the tendency to assume a trustee orientation increases. Thus personal ambition appears to be making school administrators, too, roughly accountable.

Expertise is often invoked to exclude participation by the uninitiated, and educational administrators are no exception. The more expertise school administrators believe they possess, the more they are likely to view their own trustee-like decision making as sufficient. Of those who described their own job performance as being in some fashion, expert, 72% were trustees. Of those who would not so describe themselves, only half were trustees. (Eleven of the fourteen politicos, a higher proportion than in any other group, described themselves as experts, which adds an element of self-confident trouble-shooting to the description of this group.) The data suggest that belief in personal expertise is a powerful rationale for ignoring the relevance of other people's participation in educational decisions.

Community Factors

The representation of citizen interests by administrators and the participation of citizens in school decisions are both methods for incorporating the will of the governed in public decisions. There is a clear relation between representational styles and attitudes toward lay participation, with trustees opposing and delegates favoring its increase. We were curious to know where administrators thought citizen participation could be most appropriate. Ten percent of the administrators said there were no policy areas appropriate for citizen participation. The most frequently chosen area was "budget and finance." But the emphasis was on finance, not budget; on how much to spend, not what to buy. Participation in curriculum matters and matters of student concern were about evenly chosen next most frequently, and there was real unanimity that citizens should not take part in decisions about teacher personnel. Only 7 of the 165 administrators said that area was the most appropriate. Since participation in, if not determination of, teacher personnel matters is a premier demand of community control advocates, and since school administrators are so unanimously against it, the opposition is an ominous one.

The stress on expertise and the inappropriateness of most citizen participation is consistent with a theme that ran throughout the interviews. That theme was one in which interaction with the community is seen not as shared decision making or authentic participation, but rather as an exercise in public relations. For example, when we asked administrators to list the major components of their jobs almost 40% described only bureaucratic or internally oriented tasks. Fifty-five percent did mention parents or community in their descriptions, but only as objects to be informed. About 5% felt that a part of their job responsibilities was to pursue a conscious and possibly binding relationship between the expressed preferences of the community and their own actions. And as expected, there was a strong relation between the presence of this representational role self-determination and the propensity to take delegate orientations. Trustees tended either to ignore any community-related job dimensions or to express them in public relations terms. In order to pursue this, we asked administrators to indicate to whom they were responsible. Seventy-two percent of those who felt responsible only to other educational bureaucrats were trustees, but the addition of any perceived responsibility to any part of the lay community dropped the trustee proportion to 50%.

When administrators do talk about "the community," parents are exceedingly dominant. Only about a third of school administrators recognize that there are nonparent interests with a stake in education (for example, community action agencies, government programs, business interests, and voluntary associations of all kinds). For the other two-thirds, mentioning parents exhausts their community representational responsibilities. Although this research did not deal with them, representation of student interests, even in the high schools, was noticeably absent from the administrators' concerns.

Within the recognized constituency group, there is a great deal of concentration on the supporters of the school. Seventy-three of 165 individuals either denied that there were people in the community who did not support the schools or never mentioned them. There may be some schools that are the object of that kind of unanimous adulation, but we doubt seriously that that group is as large as 44% of all schools. Rather, much of that figure should be attributed to the need to maintain the facade of unanimity by denying the presence of opponents. In minimizing or denying the presence of conflict, and in creating a simplistic image of the community, school administrators are making the task of representation in their own decisions more manageable. Although the tendency is understandable, and to some extent unavoidable, it has been carried too far. The question becomes how best to open up educational decisions. Some of the evidence presented so far points to needed changes but there are additional variables of interest.

By analyzing the way in which administrators described their communities, we were able to determine that in those places that were described as apathetic, 74% of the administrators were trustees (probably because of the tendency to interpret apathy as support). But in the communities that the administrators felt were actively involved in educational affairs, only about 60% of the administrators were trustees. In looking at the degree of organization in the various communities, we found sixteen "unorganized" communities, i.e., places where the administrator did not describe any functioning school-related interest groups. Eighty-seven percent of administrators in those places were trustees. The second, or "traditionally" organized communities had only that old standby of public relations, the Parent Teacher Association. Although many PTAs are extensions of the principal's mimeograph machine, the tendency to take trustee orientations still fell to 69%. "Highly organized" communities had two or more continuing education-related interest groups that were independent of the school. In the 33 highly organized communities, only 55% of the administrators were trustees. Thus, moving past the PTA stage to a situation in which there are independent and continuing agencies interested in the conduct of school affairs seems to be highly associated with the responsiveness of the administrator.

The visibility of the administrator's decisions is the final factor considered here. When the only scrutiny of an administrator's decisions came from bureaucratic superiors, 82% were trustees. When any parent or community groups also exercised regular oversight, the trustee percentage fell to 54%. Among building principals alone, the differences between those who were and were not regularly reviewed by outside groups is even more dramatic—a 30% decline in the percentage trustee. Thus, both the presence of outside watchdog groups and the visibility of the administrator's decisions (through hearings, joint meetings, review and advisory groups, and the like) press administrators away from the trustee style.

We have seen that several characteristics are strongly associated with the trustee representational style—stress on expertise to exclude the relevance of citizen participation, a concentration on internal routines and responsibilities, and an interpretation of the community as a holistic entity populated only by parents and supporters. Several things appear to reduce these tendencies, for example the power of electorally sanctioned oversight and the effect of inserting community opinion in the process of career advancement. Active, community-based, independent, and expert educational interest groups appear to be quite effective. So also is the practice of opening up administrative decisions to scrutiny by non-educators. In that regard, advisory groups and the introduction of such management reforms as programming-planning-budgeting have much to recommend them.

In all this, there is a clear implication that community interaction and community representation must be pursued at a level significantly different from public relations. The difference is the difference between being asked to help decide what is to be supported and being asked to support what has been decided.

Notes

1. David Easton, *A Framework for Political Analysis* (Englewood Cliffs, N.J.: Prentice-Hall, 1965), p. 50.

2. Hannah F. Pitkin, *The Concept of Representation* (Berkeley, University of California Press, 1967).

3. *Ibid.,* p. 4.

Part III
The Management of Conflict

Introduction to Part III

The Management of Conflict

Preceding sections have portrayed the obvious political context of schools, with alternating periods of quiescence and community conflict over allocation of resources and values. Stelzer and Mann emphasized that officials become much more open to the community when its inputs increase in volume and intensity, as they do periodically. A larger context for the analysis of these events, however, is the concept of the manifest and latent roles of the political system in the regulation of social conflict. Under most conditions, political authorities dominate the flow of policy demands, but there are occasions when that independence is challenged because an issue's intensity mobilizes the normally passive publics into action. Thus, we should expect to find the efforts of these authorities to manage conflict being affected by the kind and intensity of conflicts within which they must operate. Moreover, how well or fully they can deal with conflict may well be conditioned by the nature of the community in which they perform their duties. An understanding of the significance of the community context for the management skills of superintendents was a major contribution of David Minar, to whom this book is dedicated. The two studies in this section, particularly the first, deal directly with this thesis.

William Boyd examines eight suburban school superintendents for the mediating effect of the community context of each upon his skills in managing conflict. There emerges the understanding that the degree of autonomy of these professionals in dealing with conflict is shaped much less by his individual skills than by the class status of his district. Cultural ethos and the level of management resources seem to vary from place to place. Thus, higher status suburbs permit superintendents more freedom to deal with school conflict, while working-class districts constrain them much more; at the heart of this difference are different values concerning the professional's role.

From a major research into desegregation among 49 districts in California, Eldon Wegner and Jane Mercer have prepared for this volume a special analysis of their findings. They explore the relationships among such factors as community characteristics on the one hand, and, on the other hand, the degree of desegregation, the policies of desegregation, and the pressures for desegregation. These four sets of variables constitute different models that might explain the school policy process. They find that, despite the enormous publicity about political conflict to achieve desegregation, there is little relationship between the two factors. Indeed, there is little variation in the amount of desegregation which is explained by any of these models except community characteristics. This finding links to Boyd's, and before that to Minar's, that these local qualities form indistinct but nevertheless real constraints upon what authorities may do. Again, then, this section challenges the notion that the polity of the schools involves professionals exercising autonomous control.

7 Community Status and Suburban School Conflict
William L. Boyd *

Although public school districts represent America's most numerous governmental units, and expend the largest proportion of local public revenues, a concerted and systematic exploration of American school politics has only begun in recent years. Because of the exceptional social, political, and educational problems confronted by our large city school systems, they have naturally commanded most of the attention of researchers interested in school politics. However, with the growing concentration of Americans in suburban areas, systematic knowledge about the nature of suburban school politics becomes increasingly important. While much of the research on suburban school politics to date consists of atheoretical single case studies, whose richness in data tends to be offset by its limited generalizability, an important exception to this rule is found in a pair of related comparative studies by David Minar,[1] which raise a number of intriguing questions concerning the effects of community socioeconomic status upon conflict in educational policy-making. These questions prompted the research reported here, which used Minar's pioneering work as a point of departure for a comparative case study investigating the factors affecting the incidence and intensity of conflict in high and low status suburban school districts.

Of course, however interesting conflict and its causes may be in themselves, it is clear that not all conflict in school politics has significant immediate or long-term consequences. However, studies of American public school politics suggest that *high* levels of public conflict in educational policy-making have at least three important consequences. First, there is

This abridged, revised version of "Community Status and Conflict in Suburban School Politics" by William L. Boyd is reprinted from the *Sage Professional Papers in American Politics* series, Vol. 4, No. 025 (© 1975) by permission of the Publisher, Sage Publications, Inc. An early version of this paper was presented at the annual meeting of the American Educational Research Association, April 5, 1972, Chicago, Illinois. Readers desiring the complete footnotes (including some important qualifications and *caveats*), references, and methodological details concerning this study are referred to the Sage paper, and to the larger study, "Community status, Citizen Participation, and Conflict in Suburban School Politics" (unpublished Ph.D. dissertation, University of Chicago, 1973).

* University of Rochester

evidence that as the level of conflict in school district policy-making increases, the autonomy and discretion of school administrators is reduced
as a result of increased school board and citizen involvement in, and
scrutiny of, the policy-making process. Second, there is evidence that high
levels of conflict tend to have a debilitating effect on school officials. As
Minar notes, because of the widespread belief that the governance of education should be nonpolitical and nonpartisan,

> the [school] authority system usually is not accustomed to being opposed
> and therefore lacks resilience. Conflict is likely to be a disorganizing
> shock. Whereas, in most democratic government, structured conflict is
> recognized as the way the game is played, in school government it often
> seems to be regarded as a rude and foreign intrusion.

Finally, research shows that conflict which continues and increases over
time is likely to lead, ultimately, to the defeat of school board members
seeking reelection, followed by the replacement of the school superintendent and the adoption of new educational policies. Since most recent
studies have concluded that educators generally dominate most aspects
of public school policy-making, the reduction of the autonomy and influence of school administrators is in itself a significant development,
making possible—but by no means ensuring—a more democratic policy-
making process.

If the consequences of high levels of conflict in school politics are
significant, then knowledge about the factors causing and influencing the
course of such conflict is important. Although the literature on school
politics and community conflict suggests a variety of factors affecting
conflict, Minar has presented data indicating that the likelihood of high
levels of conflict and reduced discretion for school administrators varies
primarily with the socioeconomic status of communities. In a study of
forty-eight Chicago suburban elementary school districts, Minar found
that the twenty-four higher status districts had substantially lower levels
of electoral *conflict* (as measured by votes cast for losing candidates) and
electoral *participation* in school board elections than did the twenty-four
lower status districts. In addition, he found that the school superintendents
in the lower status districts were much more likely to have minor administrative decisions and policies questioned by their school boards than
were their counterparts in the higher status districts.

From these and other related data, Minar concluded that the variable
which could best account for his findings was the differential possession
by higher and lower status school districts of resources of conflict management skills in their respective populaces. By conflict management resources, Minar meant the aggregate organizational and management skills

and associated attitudes derived from the level of education and the kinds of occupations of a given populace. Minar hypothesized that the greater possession of management resources (including skills in such areas as "communication, negotiation, persuasion, division of labor and delegation of function") by higher than by lower status districts promoted deference to expertise (i.e., deference to professional administrators) in the former districts and tended to lead to a controlling and channelling of the educational decision-making process (especially by means of the use of nominating caucuses for the selection of school board candidates) in such a way as to minimize conflict. Conversely, Minar argued that the paucity of management resources in lower status districts is likely to reduce deference to expertise, increase school board and citizen interference in essentially administrative, as opposed to policy, matters, and reduce the community's ability to contain and control conflict.

In a follow-up comparative case study of four of the original 48 districts, Minar explored the validity of his hypothesis and concluded that it was essentially correct. However, because Minar chose to select for in-depth study two high status-low conflict districts and two low status-high conflict districts, there was no common effect between the pairs of districts. By not including what according to the *conflict management resources* hypothesis would be the *deviant* cases (i.e., high status-high conflict districts and low status-low conflict districts), the design of the study tended to make the rejection of the hypothesis unlikely. This is a troublesome point, for although the logic of the hypothesis is quite appealing in some respects, it seems to provide almost too simple an explanation for such complex phenomena.

In fact, political and sociological theory suggest a number of plausible rival explanations, some of which Minar acknowledged and considered, within the limitations of his data and research design. It could be argued, for example, (1) that lower status communities are more likely to be conflictual because, unlike in their more affluent higher status counterparts, the cost of governmental services is a continuing and burdensome issue; (2) that the higher levels of education of higher status populaces lead them to value education and other governmental services more and hence be more willing—as well as able—to spend for these services than lower status populaces; (3) that higher status populaces tend to be "civic-minded" and supportive of government, while (4) lower status populaces are inclined to be "alienated" and hostile toward government; and (5) that lower status communities may be less well integrated due to their low levels of citizen participation and the concomitant weakness of their organizational networks and, hence, they may be more susceptible to conflict. Although Minar recognized that explanations such as these may account for some part of the variance in conflict he found, he vigorously maintained that the single most potent variable is the differential possession of conflict management resources by higher and lower status districts.

Minar, of course, did not claim that his hypothesis could account for all phenomena of school politics, but instead argued for its general applicability. As he noted, "such questions as what happens to low-conflict communities in the event of a deep ideological schism or what happens to a high-conflict community in the presence of extraordinarily skilled technical leadership remain substantially untouched." Thus, the present study sought to test Minar's hypothesis through a design which included *deviant* as well as *non-deviant* cases. By this approach, it was possible to investigate both the factors operating in the absence of plentiful management resources to minimize conflict in low status–low conflict districts and the factors appearing to account for the ineffectiveness of the abundant management resources in high status–high conflict districts. Equally important, the study was designed to provide a more adequate test of possible alternative explanations for Minar's findings, such as those enumerated above.

Design and Methodology of the Study

In order to study the effects of community socioeconomic status upon citizen participation and the incidence and intensity of conflict in educational policy-making, a sample of eight districts were selected from the 118 Cook County [Chicago] suburban elementary school districts to provide pairs of districts to fill the cells of a fourfold typology (see Figure 7-1) of community status (as measured by 1960 median family income) and known conflict (as indicated by performance in tax and bond referenda from 1963 through 1968). Because of space limitations, we can suggest only the rudiments of the conceptual and methodological approaches employed in the study. Suffice it to say that the theoretical framework which guided the collection and analysis of data drew upon Minar's work and, in addition, included an effort to take account of the extent to which certain structural features of the school districts' communities—which on the basis of theory and research might be expected to promote or inhibit the incidence and intensity of community conflict—were correlated with the levels of conflict the respective districts experienced.

Specifically, three interrelated structural categories suggested by Gamson were investigated.[2] *Structural strain,* which refers to tensions arising from change in the community which may lead to conflict, was measured by the magnitude of variation in school district average daily attendance (A.D.A.) and assessed valuation over the decade from 1959 to 1969.

Conflict in Referenda

		Low		High	
Community Status	High	Northview *	(1)	Greenwood	(2)
		Oakton	(4)	Camden	(3)
		TYPE I		TYPE IV	
	Low	Smithville	(6)	Alton	(5)
		Trenton	(8)	Weston	(7)
		TYPE II		TYPE III	

* Pseudonyms are used for the districts studied.

Figure 7-1 Districts Selected Classified According to Community Status (ranked by number) and Conflict in Referenda.

Structural conduciveness to conflict, which refers to structural features which could provide potential lines of cleavage in the community, was measured by the extent to which the school districts possessed distinct solidary groups (such as religious or ethnic groups). Following Gamson's method, groups within the districts were classified as distinct solidary groups if over half of the respondents interviewed mentioned them and attributed to them some common outlook. Districts were ranked on the number and degree of solidarity of solidary groups, the latter dimension being determined according to four criteria suggested by Gamson. *Structural integration,* which refers to the extent to which the districts possessed networks of interlocking and cross-cutting ties, both formal (organizational) and informal, which might tend to bind together inhabitants and constrain and inhibit their behavior in issues and affairs of community concern, was measured indirectly, insofar as possible, by gathering data on the number of local organizations, the extent of their activity and the level of citizen participation within them, and the extent to which they were district-wide and broadly representative in their membership. According to Gamson's theory, the three categories of structural determinants —strain, conduciveness, and integration—are highly interrelated and operate only in conjunction to predict the likelihood and level of community conflict. Thus, "high conduciveness will not produce rancorous conflict if unaccompanied by strain nor if, although accompanied by strain, structural integration is great."

Following, Minar, conflict was defined as the "public confrontation of competing demands" and included all such demands pertaining to school affairs publicly manifested, for example, in public meetings, in the newspapers, by picketing, and in elections. The dependent variable, conflict in educational policy-making, was measured by developing rankings (on the basis of analyses of case study data, including voting behavior in school board elections and tax and bond referenda) of the districts studied on the *incidence* and on the *intensity* of the conflict they experienced during the five year period, 1964-1969, for which data were collected. From these two rankings, an average or overall conflict ranking was established. Data on participation and conflict in each district were collected by means of interviews with the principal participants (i.e., school board members, superintendents, and citizens active in school affairs) and by a review of the minutes of school board meetings and newspaper coverage for the five year period studied.

FINDINGS

Since space limitations prohibit the presentation of a summary of the case study data supporting the ranking of the districts on overall conflict, we will simply begin by stating that the overall conflict ranking proved to be strongly correlated with the ranking of the districts on referendum dissent (i.e., proportion of total votes which were cast against referenda over the period 1964-69). This correlation tends to validate the method of selecting the districts, suggesting that performance in tax and bond referenda is a good proxy for a measure of overall conflict.

Significantly, our analysis of school district conflict revealed that in both the higher and lower status districts the principal issues producing conflict included a range of substantive matters (e.g., the location of new schools, changes of school attendance boundaries, educational philosophy, and desegregation) that went well beyond simply those primarily related to economic considerations. Indeed, in only one of the districts (Weston) were a majority of the issues clearly related to cost factors. Thus, it appeared that much of the conflict in the lower as well as the higher status districts derived from considerations other than simply the ability or willingness to pay for educational services.

Turning briefly to the question of structural effects upon the incidence and intensity of conflict, as shown in Table 7-1, the rankings on the structural variables selected as indicators of structural strain, conduciveness, and integration proved to be unreliable predictors of overall conflict. For example, while Northview's conflict ranking matches our expectations based on Gamson's theory, Smithville should rank higher on conflict and Alton, given its low level of growth, should rank lower. In the case of the variable of growth, there were notable and easily measurable differences in "structural strain"—for example, Oakton's growth of 290% in A.D.A. from 1959 to 1969 as compared with Alton's growth of 17% for the same

Table 7-1

Rankings and Ratings of Districts on Overall Conflict, Growth, Solidary Groups, and Strength and Scope of Organizational Networks

District	Type	Overall Conflict	Growth in A.D.A. & Assessed Valuation (Strain)	Number and Degree of Solidarity of Solidary Groups (Conduciveness)	Strength and Scope of Organizational Networks (Integration)
Alton	IV	1 High	7 Low	2 High	5 Low
Weston	IV	2 High	2 High	6 Low	6 Low
Camden	II	3 High	5 Medium	4 Medium	3 High
Greenwood	II	4 Medium	6 Medium	7 Low	2 High
Trenton	III	5 Medium	4 Medium	1 High	8 Low
Smithville	III	6 Low	3 High	3 High	7 Low
Oakton	I	7 Low	1 High	5 Low	4 Medium
Northview	I	8 Low	8 Low	8 Low	1 High

period—which seemed to have no bearing on the level of conflict. This result, of course, may be due to the utilization of only a few of the many possible indicators of the numerous variables falling into the three structural categories. Gamson, who used very similar indicators in his own research, also had very limited success in differentiating high and low conflict communities according to his scheme. Nevertheless, to the extent that the indicators chosen are representative of their structural categories, the fact that they neither individually nor in combination reliably "predict" the level of conflict experienced suggests that we need to look elsewhere for much of the explanation we seek.

Political Culture and Conflict

In the comparative analysis of the case study data assembled, two variables, leadership by the school authorities and political culture, appeared to account for most of the variation in conflict levels. Taking the latter variable first, among both the districts selected as "deviant" and as "nondeviant" cases, striking and systematic differences in political behavior were clearly apparent and seemed to flow from differing political cultures in, on the one hand, the higher status, predominantly white collar districts and, on the other hand, the lower status, predominantly blue collar districts. The existence of distinctive political cultures was indicated both by extensive data linking the differences in political behavior to norms, attitudes, and values concerning the conduct of politics, and by the nature of the systematic patterns of behavior, which conformed to behavior associated with what Banfield and Wilson describe as the *public* and *private-regarding* political cultures.[3]

Banfield and Wilson contend that the various social cleavages in American cities and metropolitan areas tend to coalesce into two basic opposing patterns (or political cultures) deriving from the "fundamental cleavage between the public-regarding, Anglo-Saxon Protestant, middle-class ethos and the private-regarding, lower-class, immigrant ethos." The public-regarding political culture emphasizes the values of the Reform movement, e.g., "good government," efficiency, and the disinterested support of the broad public interest. By contrast, the private-regarding culture, which is associated with "machine" politics, seeks personal benefits and favors from the political system and identifies with the ward or neighborhood rather than the community as a whole. While the private-regarding culture recognizes the legitimacy of competition and conflict between groups concerned with narrow and special interests, the public-regarding culture takes "the view that politics, rather than being a struggle among partial and private interests is (or at any rate ought to be) a disinterested effort to discover what is best for the community 'as a whole'."

As the short description above suggests, these two political cultures tend to produce different types of citizen participation which are likely to affect the incidence and intensity of conflict. Indeed, this proved to be the case in the blue collar and white collar districts studied. Thus, in relation to theories of participation and conflict, a rather surprising finding of the study was that, in terms of conflict, the *type* of citizen participation was more important than the *volume* of participation, the dimension of participation which has traditionally received the most attention.

Minar, in his explanation of the differing levels of conflict in white collar and blue collar districts, has emphasized the importance in their respective political cultures of the distinctive norms and values associated with their differential possession of resources of "conflict management skills" (i.e., "perspectives and experiences that prize specialization, division of labor, delegation of authority, and technical expertise," thus affecting the way they conduct public business). However, the findings of the present study indicate that a satisfactory explanation of the incidence of conflict must also take explicit account of their norms and values concerning the nature of *politics* itself—in other words, the norms and values at the *heart* of their respective political cultures. While on the basis of the data we certainly agree with Minar about the importance of conflict management resources, we believe that they represent only half, and probably not the most significant half, of an adequate explanation of the differences in the incidence and intensity of conflict in blue collar and white collar suburban school districts. In other words, if, as Minar recognizes, "the application of these conflict management skills reflects (a) their availability in the community context, and (b) community expectations as to the means and ends of doing public business," then the nature of these community expectations becomes a vital part of a complete explanation of the variance observed in political behavior. This point becomes more apparent when one recognizes that the organizational and management skills of citizens can be, and not infrequently are, utilized to mobilize political opposition and aggravate conflict rather than to minimize conflict and maximize support for the authorities.

To summarize our position, we agree, on the basis of the data, that the availability of management resources clearly has a great deal to do with the *structuring* of the political process of school district governance. The crucial "rules of the game" affecting the process, however, appear to derive more from the cultural ethos than from perspectives associated with the level of management resources available. According to Banfield and Wilson's description of their "ethos theory," the "rules of the game" which differentiate the public and private-regarding political cultures appear to vary along four major dimensions: (1) the extent to which competition and "politics" are viewed as legitimate; (2) the extent to which the public interest is defined in terms of the whole community; (3) the extent to which honesty, impartiality, and disinterested participation are expected; and (4) the extent to which efficiency and expertise in governance are valued. In order to support these conclusions, we will now present a summary of the data pertaining to the above dimensions. Following this, we will discuss our analysis of the "deviant" cases which helps clarify the relationship to conflict levels of aggregate management resources, norms and values concerning "politics" (i.e., political culture), and the quality of leadership provided by the school authorities.

The Legitimacy of Competition and "Politics"

Although the populaces of both the white collar and blue collar school districts accepted and professed the view that politics should be "kept out" of education, there was a significant difference in terms of the general attitude toward, and meaning ascribed to, "politics," as well as in what went on in practice. While in the white collar districts "politics" was shunned as unseemly, unnecessary, and improper because it was believed that a common interest could and should be defined, in the blue collar districts competing interests and points of view tended to be an accepted fact of life. In the latter districts, keeping politics out of education chiefly meant that political parties should not interfere in school affairs and that the administration and governance of education should be free of patronage and corruption. In the white collar districts such occurrences were virtually unheard of. The emphasis on these points in the blue collar districts, however, was more than theoretical. In at least one of the districts, payoffs and patronage were not entirely things of the past. In the others, "machine" style political behavior and periodic revelations of corruption in municipal or township government were a constant reminder of the dangers of the coarser side of politics. Unlike the white collar districts, in three out of four of the blue collar districts political parties (often nominally "nonpartisan") were judged to be the most important local organizations and appeared to reach a larger proportion of the inhabitants than any other organizations.

Although overt activity in education on the part of local political parties and politicians was rare in both white collar and blue collar districts, informal and indirect linkages between the school systems and the local political parties tended to be much more important in the blue collar districts, mainly in terms of the recruitment of school board members. In the absence of effective nonpartisan structures for the recruitment and support of board members, blue collar school boards were inclined to be self-recruiting and often turned to local politicians and political parties in seeking new board members. This practice was reflected in the fact that three out of four of the blue collar districts had persons on their school boards who were also active in leadership roles in local political organizations. This state of affairs was not found to be the case in any of the white collar districts, where influence tended to be concentrated in local civic organizations rather than in local political parties.

The pre-eminence of the political parties in the blue collar districts seemed accountable to the traditions and values of their citizens, large numbers of whom are foreign born or first generation Americans. In part, the parties appeared to be supported in order to protect and enhance the interests of groups and community areas within the districts. In part, the popularity of the parties seemed to flow from an approach to politics as a form of "play," as an enjoyable diversion and sport. Interview data suggesting this attitude included descriptions of the boisterous character of citizen participation in political parties and political clubs, and of the interest and fascination commanded by community controversies. For example, during a teachers' strike in Weston, citizens turned out in droves to attend heated negotiations between the teachers' union and the school board which were open to the public and were described as being "more entertaining than television." Another manifestation of this attitude toward politics may be found in the response of a blue collar school board member, who, when asked why he served on the board, said, "I looked on it initially as a form of recreation, a hobby, and I still see it this way to some extent. It's interesting and less expensive than bowling." The data indicate that, as a result of this attitude toward politics, hotly contested school board elections in blue collar districts were rather widely enjoyed rather than being viewed as a sort of social disaster, as such elections tended to be perceived when, on occasion, they occurred in white collar districts.

The norms against political competition and conflict in white collar districts can be illustrated by two examples. In Northview, the formation and activities of a self-appointed citizens group critical of the school system (the first such group in the history of the district) were greeted with an icy response from the public despite the fact that it was admitted in private that the group had identified many legitimate problems. It was felt that this "just wasn't the way to go about things," that is, to seek change, especially since the incumbent superintendent was near retirement. The group soon began to disintegrate as its members began to respond to the cues they were receiving. Eventually, several members of the group worked their way up to leadership positions within the school district "establishment." Similarly, in Greenwood, when a controversy led to a situation in which two independent candidates decided to run for the school board in competition with the slate of candidates endorsed by the district nominating caucus, the independent candidates—who were not aligned—felt called upon to publicly apologize for and justify their decision to challenge the caucus, since their action was virtually unprecedented. By contrast, in Alton, a blue collar district employing a caucus, independent candidates regularly ran against the caucus slate and no need was seen for any apology for this.

The functioning as well as the existence of nominating caucuses to select school board candidates—which in the Chicago suburbs appears much more likely to occur in white collar than in blue collar districts— seems accountable to cultural values *vis-a-vis* politics as well as to the level of management resources available. Indeed, caucuses of this type appear to be inventions of the middle class reform movement and are often associated with nonpartisan systems. The avowed purposes of caucuses appear to be very public-regarding ones. Caucuses are said to exist as mechanisms for seeking the best qualified persons available for school board service and they operate on the assumption that "the job should seek the man" rather than *vice versa*. While it could be easily argued that it would be more democratic for the caucuses to offer the voters a choice between several well qualified candidates, in practice the caucuses in white collar Chicago suburban districts overwhelmingly choose to present the voters with single slates of candidates which typically run unopposed, a procedure and response which may be more accountable to a desire to avoid political competition and conflict than to the inexorable workings of the plentiful management resources of white collar districts. As one of the white collar school board member respondents put it, "the whole point of the caucus is to *avoid* having to run for office," an undertaking which he went on to indicate was viewed as onerous, immodest, and potentially embarrassing. In contrast to the white collar districts, the few blue collar districts which employ caucuses are more likely to face opposition from independent candidates, a fact which may be as much a result of cultural values as of a deficiency of managerial resources. The fact that the caucus nominees in white collar districts are typically unopposed accounts not only for the low levels of electoral *conflict* in these districts, but also for their low levels of electoral *participation* in settings where one would otherwise expect high levels because of the "participativeness" associated with higher status populaces.

Honesty, Impartiality, and Disinterested Participation

While the moderately to highly affluent citizens of the white collar districts studied for the most part had little to nothing to gain in the way of *material* personal benefits from their school systems, and, further, professed or accepted an ideology which prohibited such self-seeking, the same was not true of many of the citizens of the blue collar districts studied. Interview data from blue collar district board members and superintendents indicated that board members tended both to expect and to receive requests for favors from their constituents, and that some members tried to grant these requests toward the end of building their political following. In particular, school board members frequently mentioned receiving personal requests from citizens for custodial and other noncertified positions for themselves or their friends or relatives. Further, board members in three out of four of the blue collar districts alluded to the days in the not too distant past when noncertified positions in their systems were objects of patronage. Indeed, in Weston one of the largest controversies in fact involved allegations against the school board concerning the use of custodians' jobs as "political plums," reputed "ghosts" on the district's payroll, and suspicion of bribery in the case of the retention of an attorney. The majority of this particular board, which became completely discredited, was also accused of holding secret "bootleg" board meetings at which they plotted their machinations. Interestingly, in regard to "explaining" observed political behavior, a subsequent "reform" member of this board remarked that he felt that the competitiveness of board elections and the greater turnout of voters for board elections than for referenda in his district was at least partly accountable to the tradition of patronage associated with the board.

The history of patronage and occasional revelations of corruption in local government, and in a few cases in the school systems themselves, tended to make the residents of blue collar districts suspicious of public officials, including both school administrators and school board members. Three out of four of the blue collar districts studied had had scandals in local government within the past decade. One of the districts, already alluded to, had also unquestionably had cases of improper behavior involving school authorities. On the other hand, none of the white collar districts in the study had such histories to undermine trust in public officials. Thus, the reluctance to delegate authority and defer to expertise common in the blue collar districts derived not only from the paucity of managerial experiences and attitudes in the populace but also from aspects of the political culture which generated suspicion of public officials.

The Broad Public Interest

In general, in the blue collar districts there was a greater allegiance to sub-communities and groups within the districts than to what was "best" for the *whole* school system. This tendency was often aggravated by the fact that three out of four of the districts subsumed several villages or communities within their boundaries. Although the same was true of two of the four white collar districts, in these districts potential lines of cleavage seldom interfered with the pursuit of the "best interest" of the whole school district. These points are illustrated by the fact that while in the white collar districts the PTAs tended to work together well to promote projects, including referenda, which benefited the whole district, there was a notable lack of unity among the PTAs within the blue collar districts. This lack of unity was clearly partly accountable to the pronounced allegiance, apparent in both actions and words, of blue collar PTAs to their own schools and sub-communities. At the same time, insufficient managerial and leadership skills, and the general weakness of the PTAs themselves in the blue collar districts, were also factors which contributed to the lack of unity.

Other evidence suggesting allegiance to sub-communities and groups in the blue collar districts included aspects of voting behavior and the performance of school board members. The citizens of the blue collar districts manifested certain of their "attachments" in the phenomenon of "name-voting," a practice not detected in the white collar districts. In all four of the blue collar districts, respondents volunteered that having a name associated with certain ethnic groups would attract votes in board elections. As one board member put it, "Being Bohemian will draw votes; being Bohemian and Catholic is even better." In the case of the performance of board members, although the board members in all districts studied are elected at-large, those in the blue collar districts appeared more inclined than their counterparts in the white collar districts to represent and serve the interests of sub-communities or areas within their districts.

Finally, the difference between the blue collar and white collar districts in terms of their ideology regarding the definition of the public interest can be depicted in the manner in which competing demands were presented. When, on occasion, the consensus regarding what was "best" for the whole district broke down in the white collar districts (and, of course, this happened most frequently in the "deviant" white collar districts), there was a tendency for competing views to be couched in the rhetoric of "the broad public interest" even when in substance they clearly reflected the desires of sub-communities or special interest groups. On the other hand, in the blue collar districts, demands generally were simply presented from a neighborhood or sub-community point of view with little or no attempt to justify them in terms of what was "best" for the whole district. The former pattern occurred, for example, in Greenwood during the controversy over the site for the new junior high. Neighborhood groups near the old junior high argued that a nearby vacant lot on which they feared an apartment building might be constructed (to the detriment of their neighborhood, as they saw it) was the "best" site despite the fact that a larger and more conveniently situated lot nearer the old school was preferred by the school authorities and their architects. By contrast, during the controversy in Alton over the adjustment of school attendance area boundaries to equalize class size, neighborhood groups simply demanded the restoration of their former neighborhood school patterns, although they knew this would recreate overcrowding problems in some schools.

In regard to the final dimension of interest, it should be clear from what we have said above that *both* the paucity of management resources in blue collar districts *and* the character of their political culture combined to minimize the extent to which efficiency and expertise in governance were valued. By contrast, plentiful management resources and a strong sense of "public-regardingness" tended to maximize the emphasis on these values in white collar districts.

So far, we have shown that our data strongly suggest that differences in *both* the political culture and management resources of white collar and blue collar school districts lead to different types of citizen participation and political behavior, which in turn tend to cause predictable differences in the incidence and intensity of conflict in school politics. Since the systematic differences in political culture from higher to lower status districts were readily apparent in deviant as well as nondeviant cases, we are left with the problem of explaining the failure of the deviant cases to "behave," with regard to conflict levels, in the manner expected on the basis of our theoretical analysis.

Analysis of Deviant Cases

In their comparative analyses of the four school districts they studied in collaboration, Minar and Snow found that the quality of leadership by school authorities seemed to account for much of the variance in conflict levels not readily attributable to contextual factors, such as the availability of management resources. The same was true in the present study. As compared with the high status-low conflict districts (Northview and Oakton), many of the difficulties of the high status-high conflict districts (Greenwood and Camden) seemed to stem from naive, unrealistic, or unresourceful leadership behavior with regard to school and community relations by their authorities. On the other hand, as compared with the low status-high conflict districts (Alton and Weston), astute and enterprising leadership by the authorities in the low status-low conflict districts (Trenton and Smithville) appeared to partially offset their many contextual disadvantages and contribute to their relatively low conflict levels. Finally, although there were numerous and frequently important differences among the eight districts, the four districts lowest on overall conflict appeared generally to have more resourceful leadership from their authorities than did the four districts highest on overall conflict, three of which witnessed provocative behavior by their authorities which intensified or precipitated conflict.

It would, of course, be simplistic and far-fetched to suggest that more effective leadership by the authorities by itself could have brought the high conflict districts down to the conflict levels of the low conflict districts when many other variables than the quality of leadership obviously were involved. However, it does appear that in many instances conflict might have been appreciably reduced by more resourceful leadership. In particular, in the comparative analysis two dimensions of leadership seemed to be especially important: politically sensitive behavior (as opposed to apolitical behavior) and proactive behavior to retain the initiative (as opposed to reactive behavior in which the authorities tend to be on the defensive). Due to space limitations here, we shall have to confine ourselves to a brief summary of the data supporting these conclusions, focusing mainly, for illustrative purposes, on two of the four deviant cases.

To begin with the high status-high conflict cases, Greenwood provides a striking example of the effects of unrealistic and apolitical leadership behavior. Although Greenwood is remarkably similar to Northview (the district lowest on overall conflict) in terms of the composition of its population, its size, and its advantageous resources and structural features, the Greenwood school board precipitated a crisis by ignoring the recommendation of a citizens advisory committee it had appointed to consider the question of whether the district should enlarge its existing junior high or build a new middle school. Four members of the citizens committee opposed the board's decision to build a new school and formed an *ad hoc* group of about forty citizens which very skillfully fought the necessary bond referendum, which was defeated. Board members interviewed stated, in retrospect, that they had realized that their decision might not be popular in some quarters, but that they had counted on majority support for their bond referendum because they were convinced that it was in the "best" interest of the district from an *educational* standpoint. However, although cost was not a factor in this affluent suburb, it is apparent from our data that at the time of the issue a number of values in addition to educational ones (e.g., convenience of location) were being weighed by large segments of the populace.

In the aftermath of the referendum defeat, with both the consensus concerning what was "best" for the district and the local norms against conflict temporarily shattered, the school board groped for a solution to the junior high issue. They next proposed a bond referendum to authorize an addition to the existing junior high, but this proposal became embroiled in a new dispute over which property adjacent to the existing school should be utilized. Again, the board had chosen to disregard the advice and requests of citizens involved—this time on a self-appointed basis—in favor of doing what it thought was best *educationally,* and again many of these citizens joined together to organize an effective *ad hoc* opposition group. Following the defeat of the second referendum, the board capitulated and delegated the resolution of the issue to a new citizens advisory committee made up of opponents and proponents of the previous referenda. The "compromise" referendum proposal which emerged, and which was successfully passed, simply revised the second proposal to satisfy citizens' demands regarding the property to be utilized.

The intense controversy which Greenwood experienced was certainly not brought about by any deficiency in management resources—either in the populace or upon the school board, which was loaded with executives —or by a lack of general commitment to public-regarding values. Nor did the controversy seem to spring from ideological differences within the community, which was the case in the instance of Camden (the other high status-high conflict district), where much of the conflict derived from a fundamental ideological clash—exacerbated by inept behavior on the part of the school authorities—between advocates of conservative and liberal educational and governmental philosophies. However, it did appear that the unrealistic and apolitical behavior of the Greenwood school board —derived ironically from an *excess* of public-regarding zeal for what it thought could be demonstrated to be "best" for the district—triggered the conflict by destroying (temporarily) the credibility of the assumption of a *single* public interest upon which the public-regarding culture rests. In Camden, on the other hand, ideological differences within the populace made a public-regarding consensus regarding the school system difficult to maintain despite widespread lip service to this value.

Moving now to the low status-low conflict districts, in addition to astute leadership Smithville and Trenton also had in common a distribution of the electorate within their boundaries which enabled the largest sub-community within each district to control district decision-making, an accomplishment which was facilitated by the presence of a single dominant local political party in each district. Both of these sub-communities consistently utilized the voting advantage they enjoyed to dominate district affairs toward the end of protecting their own interests, not the least of which was to try to maintain the separation existing between themselves and all-black sub-communities within the districts.

In Trenton the situation in several important respects resembled that described by Vidich and Bensman in their celebrated study of "Springdale." [4] Like Mr. Peabody in Springdale, Trenton's superintendent operated under heavy constraints imposed by an uncooperative school board dominated by a very conservative sub-community. Like Mr. Peabody, the superintendent nevertheless exerted what appeared to be the maximum possible influence, under the circumstances, by means of full and strategic use of his limited resources. For example, to contend with the lack of deference from his all-blue collar board, their propensity to meddle in routine administrative matters, and their inclination to caucus informally prior to meetings in order to decide how they would vote on certain matters, the superintendent intentionally made the agendas he sent out in advance of board meetings as sketchy as possible and then allowed the board to bog down whenever they liked in "administrivia." This approach tended to leave open to the superintendent the opportunity to move ahead somewhat independently, in a quiet and cautious fashion, in more substantive areas, such as curriculum development. Again, like Mr. Peabody, the superintendent knew his community and made maximum use of the rather weak PTAs as support organizations, for example, in getting out the vote for referenda the board had approved but had done little campaigning for.

In sum, however, as much as the superintendent's skills contributed to the reduction of conflict, it was the combination of his leadership with the strong dominance of the main sub-community (together with the dominant local political party which structured this power and acted, as in Smithville, as a conflict reducing mechanism) that appeared to account for the moderate level of overall conflict in a setting which otherwise might have produced intense conflict.

To conclude, if it is safe to assume, as suggested by Minar's study of forty-eight districts, that high status districts tend to be low on conflict and low status districts tend to high on conflict, the present study suggests that, at least in the Chicago suburban area, this is due both to differences in political culture and management resources. It appears that in "normal" cases, higher status districts will tend to have public-regarding cultures (which tend to lead to harmony and the avoidance of conflict) as well as plentiful management resources while lower status districts will tend to have private-regarding cultures (which tend to lead to tension and conflict) coupled with meager management resources. In "deviant" cases, the public-regarding tendency toward consensus of high status-high conflict districts will have broken down, most likely because of ideological tensions and/or as a result of inept leadership, and management resources will be used to mobilize conflict. Low status-low conflict districts may exist as a result of unusually skilled leadership behavior by the authorities and/or as a consequence of a distribution or control (perhaps through the existence of political machines) of power within the districts which tends to suppress conflict.

IMPLICATIONS

Although it will come as no surprise that the four districts highest on overall conflict faced significantly more *organized* opposition than did the four districts lowest on overall conflict, it is noteworthy that in two of the four high conflict districts (Alton and Greenwood) the formation of organized opposition was precipitated by apolitical and provocative behavior by the authorities. In light of the impact that even quite small opposition groups can exert in school districts—given the structural and political vulnerability of nonpartisan school government—it would seem that school authorities would benefit by more attention and sensitivity to the political realities of the world in which they operate.

Of course, conflict is not always dysfunctional, and for this reason "good" administration cannot simply be equated with the avoidance of conflict. Indeed, in some instances progress may require that conflict be joined. Nevertheless, where high conflict seems unnecessary or counterproductive, careful consideration of the *political* as well as the more *substantive* (e.g., educational) merits of alternative policies seems in order. Here, however, the phoenix-like myth of the "non-political" nature of educational policy-making often seems to delude both school board members and superintendents. Hence, an obvious implication of our findings is that school authorities might find training designed to increase their political sensitivity very useful. In addition, training which focuses upon conflict management skills should emphasize the analysis and anticipation of problems and issues and proactive leadership behavior.

Moreover, to the extent that predominantly blue collar school districts indeed tend to have private-regarding political cultures—and further research on this point is much needed, especially in areas which, unlike the Chicago region, are not known for their private-regarding, machine politics traditions—it appears that the training and expectations of school administrators who may serve in such districts should be adjusted accordingly. Our data suggest that school superintendents in blue collar districts—where, because of the cultural ethos and available management resources, there is less deference than in white collar districts to expertise —are often forced to play the role of pragmatic political strategists while their counterparts in white collar districts are more often able to play the role of educational statesmen more consistent with the ideology of their profession and training. While both roles are political ones—that of the statesman simply requiring a different and more covert brand of politics— school superintendents in blue collar districts should be less burdened with the constraining baggage of a professional ideology which is ill-suited to their situation and which in some cases, as our data revealed, tends to incapacitate them with role conflict.

Notes

1. David W. Minar, "The Community Basis of Conflict in School System Politics," *American Sociological Review,* 31, 6 (December 1966), 822-834; and Minar, *Educational Decision-Making in Suburban Communities,* Cooperative Research Project 2440 (Northwestern University, 1966).

2. William A. Gamson, "Rancorous Conflict in Community Politics," *American Sociological Review,* 31, 1 (February 1966), 71-81.

3. Edward C. Banfield and James Q. Wilson, *City Politics* (New York: Vintage Books, 1963).

4. Arthur J. Vidich and Joseph Bensman, *Small Town in Mass Society* (Princeton University Press, 1958).

8

Dynamics of the Desegregation Process: Politics, Policies, and Community Characteristics as Factors in Change

Eldon L. Wegner and Jane R. Mercer *

The Civil Rights Act of 1964 established the first statutory basis for school desegregation with administrative procedures for enforcement. Schools at all levels of education that were supported by any federal funds were prohibited from employing racial or ethnic criteria as a basis for attendance. The Department of Justice was authorized to file suit against districts found in violation of this policy and these districts could be denied all financial support from the federal government. In addition, the U.S. Office of Education was authorized to make grants available to districts and state departments of education for the purpose of assisting school desegregation.

Between 1966 and 1971, there was considerable judicial, legislative and executive initiative favoring school desegregation in the State of California. In 1965, the Department of Education obtained a grant from the U.S. Office of Education to establish a Bureau of Intergroup Relations (BIR) to conduct an annual ethnic survey of all schools in the state and, upon request, to assist districts in developing programs to accomplish school desegregation. The state guideline for determining racial balance in a school was whether the proportion of any racial or ethnic group in the school differed by more than 15 percent from the proportion of that group in the total district. No sanctions were established for noncompliance with this policy. However, the policy received formal recognition by being incorporated into the California Administrative Code in 1969. It was passed into law by the California State Legislature in 1971. Subsequently, a proposition was approved by 60% of the voters in November, 1972, which prohibited pupil assignments based on "race, creed, or color." By 1972, all legislative initiative for school desegregation had stopped and

The work presented or reported herein was performed pursuant to a contract from the U.S. Office of Education, Department of Health, Education, and Welfare. However, the opinions expressed herein do not necessarily reflect the position or policy of the U.S. Office of Education, and no official endorsement by the U.S. Office of Education should be inferred. Funded by the United States Office of Education, OEC-9-73-0137. Under the provisions of Title IV, Section 403, of Public Law 88-352, The Civil Rights Act of 1964.

* University of California, Riverside

the issues involved in these conflicting acts were pending before the California State Supreme Court.

The Bureau of Intergroup Relations was very active in working with districts to desegregate their schools between 1966 and 1972. Every fall the BIR conducted an annual ethnic survey of all schools. All schools violating the state guideline, using the 15 percent criterion, were reported to the district as ethnically imbalanced, and their imbalance became a matter of public record. The BIR then asked the district to develop a plan to bring about compliance with the state policy and offered its assistance in developing desegregation programs. Thus, districts felt considerable formal and informal pressure to take some action, and the BIR was an important source of external pressure for desegregation in many districts during the period studied. Yet, between 1966 and 1971, the percentage of schools meeting the state guideline for ethnic balance changed from 75.2% to 78.2%, a gain of only 3%.

Four Models of the School Desegregation Process

This paper examines four different models of the school desegregation process. Each model focuses on different sets of factors hypothesized to be critical in determining changes in the ethnic balance in a district. Each model oversimplifies a complex reality in an attempt to identify which specific factors are most crucial in the movement toward desegregation.

The Desegregation Action Model

The desegregation action model views the educational administrator and school board as the key actors in the desegregation process. It hypothesizes that school desegregation results from a series of actions taken by the school board and educators in a district. A critical assumption of this model is that board members and administrators effectively control those resources and processes which determine the degree of racial balance in a district and that effective school desegregation is primarily a technical problem which involves developing and implementing appropriate strategies for desegregating the schools. Thus, school desegregation depends upon the willingness of school officials to adopt measures designed to bring about racial balance, such as changing school boundaries, busing students out of their neighborhood schools, pairing schools, establishing an open enrollment policy, and so forth. Desegregation efforts are directed at getting the board and administration to act.

A recent volume, directed to educators, is based on a desegregation action model.[1] It provides "practical detailed suggestions to various educational and community groups most directly involved in desegregation efforts." These recommended procedures "take into account traditional educational processes which over the years have assured educational progress . . ." The belief of the authors is that "positive, dedicated leadership can mean the difference between success and failure of the desegregation process." The volume then proceeds to develop a prototype model describing the actions which the board and superintendent should take to achieve "effective desegregation."

A study by Kirby, Harris, Crain, and Rossell is also based on an implicit desegregation model.[2] Their study included ninety-one non-southern cities of over 50,000 population and at least 3,000 blacks. They used the "desegregation actions" of the school board and superintendent as a major dependent variable. The implicit assumption is that "desegregation actions" are correlated with the amount of actual racial balancing that takes place in a district. However, their measure of "desegregation actions" was correlated only .29 with "percent blacks moved," accounting for only 8.4% of the variance in actual relocation of students.

The Political Pressures Model

This model theorizes that school desegregation is a political process and will occur if sufficient political pressures for change are mobilized within the school district. In this model, the critical factor is not so much the activity of school officials, but actions taken by groups in the community to force officials to desegregate the schools. The major assumption of this model is that the school district exists in a state of dynamic equilibrium. Representatives of the dominant Anglo-American community control the district and district policies reflect their particular interests and values. Change, therefore, is not likely to be initiated spontaneously by the school board or by administrators, but they will respond to political pressure.

Political pressures may be internal or external or both. In some districts, the minority community becomes dissatisfied because of some local event and disturbs the equilibrium of the district by creating internal pressures for change. A building program that would increase or maintain segregation in the district may trigger action. The low scholastic achievement of minority students may become public information. Racial tension may develop into open conflict between students. Discriminatory disciplinary or personnel practices may become the basis for protest. As a result of some precipitating event, a citizen organization is often formed to present minority grievances to the school board or to take more direct action, such as organizing school boycotts or sit-ins. In other cases, external forces play an important role in producing political pressures on the administration, court orders, national civil rights groups, and state education officials.

According to the political pressures model, once the old equilibrium has been destroyed, school officials must search for a new accommodation that will satisfy the political pressures being mobilized against them if they are to maintain their control. Thus, school desegregation will occur in those districts in which minority discontent has disturbed the status quo by mobilizing political pressures favorable to desegregation.

The District Characteristics Model

This model theorizes that the economic, demographic, and organizational characteristics of the district are the most critical variables determining the extent of desegregation in a district. The major assumption of this model is that impersonal, demographic factors operate as constraints more powerful than the actions of persons in official positions or the political pressures mounted by any particular segment of the community. For example, in some districts, the size and racial distribution of the district makes school desegregation very costly. A poor district may not have the resources for new construction or for the transportation of students to implement desegregation. The district characteristics model hypothesizes that political pressures and desegregation actions will have only a limited, independent effect on desegregation once district demographic characteristics have been controlled.

A Composite Model

A composite model pictures school desegregation as the outcome of a particular configuration of community characteristics, political pressures, and actions by the school board and administration. In particular types of communities, the minority population will be more likely to exhibit discontent with traditional patterns of separatism and will be able to organize and bring political pressure to bear. This pressure will force the district to respond. The result is a series of desegregation actions that lead to a program of racial balancing in the schools. This model predicts high correlations between certain community characteristics, the development of political pressures for desegregation, adoption of district actions to implement desegregation, and the achievement of racial balance in the schools of the district. We will examine each of these models in relation to school desegregation between 1966 and 1971, in a sample of California school districts.

Methods of Procedure

The sample includes all 49 California unified districts (kindergarten through twelfth grade) that had a minimum average daily attendance (ADA) of 2,500 students, at least 10 percent total minority student population (black, Spanish surname, Oriental, other), and less than 80% of their schools balanced according to state guidelines in 1966. The Los Angeles Unified School District was omitted because of its unusual size (over 600,000 students) and some problems in obtaining data.

A number of sources of information were used to develop a detailed picture of each district and an account of events of each district relevant to school desegregation over the six-year period. Quantitative data were available from the annual ethnic survey regarding the school attendance patterns of each ethnic group during the period (California State Department of Education, BIR surveys). In addition, California Department of Education publications provided information about tax rates, achievement test scores, average class size, and other organizational characteristics of each district (*California State Testing Program 1969-70*). A large amount of information was obtained from 1970 U.S. Census data tapes describing such population characteristics of each district as the proportion of high school graduates, the occupational distribution, average family income, the number of female-headed households, and so forth. This information was available both for the total population in the district and for the Anglo-American, black, and Spanish-surname populations separately, on data tapes which the California State Department of Education made available to us, at cost, on which the fourth-count population characteristics had been re-categorized to conform to school district boundaries. The Bureau of Intergroup Relations permitted us to study historical materials in their records and provided additional material through interviews with their staff.

The Measure of Change in Ethnic Balance 1966-1971

The state of California classifies each school in a district as balanced or imbalanced, according to the 15 percent criterion in the state guidelines. This measure, however, does not actually reflect the proportion of minority children in the district attending segregated schools. It is possible for a small number of schools in a district to be classified as imbalanced, but the overwhelming proportion of minority children may be concentrated in these schools. For this reason, we calculated the actual proportion of black and Spanish-surname children attending ethnically balanced schools and subtracted the proportion for Fall 1971, from the proportion in Fall 1966, in each district. We then added 100 to the difference to allow for minus scores. The difference between these proportions plus 100 is the measure of change in ethnic balance that we used as the dependent variable in our analysis.

Ten districts had a smaller percentage of their black and Spanish-surname students in desegregated schools in 1961 than in 1966, but 39 districts had made some headway. Fifteen districts had an additional 20% or more of their students in desegregated schools in 1971 than in 1966. The average ethnic balance score for the sample was 111.39 with a standard deviation of 19.80. Scores ranged from 79 to 164.

The Measure of Desegregation Actions

Information on desegregation actions taken by a school district between 1966 and 1972 was secured from three sources. First, a questionnaire was sent to the superintendent of each school district asking about specific actions which had been taken to desegregate their schools. Second, a narrative account of events relevant to desegregation in each district was constructed from qualitative data available in the files of the Bureau of Intergroup Relations. Those files contained correspondence with the BIR, accounts of action taken by the school board and administration in the district, reports by BIR officials, and newspaper clippings and other items of information. Third, members of the BIR staff were interviewed regarding their perceptions and experiences in the school districts in which they had worked as consultants. Six major types of desegregation actions were identified.

(1) *Relocation of Schools.* Old school buildings may be abandoned in favor of a new site which would draw upon a more ethnically diverse population. A number of California districts have abandoned older buildings that do not meet acceptable earthquake standards and have used the opportunity to relocate schools to achieve greater ethnic balance in enrollment.

(2) *Construction of New Schools.* Many California communities had a major increase in population between 1966 and 1969. Some of these school districts built new schools to accommodate their increasing enrollment in locations which would improve the ethnic balance of the district.

(3) *Changing School Boundaries.* A fairly common approach to desegregation is to change the attendance boundaries of existing schools to encompass more ethnically diverse neighborhoods. The effect of changing boundaries is potentially great, especially in those instances in which there

has been gerrymandering aimed at maintaining racial homogeneity of schools. Altering attendance boundaries is most likely to be productive in small and medium sized districts where the population is geographically concentrated.

(4) *Open Enrollment Programs.* Some districts have adopted programs that allow parents to request a transfer for their child to another school, if the transfer will improve the ethnic balance in the district. Sometimes, the school district provides transportation for these students and in some cases the parents must provide transportation. Usually transfers are contingent upon space being available in the receiving school. This policy has enjoyed some popularity because of its voluntary nature. Children are not sent out of their neighborhood for school unless the request is initiated by the parents.

(5) *Mandatory Busing.* Without doubt the most controversial action taken to desegregate schools is mandatory busing. This policy has the potential for accomplishing total school desegregation by ignoring patterns of residential segregation in making school assignments of children. Those districts that employ busing differ substantially in the extent of their programs and in whether there is cross-busing rather than one-way busing for only minority children.

(6) *Pairing of Schools.* Some districts have improved their ethnic balance by pairing elementary schools and reorganizing their grade structure. For example, two elementary schools that offer kindergarten through sixth grade could be paired such that one school offers grades kindergarten through three to all children in the combined attendance areas, while the other school offers grades four through six. The effect of the policy is to broaden the attendance boundaries of both schools to encompass more heterogeneous and ethnically diverse neighborhoods. Pairing schools may or may not involve busing, depending upon the distances involved.

Over half the districts (61%) changed the attendance boundaries of some of their schools. More than a third of the districts reported having open enrollment programs (39%), and almost the same number (37%) employed some mandatory busing to accomplish desegregation. A few districts relocated schools (14%), constructed new schools so as to reduce racial imbalance (18%), or paired schools (18%).

The six major types of desegregation actions were combined to form a summated measure, the Desegregation Actions Index. The index was constructed by counting the number of different types of policies each district adopted during the period of the study. Scores ranged from 0 through 5 with a mean of 1.88 and a standard deviation of 1.36. This measure does not take into account the extensiveness of the policies adopted or the degree to which they were implemented.

The Measure of Political Pressures

Both internal and external political pressures were evident in the history of events in the school districts in this study. However, these pressures were so interdependent that the analytical distinction between internal and external pressure was difficult to maintain. Groups within the district desiring change often had little effect until they obtained the support of external agents, such as the courts. Likewise, external agencies, such as the Bureau of Intergroup Relations, found it difficult to make headway unless there was internal pressure for change in a district. Our review of the history of events in the 49 school districts in this study revealed six sources of political pressures.

(1) *Court ordered desegregation.* The most compelling external pressure on a school district is a court order. Such orders are the outcome of a long period of controversy in the district in which desegregation is finally implemented by binding legal pressure from outside the district. Once a court orders desegregation, the district is required to submit a plan for achieving racial balance in its schools for the court's approval. The court usually retains authority to monitor the district to insure compliance with its order.

(2) *Pressures from the Bureau of Intergroup Relations.* A second source of external pressure on California school districts during the period studied was the Bureau of Intergroup Relations. Although the BIR had no sanctions at its disposal, it played an important role in stimulating school districts to address the desegregation issue. Each year it reported which schools were ethnically imbalanced in each district, according to the state guidelines, and asked each district to submit a plan to correct any imbalance. In the process of this exchange, school desegregation often became publicly defined as an issue with the BIR providing aid and reinforcement to those in each district who favored school desegregation. Information about the number of visits made to each district by a member of the BIR staff was available and serves as a crude measure of the extent to which the BIR was involved in each district. This measure was dichotomized with districts receiving less than five visits in one category and those receiving more than five visits in the other.

(3) *Interracial conflict in the schools.* Interracial conflict between students in the schools may serve as a catalyst for bringing about change. Student conflict forces a school board to consider change because such incidents polarize racial attitudes, demonstrate the discontent of the minority students, and pose a threat of physical harm. Such incidents often lead minority group parents to present grievances to the schools. State authorities may be asked to intervene to help calm the local situation, and other efforts to desegregate the schools may follow.

This pattern of events is illustrated by one southern California district in which a citizens' committee had been working on a school desegregation plan without success for several years. In the spring of 1969 violence between Black and anglo students in the high school resulted in numerous injuries and a police confrontation. School officials contacted the state Superintendent of Schools for aid, and the Bureau of Intergroup Relations was asked to study the situation. The BIR argued that racial tensions were in part a product of segregated conditions in elementary schools. Their report reinforced efforts by the NAACP and other pro-integration forces in the community and, subsequently, the school board agreed to desegregate its schools.

While interracial conflict does not articulate underlying problems, in many cases it destroys the status quo and mobilizes forces in the community to work toward a new accommodation between minority and white communities. Each district in our sample was classified according to whether it had or had not experienced interracial conflict in the schools.

(4) *Organized complaints by blacks.* Complaints by black parents and black civil rights groups are often instrumental in stimulating school desegregation. In most districts, these complaints do not initially involve a demand for school desegregation. They demand that steps be taken to improve the level of learning of black children. However, parental complaints become politically channeled and reformulated into a demand for school desegregation by organizations and agencies, such as the NAACP, the BIR, and the courts, which view ethnic imbalance in the schools as the underlying problem.

The organized complaints of blacks took many forms in our sample. For example, in one suburban district black parents and the NAACP actively protested the gerrymandering of school attendance boundaries by the district to maintain racial segregation. A court case in 1962 was the result. A quite similar case in 1969 led to court-ordered desegregation in 1970. In another district, a series of confrontations between black parents and the district centered on concern over low achievement of blacks in the schools. Finally, black parents organized a school boycott which resulted in a state Department of Education recommendation to desegregate the schools. In a third district, a group of black parents wrote to the state superintendent of schools in 1968 outlining complaints regarding the low academic achievement of minority children, unfair discipline practices in the schools, and efforts to discourage black children from participating in school activities. The BIR was asked to investigate these charges and subsequently encouraged the district to desegregate its schools.

Each district in the sample was classified as having experienced organized complaints by blacks or as not having experienced organized complaints by blacks. This determination was based on whether there was any indication of an organized effort to influence the schools in the historical records irrespective of the nature of the complaints or the method of protest.

(5) *Organized complaints of Mexican-Americans.* Mexican-American parents may also request changes in the schools. Like black parents, they are often disturbed by the low level of academic achievement of their children. However, their demands are more likely to ask for bi-lingual and bi-cultural programs for their children. Such programs have the effect of maintaining the separate treatment of Mexican-American children by the schools and, consequently, run counter to desegregation efforts.

For example, one rural district illustrates the pattern in many agricultural areas of the state. The relatively large Mexican-American population is primarily engaged in farm labor and lives geographically isolated from the white community. In recent years, Mexican-Americans have organized and have pressured the school district for improved schools and special programs for their children. However, they do not wish their children to leave their community schools. Compensatory education programs have been instituted in the schools but little school desegregation has occurred. A different result is illustrated by a district near Los Angeles. Mexican-American parents complained that the schools were not paying enough attention to their children and they requested counselors and special programs. Anglo-American liberals and the Bureau of Intergroup Relations used these complaints to push for school desegregation. However, the Mexican-American community responded with resistance to this plan.

A district was coded as having organized Mexican-American complaints whenever there was evidence in the historical documents that a group of parents or a Mexican-American organization had requested changes by the school district, irrespective of the nature of these changes.

Court orders were issued to only four districts during the period of the study. On the other hand, the Bureau of Intergroup Relations was very active and minority discontent was relatively prevalent. The Bureau sent a staff member on more than five occasions into more than three-fourths of the districts and nearly half experienced some racial violence in their schools. About one-third of the districts had black parents and Mexican-American parents who registered organized complaints against the schools.

A political pressures index was constructed by doing a principal components factor analysis on the five items. Factor loadings were court orders, .58; BIR contacts, .79; conflict in schools, .50; black complaints, .74; and Mexican-American complaints, $-.21$. A political pressures score was computed by multiplying the response to each item in the scale by its factor loading and summing the results. It should be noted that political pressures from Mexican-American organizations is *negatively* correlated with the other pressures. Scores were positively skewed and ranged from 2 to 210 with a mean of 36.0 and a standard deviation of 44.79.

District Characteristics

Over one hundred variables were examined relating to the economic base and population characteristics of the community and the schools, using data from the 1970 U.S. Census, the California ethnic survey, and reports of the California State Testing Program. Linear correlations were calculated with each of the three dependent variables, the Political Pressures Index, the Desegregation Actions Index, and the Change in Ethnic Balance Index. Eighteen variables were selected for further analysis: number of schools in the district; total assessed evaluation of taxable property; district tax rate; expenditures per average daily attendance; number of black students; percent black students; number of Mexican-American students; percent Mexican-American students; proportion of white male college graduates; proportion of black families with an annual income of over $10,000 per year; proportion of Mexican-American men in professional or managerial occupations; proportion of Mexican-American families earning over $10,000 per year; percent employed in agriculture; proportion of female-headed families with children; scholastic achievement of 12th grade students; ratio of administrators per 100 teachers; percent blacks in same house since 1959; and percent general population in same house since 1959.

Findings

Relationship between Desegregation Actions and
Change in Ethnic Balance

We used three approaches to examine the relationship between each of the six desegregation actions and district change in ethnic balance between 1966 and 1971. First, we computed the average change in ethnic balance score for those districts reporting a particular desegregation action and compared that with the average change score for those districts which did not employ that policy. Although the average change score tended to be higher for those districts that relocated schools (118 vs. 110), changed boundaries (112 vs. 110), paired schools (114 vs. 111), or used mandatory busing (117 to 108), none of these differences was statistically significant. Districts that constructed new schools or used open enrollment actually had slightly less change in ethnic balance than those districts that did not use these mechanisms.

Second, we computed a stepwise multiple regression to determine the multiple correlation between desegregation actions and change in ethnic balance. The multiple correlation was .30, not statistically significant. Finally, we correlated the Desegregation Action Index score based on the total number of different desegregation actions taken by each district with the amount of change in ethnic balance. It was an insignificant .14. We concluded that the number and kind of Desegregation Actions taken by a district does not significantly influence the extent to which that district will experience a change in the percent of minority children attending racially balanced schools. Our correlations are similar to the correlation of .29 reported by Kirby et al., between their measure of Desegregation Actions and the percent black students moved in the 91 districts they studied.

Relationship between Political Pressures
and Change in Ethnic Balance

We used the same three approaches to examine the relationship between specific political pressures and change in ethnic balance in a school district. First, we computed the average change in ethnic balance score for those districts reporting a particular type of political pressure and compared that with the average change score for those districts not experiencing that particular pressure. The only statistically significant difference was found when we compared communities experiencing Mexican-American protest with communities not having protest; the difference was in a *negative* direction. Districts experiencing Mexican-American protest had a mean score of 103 compared to 116 for those without protest ($p < .05$). The linear correlation between Mexican-American protest and change in ethnic balance was $-.31$ ($p < .05$).

Second, the six political pressures were entered into a multiple correlation analysis with change in ethnic balance as the dependent variable. The multiple correlation coefficient was an insignificant .35.

Finally, we correlated the Political Pressure Index score based on the weighted sum of each item with Change in Ethnic balance. The correlation was an insignificant .24.

We conclude that political pressures do not automatically translate into changes in ethnic balance. The most potent political effect in the districts we studied was the power of Mexican-American parents to slow desegregation efforts. This finding confirms the negative loading that Mexican-American complaints received in the factor analysis of the Political Pressures Index.

Relationship between Desegregation Actions and Political Pressure

We examined the relationship between specific desegregation actions and specific political pressures and found only one statistically significant relationship. The BIR was significantly more likely to be involved in districts which had adopted an open enrollment program ($p < .01$). This finding suggests that the BIR was very instrumental in establishing open enrollment programs. Open enrollment actually had little impact on achieving racial balance ($r = .03$) and, consequently, much of the political impact of the BIR may have been symbolic rather than actual.

Few, if any Anglo-American or Asian-American parents request transfers for their children. Thus, the primary burden of desegregation falls on minority children because open enrollment programs are essentially one-way busing programs. In addition, only a small proportion of black and Spanish-surname parents are likely to participate. For example, in the two districts in California which made the most strenuous efforts to encourage participation in open enrollment programs, only 11% of the minority children in one district and 15% of the minority children in the other district participated during the peak year of the programs.

When the Desegregation Action Index was correlated with the Political Pressure Index, the correlation was significant ($r = .29$, $p < .05$). This finding seems to indicate that there was a cumulative effect of political pressure on desegregation actions when all political pressures are combined in a single index that gives a negative weight to complaints of Mexican-American parents and a positive weight to other factors. In any case, the relationship is not strong and accounts for only 8.4% of the variance.

Relationship between District Characteristics and Other Variables

All of the eighteen district variables were examined in relation to the three dependent variables: Political Pressures, Desegregation Action, and Change in Ethnic Balance. A stepwise multiple regression procedure was used to identify which variables had the highest independent effects on the respective dependent variables. Ten variables proved to be significantly related to at least one of the dependent variables. These variables are presented in Table 8-1 together with the results of the three computations. Only those district characteristics having a statistically significant relationship to a dependent variable are presented. Some of the variables omitted from the equations, however, have a high co-variance with some of the variables that were entered into the equation. The discussion of results will take this relationship into account by reporting co-variance in an effort to present a wholistic picture of those districts scoring high on each of the three dependent variables.

Political Pressures. Six of the variables shown in Table 8-1 have significant relationships to political pressures. The combined multiple R reaches .82. High political pressure for school desegregation has occurred in wealthier districts with relatively high expenditures on public education, relatively more residential stability, higher proportions of female-headed families and larger numbers of black families having annual incomes over $10,000. After all these other characteristics are controlled, districts experiencing political pressures have relatively fewer white college graduates.

When we examine the co-variance of other variables with those in the equation, the Political Pressures Index correlates .53 with the number of schools in the district, .33 with the percent black students and −.33 with the percent Mexican-American students. One additional finding deserves some comment. Political pressures are most likely (.39) in urban districts

Table 8-1

Linear and Multiple Correlations between District Characteristics, Political Pressures, Desegregation Policies, and Change in Ethnic Balance for 49 California Unified School Districts

District Characteristics	Political Pressures		Desegregation Actions		Change Ethnic	
	r	beta	r	beta	r	beta
Assessed Evaluation	.64	.424 [c]				
Blacks Over $10,000 Income	.42	.370 [c]				
Same House since 1959	.28	.183 [a]	−.25	−.232 [a]		
Expense per ADA	.43	.305 [c]			.40	.442 [c]
Anglo Male College Grad.	.16	−.311 [c]				
Female Head of Household	.54	.206 [a]				
Percent Agriculture			−.31	−.271 [a]		
Blacks Same House Since 1959			.26	.263 [a]		
District Tax Rate					.27	.241 [a]
Scholastic Ability Grade 12					−.20	−.229 [a]
R		.82 [c]	.46 [a]		.54 [b]	

[a] Significant beyond .05 level.
[b] Significant beyond .01 level.
[c] Significant beyond .001 level.

where Mexican-American families earn over $10,000 a year. The correlation with percent employed in agriculture is −.76. While Mexican-Americans in rural areas may be politically apathetic or even hostile towards school desegregation, these sentiments do not seem to be shared by urban, middle status Mexican-Americans.

In general, the picture emerges of political pressures for school desegregation being greatest in urban school districts that have a high proportion of black students. Political pressure is weakest in rural districts with high proportions of Mexican-American students. Thus, the top five districts on the Political Pressures Index are San Francisco Bay Area districts and Los Angeles County districts. In contrast, the lowest five districts on the scale are relatively rural districts.

The findings perhaps reveal some of the dynamics underlying the political pressures for school desegregation. The major pressure appears to come from urban blacks, a group highly involved in political pressures for equal rights and opportunities in all phases of our society during the 1960s. The presence of middle status blacks, as well as middle status Mexican-Americans, within this population is of particular importance. No doubt this segment of the minority community particularly values educational opportunity in order that their relatively high status may be passed on to their children. In addition, the relative stability and high status of these minority families in politically active districts probably reflects their ability to organize and pressure the school district for changes.

Desegregation Action. Table 8-1 shows that three variables have significant relationships to the number of desegregation policies adopted by a district. Desegregation policies have been adopted in districts experiencing residential mobility in the general population but having a residentially stable black population and few persons employed in agriculture.

In general, these are urban districts that have been undergoing ethnic residential transition during the past ten years. While blacks have been present throughout this time, the data seem to indicate that the white population has been less stable. Another finding is that urban districts experiencing Desegregation Action are not large cities. Thus, when other variables were examined, we found that number of schools in the district correlates only .14 with number of Desegregation Actions. The number of blacks correlates only −.28, and the number of Mexican-Americans correlates −.20 with the Desegregation Action Index. The six districts scoring highest on Desegregation Action were all relatively small, having less than 27,000 ADA.

Why have these districts adopted a wider variety of desegregation policies during the time of the study? First, a relatively stable black population may be more capable of influencing the school officials to adopt desegregation policies. Second, the moderate size of these districts means relatively small numbers of minority students are involved. Thus, desegregation policies can be implemented with relative ease and low cost and a wider variety of actions may be utilized. Relocating schools and changing attendance boundaries can have a major impact on the ethnic distribution of students in a smaller district. Busing involves only short distances and smaller numbers of students compared to what is necessary in large cities.

Change in Ethnic Balance. Only three variables in Table 8-1 show significant independent effects on change in ethnic balance in the schools. Districts with relatively high expenditures on public education, as indicated by a high tax rate and high expenditures per student, in which academic achievement is below average are most likely to have desegregated their schools. $(R = .54, p < .01)$.

Finding so few demographic variables related to changes in ethnic balance is somewhat of a surprise. One reason for this finding may be that change was so pervasive during this period. Thus, 22 of the 49 districts experienced a change of more than 10 percent in the proportion of minority children attending ethnically balanced schools. Change occurred, furthermore, in many types of districts. Thus, size of district and percent employed in agriculture were not related to change in ethnic balance, though these variables did have importance for the development of Political Pressures and adoption of Desegregation Action. A number of rural districts desegregated their schools without any significant Political Pressure or the development of numerous formal policies. Among those districts with the greatest change are Pasadena, Berkeley, Morgan Hill, and Pittsburgh. They include both urban and rural districts. Likewise, both urban and rural districts are found among those at the bottom of the desegregation scale.

The financial resources of the school district are important. A wealthy district can implement changes whereas districts without resources, even if they are under considerable political pressure and have formally adopted measures to reduce ethnic imbalance, will have difficulty bringing about significant change. The negative relationship of scholastic ability to desegregation adds further insight into one characteristic of districts which have undergone the most change. Scholastic ability apparently appears in the equation as a substitute for other variables. Thus, scholastic achievement correlates $-.22$ with number of black children and $-.35$ with percentage of Mexican-American children enrolled in the district. However, neither of these variables, by themselves, is particularly related to desegregation. A significant negative beta weight for academic achievement occurs after controlling for wealth. A likely interpretation, then, is that wealthy school districts undertake school desegregation when those districts include greater numbers of minority children than other districts of similar wealth. A reasonable conclusion is that school desegregation is not a product of district wealth or size of minority population, but that the joint occurrence of wealth and presence of minority population is conducive to the elimination of segregation within a district.

Conclusions

The Four Models of School Desegregation

At the outset of this paper four models of the process of school desegregation were presented. Each model emphasized one particular type of variable as most critical in determining whether or not the district would achieve greater racial balance in its schools. These models were the desegregation policies model, the political pressures model, the district characteristics model, and a composite model incorporating all these variables. The findings thus far have reported the effects of each type of variable separately.

Figure 8-1 examines the interrelationships between District Characteristics, Political Pressures, Desegregation Action, and Change in Ethnic Balance. The vectors beginning at District Characteristics represent the multiple correlation coefficients from the regression equations presented in Table 8-1. The remaining vectors are Pearson correlations between the Political Pressures Index, Desegregation Action Index, and Change in Ethnic Balance. An evaluation of the four models can be made by examining the relative strength of these vectors.

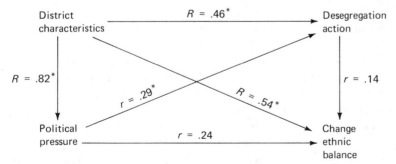

*Correlations significant beyond the .05 level of probability.

Figure 8-1. Correlations between District Characteristics, Public Pressures, Desegregation Policies and Percent Change in Ethnic Balance for 49 California Unified School Districts.

The Desegregation Policies Model. This model suggests that school desegregation depends upon the adoption by school officials of policies designed to improve racial balance in the schools. The findings do not support this model. The Desegregation Policies Index correlates with a coefficient of only .14 with actual change in the proportion of minority children attending ethnically balanced schools. Table 8-1 showed that districts adopting numerous Desegregation Actions were middle-sized urban districts undergoing ethnic transition. Figure 8-1 also shows that political pressures for desegregation tend to exist in these districts ($r = .29$, $p < .05$). A number of reasons may be advanced for the lack of effect of desegregation policies. Perhaps a large number of desegregation policies adopted by a school district indicate symbolic attempts to reduce political pressure. Physical or economic barriers to desegregation may override the ability of the district to accomplish meaningful change. Also, district officials may adopt official policies but fail to implement them effectively because they do not value racially integrated education.

The conclusion can be drawn that public policies are a complex phenomenon that must be examined in the context in which they develop and in terms of the actual consequences which follow from them. Policies are not always rational attempts to solve a problem, nor do they necessarily reflect efficient means for accomplishing some goal. Instead, they may be the product of emotionally charged conflict between parties holding incompatible values or having incompatible interests. Their adoption may represent an important symbolic victory for one side of the controversy rather than a real commitment of the district to change. Furthermore, desegregation policies may be publicly adopted by school officials in order to "cool out" opposition in the community and reduce pressure from outside agencies by publicly complying with the mandate to develop a desegregation plan.

Finally, many examples exist in the sociological literature indicating that the implementation of policies often displaces the publicly stated goals of those policies. Sometimes formidable obstacles prevent effective implementation of a policy. Thus, limited economic resources and large distances within a school district may severely restrict the extensiveness of a busing program or the ability to relocate schools or build new ones—even if school officials have publicly committed themselves to do so. The intent of a policy may also be undermined by those parties responsible for its implementation. The ineffectiveness of voluntary enrollment programs and the surprisingly small impact on racial balance of new schools intended to implement desegregation perhaps reflect a lack of commitment to the publicly stated goals of these policies. An assessment of progress towards desegregation, then, must not focus on the adoption of formal policies but instead examine the actual consequences of these policies as they are implemented in the school district.

The Political Pressures Model. This model suggests that the key events leading to school desegregation are discontent with the status quo among minority parents and mobilization of political pressures on district officials for change. The findings in Table 8-1 indicated that political pressures were most intense in wealthier urban school districts with more high income blacks and higher proportions of black students. Figure 8-1 reveals a modest overall association of political pressures with adoption of desegregation policies ($r = .29$, $p < .05$) and change in ethnic balance ($r = .24$, NS). However, these relationships are too weak to support the notion that political activism is a sufficient condition for bringing about school desegregation.

A closer inspection of the consequences of political pressures reveals two separate reasons for the modest association of political pressures with school desegregation. First, as the above discussion of desegregation policies implies, political pressures may result in symbolic victories or the adoption of public policies that "cool out" the discontent of minority parents without bringing about significant change. Thus, the correlation of political pressures with desegregation policies (.29) is twice as large as the correlation of desegregation policies with change in ethnic balance (.14).

Second, while political pressures have been strong in some districts which have achieved desegregation, other districts have reduced ethnic imbalance with little political confrontation. The latter districts have had relatively low numbers of minority population. Thus, it has been possible for the district to comply with the state mandate at relatively low cost and without creating a public controversy over the desegregation issue. In conclusion, the evidence suggests that political pressures have played a role in school desegregation in some districts but that other districts, because of favorable conditions, have been able to achieve racial balance in the absence of organized political conflict in the community.

District Characteristics Model. This model suggests that economic demographic, and organizational characteristics of the district are most important in determining whether or not school desegregation will occur. The sizable multiple correlation between district characteristics and change in ethnic balance (.54) indicates that indeed the structural characteristics of the community are of greater importance than political activism or the adoption of desegregation policies. Neither urbanism nor large size were found to be directly related to change. The findings in Table 8-1 revealed that school desegregation has occurred in moderate sized, affluent school districts where academic achievement is relatively low probably due to a larger minority enrollment than is typical of such districts. Where resources are available, and a relatively small but low achieving minority population exists, school desegregation can be undertaken in an effort to improve

142

Table 8-2

Unique Contribution of Political Pressures in Accounting for the Variance in Desegregation Policies and Change in Ethnic Balance

Dependent Variable:	Desegregation Policies		Change in Ethnic Balance		
	R	R^2		R	R^2
District Characteristics	.46	.21	District characteristics	.54	.29
District Characteristics plus Political Pressures	.49	.24	District Characteristics plus Political Pressures	.54	.29
			District Characteristics plus Desegregation Policies	.54	.29
			District Characteristics plus Political Pressures and Desegregation Policies	.54	.29

educational opportunity. The constraints of cost, size, distance, and so forth, make change less possible in districts with other characteristics.

Because of the constraints posed by the structural characteristics of the community, political activism and the adoption of formal policies can have little independent effect on the district. Table 8-2 presents multiple correlations intended to test the extent of unique contribution of political pressures and desegregation policies beyond the influence of district characteristics. The first portion of the table shows that the degree of political pressure makes only a small, unique contribution to the number of policies adopted by the district beyond the variance that can be accounted for by the district characteristics. The second portion of the table shows that neither political pressures nor desegregation policies make a unique contribution to achieving racial balance in schools apart from the variance that can be accounted for by the economic and demographic characteristics of the district. These results are our most direct evidence that the district characteristics model of school desegregation most fully accounts for the changes that occurred in California between 1966 and 1971.

A Composite Model. Finally, a composite model was proposed which suggested that school desegregation is the outcome of a particular combination of community characteristics, political pressures, and district policies. In some types of school districts, the minority population is likely to be discontent with the status quo and to exert pressure on school officials for change. This political pressure should eventually lead to the adoption of desegregation policies in order to restore an equilibrium in the community and eventual racial balance in the school should be achieved. This wholistic picture of the relationships between the variables in the study seems very reasonable. If school desegregation in fact occurred in this fashion, high correlations between all variables would be anticipated in

Figure 8-1, but no independent effects of variables, such as those tested for in Table 8-2, would be evident.

However, Figure 8-1 indicates that the composite model is an oversimplification and must be rejected. First, the low correlations of Political Pressures ($r = .24$) and Desegregation Action ($r = .14$) with Change in Ethnic Balance reveal that Political Pressures and large numbers of different Desegregation Actions do not necessarily result in change. Therefore, they are not sufficient conditions for school desegregation.

Second, the high correlations associated with district characteristics in Figure 8-1 do not, in fact, confirm the composite model. These correlations do show that the characteristics of the district are highly related to whether Political Pressures will develop, Desegregation Action will be adopted, and desegregation of the schools will occur. However, as the regressions reported in Table 8-2 make clear, *different* community characteristics are associated with the occurrence of each of these phenomenon. The characteristics of those districts with high Political Pressures are not the same as the characteristics of those which adopt numerous Desegregation Actions. And those districts which underwent the most school desegregation did not have the most Political Activism or adopt the most desegregation policies.

By far the most significant factors in explaining progress in school desegregation are the characteristics of the district. At every point in the analysis, district characteristics were found to be more highly correlated with the political pressures, desegregation actions and changes in ethnic balance in the district than these variables were correlated with each other. The most important conclusion of this paper must be that more of the variance in the dynamics of the desegregation process can be explained by community characteristics than community politics or policies.

Notes

1. Al Smith, Anthony Downs, and M. Leanne Lachman, *Achieving Effective Desegregation* (Lexington, Mass.: Lexington Books, D. C. Heath and Company, 1973).
2. David J. Kirby, T. Robert Harris, Robert L. Crain, and Christine H. Rossell, *Political Strategies in Northern School Desegregation* (Lexington, Mass.: Lexington Books, D. C. Heath and Company, 1973).

Part IV
The Pressure Context of Policy Making

Introduction to Part IV

The Pressure Context of Policy Making

Previous sections have indicated the mediating effects upon educational policy making of such forces as popular involvement and community status distinctions, but another dimension is more organized and personal. That is the pressure group matrix within which policy is shaped. This concept has a long history as an explanation of policy behavior, possibly the longest in political science, when one traces it back to Arthur Bentley. When this approach was revived after World War II by David Truman, Stephen Bailey, and others, it acted as an introduction to the later, increasingly rigorous, concepts of behavioralism. Certainly pressure group theory was more rigorous in contrast to the prior concepts of institutionalism and legal analysis that had once dominated research in this discipline. While the more highly quantifiable fields of behavioralism dominated recent decades, interest in and the use and development of pressure group theory remained. In this section we draw upon recent uses of this concept as it applies to school politics.

David Kirby and Robert Crain, drawing from a larger study that includes the data base discussed earlier in Christine Rossell's contribution, explore how 91 cities first reacted to desegregation demands in the North. They trace the degree to which conflict was functional for both the groups seeking change and the school boards facing them. While the protest politics accompanying this conflict has dominated publicity, Kirby and Crain find that there was no relationship between the adoption of desegregation policies and the presence, or even intensity, of protest policies in these cities; earlier, Wegner and Mercer echoed this finding among California districts of all sizes. But, unlike earlier findings about responsiveness, the present authors find that conflict does not facilitate desegregation, unless the board has a prior record of responsiveness to popular inputs. Indeed, the recalcitrant boards seem to ignore such inputs, whether from blacks or whites. Therefore this contribution is important for differentiating the conditions under which popular participation can and cannot be effective with school authorities.

The next contribution, the chapter from Harry Summerfield's larger book, recapitulates four models of politics, which are combinations of interactions among the community, principals, and central administration in a given school system. In part, these are models of administrative styles of representation, and as such might be read with Part II. But Summerfield's contribution is more significant for illuminating the theory of school interest groups, as each school within the district system is conceived as

147

an interest group, with its neighborhood constellation of groups. Each of these schools interacts with the others and with the central political authority in seeking allocation of resources to forward its own goals. This selection argues, as do others in this book, that school systems are not as fully closed as popularly believed, for they can be opened by increased public pressure.

The development of organizational theory in the last two decades has united many disciplines having interest in the structural and role behavior qualities of social life. Willis Hawley, in a contribution specially prepared for this volume, reviews that literature to demonstrate the concept's application to another interest group within the matrix of school politics, namely, the professionals. The reasons for this group's purported rigidity in system maintenance arise out of the fact of organizational life and not because its members are imbued with some particular ideology. In a full review of this concept, Hawley modifies the thesis of Summerfield and others about the openness of school professionals noted earlier. Indeed, this contribution illuminates a prevalent interpretation of school bureaucracy, a phenomenon against which many school reform measures (like community control, desegregation, teacher militancy, and student rights) are currently directed. In short, it may well be the fact that it was this rigid behavior by the professional as an actor in the pressure matrix of school politics which directly politicized other constituencies of the school and thus transformed urban school policy making in the early 1970s.

The Functions of Conflict: School Desegregation in 91 Cities

David J. Kirby * and Robert L. Crain †

Is conflict functional or dysfunctional? This vague question is central to a number of debates in political science and sociology. In this paper we focus on one specific version of this general question: When is conflict functional to a change agent who is attempting to change the *status quo* and who does not have a large amount of resources? Our data deal with the *de facto* school desegregation issue in Northern cities, which is a good example of this common situation.[1] We hope this paper will encourage others to consider the question as it applies to other types of change agents and other types of issues.

We are here concerned with the common-sense interpretation of conflict: disagreement which results in the participants becoming angry, upset, inconvenienced, or otherwise uncomfortable because of the conduct of the debate. It is this kind of community conflict with which James Coleman's *Community Conflict* is concerned, and which, above a certain threshold, becomes what William Gamson has called "rancorous conflict." That this sort of conflict intuitively is considered dysfunctional is reflected in the necessity for Coser to write a book entitled *The Functions of Social Conflict.* Let us assume that the participants in a decision have at least some latitude to increase or decrease the level of conflict; they can choose whether to attack an opponent on a personal level or not, to call a traffic-jamming demonstration as opposed to a private negotiating session, etc. Given this assumption, we can ask two questions: (1) Was school desegregation more likely to occur where participants did or did not engage in conflict-increasing tactics? (2) One tactic which is almost always conflict-increasing is the use of grass roots demonstrations either for or against desegregation. Were these generally effective or not?

Reprinted with permission of the *Social Science Quarterly* from David Kirby and Robert Crain, "The Functions of Conflict: School Desegregation in 91 Cities," *Social Science Quarterly,* 55, no. 2, September, 1974. See original for footnotes omitted here.

* Memorial University, St. John's, Newfoundland

† The Rand Corporation

Sample and Data Collection

The data on which this paper is based are part of the data collected for a research project which examined *de facto* school segregation controversies in 91 northern U.S. cities.[2]

We wanted as large a sample of school desegregation controversies as possible, and chose our sample cities from the National Opinion Research Center's Permanent Community Sample of 200 cities. The Permanent Community Sample is a national probability sample of all American cities which had a population of 50,000 or more in 1960; the cities are sampled proportional to population, including all cities of over 150,000 persons. We selected from the PCS all cities which had at least 3,000 blacks and were "outside the South." "Outside the South" included those cities in the southern census region which ceased maintaining *de jure* segregated school systems immediately after the 1954 Brown decision.

Using these procedures, our final sample contains 91 cities, and omits only 4 northern cities of over 250,000 population; the median population in the sample is approximately 200,000.

Within each sample city, interviewers from the National Opinion Research Center administered a series of 18 interviews with selected informants (see Table 9-1). In addition, a self-administered questionnaire was completed by the Education Reporter of the major newspaper in each city. Informants were selected by a mixture of "positional" and "reputa-

Table 9-1

List of Respondents

1. City editor of a major local newspaper
2. 1955 School Board member
3. Mayor or his administrative assistant
4. Political leader of the party opposite the Mayor
5. A major civic leader in the community
6. An informed civil rights leader in the community
7. Superintendent of schools
8. PTA President
9. A "moderate" civil rights leader knowledgeable about city schools in 1963
10. A "moderate" civil rights leader knowledgeable about city schools in 1968
11. A "militant" civil rights leader
12. A black politician
13. A black businessman
14. A current member of the school board who is black
15. A current member of the school board who is knowledgeable about the desegregation issues in the city
16. A current school board member who is knowledgeable about school board elections or appointments
17. A current school board member who is knowledgeable about school finances
18. A member of the school superintendent's staff
19. Education Reporter of a major newspaper

tional" methods, i.e. some were interviewed because they held a particular job or post; others by asking informants to recommend people to us.

In summary, this technique is an effort to apply the standardized procedures of survey research to city problems, treating the city as the unit of analysis and "interviewing the city" by using standardized questionnaires administered to informants selected in a standardized way. Responses from different informants were combined in the same way that scales are built in a conventional survey.

In this paper we focus on the effects of conflict and conflict-producing tactics within the overall political context of the school desegregation controversy. Correlation and regression analysis is used in the general model shown in Figure 9-1. Various background characteristics of the city (taken from the census) are correlated against both the initial appearance of the issue and the way it was resolved; then the behavior of the school board and the superintendent, the civil rights movement, the

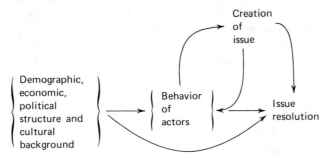

Figure 9-1. Model for Data-Analysis of School Desegregation Decisions.

mayor and the "civic elite," and white "grass-roots" groups are introduced as intervening variables to explain the outcome of the controversy. We first present four findings from the analysis, concerning the effects of civil rights demonstrations, of white grass roots support for and protests against desegregation, and of conflict within the school board. After stating the findings, we list five more general hypotheses based on these findings.

First Finding: Conflict-Increasing Tactics Seem to Have Been Necessary to Make School Desegregation an Issue

Thanks to the writings of E. E. Schattschneider, Bachrach and Baratz, and Matthew Crenson, we know to ask the question "What preconditions enabled school desegregation to become an issue?"

In each city we defined a more-or-less comparable concept, "The First Major Demand (FMD) for the improvement of black education made to the school systems in each of our sample cities after 1960." Doing this forces our data to "begin at the beginning" and gives us a sequential time-ordering of the issue that is general enough to be common to most northern cities, and yet is specific enough to allow us to make meaningful and comparable distinctions among cities.

Sixteen of our sample cities experienced no First Major Demand. At least there was nothing that our informants felt could be classified as such. Given the pervasiveness and scope of the civil rights movement in the 1960s, how did these 16 cities manage to escape the desegregation controversy?

Table 9-2 correlates the absence of a demand with selected characteristics. We see that cities which did not experience FMD's were smaller, and had populations which were more educated, more wealthy, more professional, and whiter. In essence, they seem similar to suburban communities (although they are not all suburbs). But why are these types of communities less likely to be faced with a desegregation issue? One reason may have been that there was less need. It is not true that these cities are less segregated than others. More interesting, white and black informants evaluate the quality of education minority children receive in these sixteen cities favorably. We asked nine of our informants to rate the job they

Table 9-2

Correlates of Absence of First Major Demand for Desegregation

Background Variables:	Correlation with Absence of FMD
City Size (log)	−.19
Percent white collar	.10
Percent black	−.15
Median years of school completed	.17
Ratio city to metropolitan population	−.02
"Need" Variables	
Index of segregation	.00
Perceptions of Educational Quality:	
All students	.15
Black students	.25
Expectation for quality of education in future:	
All students	−.11
Black students	.13
Militancy Variables	
Earliness of black political victories	−.17
Number of office blacks have been elected to	−.23
Civil rights groups commitment to black power	−.22
Presence of black power-type groups	−.21
Self-rated militancy of civil rights groups	−.35

thought their city schools were doing, compared to other cities like it. Even if citizens thought the schools were doing a good job when in fact they were not, this (misinformed) belief could be enough to spare the school system from outside demands. We have no reason to believe that our informants are basing their judgement on objective data; it seems more likely that they thought the schools were doing a good job in the no-FMD cities because the issue had not been raised.

Very often we don't consider anything to be a problem unless and until conflict and controversy force us to consider it. The quality of black education usually does not become an issue until blacks define it as such; if the black and civil rights organizations in a city are unorganized, weak, or conservative (reflected in these data in their later reluctance to endorse "black power" ideology) we would not expect them to make demands for the improvement of black education.

The lower part of Table 9-2 provides evidence to support this view; the correlations indicate that in the no-FMD cities, civil rights organizations were less interested in acquiring black economic and political power; black political and cultural organizations were less prevalent; blacks hold fewer city-wide offices and were elected later, and in general the local civil rights movement was not very militant. These sixteen cities may not have experienced an FMD because the civil rights organizations were not strong enough or not interested enough to mount an attack on the school system.

If we look at the variables in Table 9-2 again, we see that many of them are characteristics we intuitively associate with a black community which is not oriented toward conflict-increasing tactics. It makes sense that not all black communities either want conflict or find conflict tolerable. Our first finding therefore suggests that conflict-raising civil rights activity accomplished some of the functions Coser attributes to conflict; it made others aware of the issue, called into question norms and conditions, and brought the conflicting parties together. It was only then that relationships could be established and a dialogue begun.

The Outcome of the Desegregation Debate

School systems initially responded to the demand for desegregation in a luke-warm fashion, typically appointing a committee to study the problem. The civil rights movement replied in turn by calling for southern-style, non-violent demonstrations. The result was a debate, punctuated by further demonstrations, over the next several months, and in some cases several years. By 1969, when the issue began to burn itself out, most cities had responded by taking a wide variety of actions. The next task of the research was to create a scale of the degree to which actions taken by the schools met the symbolic goals of the movement. We are here less interested in the actual amount of desegregation (which was generally still very small in almost all of the cities by 1969) but in the degree to which the actions reflected a commitment to desegregate.

We recorded 27 actions which school systems took, and divided them into three broad categories: those actions which were only procedural or symbolic, those which required no more than voluntary participation on the part of whites, and those which compelled white participation. Within each category we ranked the actions from least radical (or least pro-integration) to most radical, based on a composite judgement of the number of students involved or the amount of opposition the typical community would mount to such an action. This enabled us to rank the 27 acts. The first column of Table 9-3 indicates the percentage of cities reporting each type of action (the least radical actions were frequently not reported). The second column gives the percentage of cities in which the research staff judged this action to be the single most significant one, in terms of amount of public attention and number of students involved. Table 9-3 shows that in 85% of the cities, the most significant action involved some degree of desegregation.

An Action to Desegregate score for each city was created by simply adding the ranks of the three most radical actions taken; the scores ranged from a low of 12 to a high of 77 (A city which assigned quotas, bused blacks to the suburbs, and bused whites to ghetto schools would have received a score of $25 + 26 + 27 = 78$).

However, most of the activity was limited to a small number of students. In 1972, Christine Rossell asked each school system to list the schools which they had intentionally desegregated, and computed the number of students involved. Only 63% of the systems claimed to have done anything (indicating that some of the actions reported earlier either never occurred or were so trivial in size as to be forgotten later). Furthermore, the typical city which did act reassigned none of its white students, and only 7.5% of its blacks, in its desegregation plan. While how much action should be considered significant is a matter of taste, we would conclude that about one-quarter of the school systems adopted a major desegregation plan. While this may be more than the reader expected, it still means that the demand for desegregation failed more often than it succeeded.

The Analysis of the Impact of Various Actors on the Decision

Since we had no satisfactory model of the time at which each actor participated in the decision, a general linear regression model was used,

Table 9-3

Percentage of Cities Ever Taking Each Action, Most Significant Action Ever Taken by a City, at Any Time, Listed in Order of "Radicalness"

Ranking of Radicalness, low to high	Percentage of cities taking this action	Percentage of cities which this action was the most significant
Symbolic-Procedural		
1. Submit anti-civil rights statement	15%	0
2. Do nothing; ignore the demand		0
3. Provide data or information about the school system	15%	0
4. Appoint a committee to study problem	55%	0
5. Submit a pro-civil rights statement	42%	0
6. Prepare a plan to attack the problem	29%	0
7. Dismiss the superintendent	3%	0
Voluntary Participation		
8. Initiate compensatory education	79%	3%
9. Initiate supplemental centers	3%	0
10. Improve facilities for blacks; reduce over-crowding	22%	1%
11. Appoint a human relations committee, establish human relations workshops	12%	0
12. Initiate Black Studies Program; improve the curriculum	54%	8%
13. Hire more black teachers and/or administrators	35%	2%
14. Integrate the faculty	15%	1%
15. Initiate a program of community control	4%	1%
Forced Participation		
16. Limit open enrollment	2%	0
17. Initiate or expand open enrollment	45%	10%
18. Do not build a school because it would become segregated	1%	0
19. Redraw school boundaries; change feeder patterns	44%	19%
20. Bus for overcrowding	37%	14%
21. Create a middle school	5%	1%
22. Bus to integrate	36%	11%
23. End tracking; integrate classrooms	3%	3%
24. Close a school	22%	19%
25. Assign racial quotas	3%	3%
26. Bus students to the suburbs	3%	3%
27. Bus whites to black schools	2%	2%
		101
		($N = 91$)

entering the background factors first (explaining 16% of the variance) followed by the six largest predictors of action to desegregate (explaining an additional 31%) from among 10 variables describing the attitudes and behavior of the mayor, superintendent, school board, the civic elite, and the civil rights movement. We then added (one at a time) the remaining 4 of the 10 variables and also measures of white citizens-group activity in support of or opposition to desegregation to produce seven additional equations. (Since analysis suggested that white "grass-roots" behavior was largely a response to other actors' behavior, these variables were not permitted to enter the general equation). The dependent variable (action to desegregate) and city size were both normalized. Comparison of the zero-order correlations of column 1 of Table 9-4 to the standardized regression

Table 9-4

Regression Equations Predicting Action to Desegregate

		Standardized Coefficients (β)	
	Zero-order r	General Regression Equation	Other Regressions [c]
Background Variables			
City Growth	.10	.10	
Population Growth	−.08	.20	
Median Educ.	−.04	−.09	
Percent Foreign Stock	.32	.24	
Percent over Age 65	.23	.23	
Eastern Region	.22	.13	
Midwest	−.18	.04	
West	.07	.02	
Border	.17	[a]	
School Board Elected	.04	.12	
Political Variables			
Superintendent Support	.28	.29 [b]	
Board Conflict	.23	.30 [b]	
Mayor Support	.16	.25 [b]	
Elite Support	.25	.27 [b]	
Elite Active	.07	.20 [b]	
Civil Rights Groups Unified	.31	.17	
Number of Black Elected	.01		(−.04)
Board Liberal Attitudes	.03		(.01)
Civil Rights Activity	−.14		(−.11)
Mayor Liberal Attitudes	.17		(.10)
White Grass-Roots Activity			
White Citizen Support	.06		(.02)
White Citizen Opposition	.23		(.23) [b]

[a] Redundant term omitted.
[b] Significant, $p < .05$.
[c] Parenthetical values are produced by adding this variable only to general

Table 9-4 (cont.)

regression equation. Thus column 3 reports the results of six separate regression equations.

Variable Definitions:

Census variables are for 1960.

Superintendent Support: report of superintendent's "leadership role" by reporter, civil rights leader, black and white board members.

Board Conflict: reports from 4 board members and superintendent to 9 questions about voting, personal contacts among board members, heated debates at board meetings.

Mayor Support: report by mayor or his administrative assistant on 12 possible actions he may have taken; score is number of pro-desegregation actions minus number of anti-desegregation actions.

Elite Support: one board member was given a list of civic leaders (generated by 5 "reputational" interviews) and asked to identify every leader who supported civil rights demands.

Elite Active: The most prominent civil leader (identified by reputational method) was asked 3 questions about activity of elite in major community projects.

Civil Rights Groups Unified: 2 civil rights leaders were asked to rate the degree of unity of the civil rights movement on each of previous 6 years.

Number of black elected officials: One black political leader was asked to report the pressure of blacks in each of eight types of offices, ranging from Congress to city council.

Board Liberal Attitude: 4 board members responded to a six-item racial attitudes scale.

Civil Rights Activity: The reporter and a civil rights leader reported number of demonstrations, sit-ins, or school boycotts directed to the school desegregation issue.

Mayor's Liberal Attitude: Mayor's response to questions about fair housing, employment discrimination, and his position on race vis-a-vis his opponent.

White Citizen Support: A board member reported number of meetings and attendance at largest meeting held by whites in support of desegregation.

White Citizen Opposition: similar to white citizen support variable.

coefficients of columns 2 and 3 indicate that multicollinearity was generally not a severe problem (the exception is population growth rate). Table 9-5, which presents a portion of the correlation matrix, indicates that intercorrelations among the political variables were not high enough to cause serious problem.

Table 9-4 contains some expected results (that the superintendent and the mayor are key figures) and some surprises (that desegregating cities have large foreign-stock populations, that the civic elite plays an important role, and that desegregating cities do not have more liberal mayors or school boards). But in this paper we are interested in examining only the five italicized variables in Table 9-4: *school board internal conflict, civic elite support for the civil rights movement, civil rights activity, and organized white "grass-roots" support and opposition to desegregation.* For clarity, these five variables are grouped together on the right of the matrix in Table 9-5.

Table 9-5

Correlations Among Independent Variables

	Size	For. Stk.	C.L. Act.	C.R. Uni.	Blk. Ele.	Bd. Lib.	Sup. Spt.	May. Lib.	May. Sup.	S.B. Con.	Elt. Sup.	C.R. Act.	Wh. Sup.	Wh. Opp.
City Size (log)	—	.12	.14	-.17	.56	.22	-.11	.35	-.01	.13	.10	.12	.22	.15
% Population Foreign Stock		—	-.20	.03	-.13	.27	-.19	.22	.01	.19	.12	7	-.05	.06
Civic Leader Activity			—	-.09	.13	-.06	.07	.20	-.02	-.14	-.04	-.05	.10	-.09
Civil Rights Groups Unified				—	-.20	-.02	.35	-.15	.01	.12	-.02	-.10	.07	.05
Number Blacks in Elected Office					—	.12	.07	.10	-.14	.26	.10	.01	.10	.15
Board Liberal Attitudes						—	-.07	.33	-.13	.01	.11	.07	.20	-.09
Superintendent Support							—	-.19	-.02	-.13	-.05	.12	.03	-.10
Mayor's Liberal Attitude								—	.13	-.02	.13	-.10	.03	-.10
Mayor's Support									—	-.18	-.03	-.03	.00	.10
School Board Conflict										—	-.03	.06	-.03	.26
Civic Elite Support											—	-.39	.18	-.13
Civil Rights Activity												—	-.08	-.08
White Citizen Support													—	.28
White Citizen Opposition														—

Second Finding: Conflict within the School Board
Facilitates Desegregation

We asked four school board members and the superintendent a total of
fifteen questions dealing with the presence of several kinds of disagreements, the frequency of heated debates, and the amount of social contact
on the board. We found that school desegregation was more likely to occur
in cities where the school board members had less friendly interaction and
more conflict. The fact that β is larger than r in Table 9-4 indicates that
school board conflict occurs in cities where the other actor's characteristics
are not conducive to desegregation. In particular, school board conflict
tends to occur in cities where the mayor did not support desegregation
($r = -0.18$) and where the superintendent of schools exerted less leadership ($r = -0.13$). School board conflict is also associated with more white
grass-roots opposition ($r = +0.26$).

It seems unlikely that the school desegregation decision, important
though it may be, could single-handedly set the tone for the school boards
internal relations on all issues. It seems more likely that conflict is a characteristic of some boards and not others (perhaps because of the political
style of the city and the way school board members are usually recruited)
and these boards are more likely to desegregate.

It should be observed that this finding, coupled with the failure of action
to desegregate to correlate with board member attitudes, clearly disagrees
with Robert Crain *et al.* in *The Politics of School Desegregation* (1968).
There are many methodological differences between the two studies, which
might explain these differences, but we are inclined to think that the differences in the time of the two studies is the key. Crain *et al.*'s interviewing
was done in 1967, when desegregation was still being debated in most of
the 8 northern cities studied; their scoring system tended to rank as most
"acquiescent" those districts which had settled the desegregation issue,
giving lower scores to those where the debate was still in progress. Since
1967, the acquiescent districts have done little to desegregate, and some
of the others (particularly Buffalo, San Francisco and Boston) have passed
them in degree of desegregation. Liberal, unified boards were able to
respond quickly and sometimes satisfy the civil rights movement with an
acquiescence which was mostly symbolic; divided boards could not, and
in the long run were forced to do more.

Third Finding: Civil Rights Demonstrations Generally
Did Not Facilitate Desegregation

Table 9-4 seems to support the argument of *The Politics of School Desegregation* that civil rights demonstrations were ineffective in desegregation

controversies. The correlation between amount of activity and amount of action to desegregate is negative. The negative relation indicates that demonstrations are more a response to a district's failure to desegregate than a cause of desegregation.

One reason why civil rights activity has little impact is that the non-violent demonstration is not a strong coercive device. Since they can really do little financial or other harm there is little reason for the school administration not to ignore a sit-in, street demonstration or boycott. Contrast this to the position of the teacher's union, which can, by going out on strike, threaten to close the schools indefinitely—for all students. If the strike runs for any length of time the mayor and the school board members can expect voters to be angry. By comparison, the civil rights movement was a weakling indeed.

It is ironic that a school boycott is less effective in a segregated system, since white students in all-white schools are unaffected by the closing down of black schools.

The Anti-Conflict Bias of the Civic Elite

Civil rights activity was ineffective for a second reason: it created a back-lash among white elites. The names of the civic elite were obtained by asking five of our informants to list the persons they considered civic leaders—"people who have been active in supporting various community programs and in bringing new programs to the city; or, on the other hand, persons who have been active in opposing or trying to significantly alter such programs." (Goverment employees or officials were not to be in-cluded.)

We then asked a school board member to review this list and identify those leaders who had been "favorably disposed," "opposed" or "pretty much neutral" toward the local civil rights groups and their demands. Few civic leaders are considered opposed to the civil rights groups, but many are neutral. On a scale from 0 (opposed) to 1 (favored) with .5 for neutral, the average score is .66—somewhere between neutral and favor-able.

One of the main findings of our study is that civic elite support for civil rights was strongly negatively related to civil rights activity ($r = -.39$). This last correlation may indicate that a lack of elite support causes the civil rights movement to demonstrate more, but we think it more likely that high levels of civil rights activity causes elites to withhold their sup-port. We think this is likely because the civic elite is unaccustomed to (and perhaps upset by) public conflict—civil rights activity is out of keeping with the elites' normal world of charitable fund-raising, testimonial dinners, and public service on behalf of public projects such as urban renewal which, while sometimes controversial, are usually handled with gentlemanly standards of debate.

This suggests a reason why the southern civil rights movement could not function successfully in the North. In the South, street demonstrations, coupled with police brutality, prompted a northern liberal reaction and the passage of civil rights legislation. When the civil rights movement tried the same tactics in the North there was no group of outside liberals to be offended by the behavior of the school boards of Milwaukee, Oakland, or Boston. If the civil rights movement was to attain its objective of being martyred and becoming a moral force it would have to do so by enlisting the support of white elites in the same city. This is precisely what they were unable to do. The correlation coefficient here, −.39, is one of the very largest in our entire analysis. Roughly, it can be translated into the statement that civic leaders were two or three times more likely to support the civil rights movement where there were fewer desegregation demonstrations than where there was a large amount.

Elite support for desegregation is strongly associated with action to desegregate; we think this means that elite support encourages the school system to desegregate.

When the elite endorses desegregation, it lends its prestige and legitimacy to it; its resources include a social network of relations with the right people, and the school officials are likely to remember the importance of the elite on financial matters.

*Fourth Finding: White Grass-roots Activity is
Also Ineffective*

We asked a school board member if there had been meetings of whites who were opposed to school desegregation; if he or she said "Yes," we asked how many meetings there were and how many people attended the largest, and combined the two responses. (The same questions were used to record opposition meetings.) Table 9-4 shows no evidence that either kind of grass-roots activity affected the outcome. Opposition meetings tend to occur in cities with high action to desegregate. Apparently white grass-roots opposition is a response to desegregation, just as civil rights activity is a response to a refusal to desegregate.

The issue is difficult, since we do not have longitudinal data which would be necessary to untangle a complex web of white activity both causing and being caused by school system action. But we do know this much: there are very few cities, if any, where a massive set of anti-integration meetings were held and no desegregation took place. Perhaps better measures of white citizen activity would show a different pattern, but with the data we have we can only draw a portrait of an elitist, decision-making machine which is either insensitive to or aliented by efforts of the masses to generate conflict. Similarly, we cannot find any evidence that grass-roots white support for desegregation made any difference, since support is not more likely to appear in cities which have taken steps to desegregate.

Generalizing to a Set of Hypotheses

We now must put these four findings into a consistent set of statements. Recall that our question is, "Does a political actor with few resources profit from using conflict-raising techniques?" The answer is sometimes yes, and sometimes no, and our next task is to develop a set of hypotheses which explain why conflict is helpful in some ways and harmful in others. Our propositions are hypotheses only; they are consistent with the data, but data on a single issue do not constitute strong evidence for them.

Proposition 1: A non-issue can be made salient by a powerless group with conflict-raising tactics. Conflict can create an issue, partly because to engage in conflict, to violate the gentleman's agreements of everyday politics, harms its opponents (through embarrassment, for example). In addition conflict serves notice that the powerless group is angry, concerned, and committed. Conflict is the expenditure of a resource (one's reputation as a "gentleman"), and creating conflict demonstrates both a willingness to risk one's reputation and a confidence that one's supporters will agree that ungentlemanly behavior is not inappropriate. To engage in conflict is to advertise that one is not embarrassed by conflict—the conflict creator is in effect saying, "I am morally right, and my constituency will support me."

Proposition 2: The presence of a tradition of conflict is a facilitator of change. This proposition is a corollary of Proposition 1; for if conflict can be used to generate an issue, disapproval of conflict by a group (such as a harmonious school board) can serve to prevent issues from being raised. Conversely, a group with a tradition of conflict (like our high-conflict school boards) encourages proponents of change, who, rather than being conflict-shy, may look forward with pleasure to making some long-time enemy in the group squirm.

Proposition 3: Grass-roots activity without the support of some elites is often ignored by other elites. Our rather convincing data on the failure of both civil rights demonstrations and white grass-roots activity merit advancing this general proposition. (We also have other data in our monograph supporting the idea that coalitions with elites are effective in producing change.) We think that this general proposition is more true than false because decision makers, whether civic leaders or city councilmen, value "face-to-face opinion"—the reaction they see from persons of their own status in informal meetings—more than public opinion and indeed often take the elitist view that public opinion is easy prey for demagogues. The social rules of courteous debate are functional because informal interaction is so frequent in the day-to-day behavior of elites that high levels of conflict would be stressful. Thus a mass movement with no elite support for legitimacy and which uses conflict-creating tactics offends the elite in two ways.

Proposition 4: Conflict is generally dysfunctional if a decision for change must be made by an informal decision rule based on consensus politics. Many major decisions in cities are made by a consensus rule which in effect requires both a commitment of effort by some leaders and near-overwhelming majority support from a number of relevant actors. For example, a typical urban renewal plan requires considerable effort by some leader inside the government and one or more civic leaders who must work with enthusiasm for some time. If they do not receive encouragement, the civic leader can withdraw, and the government official can divert his resources to some other needy area of the city. Encouragement turns out to mean the support of the mayor and a number of other leaders, and the opposition of no more than a few notables who can be dismissed as self-interested, as cranks, or as extremists. Face-to-face interaction among friends, acquaintances, and colleagues plays an important role in defining whether one has received "encouragement" to desegregate just as it does to others decisions. While technically the school board had the authority to make the decision, our data indicate they were dependent on the (volunteered) support of the mayor and civic leaders, and the (also voluntary) enthusiasm of the school superintendent.

We noted earlier that conflict is a weak form of coercive force; it is harmful to its opponents by being psychically painful, producing disagreements among friends, embarrassment, loss of status, anxieties and feelings of guilt. But such force is ineffective for producing change if change must occur by a consensual decision process, for the civic and political leaders can respond to the pain of conflict by simply withdrawing, isolating the school board and in effect preventing the formation of the coalition necessary to produce change.

Proposition 5: Conflict-increasing tactics are less likely to be self-defeating, and may be helpful, in a group with compulsory attendance and a decision making rule requiring less than unanimity. This is a corollary of Proposition 4. Examples of groups with compulsory attendance are bureaucracies, legislative bodies, and firms; in all cases a person with influence over the decision cannot withdraw except at some cost. This may turn the main disadvantage of conflict-raising tactics into an advantage; for if people cannot withdraw, then they can only escape the pain of conflict by settling the issue, which will frequently mean a compromise—and compromises usually imply some amount of change. Finally, if a written decision rule exists (requiring only a simple majority, for example) there is no disadvantage to alienating a minority of the decision-makers.

These five propositions we draw from a comparative study of a single issue—northern school desegregation. Testing their generality depends on our ability to obtain comparable data on other issues.

Notes

1. The data reported here are taken from David J. Kirby, T. Robert Harris, Robert L. Crain, and Christine H. Rossell, *Political Strategies in Northern School Desegregation* (Lexington, Mass.: Lexington Books, D. C. Heath, 1973). We would like to acknowledge Christine Rossell's and T. Robert Harris's important contributions to this project, and Laura Morlock's help in the re-analysis of data for this paper.

2. The sampling, questionnaires, and scale construction is described in detail in Kirby, *et al., Political Strategies in Northern School Desegregation.*

10 The Neighborhood-based Politics of Education
Harry L. Summerfield *

The unique flavors of four out of seventy neighborhoods in one large city have been sampled. Each of the four provides for the education of children; none bear the same responsibility or capability. Their styles differ. Each neighborhood selects and develops its own political patterns. In turn, central school decision-makers tailor their responses to each neighborhood situation. So, neighborhood-based politics of education exist.

The problem now is analytical. Since each neighborhood seems to be unique, the first analytical task is to identify conditions which cause neighborhood politics to differ. Why do certain neighborhood conditions lead to one type of politics rather than to another? (That expectations of neighborhood residents shapes the style of neighborhood politics is a finding discussed below.) Then focus shifts. Is each neighborhood entirely unique or do all neighborhoods share some critical political characteristics? (That all neighborhoods operate like educational interest groups and all neighborhood educational interest groups share crucial processes, is another finding.)

These findings in turn will lead toward a theory of neighborhood-based politics—a set of propositions about *all* neighborhoods which helps account for differences in *each* neighborhood.

Finally, neighborhoods are viewed in the world of practical politics. How do neighborhood residents affect the educational decision-making process? (That neighborhood interest groups are able to engage decision makers, i.e., that the educational decision-making system is open is the last finding.) What then is the responsibility of the public?

Differing Political Styles of Four Neighborhoods

In King (Figure 10-1), the principal, Mr. Gold, is the main advocate for school needs. He petitions the central school authorities, and wins con-

Reprinted with permission of the publisher from Harry L. Summerfield, *The Neighborhood-based Politics of Education* (Columbus: Charles E. Merrill, 1971), © 1971 by Bell & Howell. For an extended discussion of this chapter see Summerfield, "Cuing and the Open System of Educational Politics, *Education and Urban Society,* Fall 1971.
* Wright Institute, Berkeley, California

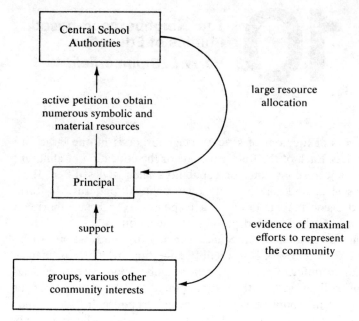

Figure 10-1. King School.

siderable allocations of educational resources. His pursuit of resources succeeds because he is skillful; his petitions are supported and supplemented by active neighborhood, community, and city-wide interests; and resources from city, state, and federal sources for which he can petition are available. Mr. Gold's success, evinced by the increased material inputs to King school, feeds back to his constituency and reinforces the support he receives from the neighborhood, community, and city.

Notably, in the case of King, successful neighborhood petitioning is not predicated upon and does not require active support of the parents. (It is doubtful, however, that much could be done in face of parental opposition.) Mr. Gold's support comes from neighborhood and community groups manned by professional organizers and from liberal spokesmen who are not residents of the neighborhood.

Conditions in King lead to the hypotheses that if the principal is to assume the role of petitioner for the neighborhood, he must be backed by an influence base of community support. (That support base—parents, groups, etc.—remains unspecified without knowledge of the make-up of a particular neighborhood.)

Further, if the community petitions the principal to seek expansion of the school's resources and if he is to maintain support of the politically active community (that is, minimize conflict between the neighborhood and the school), then he must seek and gain resources—material as well as symbolic and policy reassurance—from central school authorities.

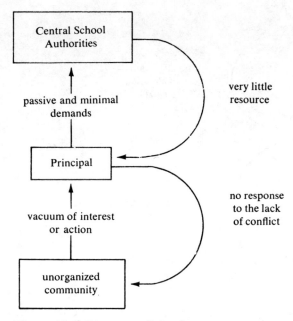

Figure 10-2. Lawrence School.

Lawrence neighborhood actors (Figure 10-2) generate no petitions of their own. Thus, the principal receives no community petition.

Further, he takes virtually no independent steps to represent neighborhood school interests to central school authorities. In the face of objective educational disadvantage, Lawrence receives a relatively small amount of the city's educational resources.

Lawrence neighborhood suggests the hypothesis that a vacuum of community interest (lack of petition) leads the principal to assume a passive role in which he does not act to represent the neighborhood's needs. Two corollaries follow. (1) Even when need is evident, if political thrust (petition) is absent from a neighborhood, then central school authorities allocate few educational resources to a school. (2) Resource allocations to such a neighborhood would have to emanate from a sense of professional commitment, noblesse oblige, or other non-political source, but, in face of scarcity, such allocation is not likely.

In Truman (Figure 10-3) despite constant intra-neighborhood debate on well-known school deficiencies, neither the principal nor the parents represent neighborhood interests to central school authorities. Parents and non-parent residents are intensely concerned about the diminishing quality of the school, but they lack consensus on what to do about it.

Rather than represent Truman's interests to central school authorities, the principal absorbs some neighborhood tension and reflects the rest back onto the neighborhood. Neighborhood petitioners have not commissioned

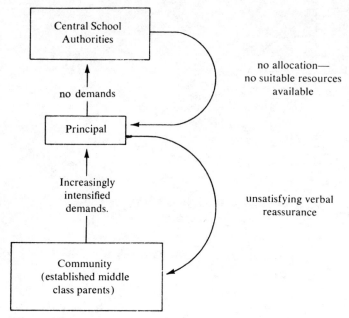

Figure 10-3. Truman School.

him to focus conflict outward. Thus, no compensatory resources come to Truman. Mr. Heard distributes only "symbolic reassurance" (verbal confirmation that everything is all right) because, without petitioning central school authorities for material, it is the only resource he can possess.[1] In Truman, symbolic reassurance hardly suffices to end conflict based on real problems; however, it is the extent of resources available given the limitations on political action allowed within the Truman system.

The hypothesis follows: if residents are aware of school problems and neighborhood political activity is high, but parents and residents cannot agree on an acceptable course of political action (petition), then the principal will be stalemated as a petitioner to central school authorities, and he will become the focus of resident anxiety. And, in lieu of new educational resources, the principal will seek to assuage parental anxiety (reduce conflict between school and community) by symbolic reassurance, and the underlying problems will not really be treated.

In Larsen (Figure 10-4) the principal does not serve as an active petitioner for the neighborhood school, and parents do not petition the principal. Generally, the intensity of Larsen political activity is low. (Whereas political quiescence in Lawrence occurs as a result of parental passivity or lack of political skill, the highly perceptive and skilled Larsen parents simply find few issues about which to be intense.) The educational service and educated product satisfy Larsen consumers. Parents support the

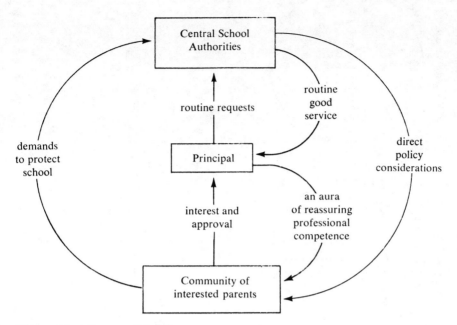

Figure 10-4. Larsen School.

school and its principal, and the principal is able to operate non-conflictu-
ally with the neighborhood and central office.

The only perceived threats to Larsen school emanate from central school
authority policies—possible bussing—or lack of policy—lack of sufficient,
special suburban-like programs. Accordingly, Larsen parents, through their
spokesman, petition the central school authorities for two purposes: to
protect Larsen from certain policies which are deemed as threatening to
school quality; to obtain extra, special resources for the school.

The hypothesis may be advanced, if clients of the school perceive delivery of adequate educational service, then parents actively support the
school, and, as petitioners, remain quiescent. If community actors perceive
a threat which emanates from outside the neighborhood school arena,
then community actors will direct their petition and raise conflict with the
appropriate authorities, probably central school officials.

Figures 10-5 and 10-6 compare the dynamics of political activity in the
four neighborhoods from the perspectives of petition and allocation.

Shared Political Characteristics

The finding that neighborhood political styles differ, helps debunk the
notion that urban school government is a homogenized structure with a
monolithic decision-making process. But, the mere finding of differences

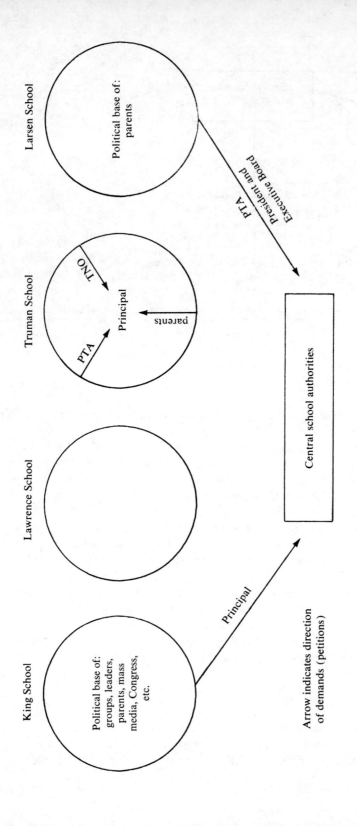

Figure 10-5. Dynamics and Direction of Political Petitions.

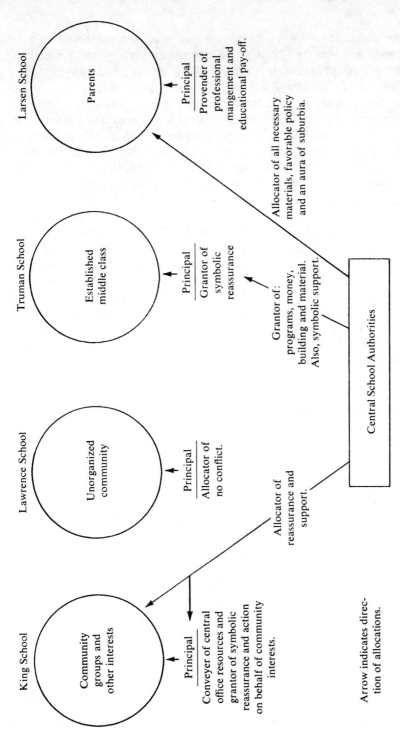

Figure 10-6. Dynamics and Direction of Political Allocations.

is also confusing. It fails to provide a systematic perspective about neighborhood political activity. To increase our understanding and predictive capability, a concept is needed which is more overriding and unifying than that neighborhoods are simply all unique political phenomena.

This section proposes to characterize each neighborhood in *one political model*. The proposal is that each neighborhood is a type of political interest group operating within the city-wide educational decision-making system. If we view each neighborhood as one basic model (interest group), then we will have a systematic way of looking at all neighborhoods.

The inquiry must go further however. If all neighborhoods act as interest groups, what interest group processes serve as determinants of political style? Three processes are proposed: (1) the tendency of each neighborhood school principal to act to minimize conflict which arises between the community and his school; (2) the manifestation of deference for the school by neighborhood residents; (3) the problem of matching neighborhood expectations for education with available educational resources.

Knowing both the political function of a neighborhood (i.e., to act as an interest group) and the determinants of interest group style has value not only in building a theory of a politics of education, but also in aiding petitioners and allocators as they assess and revise their strategies in the educational political arena.

Neighborhoods as Interest Groups

Large city schools are service centers managed on the spot, but in terms of important policy and resource allocation, they are governed elsewhere by authoritative decision-making bodies (school board, state and federal laws, and the administrative agents to whom authority is delegated, which rarely includes neighborhood principals).

To achieve goals which require an important new policy or a change in amount or pattern of distribution of the school system's resources (particularly money), neighborhood-based petitioners must ultimately focus on central school authorities, not on the neighborhood principal. The principal has little budgetary discretion, little discretion about staffing patterns, and, frequently, even severe limitations on his control of school programming. As a school official, the principal has little or no power to dramatically alter the city-wide pattern of resource allocations.

If, in terms of the political function, neighborhood schools are not governments (and principals not governors) politically what then are neighborhoods?

In the relationship between a neighborhood and the city-wide central school government, the neighborhood, as a unit of city education politics, is best conceived as an *interest group*. David Truman writes:

. . . "interest group" refers to any group that, on the basis of one or more shared attitudes [interests], makes certain claims upon other groups in the society for the establishment, maintenance, or enhancement of forms of behavior that are implied by the shared attitudes.[2]

Neighborhoods, like interest groups, face circumscribed problems which, to a greater or lesser degree, are shared by all members (residents). These problems are not necessarily shared by other neighborhoods or groups in the city. Like interest groups, if some members of a neighborhood group determine they need and want new educational resources, they also find that they have no formal authority to allocate them. Thus, the group must develop techniques to represent its interests to the authorities who are able to allocate resources. Interest groups operate in a competitive environment, and in the city-wide educational political system, the neighborhood is one group which represents its own interests in competition with others.

David Truman's definition concentrates on interest groups as active entities. Group members hold concerns which are their interests, and they make demands upon other groups (which could be government). It is noteworthy, however, particularly in reference to the politics of education, that interest groups continue to exist while in a dormant stage. The group's quiescence can indicate satisfaction of the members' shared concerns (i.e., as a group, no new educational needs are perceived), or quiescence may be a function of impotency, or political inability of the group to pursue its interests.[3]

Group Members' Participation

Elites. Neighborhood group structures vary in terms of the leadership elite and the following. Among many forms, the elite may be a lone citizen (Mr. Eathen in Lawrence), an intense group (the PTA executive board or the established middle class in Truman); a chosen representative of a large number of residents (the PTA president in Larsen); or one or more paid public officials (Mr. Gold and others in King).

Two qualities strengthen an elite and make it powerful: (1) if it is a gathering point in the funnel of community interest; (2) if, in pursuing neighborhood interest, its responsibility is unambiguous. Each in their own way. King, with public support drawn from institutions and paid leaders, and Larsen, with support coming from active residents, typify neighborhoods with strong elites.

Unsupported or confused elites seem to develop little political strength. The indecisive collegial group serving as the collective elite in Truman is unable to appoint a distinct spokesman charged to pursue neighborhood interests. With ambiguous public support, Truman's decision-making funnel is insufficiently narrowed to concentrate and activate political "clout." Mr. Eathen in Lawrence, as leader of a virtually inert group, is clear about his goals, but lacking community support, he is without either potential or actual power in dealings with central school decision makers.

Citizens. Although most parents are concerned about their children in the school, mass citizen activity directed at the school is uncommon. Sometimes, however, mass support and participation become striking. (King and Truman on several occasions and Larsen over bussing.)

But, mass participation is not always evident even when it operates intensely. Quiet support of the status quo or quiet support of elite efforts to bring change are both powerful political acts of citizens. Indeed, quiet support of the status quo has typified much of the public's role in the politics of education.

The Neighborhood Interest Group and the Principal's Role in Conflict Reduction

Regardless of the neighborhood, the principal's chief political function is to *minimize conflict between the community and the neighborhood school.* He does not necessarily act to reduce conflict between the community and central school officials. (Note especially King, but also Larsen.)

As a petitioner for King, the principal is leader of the neighborhood interest group. He must structure conflict between the neighborhood and central school authorities in order to reduce conflict between neighborhood and school. In Lawrence, the principal, as a kind of agent of central school authorities, is faced with virtually no neighborhood petition, and he completely controls conflict—where there is no conflict, none shall be raised—even though this policy seems to serve poorly Lawrence and its quality of education. At Truman, the principal is generally the exclusive target of neighborhood discontent. He seeks to reduce the endless conflict by either absorbing or reflecting it within the neighborhood setting. Although, of all principals, he is least successful at reducing dissatisfaction, he is, ironically, most intensely and most constantly involved in the conflict reduction process. At Larsen, the principal is a "nice neutral." She maintains a smooth, well-managed school house giving the alert, potentially critical community no major cause for dissatisfaction with the school. She preempts conflict.[4]

Although the political *function* of each principal—to minimize conflict between the community and the neighborhood school—remains constant among neighborhoods, the political *style* of each principal varies. Problems and resources vary, and what is a problem or resource in one neighborhood is not in another. Thus, the conflict reduction style of the principal is structured in terms of the conflict arousal characteristics of the neighborhood. Thus, *the rule of the best fit* of the principal's political style to his neighborhood setting tends to operate.

Because principals seek to minimize conflict using a well-tailored "best fit" political style, Mr. Gold, for example, would be unlikely to operate in the same manner which has been successful at King if he were assigned to Lawrence (or any of the other schools). As a dynamic petitioner in King, Mr. Gold requires strong community support, and that is markedly lacking in Lawrence. Likewise, Mr. Lowe of Lawrence could not be his passive self at King. A deafening calamity would reach the ears of central school authorities.

Interest Group Style and Its Characteristic Deference

A mighty army, a sage old man, a beloved church, a nation, or a school can be an object commanding respect and submission to its authority. This slightly reverent willingness to submit may be called deference.

Education, as a "sacred" function, typically has commanded deference from the public, and, because of the neighborhood structure of public education, citizens have had little choice except to focus that respect on their neighborhood schools.

Although deference conceivably can be withdrawn at will, withdrawal seems infrequent in regard to schools. Rather, deference is granted, and the school is "accepted," but each neighborhood sets its own standards for "acceptance of what?". The manifestation of respect and the conditions under which citizens will feel submissive to education policy take many forms and become a determinate of neighborhood interest group style.

In the potentially volatile King neighborhood, deference is granted by neighborhood actors and parents in exchange for evidence of inputs to the King school: vigorous educational programs and efforts, hard work of the principal and staff, good community relations, visible quantities of material and symbolic resources. (It is noteworthy that in the past, output—educational achievement of the children—has not been a criteria for granting deference; although, this paradox may now be changing.)

Deference in King reflects a positive awareness by community actors—they watch what is going on. Politically, the community's respect is a support which (1) unites school and neighborhood in order to (2) provide the principal with a base of influence for his dealings with central school authorities.

Lawrence is different. Residents there grant deference in part because they have scanty knowledge about the processes and goals of education, and they are satisfied with and expect no more than the minimums they receive. Their ignorance blocks development of issues and leaves the residents unreflective, without a will to organize. In this respect, deference in Lawrence is a blind faith, a non-action. Willingness to accept the status quo is also in part a conscious decision. As marginal people, Lawrence residents fear that change will destroy the little security they have. Thus, they consciously oppose movements—like urban renewal—which could dislodge them from their life style. Theirs is a problem non-solving situation.

In Truman, the manifestation of deference from the neighborhood is twofold. For the lower-socio-economic newcomers, the school is seen as better than what was known in the old neighborhood. Newcomers respect and appreciate the school, viewing it as an opportunity for educational uplift. The established middle-class grant their respect ambivalently. They manifest faith in the "basic quality" of the school in order to reassure themselves that the school is indeed worthy of their support. But, the growing signs of Truman's deterioration taint their deeper certainty. Residents support "the school," but volubly doubt critical aspects in the school's learning and moral environment. They endlessly ponder the school's problems, but do not admit that the problems are in reality manifestations of the neighborhood's social change. Failing to admit that basic change has taken place in the school, they take no effective political action which might bring educational reinforcement to Truman. Therefore, the residents' deference, in the face of their carping, represents denial of real problems—reluctance to admit to themselves the faltering character of Truman school. Politically, their deference impedes formation of effective political action directed to central school authorities.

In Larsen, deference is a function of parents' scrutinous appraisal and approval of the school program. Politically, this deference serves to support the school and defend it against deterioration of its quality.

Thus, deference may be manifested as: strong political action geared to strengthen the school (King); uncritical acceptance stemming from ignorance and lack of skill (Lawrence); fantasy solution to real problems (Truman); or satisfaction (Larsen).

The effectiveness of neighborhood-based politics of education can be tragically stunted where residents cling to unrealistic patterns of deference (Lawrence and Truman). For a neighborhood to function as an effective political unit, petitioners must blend a degree of respect for education with a component of critical, measured demand on the school. The formula combining deference and demand appears poorest in Lawrence, but optimal in the very distinct settings of King and Larsen. Larsen is mostly quiescent, King is always active. In both, neighborhood people (petitioners) respect education and look to the school for its provision. Actively, they hold the school accountable for its education program.

Interest Group Success as a Function of Matching
Expectations with Resources

The ability of a neighborhood to achieve an optimal balance of respect (acceptance) and demand is related to the ability of the political system to match expectations to resources.

Each neighborhood's unique set of problems is matched with a measure of the capability for solving the problems. Thus, the relationship between petitioner and allocator—their degree of conflict—in any particular neighborhood can be explored in terms of two political variables: (1) expectations of the petitioner and (2) feasibility of a solution to the conflict raised.

(1) Expectations have to do with the goals of the petitioner. First, what is being sought—material (money), policy decisions not involving material, symbolic reward, etc.? Second, at any stage of the goal seeking process, what gradation of goal attainment is expected? What is the schedule of rewards?

(2) Feasibility of a solution to a problem depends first upon the availability of resources which can quell conflict. The most vigorous demands to build a wall will be unmet if there are no bricks or if there are bricks but no masons. Second, feasibility of a solution depends on the effectiveness of allocative mechanisms. The political system must offer a viable format for distribution of resources. The feasibility of a solution depends on the capability for compromise to avoid polarization of petitioner and allocator.

The case studies illustrate that neighborhood expectations for education are matched to available resources in a variety of ways. Not all matches are optimal. For example, where expectations are extremely low, the level of education service is low and school authorities are disengaged from virtually all political activity (Lawrence). At the other extreme, where community expectations are vigorously expressed but unrealistically high in terms of resources available to meet the problem, the school authorities can provide only inadequate response even though the principal is politically hyperactive (Truman). Where expectations of the community are well-matched to the kinds of resources the school is easily able to provide, important conflict is infrequently activated (Larsen). Similarly, where expectations for education are vibrant and potentially conflictual, but limited within compromise goals which can be matched to available resources, then political interplay, although intense, will result in a process of conflict reduction commensurate with the conflict which is raised (King).

Material resources are always limited, thus all expectations cannot be met. In Dewitton, school officials have had to decide whether Truman or King (among other schools) would receive material resources sufficient to match neighborhood expectations. Because the least amount of resources are allocated to gain the most conflict reduction, Truman, with tensions controlled by symbolic reassurance, commands (and demands) few of the very scarce material resources while King, posing considerable threat to quiescence in the school system, commands considerable, palpable, material inputs.

Not only is there a limit to the city-wide pool of material resources, but also, in some cases, no amount of money, symbols, or policy available to the school system can, in the short run, alter the conditions which are creating conflict. For example, no resources available to the school system can stop the social change which is affecting the character of Truman. (Perhaps the effects of social change could be controlled. Even that speculation is improbable given the constraints on Truman politics.)

In many neighborhoods, particularly those with extreme educational problems, matching expectations with resources can come to border on the impossible. For example, one can anticipate a political crisis in neighborhoods like King and Lawrence. To date, the one resource not demanded by King residents is the only resource really required in Larsen— academic achievement by children. Despite all the programs and money and energy at King, the school remains at the bottom of the list in terms of pupil achievement. If community actors in King were to insist on the same payoff required by residents of Larsen, under current technology, the school system would be unable to comply. In the contemporary state of pedagogy, "learning" is not a commodity politically allocable to great numbers of people of the lower classes. Unmitigated demand for a nonallocable resource creates chronic and irreducible conflict. No political system is viable under such circumstances.

Conclusion

The process of matching expectations to resources assumes the capability of petitioners and allocators to communicate. This assumption should be examined for upon it rests the question of whether the neighborhood interest group can actually affect educational decision making. Is the educational political system open? If so, what constitutes engagement of educational allocators by petitioners?

That Education Political Systems Are Closed— A Doubtful Contention

That "Federal bureaucrats off in Washington" are out of touch with local needs is a long held, if unsubstantiated, belief sardonically held by many local schoolmen. But, recent research now asserts that *local* educational decision makers are out of touch; that they neither respond to nor reflect the public will. Quite reputable scholars report that local educational authorities are "unpublic officials" because of their insulation and autonomy. In system's theory parlance, these researchers contend that the educational decision-making system is essentially closed, that is, clients of the system have neither access to nor influence upon the educational decision making process. For example, Laurance Iannaccone, first writing in 1967 [5] and again in reconfirmation with Frank Lutz in 1969, conclude from their analysis of the research that:

> The politics of school districts, influenced by their special governmental arrangements and the emotional commitments of American society in the absence of the two-party system, have developed an unusual degree of autonomy. This has resulted in an amazing capacity among school districts for rejecting changes that would modify their usual processes and their internal status structure. The rejection of new inputs, people, ideas, activities, and technologies is hardly surprising when those who have the most to lose by this innovation constitute the internal power structure of the existing system.[6]

In a similar vein, Marilyn Gittell and T. Edward Hollander write:

> The insulation of public education is twofold: bureaucratic centralization (or more accurately overcentralization) which is a product of size, reinforced by an ideological rationale of professionalism which is a product of the vested interests of the educationists. The result is a static, internalized, isolated system which has been unable to respond to vastly changing needs and demands of large city populations.[7]

Critics who attempt to support the contention that the educational political system is closed because elites manage the decision-making process rely on faulty logic. (Whereas this discussion referred earlier to interest group elites, now reference is to decision-making elites.) The critics argue that a closed political system affords no opportunity for public petitioners to affect the decision-making process. Thus, in a closed system decisions are made by political elites who can be impervious to the public, and since the educational decision making process is managed by elites, it is a closed system and impervious to the public. But, the fact that elites direct and manage the educational decision making process is not at all a sufficient sign to indicate closedness.

In a society of mass populations, representative government, and intense division of labor, political apparatuses are necessarily operated by the few for the many. When a public commodity like education is distributed to all citizens, the vast complexity of the process requires that only a relatively few people spend the time, develop the skills, and responsibly manage the ongoing specialized governing operations. There is no practical alternative to elite management of the government of mass populations or large scale private organizations; yet, the existence of elites is compatible with representation of public interest and is, indeed, the hallmark of the perpetuated American government. As part of their function, elites condense, represent, and process the interests of various publics.

The test of openness is not whether there is elite management, but whether public education decision making elites can remain impervious to public demand. Can educational decision makers insulate themselves from engagement with interested publics?

The vote stands out as the most obvious mechanism whereby members of the public can influence educational elites. The bond issue or tax increase election is a powerful tool of the mass public.[8] Iannaccone and Lutz focus on school board elections.[9] They conclude and rightly so that the electoral defeat of an incumbent board member reflects changing expectations for education in the community. Incumbent defeat is seen by them as a crucial public input which will probably lead to significant changes in the school district governance. They find however, that there is a considerable time lag between real changes in the community and response in school government. Fundamentally, the authors argue that while social and economic changes occur gradually and steadily in the community, political change (incumbent defeat) occurs infrequently and suddenly. During the time in which the old guard holds its position the system is relatively closed.

This sort of theory of revolutions tends to blur and vastly underestimate the essence of the political process. Elections stand only as benchmarks in the ongoing public engagement with the educational political system, and more often than not, elections confirm the work of the system rather than revolt against it.

Mostly, political systems are viable for extended periods of time. Viability implies that the system obtains a relatively high level of ongoing support. Support comes for two reasons: (a) clients of the system are sufficiently satisfied with the ongoing services of the system, that is, they get at least enough of what they expect; (b) when they are dissatisfied, the stress they raise is sufficiently reduced, that is, the political process works to contain and defuse conflict. Whether clients of an educational system want more of the same or whether they are able to identify and seek change, the studies of four neighborhoods in Dewitton show that without utilizing the technique of elections, citizens regularly engage decision-makers.

Through mechanisms developed by each group—mechanisms which

are sometimes subtle; sometimes bold—demand is structured and, on occasion, conflict is created. At times neighborhood interest groups actively engage central decision makers on behalf of change (King); in another fashion, interest groups passively engage central decision makers by acquiescing to the status quo (Lawrence). (Larsen residents developed the behavior of actively seeking to preserve the status quo in the face of indications of change.) In a third mode, typified by Truman, neighborhood interest groups can structure themselves into a state of suspended conflict neither active nor passive, but just tense. Whatever the pattern, between election benchmarks, school district officials, like most other American governmental officials, obtain a reading of the "public will," respond to demands, and if necessary and possible, implement reform.

A Preferred Hypothesis—The System Is Open

Because political settings for education vary so much, no absolute statement about systemic openness or closedness is possible and exceptions to any generalization will quickly arise. But, based on the findings about neighborhood based politics of education, a preferred hypothesis would be that the decision making system of public education is essentially open rather than essentially closed.

Understanding Openness

The concept of openness emphasizes the capability of petitioners to engage a political system. At the simplest level this means communicate and be heard; make the petition known and comprehended. Each neighborhood, in its own way, based on the political style and expectations of its residents attained this engagement.

Engagement, however, is often mistakenly equated with successful use of power (ability to make another actor do what you want him to do). But, openness of the system is not measured by the ability of any particular systemic actor to win. What any particular actor gets from a political encounter is the result of the engagement (made possible by systemic openness) and is dependent upon conditions within the political system.

Conditions Within the Educational Political System

A basic premise about educational change is that it is slow. As a social and economic institution, public education largely perpetuates and carries predominate culture modes of our society. As an institution resistant to violation of societal norms, the school political system is designed to delay response to new societal demand until need and the demand are unequivocally clear. Clients of public education can disagree about the desirability of conservatism versus social activism in the school's role, but a conservative system is not necessarily a closed system. It is, if anything, overly open to the majority and defensively wary of the vanguard which always first appears as a minority. The defensive stance toward the vanguard is itself a sign of openness, for, clearly, allocators have been engaged and are responding to pressures for change.

Assuming that preservation of the status quo is only a part of the function of a government and that change is also desirable, the finding that interested publics can petition for change and engage educational decision makers does not indicate that such a petitioner must win any or all issues he raises. Demands always exceed the limited resources and reasonable (as well as unreasonable) people differ about what is the "best" solution to a problem. Simply stated, people often conflict with each other.

The management of conflict by decision makers is a responsibility of the job, not a sign of closedness. Decision makers must develop coping behaviors as an aide to decision making and as a source of stability for the system. E. E. Schattschneider writes:

> The crucial problem in politics is the management of conflict. No regime could endure which did not cope with this problem. All politics, all leadership and all organization involves the management of conflict. All conflict allocates space in the political universe. The consequences of conflict are so important that it is inconceivable that any regime could survive without making an attempt to shape the system.[10]

Coping behaviors, which frequently amount to use of the power of public office (1) to forestall decisions and actions; (2) to bring compromise; and (3) to reach decisions when timing is right, are highly functional to even the most reform-minded political system. A petitioner has no chance of victory if he does not enter the political arena, but because decisions are not rendered immediately and to his entire or even partial satisfaction is not necessarily a sign of closedness.

The fervent activity of petitioner groups within a big city can lead to stalemate. Large urban school systems have shown themselves unable to meet some important, intense demands. Under this considerable stress, the resultant coping behavior by decision makers is sometimes interpreted as bankruptcy or rancidness of the system. Certainly the accusations that some large city educational systems are politically archaic is in portion true; however, a simpler fact is more explanatory: the urban system lacks the money and technology to act on many of its most severe problems. Despite the mythology of American capability to solve any problem, the hard fact of failure—at least temporary failure—must occasionally be admitted.

Faced with failure, three choices are available: (1) Petitioners may seek new resources by broadening the scope of the education political system. It has many portals of entry from the neighborhood to the federal government. Merely because one level of the system fails to provide relief is not necessarily an indication that the system is closed. If the local level of the decision-making system has been engaged and has failed, petitioners can then focus upon and seek resources from the state or Washington, D.C., (2) Failure can be accepted for the time being and petitioners can modulate their demands, and, for a while, pursue lower level expectations with anticipation of gradual reform, (3) If feelings of urgency are great and sense of desperation dominating, then petitioners may ignore obvious perils and press extreme demands seeking to destroy the system in the revolutionary hope that a new system will solve problems previously considered insurmountable.

Public Will. Because decision makers interpret passive engagement (acquiescing acceptance of the status quo) as affirmation of operating policies, in a passive political environment educational decision-makers can be expected to make few changes or only those changes dictated by "professional discretion." Politically, professional discretion is exercise of the authority and power granted by continual public acquiescence. This power is in part used to preempt conflict—solve problems before they become public issues—thus, allocators avoid confrontation and challenge to their authority. Or, the power is manifest as leadership which brings public support.

Because educational decision makers typically have been granted considerable power by acquiescing publics, some critics condemn the authorities as recalcitrants. But, what passes as recalcitrance can also be interpreted as representation by authorities of public opposition to change; or, stated differently, public support of the status quo.

Sometimes occasions arise for petitioners to create an issue in the realm of public education. At that time, rather than view educational decision makers as autocratic ogres, a more fruitful and optimistic perspective for petitioners would be to put decision making elites on the defensive. Petitioners can approach decision-making elites, viewing them as political actors who can, do, and should face a public demand. (Optimally, the demand pattern of petitioners will respect the fact that the educational political system, like all political systems, is fragile and should be approached responsibly.)

With this view, a share of the burden to initiate change or preserve the status quo shifts to the public. If interested publics (neighborhoods for example) want change, they must be willing and able to properly organize to pursue their goals. They must endure frustrations and be willing to counter competition such as strong support for continuing the status quo.

To the question of "who shall be accountable for education?" the reflex answer "professional educators" taps only a facet of the problem. The public, guided by tacit or formulated expectations for education, bears considerable responsibility for the shape of its educational institutions.

Political activity begins with demands. (A problem is not a political problem without demand.) The consumer of public education services is responsible for deciding and making clear that he is demanding either more of the same or change. For public education is more than education. It is public.

Notes

1. The phrase "symbolic reassurance" was coined by Murray Edelman in his extremely valuable book, *The Symbolic Uses of Politics* (Urbana: University of Illinois Press, 1964).

2. David B. Truman, *The Governmental Process* (New York: Alfred A. Knopf, Inc., 1951), p. 33.

3. Peter Bachrach and Morton S. Baratz, "Two Faces of Power," *American Political Science Review,* 56 p. 948, December 1962, discuss aspects of political inaction as a function of the larger political process.

Of course power is exercised when A participates in the making of decisions which affect B. But power is also exercised when A devotes his energies to creating or reinforcing social and political values and institutional practices that limit the scope of the political process to public consideration of only those issues which are comparatively innocuous to A. To the extent that A succeeds in doing this, B is prevented, for all practical purposes from bringing to the fore any issues that might in their resolution be seriously detrimental of A's set of preferences.

4. Principals are differentially equipped to respond to neighborhood petition. Some resources available are (1) verbal reassurance directed to anxious residents that problems are being solved (this is the least costly and most abundant resource); (2) activism: the ability, as representative of the neighborhood, to petition central school officials on behalf of neighborhood interests; (3) passivity: reluctance to take any action which would stir conflict where none exists; (4) the school's reputation: its reputation and performance record which, if satisfying, in effect keeps conflict down; (5) support the principal receives from central school authorities.

5. Laurance Iannaccone, *Politics in Education* (New York: The Center for Applied Research in Education, Inc., 1967).

6. Laurance Iannaccone and Frank W. Lutz, *Politics, Power, and Policy* (Columbus: Charles E. Merrill, 1970), p. 28.

7. Marilyn Gittell and T. Edward Hollander, *Six Urban School Districts* (New York: Frederick A. Praeger, 1968), p. 197.

8. Bond issue or tax increase proposals which are defeated may indicate simply that taxpayers have reached a point of exhaustion even though they generally support the work of the school. However, revenue referendum defeat could indicate more profound issues. Louis Massoti, *Education and Politics in Suburbia* (Cleveland: Press of Case Western Reserve, 1967) found that defeat of a bond referendum in a wealthy school district reflected profound community conflict over where the new school was to be built. Settlement of the conflict brought passage of the bond issue.

9. Iannaccone and Lutz, *op. cit.*

10. See E. E. Schattschneider, *The Semi-Sovereign People* (New York: Holt, Rinehart and Winston, 1960), p. 71.

11

Dealing with Organizational Rigidity in Public Schools: A Theoretical Perspective
Willis D. Hawley *

Introduction

Books criticizing the dysfunctional consequences of organizational rigidity in public schools are so numerous as to give the publishing industry a stake in resisting educational reform. Research by academicians, analysis by social critics and journalists, and attacks by aroused citizens, all argue that the failure of public education to meet the needs of society and, especially, of children, is related importantly to the rigid, excessively bureaucratic, ways that schools are organized.

Certainly, such attacks are more easily justified in some school systems than others. And, in very recent times there does appear to be a new readiness among professional educators to entertain ideas for restructuring the learning process such as "open classrooms," "multi-age grouping," various forms of "individualized instruction," in-the-community learning," and the like. Nonetheless, organizational rigidity of public schools has been the source of pervasive and enduring criticism for more than fifty years, and predictions of its rapid or widespread dissipation seem overly optimistic, if not naive.

The purpose of this discussion is not to indict public schools; such accusations already have attained the status of popular sport. Indeed, a major reason why I was moved to undertake this analysis was my wonderment at the staying power of school bureaucracies in the face of what appears to have been a whirlwind of criticism. Moreover, it seems to me that much of the so-called school reform literature seems satisfied with explanations for the rigidity it reports that were overly simplistic, educationally misleading, or without many implications for feasible, lasting, and potentially effective restructuring of public schools systems.

There are many potential sources of organizational rigidity in public schools. Some of these have to do with the role, past and present, of education in American society, some with the unionization of teachers,[1]

Prepared for original publication in this book from a paper presented to the annual convention of the American Political Science Association, September 1973. Write author for footnotes omitted here.

* Institute for Policy Sciences and Public Affairs, Duke University

some with the standardizing consequence of the state and federal governments and professional organizations, some with the fact that patterns of
school organization developed and stabilized in a period when business
values and the logic of "scientific management" seemed more pervasive
than they now do,[2] and some with the character of preservice teacher education and the content of training programs in educational administration.[3]

Still other sources of organizational rigidity in public schools have to do
with the nature of the educational process, internal procedures for structuring administrative and teaching roles, and the linkages of educational
decision making to the community served. These phenomena are the concern of this article. They differ from the others mentioned in that individual
school systems could have a *relatively* substantial impact on eliminating
them or mitigating their effects. Thus, the emphasis here is on understanding the sources of rigidity in public schools that, though not independent of cultural and other forces, could be dealt with by restructuring
the schools themselves.

As noted, schools vary in the degree to which one might fairly characterize them as organizationally rigid, non-adaptive, bureaucratic or the
like. My objective is to provide a theoretically oriented foundation upon
which one might explain why schools differ in this respect.

After defining organizational rigidity, and briefly suggesting why rigidity
impedes educational effectiveness, I will attempt systematically to outline
the structural sources of organizational rigidity in public schools. The final
section of the article briefly explores the policy implications of the preceding parts by identifying some of the components that might be included
in a comprehensive plan for restructuring the public schools.

The Impact of Organizational Rigidity in Schools

A General Definition of Organizational Rigidity

Despite the fact that the term "organizational rigidity"—or its functional
equivalents—is widely used by students of organizations, there appears to
be no generally accepted operationalization of this concept. It is not important to the purposes of this discussion that we resolve this problem here.
On the other hand, some specification of the idea will facilitate communication. Thus, I suggest that schools may be thought of as rigid to the degree
that they can be accurately described by four characteristics.

1. Centrality of Key Decision-Making. What proportion of decisions that
   affect (a) the way the defining functions of the organization are exer-

cised and (b) the allocation of formal authority, are made at the center (or top) of the organization?
2. Standardization of Organization Structures and Processes. To what extent are the procedures and processes utilized to accomplish organizational goals *essentially* similar in all of the organization's subunits or parts that have the same general responsibilities?
3. Routinization of Relationships with Clients. To what degree are the ways the organization relates to its "client" parents and students routinized and standardized (and thus impersonalized)?
4. Lack of Changefulness. How persistent over time, are the basic organization and behavioral patterns that prescribe the life of the school?

This concept of organizational rigidity embodies certain characteristics of Weber's definition of bureaucracy. Most "bureaucratic" organizations will be rigid, but we can imagine rigid organizations that would score rather low on some dimensions of the bureaucracy model. One reason for this, and a point of central importance is that organizational rigidity is not solely the result of formal organizational structures. It is also, sometimes fundamentally, the consequence of patterns of behavior that derive from the "informal organization" of an enterprise. For example, the routinization of classroom procedures is a function of limitations on behavior imposed by superiors and the way a teacher's work is physically structured on the one hand, and measures teachers themselves adopt to reduce perceived uncertainties and threats to competence and authority on the other.

Why Be Concerned About Organizational Rigidity
in Public Schools?

There are at least three general reasons one might want to study organizational rigidity in public schools. First, many types of public (and private) organizations appear to be less adaptive and dynamic than their tasks require. Looking through the eyes of theory at schools may suggest more generic explanations for service delivery failures in the public sector.

Second, while there is no way—given available data and research—to specify the number of schools in the country wherein organizational rigidity impedes effective education, one is hard pressed to find among the dozens of recent studies of school structure a commentator who does not attest to its ubiquity. I will not belabor the point here. In later sections I will cite several manifestations of rigidity which I suspect will be all too familiar to those who visit schools to do more than attend PTA meetings or "open house."

Third, in schools where organizational rigidity does exist its negative consequences can be profound. Perhaps those who choose to read this article need not be convinced, but it is essential to its purpose that the relationship between rigidity and ineffectiveness of schools be made explicit. Let us assume that the basic concern of formal education is the creation of experiences that maximize each student's learning opportunities.[4]

Unfortunately, available research and theory do not provide a foundation upon which to prescribe a definitive set of teaching behaviors that are superior to any others or to develop "teacher-proof" curricular or learning programs.[5]

What does this mean for the organization of schools? If we can agree that children's learning is the central purpose of schools, we can see from the foregoing that achievement of that purpose rests fundamentally with the quality of the teaching that takes place.

Given the complexity, stress, and uncertainty inherent in the teaching/learning process, one might conclude that the more effective teacher (vis-a-vis his or her contributions to a pupil's learning) would be intelligent, possess a flexible open personality, feel comfortable working with others, be able to see causality in multidimensional terms and have the ability to tolerate ambiguity, and enjoy spontaneous and intimate student-teacher contact.[6] Aside from the probability that most teachers sincerely like children, the available evidence suggests that many teachers do not possess these traits.

Drawing on the literature in organization theory and studies of schools themselves, one can readily see why schools characterized by organizational rigidity would fail to (1) attract able people to the profession and retain them and (2) provide an environment in which potential teaching effectiveness would be maximized.

The Facilitation of Effective Teaching. As I've implied, teaching can be characterized as a technology about which knowledge of cause and effect is meager and which must be applied to inputs (students) whose characteristics are complex and unpredictable. There is substantial agreement among organization theorists that non-educational organizations which maximize effectiveness under these conditions are generally characterized by:

1. Substantial freedom delegated to subunits so as to allow for localized adaptation and experimentation.[7]
2. Structures which increase opportunities for horizontal communication and collaboration.[8]
3. Considerable openness to environmental feedback with respect to both positive and negative reactions to the products or services it delivers.[9]

There is also agreement among many students of school administration that organizational rigidity impedes good teaching. If, as Robert Schaefer suggests, a teacher is a diagnostician, a "stalker of meaning," and a constant learner, the dysfunctions of organizational rigidity should be clear.[10]

Providing the Motivational Environment for Effective Teaching. The available literature suggests that organizational environments most effective in motivating people whose jobs require them to deal creatively with uncertainty and to respond flexibly and spontaneously to a variety of problem solving demands generally provide these people with:

1. a role in the development of organizational policies relevant to their work;
2. some autonomy in setting individual goals and substantial freedom in determining the means to achieve those goals;
3. opportunities for professional interaction.[11]

Attracting and Retaining Able Teachers. It follows that the conditions that motivate performance also lead to greater job satisfaction (though satisfaction need not increase "productivity"). Persons with the traits that appear to characterize effective teachers are likely to value self-direction, a collegial role in the organization's leadership activities, relative diversity and the avoidance of routine, and supportive rather than autocratic superior-subordinate relationships.[12]

The dysfunctions of organizational rigidity in schools have been summarized nicely by Robert Schaefer, "What seems so enervating in teaching is not the severity of the difficulties encountered but the relative powerlessness of the individual to further his effectiveness." But if rigidity is so counterproductive in education, why is it so pervasive?

Sources of Organizational Rigidity in Public Schools

The Difficulty of Measuring Organizational Outputs

Organizational rigidity tends to persist in the absence of effective information about, or penalties for, its dysfunctions. As Albert O. Hirschman explains:

The deterioration in performance is reflected most typically and generally, that is, for both firms and other organizations, in an absolute or comparative deterioration of the *quality* of the product or service provided. Management then finds out about its failings via two alternative routes:

1. Some customers stop buying the firm's products or some members leave the organization: this is the *exit option*. As a result, revenues drop, membership declines, and management is impelled to search for ways and means to correct whatever faults have led to exit.
2. The firm's customers or the organization's members express their dissatisfaction directly to management or to some other authority to which management is subordinate or through general protest addressed to anyone who cares to listen: this is the *voice option*. As a result, management once again engages in a search for the causes and possible cures of customers' and members' dissatisfaction.[13]

If, however the quality of the service provided is not readily assessed, neither "exit" or "voice" are likely to be exercised fully or efficiently. The problems of assessing school outputs are derived from (1) the multiple, vague, emotionally laden, and often conflicting nature of the goals both professionals and laymen hold for schools and (2) the fact that learning (the product of schools) involves behavioral changes influenced by many factors which we have a limited technical capacity to measure with validity.[14]

These two factors are interrelated in the sense that measurement problems give rise to further uncertainty about appropriate roles the organization can really play.

It is fairly easily seen how the difficulty of measuring organizational output might reduce the effectiveness of the citizenry's demands for change in education, though I will return briefly to the point in a subsequent section. But output assessment problems also affect the conscious internal structuring of schools in at least three important ways:

1. When organizations have difficulty measuring their products accurately, they seek to control quality by defining the processes that are intuitively related to output and measuring the effectiveness of workers in terms of their deviance from those processes.[15] This, of course, results in organizational rigidity. While we can understand why teachers, and school officials in general, have opposed measurement of school effectiveness in terms of product,[16] one wonders whether teachers understand that this stance contributes importantly to the reduction of their professional autonomy.

2. When under pressure from their environments to demonstrate their effectiveness, organizations tend to emphasize those activities that appear to be most readily measured whether or not those activities are central to the function of the enterprise. For example, in her study of 14 California school districts, Samuels concludes:

It was found that regardless of the size of the district in which teachers worked, more than fifty percent of all teachers agreed that classroom control and discipline was the most important criterion in teacher evaluation. The second most important criterion was the teaching methods used by the teacher. Pupil's achievement was ranked third, and the least important criterion was judged to be staff relations.[17]

Since discipline in schools is invariably defined as order, and is seen as an important objective of schools by parents, the consequence of substantially regulating student behavior is to reduce pressure for change and increase organizational rigidity.

When student performance is measured, assessment tends to focus on narrow aspects of cognitive development in the form of scores on tests of reading and quantitative ability. While it is important that children learn to read and do arithmetic, it may be that those dimensions of these skills measured by standardized tests can be taught as well with standardized teaching techniques as by more open and individualized instruction.

In any case, assessing overall teacher performance in terms of reading and math tends to reduce the incentives teachers have to experiment and to integrate cognitive and affective aspects of learning, and this too fosters rigidity.

3. When an individual is uncertain about the capacity to handle assigned responsibilities, he seeks to (a) reduce the apparent complexity of the task, and (b) reduce the scope of the task by minimizing involvement and disclaiming responsibility for certain problems.[18]

Thus the difficulty of measuring student learning encourages teachers to try to simplify and narrow their responsibilities by stereotyping and classifying students, by avoiding involvement with the factors outside his or her class that might affect learning (the rapid growth of counseling and "outreach" work as specialized functions is one manifestation of this), by routinizing student contact, by dismissing the student (and sometimes his parents) as a referent group, and by incorporating the student into the organization in the sense that he takes the blame for his nonperformance (consider the functions of the report card).

Limits and Problems of "Exit" from Public Schools

Hirschman argues, in effect, that a major incentive for an organization to remedy dysfunctional rigidity is that those whose support its needs will exit. That is, the organization's consumers will cease using its goods or services or its members will resign. In education, however, even more than most public services, the exit option is limited and its impact problematic.

Most obviously, the exit option is conditioned by the fact that all young people are required by state laws to attend school, and a relatively small proportion of the families in the country have the resources for private schools except, perhaps that decreasing number of schools operated by major religions. In other words, public schools enjoy a virtual monopoly in a captive market.

Since public schools face virtually no interorganizational competition, they have no self-interest in determining what other school systems are doing. This, coupled with the pressure of daily events, may be one explanation for the enormous time that it takes to diffuse an educational innovation.[19]

Not only are most public schools virtually free of competition from other educational organizations, in about 85 percent of all cities they are fiscally and politically independent of city government and thus do not compete directly for resources with other governmental agencies, and there is no threat that other agencies will significantly usurp their functions.

Unlike many organizations, most educational institutions experience no immediate loss of economic resources when those served do exercise the exit option. In some cases, the opposite may be the case. Two types of students who are most likely to exit ineffective schools are (1) those whose parents are interested enough and have sufficient resources to opt for private schools, (we can assume, I think, that such students will include among them some of the most academically able students in the community.) and (2) students who drop out of school entirely. The exit of both types of students not only increases proportionately the per student resources available to schools, but reduces the number of special programs —such as accelerated and remedial courses—thus giving the system a "bonus." Moreover, it may be that these types of students (and their parents in the case of the private school potentials) are more likely, each in its own way, to be disruptive of existing practices. Of course educators talk a great deal about the "dropout problem" and, especially since the "Coleman Report," [20] there is even discussion of the importance of "attracting the upper middle class back to the schools." But it is significant that there appears to be no comparative research on how the institutional characteristics *of schools* relate to either drop-out rates or movement from public to private school.

It is true that, in some cases at least, some state financial aid is allocated by "average daily attendence" (ADA). While a lot of fudging goes on in reporting these data, in principle they could provide an incentive for responding to student needs. No doubt funding procedures such as the ADA formula do discourage rigidity in some school districts, but there are at least two reasons why their potential is probably not realized. First, reasons for the school drop-out are not well studied and socioeconomic rather than school-related explanations have considerable currency among educators.

Second, ADA formulas are usually used to allocate funds to districts, not to schools. Thus, those who are in the best position to respond to the school related reasons for drop-out are not "punished" for student exit. As I've just argued, drop-outs may make a teacher's life more pleasant.

If client exit is a limited check on organizational rigidity, will schools respond to the exit of members? There has been, of course, enormous teacher turnover in public schools, but there is little evidence that schools have responded to this membership exit through structural change. One reason for this may be that most of the turnover occurs among very young teachers whose commitment to teaching—especially in "tough schools"—is readily doubted despite the fact that studies of teacher dropouts do show that organizational rigidity is a primary source of exit.[21] Second, most school systems do not have the analytical capacity—especially in their personnel offices—to do the necessary research on their own teacher turnover situation even if they had the will to do so. Third, there are important limits on the lateral movement among school systems of tenured teachers and administrators. (This point will be discussed further below.) Fourth, since almost anyone who applies to teacher education courses is admitted, and since there are no reasonably well-established criteria one *must* meet before teacher certification, teacher shortages in most urban areas—in practical terms—seldom exist.

Politics as a Check on Rigidity in Schools

If exit is less effective in inducing responsiveness to consumer and member needs in schools than it is in many other types of organizations, does voice—or political action—serve as an alternative? There is much talk in the literature on school organization about the political vulnerability of schools. In fact, relative to other public agencies, school officials enjoy substantial freedom from political pressures.[22] It is true that schools often seem to be embroiled in political crises, and one hears and reads about recurrent efforts to influence school boards. I submit, however, that most of the political pressures on schools, except those that tend to restrict change, have little impact on the organization of schools and that, therefore, voice—or politics—has a limited impact on the reduction of rigidity.

There are at least four reasons why politics has little impact on organizational rigidity.

1. Most people are not unhappy with the type of education their children are getting—though they seem to know little about it. Nor are they inclined to be very active in school affairs, including voting on school candidates and issues.[23] In the absence of adequate measures of learning

and personal development, it is difficult to know how much children are benefiting and most parents will recognize that what is being *taught* at any given grade level is more advanced than what they experienced at that age. Parents, like administrators, rely on process rather than product as the criteria for evaluation and, in general, schools look and feel familiar—the shape of things has not changed much.[24]

2. Since organizations have a bias toward certainty, they seek to reduce the power their environment has over the defining activities—or core technology—of the organization.[25] One way schools do this is to develop bureaucratic ideologies that tend to restrict the areas in which political action (i.e., lay intervention) is seen as appropriate.[26] The ideology most relevant to the present discussion is what some have called the "myth of professionalism"—the idea that only trained and certified educators can really understand and prescribe the ways children learn best.

To the extent that the "myth of professionalism" has failed to insulate the classroom from its environment, it appears to have failed with respect to issues which tend to reinforce traditional and more highly structured student-teacher interaction. For example, of the demands that directly affect the quality and structure of student-teacher interaction, the one that is most often before school boards and superintendents is efforts to restrict the way teachers deal with certain issues such as sex education, religious matters, un-Americanism, and student dress and appearance—which parents and other citizens see affecting the students' moral and spiritual growth. Even with respect to such volatile issues as sex education, school politics is dominated by the agenda set by professionals. Citizen protest is invariably aimed at programs already implemented.[27] One might speculate that where there is negative parent reaction to classroom innovations, this is at least in part the result of the tendency of school officials to relegate such matters to themselves so that the reasons for, and objectives of, changes are never explained. If this is true, then efforts by schools to protect their core technology from environmental pressure not only reduce external incentives to deal with dysfunctional rigidity but restrict the capacity of the organization to change when it does try to do so.

One area in which the public apparently feels it has extensive prerogatives to express its opinion is the amount of money expended, with the greatest voice being given to the need to keep costs down. Whether this balance of pressure to economize leads to a reexamination of existing activities is difficult to judge, though impressionistic evidence suggests that the more likely response to austerity is to cut or postpone new programs. In any case, programmatic changes may or may not affect authority relationships within the system or within the classroom (the "new math" was taught very much like the old math, and decreases in class size have had almost no impact on teaching style). Organizational rigidity of the type we are discussing here does not seem to be fundamentally the consequence of the amount of resources available.

There is some agreement among students of school politics that school boards themselves accept the professionalism thesis and, in effect, perpetuate the myth. This, of course, tends to reduce the scope of "external" demands placed on the bureaucracy while broadening its autonomy from the board itself.[28]

3. Formal structures for lay involvement tend to encourage the depoliticization of school policy making and to focus attention on system-wide solutions to problems. This has the consequence of minimizing the diversity within and among schools in a given system.

The most common method of selecting school board members is at-large, nonpartisan, popular election. Persons selected under such procedures tend to be homogeneously middle and upper-middle class with no strong roots in local consituencies.[29] It is not surprising, therefore, to find evidence that school board members who are centrally elected (or appointed) tend to view their school systems as a unitary whole.[30]

At the school level, the mechanisms for expressing grievances also foster rigidity in that they tend to insulate the individual teacher from demands for change. Generally, individual protest is funneled through the principal rather than direct to the teacher, and the principal serves as a buffer against parental "interference." The major institutional instrument for interest articulation at the local school is the Parent-Teacher Association, and the principal usually plays a major role in setting the agenda of these groups. Individuals are reluctant to bring their problems before a schoolwide group, and thus only matters of a crisis nature, or issues upon which there is substantial consensus are discussed. The job of the PTA, in any case, is to support the status quo.[31]

4. The multiplicity, diffuseness, and value-laden character of educational goals tends to result in the fragmentation of protest. The difficulty of assessing the immediate cause-effect relationship of teaching facilitates the substitution of process criteria (such as discipline or new programs) or fitness for future action (such as the number of graduates, honors received, or admission to college) for direct product criteria for measuring organizational performance.[32] Thus, parents or other citizens anxious about the dysfunctions of organizational rigidity, who find it difficult to confirm and verify their anxiety and demands for change, which tend to be non-specific (e.g. better teachers), can be defused by symbolic responses that make it difficult to mobilize and sustain protest.[33]

All of this is not to say that voice is not, in theory, a mechanism that might be used to counter forces that push schools toward organizational rigidity. There is some reason to believe that extensive and *intensive* citizen involvement in education would foster innovation and reduce rigidity.[34] The point is that present structures and practices at most times, in most communities, mitigate—and sometimes totally negate—demands that relate to opening up the ways the learning process is structured.

The Nature and Inadequacy of Internal Communications

Earlier, I observed that one of the dysfunctional aspects of organizational rigidity in schools was that it discouraged interaction among teachers and within the school system as a whole. While poor internal communication is a consequence of rigidity, it is also a source of rigidity. Thus, to understand why schools do not respond to functional demands for more flexibility, it is important to identify some of the structural arrangements *within* schools and the school system that reinforce other sources of organizational rigidity.

1. *Distortion in upward communications.* At least since the writings of Chester Barnard and Herbert Simon,[35] students of organizations have placed substantial emphasis on the importance to both organizational control and adaptation of effective feedback from managers and operatives. It has also been recognized that subordinates have substantial control over the volume and character of such interactions.[36] If this is true in organizations, generally, it is even more true of organizations in which operatives perform most of their duties in the absence of supervisors. Thus we would expect that in schools in which most teaching takes place in self-contained classrooms, the feedback process will work less effectively than in most other organizations, other things equal. Further, this upward communication problem is exacerbated by two conditions: (1) the incongruence between the principal's role as supervisor and his presumed role as senior colleague and advisor-consultant, and (2) the substantial status differences that exist within the organization and within the community between teachers and principals.

It is, of course, quite rational for teachers *not* to initiate interactions with principals concerning problems they are having since to do so would bring attention to the teacher's weaknesses. Thus, principals receive negative communication about a given teacher only through personal observation (during which time teachers seek to act out their expectation of the principal's definition of good teaching)—or from an occasional irate parent. As Sarason observes:

> The principal views going into the classroom for purposes of evaluation and change as an act that will be viewed by the teacher as a hostile intrusion. The presence of the principal in a classroom, particularly if it is in the context of a problem in that classroom, is experienced by the teacher with anxiety and/or hostility.

. . . . From the standpoint of the principal there is little that he feels he can do about what goes on in a classroom, particularly if the teacher has tenure or has been a teacher for a number of years. As a result, the principal tolerates situations that by his values or standards are "wrong." Because this toleration is frequently accompanied by feelings of guilt and inadequacy it frequently has an additional consequence: the tendency to deny that these situations exist in the school.[37]

In most schools, principals make almost all of the important new decisions not already made by the superintendent, and usually enjoy a salary substantially above their highest paid teacher, and perhaps twice the average salary of teachers. This status schism is likely to result in the exclusion by teachers of the principal from the informal communication process and the adoption of conventions aimed at requiring him to take teachers into account. As Sarason says, for most principals, the only options they see in this situation are to assert authority or withdraw from the fray, and either response is likely to widen the status schism and feeling of mutual isolation.

2. *The importance of horizontal interactions.* Individuals charged with responsibilities to which a technology can be applied with reasonable certainty of outcome require information about the variables they must deal with, the accumulated knowledge on the wisdom of alternative ways of dealing with such variables, and evaluation of the results of their efforts. In the absence of such information, they are likely to over-simplify the task, misjudge the results of their effort, and—when under pressure of new demands—over-generalize the applicability of their experience to new situations.[38] All of this fosters organizational rigidity.

For reasons just noted, teachers have few interactions with principals that might improve their effectiveness. An alternative to supervisorial feedback could be consultation with colleagues, but such horizontal communications are almost nonexistent in most schools. In addition, there is often no contact among schools within the same system. It might be that staff awareness in a given school of successful innovations or program failures in one or more other schools would stimulate innovation or facilitate the understanding of problems, thus encouraging a greater likelihood of countering the forces that induce rigidity.

3. *The lonely teacher, insecurity, and dysfunctional adaptation.* The impact of the professional loneliness that most teachers experience, especially those in elementary schools, not only isolates them from information needed for effective instruction, it is liable to contribute significantly to the uncertainty and anxiety they feel when confronted with 25-35 students with different learning needs that may vary with different subjects.[39] In the absence of supports for checks on their judgments, they are likely, as Michael Lipsky suggests, to adopt one or more of several

coping mechanisms that increase organizational rigidity: development of simplifications and routines to reduce uncertainty and save time, stereotyping of students, reduction of personal involvement, or transferal of responsibility upward or to other institutions (e.g., the family, social workers, etc.) or to school "specialists." [40]

4. *The social status of teachers and rigidity.* Public school teachers rank relatively low in the citizenry's perception of occupational status as compared to other professionals with whom teachers like to be associated.[41] This relatively low status probably affects the esteem received from parents and other citizens, including the teachers' extra-school referent groups. This, in turn, may affect the teacher's self-image and the extent to which he or she is willing to invest in the development of his or her professional skills. Moreover, low self-esteem may lead to defensive behavior vis-a-vis parents or to efforts at reducing, or carefully structuring, task related contact with parents and others interested in education.

In short, it seems reasonable to assume that the organizational pattern of most schools contributes to the low social status of teachers (by limiting their autonomy and relative economic condition vis-a-vis superiors) and in this way, too, reinforces its own rigidity.

Lack of Clarity about Role Expectations of
Teachers and Principals

In various contexts throughout this part of the article, especially with respect to the problem of measuring output, the multiplicity, ambiguity, and diffuseness of goals in public education has been noted.[42] The lack of clarity about goals results in confusion concerning role expectations of both teachers and principals. Such confusion allows, and probably encourages, a tendency to avoid risk taking and to adopt other security producing mechanisms discussed earlier.[43]

No mechanisms exist within schools for clarifying goals and defining roles aside from the principal. In addition to the limits of his capacity to do this associated with the status schism within the school, principals may be inappropriate agents for clarifying the role of teachers, in that among the criteria for appointing principals in most districts, effective teaching does not rank very high.

How Personnel Policies Condone or Foster Rigidity

Procedures for awarding salary or pay increases, and patterns of career advancement with respect to attaining greater status and power, are key instruments organizations may use to induce their members to contribute to the attainment of organizational objectives. In education, these instruments are structured in ways that tend to condone or foster organizational rigidity.

1. *The salary schedule is not tied to performance.* Movement "up" the salary schedule in most school systems is determined solely by two criteria: (1) the number of years taught and (2) the number of academic units taken. Neither of these criteria is necessarily associated with effective teaching, except, perhaps, for very inexperienced teachers. Since the salary schedule is not tied to performance, it in effect provides no incentives to the teacher to examine alternative approaches to structuring the learning process and thus does not reward behavior which would reduce organizational rigidity.

2. *Teacher evaluation is based on process, not performance, criteria.* While teacher evaluations play no role in salary advancement, they invariably play a role in the decision whether to retain a probationary teacher. Thus, early in one's career, teachers are provided with a standard model—in the form of an evaluation check list of traits—of what good teaching looks like, presumably in all types of contexts. The message is clear—it is style, not result, that is rewarded.

The tendency for "performance" evaluation procedures to foster rigidity may be enhanced if the principal does the evaluation since (1) as noted, people are not often made principal because of their reputations as teachers and (2) if the principal is a man, he almost certainly has had little contact with lower grades.

3. *Constraints on the selection of administrators.* Overall, students of educational bureaucracy draw a rather bleak picture of administrators. They are generally seen as timid, submissive, resistent to change and predisposed to autocratic leadership style.[44] The rigidity they contribute to school systems seems related, at least in significant part, to the place of principals in the schools and to certain rather widely accepted conventions that govern the selection of principals and other administrators.

I noted above how the lack of clarity about teachers' roles contributed to organizational rigidity. The role expectations for a principal are at least as ambiguous, and the tensions he may sense as "the man in the middle" can be immobilizing. Because the appropriate role of the principal is usually so ill-defined, it may be difficult to establish criteria for selection that are likely to have much validity. Thus, certain barriers one must cross are usually established to screen candidates. For example, a certain number of academic units usually must be secured and one must obtain an administrative certificate or pass qualifying examinations. However, traversing neither of these types of hurdles has any demonstrated relationship to administrative effectiveness. In the absence of any clear understanding of what an effective principal might look like, most school systems apparently resort to their own stereotypes. One persistent consequence of these stereotypes is a profound bias against women, despite some evidence that both teachers and administrators rate women principals as high or higher on performance, knowledge of teaching methods, and democratic behavior.[45]

But the constraint on the selection of administrators that undoubtedly contributes most to organizational rigidity is the practice of recruiting administrators almost exclusively from the teaching ranks and, in most districts, appointing persons from within the local system, except perhaps in the case of the superintendent and (less frequently) certain technical specialists. As a result, schools, like few other nonuniformed work organizations, experience little infusion of new blood, so that the questioning of old routines, insight to new applications, and the motivating power of new expectations are minimized. Not surprisingly, studies comparing administrators appointed from the ranks with those appointed from outside show that the latter are more likely to seek, and effect, organizational change.[46]

This general policy of selection and promotion from within limits the perspectives of those who ultimately become superintendents, even if they secure office in another city. And, where "new blood" is brought to the superintendent's office, the new man is often saddled with much—sometimes all—of his predecessor's staff, the consequence of which is, obviously, to minimize the impact of the new entry on existing rigidities. In effect, through the closed-system pattern of administrator selection, schools limit their future ability to adapt. Schools are, in short, a classic case of the tendency of bureaucracies to develop "trained incapacities."

The Absence of Research and Analytical Capacity in Schools

One of the major ways to induce change in organizations is the programmed feedback of the results of research on the organization's functioning. The relatively small amount of money invested in educational research and evaluation is widely noted.[47] Moreover, most of the money that is expended is not spent by school systems themselves. In short, a miniscule amount of money and talent is invested in research and evaluation that is directed at solving problems in schools and very little of the research that is done actually gets to school administrators, much less teachers.[48] And, few teachers receive any helpful training in even rudimentary techniques of evaluation.

The impact on organizational rigidity of this neglect of research and evaluation in education has several consequences:

1. The small knowledge base in education impedes the development of strategies for change on both the systemwide and classroom levels.
2. In the absence of reliable feedback about the effectiveness of educational programs, (a) old programs are favored over new ones, especially in times of austerity, and (b) the capacity to develop support for the schools is undermined (assuming the school is performing well).
3. In the absence of training and resources to undertake program evaluation, teachers are not in a position to examine the impact of the various techniques they employ. A capacity to evaluate the impact of their behavior on students might tend to diminish the tendency of teachers to resort to rigidifying mechanisms in the face of uncertainty. This capacity could be personal or the result of consultation.
4. Systematic research programs would encourage school systems to clarify their objectives. This in turn may facilitate the clarification of role expectations and facilitate the expression of "voice."

Conclusion

This paper has attempted to identify various sources of organizational rigidity and their consequences. The sources discussed include (1) the difficulties in, and resistance to, measuring school outputs, (2) the restrictions on, and consequences of, "exit" by the clients and personnel of schools, (3) distortion in, and mitigation or dimunition of, the demands ("voice") that school systems must confront, (4) the nature and inadequacy of internal communication networks, (5) the diffuseness of educational goals and teacher role expectations, (6) personnel policies and practices which do not reward performance, and which constrain the input of new ideas, and (7) the absence of research on, and evaluation of, educational programs. These sources of rigidity are, of course, interrelated, and emphasis has been given to the way one source of rigidity in education tends to reinforce others and why, in effect, "routine work tend to drive out nonroutine work."

Awareness of the various sources of rigidity in schools should enhance one's ability to formulate a comprehensive redesign of organizational structures that would assure more openness and flexibility. My purpose here is not to present such a design, but I will suggest some of the general directions of restructuring that seem to follow from the preceding analysis. This outline assumes that reduction of organizational rigidity is our primary objective. There are obviously situations in which we would tolerate substantial rigidities in exchange for the attainment of some other value.

1. We should vest major authority for administration and policy making in individual schools. Overall, the functional necessity of centraliza-

tion to most things that go on in schools is usually overrated. On the other hand, some balance between centralization and decentralization will probably minimize the tendencies toward rigidity. For example, centralization can facilitate the redistribution of resources from strong to weak, force some competition for scarce resources, provide a mechanism for systemwide diffusion of innovation, allow for more professional research capacities than localized units could justify, and facilitate the coordination of educational objectives and programs with those of other public agencies.

2. Teachers should play a much greater role in the making of schoolwide policies. Such a role might include a say in the selection of the principal. This means, of course, that the sources of status schism between teachers and principals would lessen, and the latters' role change from control and unilateral direction to goal integration and articulation, and facilitation.

3. Teacher performance should be measured by product rather than style or process. There are substantial measurement problems involved with this, which suggests a fourth direction of change.

4. Structures need to be developed for articulating objectives at all organizational levels, and more research on appropriate measures of learning needs to be undertaken. While more sophisticated measures are being developed, we might adopt simple devices like subjective reporting by teachers to parents and nonpunitive evaluation by colleagues.

5. The professional isolation of teachers from their colleagues should be ended.

6. We should develop in-service training programs aimed at (1) individual needs and (2) facilitating the acceptance of responsibility.

7. School systems must develop greater in-house research and evaluation capacities that are organized so that a major part of their responsibilities would be to provide research support and training to teachers.[49] Smaller districts may find cooperative arrangements with other school systems or with colleges and universities advantageous.

8. We should acknowledge that many aspects of educational policy making are fundamentally political, and thus we should avoid at-large elections and nonpartisanship while taking steps to eliminate the depth of the traditional separation of education from other public services.

9. Lateral entry to administrative and teaching positions should be facilitated, and the recruitment of non-educators to many administrative posts should be undertaken.

10. We should provide mechanisms which more fully introduce student evaluation and suggestions to the policy making process "down" into the elementary school.

11. Publicly supported alternative educational environments should be available to parents, though such alternatives might exist entirely within the public school system.[50] We should recognize that education takes place outside of schools too. Similarly, the use of course or grade equivalency examinations should be considered so that schools would have to offer students more than credits to attract them.

The central dilemma in dealing with organizational rigidity is to promote professionalization of teaching while maintaining a creative tension between the school, its clients, and the larger environment. Given the variety of social and political contexts in this country, there can be no specific strategy that will be an appropriate response to rigidity in all, or even most, school systems.

Let me emphasize that the general directions of change set out here do not pretend to be an outline for comprehensive educational reform. However, while these proposals are not the only ones that might be derived from the preceding analysis, they do, I think, begin to suggest the types of steps that will be necessary to deal with organizational rigidity in public schools. Of course, each of these proposals has had previous advocates. Perhaps this chapter will provide a new logic for them.

Notes

1. Collective bargaining agreements, regardless of the motives involved, tend to rigidify relationships and delimit the discretionary use of authority. See James G. Anderson, "The Teacher: Bureaucrat or Professional," *Educational Administration Quarterly,* 3 (Autumn 1967), p. 298. Even such union demands as maximum class-size, for example, introduce constraints on organizational structure. (Such constraints would be minimized if the demand were for reduced teacher-pupil ratio but it seldom is.)

2. See Raymond E. Callahan, *Education and the Cult of Efficiency* (Chicago: University of Chicago Press, 1962). Also see Michael Katz, *Class, Bureaucracy and the Schools,* (New York: Frederick A. Praeger, 1971).

3. See Andrew Halpin, "Administrative Theory: The Fumbled Choice," in Arthur M. Kroll, *Issues in American Education* (New York: Oxford University Press, 1970), 156-184.

4. Cf. Charles C. Jung, Robert Fox and Ronald Lippett, "An Orientation and Strategy for Working on Problems in School Systems," in Gordon Watson, ed., *Change in School Systems* (NEA National Training Laboratories, 1967), 69.

5. Winfred F. Hill, "Learning Theory," *Encyclopedia of Education, Volume 5,* (New York: Macmillan Publishing Co., 1971), 471; Norma Furst and Russell A. Hill, "Systematic Classroom Observation," *Encyclopedia of Education, Volume 2* (New York: Macmillan Publishing Co., 1971), 181. On the same point, see David R. Krathwohl, "Cognitive and Affective Learning," *ibid.,* 198; and David W. Ecker, "Affective Learning," *Encyclopedia of Education, Volume 1,* 114; Norman E. Wallen and Robert M. W. Travers, "Analysis and Investigation of Teaching Methods" in N. L. Gage, ed., *Handbook of Research on Teaching* (Chicago: Rand-McNally and Co., 1963), 500. The absence of empirically based theories of instruction is the recurrent theme of over half of the thirty articles on teaching collected recently by Ronald Hyman under the title, *Contemporary Thought on Teaching* (Englewood Cliffs, N.J.: Prentice-Hall, 1971); and Harvey Averch, *et al., How Effective is Schooling? A Critical Review and Synthesis of Research Findings.* (Santa Monica: The Rand Corporation, 1972).

6. Cf. David G. Ryan, *Characteristics of Teachers: Their Description, Comparison and Appraisal* (Washington, D.C.: American Council on Education, 1960); Norman A. Sprinthall, John M. Whitely and Ralph L. Mosher, "A Study of Teacher Effectiveness," *Journal of Teacher Education,* 17 (Spring 1966), 93-106; Richard Jones, *Fantasy and Feeling in Education* (New York: New York University Press, 1968); and Philip Jackson, *Life in Classrooms* (New York: Holt, Rinehart and Winston, 1968) chap. 4.

7. See, for example, James D. Thompson, *Organizations in Action* (New York: McGraw-Hill Book Company, 1967); Claggett G. Smith, "Consultation and Decision Processes in a Research and Development Laboratory," *Administrative Science Quarterly,* 15 (September 1970); Warren Bennis and Philip Slater, *The Temporary Society* (New York: Harper and Row Publishers, 1968) chap. 5; Ronald G. Havelock, *et al., Planning for Innovation Through the Dissemination and Utilization of Knowledge* (Ann Arbor: Institute for Social Research, 1969), 6/35-6/36 and the several sources cited there.

8. See, for example, Thompson, *op. cit.,* 56-61; Donald C. Pelz, "The Innovating Organization: Conditions for Innovation," Warren Bennis, ed., *American Bureaucracy* (Chicago: Aldine Publishing Co., 1970), 144-148; Victor A. Thompson, "Bureaucracy and Innovation," *Administrative Science Quarterly,* 10 (June 1965) 1-20; Stanley Udy, "The Comparative Analysis of Organizations," in James G. March, ed., *The Handbood of Organizations,* (Chicago: Rand-McNally and Co., 1965) p. 700; Daniel Katz and Robert L. Kahn, *The Social Psychology of Organizations* (New York: John Wiley & Sons, 1966), 214; and Havelock, *et al., ibid.,* 6/22-6/23 and the several sources cited there.

9. Much of the second part of this article is related to this theme. See the

evidence cited there. A thorough review of the dysfunctions of bureaucracy in settings like schools can be found in Willis D. Hawley, "The Possibilities of Nonbureaucratic Organizations", in Hawley and David Rogers, *Improving the Quality of Urban Management,* (Beverly Hills: Sage, 1974), 371-426. See Jackson, *op. cit.,* chap. 4; Sprinthall, *et al., op. cit.;* Wayne J. Doyle, "Effects of Achieved Status of Leaders on the Productivity of Groups," *Administrative Science Quarterly* 16 (March 1971), 40-50.

10. See Schaefer, *The School as a Center of Inquiry* (New York: Harper and Row Publishers, 1967). Also see, Mark Chesler, *The Teacher as Innovator, Seeker and Sharer of New Practices* (Ann Arbor: Institute for Social Research, 1963).

11. This literature is summarized by Hawley, *op. cit.,* 375-379.

12. Andrew Halpin, *Theory and Research in Administration* (New York: Macmillan Publishing Co., 1966), chap. 4; Arthur F. Corey, "Overview of Factors Affecting the Holding Power of the Teacher Profession," in T. M. Stinnett, ed., *The Teacher Dropout* (Itasca, Ill.: F. E. Peacock, 1970), 2-3, 8-9; Jackson, *op. cit.,* chap. 4; C. Mashburne "Teacher in the Authority System", *Journal of Educational Sociology,* 30 (1957), 390-394; Seymour Sarason, *The Culture of the School and the Problem of Change* (Boston: Allyn & Bacon, 1970), 169.

13. Albert O. Hirschman, *Exit, Voice, and Loyalty* (Cambridge: Harvard University Press, 1970), p. 4; cf. Anthony Downs, *Inside Bureaucracy* (Boston: Little, Brown and Co., 1967), chap. 16.

14. Cf. Matthew Miles, "Some Properties of Schools as Social Systems" in Watson, *op. cit.,* 7.

15. Cf. Thompson, *op. cit.,* p. 95. On how this applies to schools see James G. Anderson, "The Authority Structure of the School: Systems of Social Exchange," *Educational Administration Quarterly* 3 (Spring 1967), 136.

16. Ralph W. Tyler, "National Assessment: A History and a Sociology," in James Guthrie and Edward Wynne, eds., *New Models for American Education* (Englewood Cliffs, N.J.: Prentice Hall, 1970), 20-34.

17. Joanne Jenny Samuels, "Impingements on Teacher Autonomy," *Urban Education* 5 (July 1970), 166.

18. This formulation is a minor adaptation of some of the central themes in Michael Lipsky's, "Toward a Theory of Street Level Bureaucracy" in Willis D. Hawley, Michael Lipsky, *et al., Perspectives on Urban Politics from a Step Back* (forthcoming). See also Isabel Menzies "A Case Study in the Functioning of Social Systems as a Defense Against Anxiety", *Human Relations* 13 (1960), 95-121.

19. Paul Mort's studies of the rate of change in schools are perhaps the most extensive available. He found that important educational change is very difficult to achieve and that the time span for thorough diffusion of an

innovation is 30 to 50 years. Mort, "Educational Adaptibility" in Donald Ross, ed., *Administration for Adaptability* (New York: Metropolitan School Study Council, 1958), 32-33.

20. James S. Coleman, *et al., Equality of Educational Opportunity* (Washington, D.C.: Government Printing Office, 1966). This report gave extensive exposure to the importance of cohort effects on school children.

21. See Corey, *loc. cit.* For example, Corey cites a study of California schools showing that more than half of all teachers leave teaching (much less an individual school system) within 10 years and more than half of these leave before five years.

22. Analyses which support this conclusion include: Thomas Eliot, "Toward an Understanding of Public School Politics," *American Political Science Review,* 53 (December 1959), 1032-1051; Roscoe Martin, *Government and the Suburban Schools* (Syracuse: Syracuse University Press, 1963); Harmon Ziegler and Michael O. Boss, "School Boards and Superintendents: An Analysis of Political Resources," paper delivered to David W. Minar Memorial Conference, Northwestern University, October 31, 1974; and David W. Minar, "The Community Bases of Conflict in School System Politics," *American Sociological Review* 31 (December 1966).

23. Cf. George Gallup, *How the Nation Views the Public Schools* (Melbourne, Fla.: Institute for the Development of Educational Activities, 1969); Richard F. Carter, *Voters and Their Schools* (Stanford: Institute for Communication Research, 1960), 73-76; and Harmon Ziegler, M. Kent Jennings, and Wayne Peak, *Governing American Schools* (N. Scituate, Mass: Duxbury Press, 1973). On the low participation of the poor in school affairs, see Richard A. Cloward and James A. Jones, "Social Class Attitudes and Participation", in A. Harry Passow, ed., *Education in Depressed Areas* (New York: Teachers' College Press, Columbia University, 1963), 197.

24. See Colin Greer, "Public Schools: The Myth of the Melting Pot," *Saturday Review* (November 1969), 84-86ff.; and Robert Dreeben, *The Nature of Teaching* (Glenview, Ill.: Scott Foresman and Co., 1970), 100.

25. This proposition was formulated by Thompson, *op. cit.,* 24, 39-40.

26. The concept of "bureaucratic ideology" and its implications are developed by Downs, *op. cit.,* chap. 19. There seems little doubt that school officials regard organized citizen involvement in school affairs with great suspicion. See Sexton, *op. cit.,* p. 28; Becker, *loc. cit.;* Eliot, *loc. cit.;* and especially Ziegler and Boss, *loc. cit.*

27. Cf. James W. Hottois, and Neal A. Milner, *The Sex Education Controversy* (Lexington, Mass: Lexington Books, D. C. Heath and Company, 1975).

28. Cf. Norman D. Kerr, "The School Board as an Agency of Legitima-

tion," *Sociology of Education,* 38 (1964), 34-59. Also see Eliot, *loc. cit.;* Mario Fantini, Marilyn Gittell, and Richard Magot, *Community Control and the Urban School* (New York: Frederick A. Praeger, 1970), 67-71; Frederick Wirt and Michael Kirst, *The Political Web of American Schools* (Boston: Little, Brown & Co., 1972) chap. 5; and Zeigler and Boss, *loc. cit.*

29. See Wirt and Kirst, *loc. cit.,* and Robert Bendiner, *The Politics of Schools* (New York: Harper & Row Publishers, 1969), chap. 1; and Zeigler, et al., *loc. cit.*

30. Robert Salisbury, "Schools and Politics in the Big City," *Harvard Educational Review* 37 (1967), 408-424.

31. On the PTA, see Patricia Sexton, *The American School* (Englewood Cliffs, N.J.: Prentice Hall, 1970) p. 30, and the sources cited there. The importance of the PTA as the agent for citizen demands is noted in Neal Gross, *Who Runs Our Schools* (New York: John Wiley & Sons, 1958); and Zeigler and Boss, *loc. cit.*

32. Again, cf. Thompson, *loc. cit.,* 91-93.

33. See Michael Lipsky, *Protest in City Politics* (Chicago: Rand-McNally and Co., 1969) chaps. 6 and 7.

34. See Marilyn Gittell and J. Edward Hollander, *Six Urban School Districts* (New York: Frederick A. Praeger, 1968).

35. Chester Barnard, *The Functions of the Executive* (Cambridge: Harvard University Press, 1938); and Herbert Simon, *Administrative Behavior, 2nd Edition* (New York: McGraw-Hill Book Company, 1957 (1947)).

36. See Theodore Caplow, *Principles or Organization* (New York: Harcourt, Brace & World, 1964), 97-101; Herbert Kaufman, *Administrative Feedback,* (Washington, D.C.: The Brookings Institution, 1973); and David Mechanic, "Sources of Power of Lower Level Participants in Complex Organizations," *Administrative Science Quarterly* 7 (1962), 349-364.

37. Sarason, *op. cit.,* 120.

38. See Harland Bloland, "Sources of Professional Autonomy: The Physician and the Public School Teacher," *The Educational Forum* 33 (March 1969), 368.

39. On teaching as a lonely profession, see Sarason, *op. cit.,* p. 152; Morris Janowitz, *Institution Building in Urban Education* (New York: Russell Sage, 1970), 29-31; and Peter Knoblock and Arnold Goldstein, *The Lonely Teacher* (Boston: Allyn and Bacon, 1971).

40. See Lipsky, "Toward a Theory of Street Level Bureaucracy," *loc. cit.* Also see Thompson, *op. cit.,* chap. 9; and Peter Blau, *The Dynamics of Bureaucracy* (Chicago: University of Chicago Press, 1955), 203-219.

41. Albert J. Riess, Jr., "The Nature of the American Public School System," in T. M. Stinnett, ed., *op. cit.,* 22.

42. Almost every writer on educational administration notes this situation. One study which actually identifies the variation among a large number of school systems in the priorities placed on different objectives is Robert J. Havinghurst, *et al., A Profile of the Large City High School* (Washington, D.C.: National Association of Secondary School Principals, November 1970), chap. 3.

43. See Lipsky, "Toward a Theory of Street Level Bureaucracy," *loc. cit.,* on this point; and Robert Merton, *Social Theory and Social Structure,* rev. ed., (New York: The Free Press, 1957), 369-379.

44. See, for example, Carl Steinhoff, "Organizational Climates in a Public School System" (USOE Comparative Research Program Contract No. OE-4-10-225, Project No. S-083, Syracuse University, 1965), 104; Robert Owens, *op. cit.,* 132; Sarason, *op. cit.,* chaps. 8-9; *Organizational Behavior in Schools* (Englewood Cliffs, N.J.: Prentice Hall, 1970); Julius S. Brown, "Risk Propensity on Decision Making—A Comparison of Business and Public School Administrators," *Administrative Science Quarterly* 15 (December 1970), 473-481; and Marilyn Gittell, "Urban Schools: Organization," *Encyclopedia of Education,* Volume 9 (New York: Macmillan Publishing Co., 1971), 403.

45. Sexton reports that men make up seven percent of elementary school teachers and 59 percent of all elementary principals, *op. cit.,* p. 29. See J. K. Hemphill, D. E. Griffiths, and N. Fredericksen, *Administrative Performance and Personality* (New York: Columbia University Press, 1962).

46. Richard O. Carlson, *Executive Succession and Organizational Change* (Chicago: Midwest Administration Center, University of Chicago, 1962); and Laurence Iannacone and Frank Lutz, *Politics, Power and Policy* (Columbus, Ohio: Charles Merrill Books, 1970).

47. Less than *one-tenth of one percent* of the total education budget is invested in research and development. This compares to research investment rates in some industries exceeding 15 percent. See Sexton, *op. cit.,* chap. 10; and Lee J. Cronbach and Patrick Suppes, eds., *Research for Tomorrows Schools: Disciplined Inquiry for Education,* (New York: Macmillan Publishing Co., 1969), esp. chap. 6.

48. Bernard C. Watson, "Urban Education: Its Challenge to the Research Community," *Urban Education* 5 (July 1970), 109-127.

49. See Schaefer, *loc. cit.*

50. See the different proposals summarized by James S. Coleman, "New Models for School Incentives," in Guthrie and Wynne, *op. cit.,* 70-90; and John E. Coons, *et al., Private Wealth and Public Education* (Cambridge: Harvard University Press, 1970).

**Part V
School Policy within a Federal System**

Introduction to Part V

School Policy within a Federal System

"Local" politics is never fully local in this nation because it is conducted within a framework whose limits have been set by state and national governments. Therefore, the shape of the local politics of education—its actors and their resources, the distinctive agenda of issues, the interplay of group demands—is modified by having to operate within a federal system. In the next section we will see what difference this federalism makes for school expenditures, compared to a unitary system. But in this section the contributions seek to demonstrate the filtering effect upon school policy when it emanates from the national government. That effect stems from the presence of diverse jurisdictions, each with its different reinforcing institution and ethos, through which the national effort must flow. Both contributions also demonstrate the considerable power still available to local districts, even though dependent upon higher governments. Too, while these selections focus upon variations of school policy making in an intergovernmental system, it should also be noted that there is evidence of cooperation across this system's levels; it is all not a story of conflict alone. But the ethos of "local control" of schools is a variant on the ideology of "states rights," which has generated much of the intergovernmental friction in our history.

Joel Berke and Michael Kirst trace the differentiating effects of state political cultures upon one of the major national ventures in school policy during the 1960s, federal aid to education. They studied 575 school districts in five metropolitan states and the effects upon their school finances of various federal aid programs, particularly the large-scale Title I of the Elementary and Secondary Education Act of 1965. On this base, expanded upon in these authors' book, they develop recommendations for the implementation of future aid programs. This policy recommendation phase, with its roots in substantial empirical analysis, typifies a new direction in research upon the polity, in which scholarship does not end with analysis but builds from this base to recommendations justified by the research.

Frederick Wirt and Michael Kirst offer a contribution on a second area of federal policy involvement with local education during the 1960s—desegregation in the South. While the first selection examines the Congress and administrative agencies as national instruments of involvement, in the case of desegregation, it is the courts which perform that role. The Wirt and Kirst contribution demonstrates what occurred in the first twenty years after the landmark *Brown vs. Topeka Board of Education* decision

213

in 1954. In the process of this judicial output being converted into a diverse set of local outcomes, there is evidence of the limits of the judiciary as a change agent if it acts alone. But there is also evidence of its effectiveness when it is joined by other branches. This selection is cast within a systems analysis framework and is a contribution to the contemporary scholarly interest in the impact of law upon society.

12

The Federal Role in American School Finance: A Fiscal and Administrative Analysis

Joel S. Berke * and Michael W. Kirst †

Since its inception, federal aid to elementary and secondary education has pinched the most sensitive nerves of the American body politic. During the present period of potential change and reform in the governance and finance of American public education, the role of the federal government is debated more heatedly than ever. While a number of familiar factors— the "financial crisis," the "taxpayer revolt," the "crisis of confidence" in American public education—have all contributed to the nationwide re-examination of state and federal programs supporting public education, the greatest catalyst has been a recent series of court decisions. These cases have held that state school finance systems characterized by disparities in spending among school districts based upon their relative wealth violate the fourteenth amendment's equal protection clause. Since the first of these decisions, *Serrano v. Priest,* was handed down August 30, 1971, there has been widespread interest in efforts to develop a federal response to the newly emerging judicial doctrines. Plans to provide federal relief from property taxes, incentive plans to encourage states to lessen wealth-based disparities in educational spending, and programs designed to foster greater equality of educational opportunity through compensatory spending on the disadvantaged have been prominent among proposed remedies.

As these programs are developed and debated, discussion is handicapped by critical information gaps. A deplorable paucity of useful information concerning either the fiscal impact of federal contributions to American educational finance or the administrative and political processes which shape the patterns of those contributions seriously impedes effective reform of the federal role.

This article is a summary of the first intensive and comparative attempt to investigate these information gaps. The article is based upon a three-year

---

Reprinted, with permission, from Joel Berke and Michael Kirst, "The Federal Role in American School Finance: A Fiscal and Administrative Analysis," *Georgetown Law Journal,* 61, no. 4, March 1973. © 1973 by the Georgetown Law Journal Association. See original for footnotes omitted here.

* Syracuse University Research Corporation

† Stanford University

investigation by the authors and their colleagues, which encompassed aspects of public and educational finance, political science, and educational administration. The fiscal portion of the study examined the finances of local governments in the 37 largest standard metropolitan statistical areas and a sample of 575 school districts in five populous states. The accompanying examination of the decision-making process in the allocation of federal aid focused on six states, more than 20 representative school districts, and federal agencies concerned with education. Taken together, the fiscal and administrative aspects of this study describe the patterns of federal aid distribution and the processes which governed those allocations.

The Current Fiscal Context of Public Education

The problem of raising adequate revenues for the support of education is a serious one for a large number of school systems. In most cities, suburbs, and rural areas, heightened demand for educational services and teacher salaries meets directly with taxpayer resistance, state economy drives, and a slowed rate of increase in federal spending. In many areas of the country, school boards with fiscal crises have resorted to school shutdowns, the elimination of special projects, and increased class size.

Large cities suffer most severely, particularly in the Northeast and Midwest, due to the presence of three interacting phenomena—(1) a declining tax base which makes it increasingly difficult for cities to support educational services from their own tax resources; (2) higher educational costs caused by the composition of the student population, inherently higher urban cost factors, and aggressive and effective teacher unions; and (3) state aid laws that are frequently far more restrictive and less generous to the cities than to suburban and rural areas. A financial comparison of central cities with their suburbs clearly reveals a demographic and economic "sorting out" process. Central cities have proportionately poorer populations with a greater percentage of ethnic and racial minorities than the suburbs. Pupil populations in cities include disproportionate numbers of foreign born, handicapped, racial minorities, and poor—students whose education requires greater resources than does that of the more socially advantaged pupils in the suburbs. However, central city per pupil expenditures frequently are less than or only marginally greater than those of the surrounding suburbs. Even where per pupil expenditures are marginally greater, the generally higher price and salary levels in the city still mean that more money will provide less education.

To compound the disparity, state regulations and state aid often leave cities at a disadvantage in relation to suburban and rural areas. The costs of school retirement systems, for example, are often assumed by state governments; but in many states the large school districts are omitted from the state program and must finance retirement costs primarily from local revenues. Further, state aid formulas regularly allocate lesser proportions of aid to cities than to suburban or rural areas. A recent study conducted by the United States Office of Education of 84 large city school systems in 1967-1968 found that 70 of the cities received less than the average amount of state aid per pupil. Even where the total of both local and state funds was considered, 51 of the cities received less revenue per pupil than the statewide average.

Why do these discriminatory state aid patterns exist? Historically, the cities were relatively wealthy and the prime need was to provide a state minimum floor for rural areas. Rural dominated legislatures made possible by malapportioned legislative districts preserved this initial rural favoritism. Subsequently, widespread reapportionment under the one man, one vote rule has replaced the rural dominance with coalitions of rural and suburban interests that presently control most state legislatures. Thus, while the recent state and federal court cases on school finance, if upheld by the Supreme Court, will require revision of state school finance systems, that revision may not result necessarily in formulas more favorable to urban interests. Thus, discriminatory aid patterns may continue to characterize school finance for some time to come.

These complex difficulties affecting large cities will serve as the chief backdrop for the following examination of the fiscal impact of federal aid to education. Although the primary focus of this study is the impact of federal aid within metropolitan regions, problems of rural school finance deserve serious consideration as well. Comparisons are complicated by the significantly different cost levels between most urban and rural areas, but the low level of taxable property in many sparsely populated regions poses very real problems in providing adequate school services. Thus, the following discussion will not ignore the plight of poor rural districts.

The Pattern of Federal Aid to Education

Federal aid to education dates from the Northwest Territory Ordinance of 1787. Even the modern form of assistance, categorical programs of grants-in-aid, has a continuous tradition which stems from the Smith-Hughes Vocational Education Act of 1917. However, the largest and most ambitious federal program of aid to education was authorized in 1965. In that year, Congress passed the Elementary and Secondary Education Act of 1965. Over the last decade, aid quadrupled from just under $800 million to over three billion dollars. However, during the last five years this overall growth pattern has slowed and, in light of inflation, has probably declined in real terms. Furthermore, as a proportion of total local, state, and federal educational revenues, federal aid rose to a high of 8.8 percent in 1967-1968, but has since slipped steadily to 7.1 percent in 1971-1972.

While the proportion of ederal support has not been impressive, it has exerted important programmatic or financial leverage in certain areas of national policy. In the areas of vocational and agricultural education, and more recently, science and language instruction and education of the disadvantaged, federal funds have had a significant impact. Federal aid thus provides a small but strategic proportion of total revenues for American public education.

The Concept of Equity and Federal Aid

The authors see a basic inequity in the way in which educational services in American public education are distributed. This inequity arises primarily from the fact that expenditure levels are determined by the wealth of the more than 17,000 individual public school districts in the nation. Local taxable resources, which provide more than one-half the revenue for public schools, vary immensely from district to district. For the children who live in those districts, the quality of education varies accordingly. State aid, which supplies an additional 41 percent of school revenues, fails to overcome the disparities among districts, and in many states actually reinforces them. It was the perception of this discrimination against pupils in poor school districts that underlay the decisions in *Serrano, Rodriguez v. San Antonio Independent School District,* and similar cases.

That the level of financial support devoted to one's schooling should vary markedly depending upon where one lives is both rationally and ethically questionable. But when the variations in school spending bear an inverse relationship to the need for educational services, the inequity is compounded. As discussed previously, the greatest need for educational resources exists where handicaps to learning are the greatest—among the poor, the physically handicapped, and the victims of prejudice and neglect. These groups tend to be concentrated in impoverished rural and highly urban areas where taxable resources are least available for education.

In analyzing the pattern of federal aid to education, therefore, the authors consider aid to be distributed equitably when it tends to offset disparities among school districts with regard to wealth, when it provides assistance to urban areas in proportion to their disadvantages, and when it supplies proportionately more money to districts with higher numbers of educationally disadvantaged pupils.

Federal Aid Distribution

The focus of the study conducted by the authors and their colleagues concerned the impact of aid programs upon school districts in five metropolitan states—California, Massachusetts, Michigan, New York, and Texas. The study investigated the finances of 575 school districts containing more than 50 percent of the pupils in those states and approximately 30 percent of all pupils in the United States.

Rural Versus Metropolitan. One of the most consistent patterns of impact to emerge from the data is that rural and small town school districts received more federal aid per pupil than did school districts in metropolitan areas. In California, Texas, and Michigan, such non-metropolitan districts received an average of 50 percent more aid per pupil than did the metropolitan districts. Further, such aid provided a consistently larger proportion of educational revenues there than it did in metropolitan school districts.

Central City Versus Suburbs. Although central cities received more federal aid than their suburbs, these amounts were generally insufficient to overcome the suburban advantage in locally raised revenues and state aid. With the exception of Michigan, where there was a $17 total revenue advantage in favor of the central cities, suburbs in the five states had an average of $100 more available per pupil than did the central cities.

In Massachusetts, for example, central cities received almost twice as much federal aid per pupil as received by the suburbs. Federal aid accounted for 10.2 percent of all central city school revenues, compared with 4.8 percent in the suburbs. Despite this difference, suburban school districts still received 15 percent more revenue per pupil from all sources than did central cities. Thus, while central cities in three of the five states—New York, Michigan, and Massachusetts—received more federal aid per pupil than did their suburbs, federal aid failed to close the wide gap between cities and their suburbs with respect to total revenues available for education.

Central City Versus Rural. In comparison with the non-metropolitan or rural portions of the five states, central cities again fared poorly. A clear advantage to the central city existed only in New York. In both California and Texas, rural areas received considerably more federal aid, and in Michigan the two areas received virtually the same amounts. Regarding total revenues, there emerged no clear pattern. Non-metropolitan areas had higher revenues in two states, central cities in two others.

Title I of the Elementary and Secondary Education Act of 1965. As the largest federal aid program, title I of the Elementary and Secondary Education Act of 1965 deserves special mention. Although its educational impact and administration have been criticized, it appears to be an immense success as a fiscal device. Decidedly larger amounts of title I funds are distributed to school districts with (1) central city or rural location, (2) higher proportions of minority pupils, (3) lower income levels, and (4) greater educational need as measured by average achievement scores.

Title I aid in 1967 averaged $17.26 per pupil in the five states sampled, amounting to almost 50 percent of the total federal aid received. Further, non-metropolitan areas received 85 percent more title I funds per pupil than did metropolitan areas, easily accounting for the overall disparity between metropolitan and non-metropolitan areas in amounts of federal funds.

When distribution of title I funds within metropolitan areas was examined, the central cities fared almost uniformly better than their surrounding communities. Title I clearly has responded to central city and rural school finance problems.

Other Major Federal Programs. An internal study by the United States Office of Education examined entitlements under five federal programs in order to compare the share of state allocations to large cities with the share of the state's student population in those cities. Except for title I, the study found that large cities were receiving less aid than their proportionate share of the state's population would indicate.

Capacity to Support Education

Proper analysis of the impact of federal aid requires an examination of its relationship to various indicators of a school district's capacity to support education, such as median family income and state equalized property valuation.

Median Family Income. In the five states studied, a mild trend became apparent. In every state sampled, federal aid tended to be higher where incomes were lower. The relationship between income and federal aid was examined more extensively in the largest metropolitan area of each of the five states. Core city school districts were consistently among the lowest in average family income but received more federal aid than any of their surrounding school districts in three of the states. Moreover, in all states except Massachusetts, the wealthiest suburban school districts received the least federal aid per pupil, and the poorest suburban districts received the most. However, there existed no consistent equalizing effect; in

Houston and Detroit, for example, districts with moderately high family incomes received more federal aid than districts with moderately low income.

Glaring examples of disequalization can be found in each of the large metropolitan areas. Beverly Hills, the wealthiest district in the Los Angeles area, received $17 per pupil in federal aid, whereas the Hudson district with half the median family income, received only $14 per pupil. In Massachusetts, Quincy, which qualified for large amounts of Impacted Areas aid, received $123 per pupil in federal money, whereas Salem and Malden, with lower average family incomes than Quincy, received only $9 and $18 respectively. As noted earlier, the inverse relationship between income and aid was due entirely to the effect of title I. Without that program, federal aid was essentially disequalizing.

Property Tax Base. The concept of equalization traditionally has been linked to the real property tax base of school districts. The uneven location of valuable real property has long been accepted as a major cause of inequality in the educational opportunities provided in different communities. To overcome these disparities, equalization formulas for the distribution of state educational aid frequently allocate funds to some degree in inverse proportion to the property value per pupil. Does federal aid offset disparities in local property tax bases? In the five major metropolitan areas studied, federal aid had at best a neutral impact. In many instances, the districts with higher property values garnered more federal aid than any others, with the exception of central city districts.

It should be recognized that the use of property value per pupil as a meaningful measure of fiscal capacity creates major problems. While property value may serve as a realistic yardstick of comparative fiscal ability among school districts in suburban and rural areas, its usefulness is limited in measuring the entirely different fiscal position of large cities and highly urbanized areas. The greater service needs—police, fire, sewage, and welfare—of an urban population impose a far heavier demand upon the property tax base than is the case in less densely populated areas. Given an equal base of taxable property, large cities can devote less locally raised revenue to education than can suburban and rural areas.

Non-white Enrollment

A significant relationship was found to exist between the flow of federal aid and the proportion of non-white students, primarily black and Puerto Rican, in a school district. The higher the proportion of non-white students, the more federal aid a district tended to receive. This in fact represented the strongest statistical relationship to emerge from the many variables tested in the study.

Offsetting higher costs of education for the disadvantaged is an important form of equalization. Since non-white populations tend to have a significantly higher proportion of educationally disadvantaged pupils, this pattern of revenue distribution reflects a distinct and important equalizing impact.

The Trend in Federal Aid

One important factor in evaluating the impact of federal revenue is the pattern of aid over time and its effects in educational policy. When school districts are confident of steadily rising amounts of aid, those aid programs are likely to form an integral part of the planning of administrators and school boards. However, when aid varies from year to year, educational planners are handicapped by uncertainty as they develop future academic programs, contract for equipment, and hire additional staff. During the years covered by the study, federal aid to school districts varied from year to year and followed no discernible pattern.

State Decision Making for the Distribution of Federal Aid to Education

Having charted the pattern of allocation of federal aid to education, this article will now examine the state decision making processes which shape that allocation. As a preliminary matter, it is important to understand that states have vast discretion over the amounts and use of federal aid received by local education agencies.

State Political Culture

The variety of ways by which federal aid is administered stems primarily from differences in state political cultures. Federal aid is channeled into an existing state political system and emerges as a mixture of federal priorities and frequently quite different, if not conflicting, state priorities. This combined delivery mechanism ensures that the implementation policies will not be uniform among the states, especially since the sanctions and incentives available to the federal government are insufficient to alter significantly the traditional patterns of state educational policy. Yet, over a long period of time, federal administrators and guidelines do exert a perceptible impact on state policies, so long as federal objectives are not changed. For example, the title I guideline for targeting aid to the disadvantaged gradually has altered some state and local behavior sufficiently to reorient traditional distribution patterns. Too often, however, federal policies change in mid-course.

The six-state study revealed that differences in state political cultures produce many interesting effects. With regard to urban-suburban-rural priorities, state allocation decisions are embedded in a tradition of political relationships. The study of New York, for example, highlighted the traditional hostility between the state government and New York City. In some states—Virginia, Texas, and California—the researchers found urban alliance. In all of the states, the cities were attempting, in varying degrees, to create alliances as they gradually became more aware of the potential impact of federal aid.

The administrative styles of different state education agencies differ greatly, ranging from aggressive leadership to passive technical assistance. In some states, particular administrators—Wilson Riles in California and John Porter in Michigan, for instance—can move a state from one administrative style to another. But in other states, such as Massachusetts and Texas, the overall state political culture imposes such great constraints that a more activist-oriented state education agency would hardly seem feasible.

The states also vary enormously with respect to the partisan political image of the state education agencies. The apolitical image, paramount in Texas and Virginia, served to deter gubernatorial and legislative interest and intervention. On the other hand, former California Superintendent of Schools Max Rafferty was considered a politician rather than an objective educational expert, and the legislature interceded strongly in the administration of federal aid.

The study also revealed that discordant educational interest groups fragment educational policies in California, Michigan, and New York: administrators feud openly with teachers' and citizens' groups. In Texas, however, the Texas State Teachers Association includes state administrators and urban school district personnel under one roof. Generally speaking, discordant educational interest groups encourage gubernatorial and legislative intervention in federal aid policy. Only in California, however, was there sufficient staff to enable the legislators to oversee the implementation of federal aid. In other states, governors and legislators lacked sufficient information and analysis to intervene in federal aid administration.

Thus, the study produced significant findings with respect to: (1) the importance and diversity of state political culture and state education agency operating procedures in the determination of federal aid allocation policies; (2) the consequent lack of standard federal aid policy; (3) the substantial leadership of the state agencies in some states, and the overwhelming constraints on state leadership in others; and (4) the traditional estrangement of city lobbies from state agency decisions, coupled with the very recent awareness of the potential for changing state policies to enlarge the flow of federal money to cities.

Intergovernmental Relations

A discussion of the politics of federal aid distribution would not be complete without a broad view of the entire federal-state-local intergovernmental chain. As shown above, major federal programs are administered substantially by the states. The formulation of the Elementary and Secondary Education Act of 1965, for example, was based on "creative tension" between federal administrators wielding general guidelines for local programs and state departments of education approving specific local project proposals.

The United States Office of Education exercises control through regulations which have the force of law and guidelines which interpret these regulations. These guidelines also contain a mixture of advice and suggestions that are not legally binding. Additionally, some Office of Education programs utilize periodic and supplementary program memoranda, which presumably clarify regulations but in fact are effectively legal mandates. These three different instruments of federal control—regulations, guidelines, and memoranda—confuse state and local education agencies and permit slippage and evasion, particularly when the supplementary federal program memoranda indicate changes in long standing policies.

In sum, the limits of federal legal authority are undefined. Since funds are rarely withheld, no meaningful court precedents on the "gray areas" in binding or non-binding guidelines or memoranda exist. Occasionally, federal auditors recover funds where state or local agencies have violated explicit regulations, but more often suspected or actual violations are negotiated informally among professional educators at local, state, and federal levels.

Except for title I of the Elementary and Secondary Education Act of 1965, all large federal categorical programs are administered through state plans. These plans consist primarily of a repetition of the federal regulations and therefore contain little specific information on the intrastate allocation of money, the preferred thrust of education programs, or the criteria for approving or rejecting local agency proposals. Consequently, the state plans reveal little about the operation or funding criteria of federal-state programs.

Negotiations between the state and local levels reflect varying degrees of the "religion of localism." Local agencies frequently try to reword their own priorities so that they fit loosely within the federal categorical regulations. Open conflict with the state agency is rare, and substantive disagreements are ironed out among professionals.

One difficulty in funding, however, results from what may be called "multi-pocketed budgeting." Federal aid must be seen as one part of the local district's entire education funding structure. School districts have many other sources of revenue besides federal aid, including bonds, property taxes, and several categories of state aid. As the number of income sources increases, the significance and impact of any single source decreases. Administrators have a propensity to conserve all-purpose resources; they tend to use those resources with the greatest number of restrictions first, saving those with the fewest restrictions until last.

Federal policymakers often assume that local administrators plan their own programs, fund them, and then seek new programs and funds available from the federal government; that is, they undertake federal programs only after the local budget has been obligated. As a practical matter, however, local administrators appear to use the strategy of multi-pocketed budgeting. They plan programs and review all income sources, including federal grants, to find the needed resources. As can easily be seen, this procedure tends to promote local priorities at the expense of federal priorities.

When all of the local, state, and federal income sources are aggregated, only the smallest school districts have fewer than 15 different sources; large districts have nearly 100. As the total number of income sources increases, the apparent restrictions imposed by a particular source become less stringent. If a federal categorical grant is restricted to an area in which the district feels that it is already doing an adequate job, the district will substitute the federal grant for local funds, which then will be used elsewhere. Naturally, the complexities of school accounting make it difficult to discover these "symbolic allocations."

As a final matter with respect to intergovernmental relations, it is important to observe that state and local education agencies existed long before the Office of Education and consequently have vested interests to protect. Thus, it has been impossible for the Office of Education to create an ally in state and local agencies, as has been the case in other areas of state endeavor initiated by federal grants, such as welfare and urban renewal.

The Administrators and Their Agencies

Behind the processes and dynamics of the chain of intergovernmental relationships are the organizations and individuals who draft the regulations and conduct the negotiations. Without an understanding of these bureaucrats and their bureaucracies, any view of federal aid administration would be incomplete.

Federal Administrators

Federal civil servants are a conscientious group who for the most part endeavor to adjust as top policymakers change, elections approach, or Congress amends established programs. But when priorities change, a federal civil servant will be in better position for promotion if he is not identified solely with an outmoded cause; at the same time, promotions within grade are automatic and job security is assured. In sum, the economic incentives for civil servants to implement new policies rapidly and completely are at best unclear.

With the emphasis on the poor and non-whites that emerged in the 1960s, a particular problem became apparent. Civil servants knew very little about problems of disadvantaged minorities. The lack of minority representation in top federal grant administrative positions demonstrated one aspect of this problem—the minority groups were neglected in professional training as well as in public policy.

A still more pervasive problem relates to the lack of effective monitoring of program implementation. The White House staff concentrates on new legislation and overall budget decisions, and little manpower is available to supervise the implementation of individual grants. Because the aggregate of individual grant decisions has caused the gap between promise and performance of federal categorical aid, revised legislative provisions alone cannot resolve inadequate implementation.

To fill this gap, supervision of categorical grant administration is left to the Office of Management and Budget. The Office of Management and Budget has no field staff, yet it is in the field where programs reach the intended beneficiaries and where political compromises are made. Ultimately, it is in the field where the overlap and confusion of federal programs leads to funding delays and fragmentation of effort.

Steps have been taken to improve executive supervision of education programs. Acknowledging the weaknesses in this area, the Bureau of the Budget was reorganized into the Office of Management and Budget in 1969. It is too soon, however, to evaluate whether the formation of a management branch will make a significant difference, particularly in view of the continued absence of any field staff.

As far as auditing is concerned, the General Accounting Office analyzes administrative procedures and program effectiveness and also verifies vouchers. Because it has a limited staff available to perform these comprehensive audits, many years often elapse before a new categorical program is audited, and even then auditing is frequently conducted on a spot check basis only.

Another defect in supervision is the emphasis which domestic agencies attach to post facto evaluation of programs—have children learned, have job trainees been placed, and have new jobs been created? Not only does this orientation result in a time lag between program implementation and assessment, but more importantly, it frequently overlooks a detailed examination of the political and administrative processes and delivery services. Thus, while such evaluations can reveal whether a program has fulfilled its goals, they can rarely explain why a program has succeeded or failed.

State Administration

As noted earlier, federal categorical programs for the disadvantaged are filtered through a specific state and local administrative process. The performance of state officials varies so greatly that sweeping generalizations are impossible, but it is evident that some state and local agencies are hostile or at least indifferent to many federal categorical programs aimed at urban areas and the disadvantaged.

Another danger to federal programs designed to aid the poor is the fact that, in many states and localities, the political and administrative structure offers little reward to the bold administrator who favors the disadvantaged. The inherent difficulties of the merit system and professional working relationships apply at the state level as well as at the federal level. State administrators understand that federal priorities are likely to change; and when federal policies are in conflict with, for example, the state orientation to the disadvantaged, it is the long term state policies that are most likely to determine an administrator's job security and advancement.

For many years, state administrative pay scales have lagged far behind federal and private salaries. It is not unusual for a federal administrator of a categorical program to be paid more than $20,000 while his state counterpart earns less than $15,000. To compound this disparity, grade promotions for state administrators are rarely as frequent as are those in federal service. All of these actors tend to militate against a first-rate administrative staff, thus creating additional difficulties for the administration of federal programs.

State governments have a tradition of limited gubernatorial supervision of state administration. Governors have rarely taken an interest in the day-to-day management of government, since political rewards rarely lie in that direction, and central budget and management resources are meager and inadequate. State agencies often remain relatively free to proceed without gubernatorial or legislative supervision in dealing with federal funds, thus making state administrators effectively responsible to neither federal officials nor state governors.

A further complication arises from the differing relationships of state education agencies, school boards, legislatures, and governors. For example, in 12 states education agencies are responsible to an elected board of education; however, state boards are sometimes elected by the legislature, as in New York, or appointed by the governor, as in California. In 21 states, the chief state school officer is elected directly, and thereby maintains a political base distinct from the governor.

The policy consequences for categorical aid amid this administrative independence are difficult to assess. In some cases, independence from the governor may allow state agencies to reach disadvantaged populations constituting a minority of the electorate. In other instances, a governor may be unable to bring his agencies into line even though he desires to enforce the objectives of categorical aid.

Local Educational Agencies and Federal Categorical Aid

Local educational agencies provide the cutting edge of federal aid—the contact with the teacher and child. Federal aid is designed to be a catalyst and stimulus for local attention to particular national objectives, and in many instances it has fulfilled this goal by having a significant impact. Among other things, federal aid has helped to create a new breed of teachers and administrators who possess special concern for and expertise in dealing with disadvantaged youth. But while there are numerous instances where federal projects have had significant effects on specific local programs, it is not known how often they have provided a stimulus to broad and permanent change in the outlook of an entire school district. Even in these federal "showcase programs," business as usual is normally resumed after federal funds are phased out or have become so permanent that districtwide routine takes over.

As with state government, local and federal goals may differ greatly. A federal goal of innovative programs for particular target populations may conflict with a local goal to provide a teacher salary increase and at the same time stabilize property tax rates. In such cases, the administrative muscle of federal and state governments may be insufficient to overcome local priorities.

Even if a local school board and superintendent of schools enthusiastically support federal categorical goals, several other factors may intervene to defeat the aims of the program. For instance, most key administrators in a large local education agency have risen through a lengthy bureaucratic career. Few of them would be likely to revolutionize traditional methods of allocating money or educating children simply on the strength of federal funds which constitute only a small portion of their total revenue. Furthermore, the lack of predictability of federal funding causes the involved programs to be administered like soft money, so that its withdrawal will not upset the basic program. The end result clearly is a lack of lasting impact.

Finally, at the bottom of the implementation chain is the teacher, who in effect has a pocket veto on the instructional goals of federal programs. Even where teachers may be willing, federal funds are rarely accompanied by the lead time, planning, and in-service training necessary to effect the appropriate changes in teaching behavior.

Recommendations

The purpose for which the foregoing study of federal aid to education was undertaken was to help make future educational policy more enlightened and effective than present policy. The results of the study have been presented in some detail, so that readers can draw their own conclusions with respect to needed changes. The authors urge the reader to bear in mind not only these findings but also the reasoning and values which have gone into this work, all of which contributed to the series of recommendations which follow.

Differential Administration

There is a vast range of administrative and fiscal behavior among the states which dooms any federal administrative approach that would employ one set of regulations to cover the wide variety of state practice. More flexible approaches are needed. Flexibility would permit those state education departments capable of supervising and guiding their local agencies to administer programs, while at the same time programs could be administered through direct federal-local relationships where state agencies are less capable. Certainly, the United States Office of Education is not equipped to administer federal aid programs for the entire nation; nevertheless, it could develop a capability superior to that of many states. Indeed, this would seem little more than its basic responsibility.

Wider Participation in Allocation

The implementation strategy of federal aid since 1958 has been essentially top-down. Federal and state standards were supposedly designed to ensure that local agencies responded to federal categorical priorities. The program negotiations were conducted among professional administrators at all three levels with little involvement of parents, teacher organizations, students, and community agencies. This top-down strategy of regulations and guidelines contains neither the sanctions nor the incentives sufficient to accomplish the categorical purposes of federal aid in all 50 states. Moreover, the top-down strategy does not have sufficient leverage to reorient classroom practice or to ensure that money always reaches the intended targets.

A potentially more effective strategy would be to reverse the flow of sanctions and incentives substantially so that students, parents, and teachers who seek to effect changes would be provided with access to the means to accomplish federal purposes. Further, federal aid must be designed so that the growing influence of teacher organizations is channelled toward some of the same goals as federal categorical legislation.

If federal aid is to be coordinated with other government programs, particularly with state priorities for education, government officials and broadly based coalitions of individuals with an interest in education must be involved in the allocation process. At present, even state legislators and governors are frequently unaware of the vast discretion that may be exercised in allocating federal funds. Similarly, urban interests, whose stake in federal aid is critical, are often unorganized, uninterested, and therefore, ineffective in influencing the administration of discretionary federal programs within their state. Until these present patterns of participation are changed, states are unlikely to allocate resources in proportion to pressing educational needs.

Increased Funding of Title I

Despite the host of problems related to title I, its funding should be vastly increased, perhaps tripled, to bring appropriations up to the levels envisioned in the original legislation. Only when title I is funded to that extent can the program be judged fairly. While evaluations of the educational benefits of title I thus far have been mixed, its record as a fiscal device is clearly the best of any program in American educational finance. Its funds are concentrated on overburdened central cities and impoverished rural areas. Nevertheless, the greater resources originally envisioned in title I should be made available to teachers of disadvantaged pupils.

Further measures should be taken to improve title I: comparability requirements must be enforced; resources should be focused more carefully; program priorities should be implemented by state education departments; and evaluations of the effectiveness of programs should be made more useful. Despite its faults, however, title I has succeeded admirably in serving one of the legislative purposes enunciated in the Act, namely to assist school districts in meeting the costs occasioned by heavy concentrations of educationally disadvantaged students.

New Federal Aid Programs to Affect State Policy

While recommendations for untied block grants or for general aid to education are currently popular, the authors oppose such aid. The record of the states, as shown in this article, does not warrant confidence that their allocation of federal funds will be any more rational or equitable than it has been in the past. Instead, aid should be given for general educational purposes only so long as the state meets certain requirements.

Such requirements would have to accommodate the wide range of state political and fiscal traditions and preferences by utilizing flexible federal standards. Under such a plan, the federal government could, for example, monitor expenditure disparities caused by differences in district wealth, as opposed to differences caused by local choices of tax rates or differential funding for disadvantaged pupils. If the wealth-based disparities were greater than a specified target amount—for example, ten to 15 percent of the mean—federal aid would be reduced or eliminated. Such a plan would permit states to utilize any one of a number of financing approaches, such as full state responsibility for the funding of education or equalizing state aid formulas. The federal government could also require some differential state funding for disadvantaged children and urban areas.

In addition, to encourage changes in the quality of education rather than simply educational finance, the federal government could require that states engage in some form of comprehensive planning or priority setting as they seek to meet the educational needs of their citizens. Again, no particular method need be adopted for the nation as a whole, but encouragement should be given to different processes in a number of states that would yield real benefits. Similarly, a federal requirement that states systematically assess the performance of their educational programs would be another of these broad but highly needed changes. Clearly, the states would require technical assistance and additional funds to improve achievement testing and longitudinal evaluation, but once again, encouraging a more sensible method of resource allocation would be a long range benefit.

Eliminate Wealth- and Need-Based Disparities
in State Finance Programs

American school finance, on both the revenue and expenditure sides, is riddled with inequity and irrationality. Data on the distribution of revenues show a strong correspondence in state after state between the property wealth and income of the district on the one hand, and the level of spending on education on the other. If greater resources are to be allocated for the education of children who are demonstrably the least likely to succeed, then the present pattern of resource allocation must be changed. At present, it is communities that are the richest, whitest, and the most socially advantaged that supply the greatest quantity and best quality of school services. Large cities and heavily urbanized areas seldom receive school revenues in proportion to the more difficult educational tasks they must perform, the higher cost levels that prevail there, or the heavier demands that are placed upon their tax bases for municipal services. Poor rural areas, too, almost invariably lag far behind the rest of the state in the quality of schooling they provide. In short, the authors believe that the current distribution of educational resources does not correspond to the highest priority educational needs of the nation.

Taxation for education is basically inequitable. The property tax rates for education are generally lower in those districts with highest property valuation, yet the yield of those rates is frequently far greater than the yield of the higher rates of poorer districts. In short, education tends to place a heavier burden upon those who are the least able to bear it. Revenue policies of this sort violate the most elementary concepts of fairness in taxation.

Since the fall of 1971, courts in at least five states have declared that the fourteenth amendment of the Constitution prohibits finance systems that manifest these characteristics. In particular, they have laid the responsibility for eliminating wealth-based disparities upon the states. While the outcome of these cases in the Supreme Court is undetermined at this writing, and while none of the courts has yet formulated standards as to what will pass constitutional muster, it is obvious that the winds of change are blowing strongly.

The authors propose that it should be the responsibility of the federal government to assist the states in meeting the dictates of equity and rationality in school finance. This responsibility is consistent with the direction of the major federal education programs to date, which, as has been shown, are far more equitable and rational in their distribution than are state funds or local revenues. While the magnitude of federal aid required will be far in excess of that provided in the past, such increased funding would benefit from and be consistent with the national interest in high quality education for all citizens.

13

Southern School Desegregation
Frederick M. Wirt * and Michael W. Kirst †

Teachers, parents, board members, administrators, and ethnic groups all share implicitly the notion that federal aid to local schools is desirable. The primary reason for this, of course, is that the program is essentially supportive of the goals that these participants have in common. What occurs, however, when they do not agree because a policy's regulatory aspect dominates its supportive aspect? Because local schools do not get all that they want in life, it is well to understand their politics when compelled by the superior power of intervening authority to change old and favored ways. Many examples of this might be noted, particularly in the enlarged role of the state in school policy in this century, e.g., directives on budgets and audits, teacher certification, curricula, student attendance, health and safety, administrators' responsibilities, and taxation. In California, these run to numerous volumes of 2300 pages.

Instead of these, however, we choose as an illustration of such regulation the most publicized case in our time—the pressures by Washington for Southern school desegregation. A generation or more ago it would have been better illustrated by the school consolidation movement; the arguments over values in both cases have a surprising similarity. Our purpose in this selection is to demonstrate aspects of the schools as a political system: the difficulties of intergovernmental relations in a federal system, the clash of values in a pluralistic society, and the evolving nature of the American creed. What is emphasized here is the reaction of local school systems to the thrust of outside regulation and in particular to the role of the judiciary, as distinct from administrators.

At first thought, courts seem an unlikely adjunct of schools and, for the naive, an unlikely adjunct of politics. But the history of education has been shaped by important court decisions on the duties and responsibilities of school components; even though trivial, the right of students not to have their hair cut is only the latest of many such contributions. At a more

Reprinted with permission of the publisher from Frederick M. Wirt and Michael W. Kirst, *The Political Web of American Schools* (Boston: Little, Brown and Co. 1972), chapter 9. See original for footnotes omitted here.

* University of Illinois at Champaign-Urbana

† Stanford University

significant level, the United States Supreme Court has been directly involved in the question of religion in our schools: Bible reading, required prayers, flag salutes, transportation and other expenses of parochial students, etc. Court involvement can be as direct—but narrow—as whether schools can be prohibited from teaching German, or as indirect—and extensive—as whether schools can be segregated by race. Schoolmen may react by massive noncompliance, as with the Bible and prayer decisions, but to be indifferent is very difficult.

Court involvement in such matters surprises only those who view the bench as a political eunuch. Contemporary analysts of the judiciary emphasize not merely its behavior but the values that its behavior implements. Judges are political because they must choose between competing values brought before them in conflict. As early as 1840, Alexis de Tocqueville was noting that "scarcely any political question arises in the United States that is not resolved, sooner or later, into a judicial question." The reason is that when men differ in the political arenas, one site where that contest may be transferred is the courtroom. As we shall see, the form and rules of such contests may differ from those in other sites. But they are still essentially political because contenders seek the authority of the political system to justify and command the distribution of resources—such as rights and property—that each deems desirable. The allocation of resources that follows from a court mandate can be as effective in reality as that which issues from a legislature.

What, then, are the relationships between the judiciary, as part of the political system of the state, and the political system of the school? What are the constraints and strengths in this relationship? What is the form of accommodation and conflict in the input, conversion, feedback, and outcome phases of the political process here? How does federalism filter (Easton would say "shape") the outcome? What values are reflected among participants? These are the questions we pursue as we illuminate national efforts after midcentury to expand the American creed to include those excluded from it since Jamestown.

The Judiciary as a Political Subsystem

In our perspective, the judiciary shares attributes of a system in Eastonian terms, although it is also a subsystem of the larger political system. Like other such subsystems—legislatures, agencies, and executives—the judiciary's environment presents it with demands which it may convert into outputs; these interact with the environment to be transformed in time into outcomes and thus generate later inputs to the court. This assumes no distinct boundaries of the judicial subsystem marking it off from others. Instead, we assume it interacts with legislative and executive subsystems continuously, as well as with private systems in the social environment. In this view, as Schubert notes, the important action is not in the courtroom but is outside "in the interplay between judicial, legislative and executive systems, and between national and state judicial systems; and in the effect of judicial decisions upon society and the economy, and vice versa."

That environment within which judges operate marches constantly into their chambers, sometimes unobtrusively and sometimes loudly. For example, a historical constitutional framework imposes certain constraints upon the selection of judges and their procedures, and these forces from the past shape who is made a judge and what he does. Professional canons have their effect on who is selected or even considered; institutional traditions require procedures that shape the pace and division of labor. Further, the partisanship of extramural party life, which has affected a judge's recruitment as well as his deliberations in our past, is not without influence even today. Changes in the social order outside the chambers bring changes inside to the courts' issues, structures, and attitudes.

The value conflict thrust into the court seeks authoritative allocation of resources to implement those values. For this reason, courts—and particularly the United States Supreme Court—have a manifest function of resolving conflict. Such allocational decisions have an impact—not always favorable—on all branches of the national government and at all levels of the federal system. This task of conflict resolution performs latent functions for the values underlying the conflict. Thus, the Supreme Court legitimizes national policies and the values they reflect. Conversely, such action serves to illegitimize policies and values favored by some. The trick, of course, is for the Court to do this in a way that does not decrease support for the courts as an institution while assuring that their decisions are accepted.

Further, the Supreme Court must maintain some kind of balance with other national subsystems so as to reduce potential conflict among their respective policy decisions. In the process, the judiciary provides signals to litigants, general public, and political subsystems and their actors (including their own local courts) as to the policy-value outputs it will reinforce. The issuance of such signals is not the same as their acceptance, however. So the Court through its history has had to balance itself carefully at key intersections of a nationally separated government, a federally divided nation, and a diverse population. Yet judicial policy making has shown more consistency than the preceding might imply. Whether at the trial or appellate level, distinguishable behavioral processes are commonly at work: initiation of controversies, accommodation via out-of-court settlement, persuasion of judge or jury, decision making, implementation of decisions, and their reconsideration.

All of this is understandable as a facet of systems analysis. Inputs for the judicial subsystem are evident as reflections of environmental demands. Their form and presentation differ for this subsystem, however. The lobbyist gives way to the lawyer, buttonholing to law review articles, and publicity campaigns to litigants' briefs. The demands are presented formally, dealing with matters of logic and legal precedent. The political authority to whom all this is addressed operates within a matrix of constraints, including its own values aroused by the issues. Recent research stresses the independent role of such values in the conversion process; outputs are seen as a function of the interplay of judicial values within the social process of court procedures, all of this with political consequences for the environment. In this view, legal precedents are only partially controlling, and only when judicial values agree. But when the issue is new or has new applications, then the psychological impact of values on the bench exerts an independent force as an explanation of judicial outcomes.

However such decisions are derived, they constitute outputs for society. They are something more than a statement of which litigant won and lost. Rather, they instruct a larger circle as to the value norms that the judicial subsystem seeks to impose upon the environment. At different periods in our history, the norms of political, social, and economic freedom have assumed different judicial priorities. Most recently, the economic norms have seemed least important to the Supreme Court, the political next, whereas the social—particularly civic equality—have dominated the era of Chief Justice Earl Warren. We will shortly turn to one of these.

The final need is to understand the impact of judicial outputs on society. While the Court may signal authoritative norms, what if no one notices, or if noticing, defies them, or if obeying, misinterprets them? When the Court confirms what is widely accepted already, as with its nineteenth-century opposition to polygamy, output and outcome are similar, for compliance is very high. When, however, the Court innovates in accepted norms, some gap between output and outcome is to be expected, and compliance will be less than complete.

The conditions under which the judiciary can innovate, as Schubert has defined them, are very constraining. Given a majority of justices favoring a change, a national majority in similar agreement, and the chances that the Court's decision would not hurt it in other policy areas, then innovation would be forthcoming. But these combinations have not existed often in our history, and indeed, they have not in other political subsystems. Such an absence accounts for much of the inertia and procrastination in facing emergent demands in the American political system. If the Court

moves when the maximum conditions do not exist, considerable dissonance arises from other political subsystems. Then the Court is said to
lack "self-restraint" and is accused of being "activist."

More importantly, when that output does generate dissonance, the feedback will show evasion of the original decisions. So it was in the Dred
Scott case in 1857, and so it was in the case of *Brown vs. the Board of
Education of Topeka* in 1954. Not until the Court was joined by a national majority and by other elements of the national political system was
there compliance with the Court's insistence on the social norm of racial
equality in the education of children.

Input and Conversion in the Brown Cases

Such a conceptualization of the judicial process is illuminated in each
stage of the 1954 *Brown* case. We begin with environmental forces prior
to the decision that generated stress and the resulting demands. A major
constraint on this decision was a constitutional principle derived from
Plessy vs. Ferguson in 1896 that separation of the races was not a denial
of equality; one justice had dissented bitterly that "our Constitution is
color blind and neither knows nor tolerates classes among citizens." This
decision must be seen as part of a set of Southern forces capping the Reconstruction and separating Negroes from any form of power. For over a
half century, this decision legitimized a "separate but equal" condition for
all blacks in all aspects of a white-controlled Southern society.

In the 1930s, though, small indicators of change, if not of mind, then
of emphasis, appeared in the Court. Over a ten-year period it increasingly
insisted upon a meaningful equality in the quantity of facilities, even
though still separate, in Southern law schools. This quantitative emphasis
was joined in 1950 with insistence upon qualitative measures of equality,
raising the interesting possibility that mere separation itself was a barrier
to a qualitative equality, a foreshadowing of the *Brown* decision in 1954.
That hint set off a Southern reaction of energetically improving Negro
schools, sometimes spending more on them than on white schools.

It was out of this constitutional and social milieu that cases arose in
Kansas, Delaware, the District of Columbia, South Carolina, and Virginia
that challenged segregation, not merely in law schools or colleges, but at
the very base of Southern education—the primary and secondary public
schools. The challenge could not rest fully on legal precedents, for there
were none. Instead, social science evidence was introduced at the trial-
court level to support the charge that segregation had deep qualitative,
psychological consequences for Negroes that were not erased by quantita-
tively equal facilities. The Delaware courts actually agreed with the Negro

challenge, although only on grounds that a quantitative inequality existed in fact. But over several years all these cases wended their separate ways to the Supreme Court, which announced in June, 1952, that it would hear them in the 1952-53 term. Thus after years of effort, the main legal spokesman for Negro rights, the National Association for the Advancement of Colored People, had through its legal arm brought squarely to the highest court a challenge against the "separate but equal" doctrine of *Plessy vs. Ferguson.*

But the NAACP was not alone in this contest, or in providing inputs to the Court, for many other actors were involved directly or indirectly. Some twenty-four *amici curiae* filed briefs, nineteen of which supported the NAACP—e.g., the ACLU, the CIO, etc. One of these was from the United States solicitor general; although the federal government was not a party to the case, both Presidents Truman and Eisenhower (whose terms overlapped the argument before the Court) felt a federal interest was involved. However, this brief did not call for overturning the "separate but equal" doctrine but attacked only quantitative inequality.

These inputs were focused in oral arguments for three intense days in December, 1952. For the Negro cause it was insisted that the Fourteenth Amendment's "equal protection of the law" guarantee extended to school segregation, that school conditions had changed since 1896 when public schools were few; now the inequality was widespread, and segregation created a qualitative damage. On the other hand, counterdemands from the states emphasized that courts must not overturn established concepts of law if the legal system is to provide certainty in men's lives, that school segregation affected as many as twenty-one states (seventeen required it), and that white resistance to abolition of segregation would damage the school system for all.

The conflicting press of these arguments was powerful, for the Court could not make up its mind. No decision was handed down that term, but instead the participants were asked in June, 1953, for additional answers in the next term to questions obviously disturbing the justices on the Fourteenth Amendment framers' intent and how desegregation might be implemented. Some months of curious scholarship followed, as each side sought to use history and constitutional law to shape the decision desired. The federal government, when asked to contribute its views, was divided, because some Republicans in the new Eisenhower administration wanted to build a party base in the South. Its final presentation equivocated on abolishing desegregation, but the attorney general, when asked in oral argument, did support its abolition. Other participants in the December, 1953, reargument offered answers supporting their assertions. The advice on implementation was not so clearly drawn, however.

Again, decision was delayed, this time until May, 1954, but when it came it was unequivocal. School segregation, even where facilities were equal, deprived children of equal educational opportunities and hence was unconstitutional. History threw little clear light on what the intent of the framers of the Fourteenth Amendment had been in this respect, but certainly the scope and importance of education had changed since then. Separation of children in this important aspect of their lives "generates a feeling of inferiority as to their status in the community that may affect their hearts and minds in a way unlikely ever to be undone." While such psychological knowledge may not have been available in 1896, it was today, so its weight should not be denied. Nullifying the *Plessy vs. Ferguson* edict, the Court wrote that "we conclude that in the field of public education the doctrine of 'separate but equal' has no place. Separate educational facilities are inherently unequal." As to the implementation of this opinion, new arguments were again requested from the federal and state governments for the fall of 1954.

Few opinions in Court history have had such dramatic impact upon American institutions, and yet the document was brief, the language clear, and the legal jargon missing. Few previous cases were cited, but instead the Court made reference to scholarly studies on the history of education and the psychological effects of segregation upon children. Most important, however, and remarkable given the controversy involved, the decision was unanimous. Only the justices know the factors that moved each to this common stand, for not all of them were of a mind when the case began. As major reasons for arriving at unanimity, some outsiders cite the effective persuasion of the new chief justice, Earl Warren, others the broad nature of the wording, and yet others the argument that precedent may be changed when preceding conditions in the environment have changed.

Whatever its content and origin, the decision was still only an affirmation of social norms, even though buttressed by interpretation of the Constitution. Implementation was another matter, which required new decisions about strategies of enforcement. Almost a year later, the Court laid down the enforcement guidelines in what can be called *Brown II*. It was no sweeping set of deadlines, but a call for "all deliberate speed" by Southern schools to desegregate under administration of local federal district courts *after* Negroes had brought suits in a school district. The work should begin promptly, delays had to be justified by the districts, and local hostility was not a justification. However, little substantive guideline was provided for the district courts as to what constituted desegregation or to what was meant by "all deliberate speed" (*deliberate* can mean both "intentional" and "slow").

Some facets of this conversion process are of great consequence for what followed in the next decade, particularly the delay of the Court in reaching any decision and its unwillingness to require prompt desegregation. It seems that some justices, perhaps all, were concerned with how they could effect any abolition of desegregation. Although they supported social equality, they were uncertain that the nation, and particularly the South, was prepared to accept it. In that condition, then, procrastination could be seen as a strategy that might hurdle the horns of the dilemma. The Court could not then be assured of full support from any other major component of the political system, as the total political context of enforcement was not yet favorable. The procrastination strategy, however, offered time not only for shaping that context but for the Court's norms to be discussed and accepted by those to whom it would apply. As we shall see, however, the strategy did little to bring about Southern school desegregation; output and outcome were to be totally opposed.

Feedback to the Brown Decisions

In the year between *Brown I* and *II,* Southern reaction was muted; just after *Brown II* some Southern leaders and press actually expressed relief that it had not been worse. But the blunt comment of Senator James O. Eastland better expressed what was to transpire: "The South will not abide by, or obey, this legislative decision by a political court."

The Variety of Resistive Feedback

Although feedback was to be generally negative, the degree and instruments of its resistance were quite varied. Thus, it is now forgotten that feedback from the Border States was positive, for during the next decade an immense amount of desegregation took place there. In the states immediately bordering the Deep South, however, compliance was considerably less. But in the Southern heartland, compliance was almost nil—indeed, in Mississippi nothing at all happened. The patterns of this feedback ran from prompt and full compliance when *Brown I* was first announced —even before *Brown II*—to partial and delayed acquiescence, and on to a total and persistent—even contemptuous—refusal to comply that was aimed at undermining the authority of the Supreme Court.

The total resistance in the Deep South is best accounted for by a social structure so thoroughly imbued with segregationist values that the new Court norms found no access there. This is what Southern spokesmen said and what scholars confirmed. It was not merely that the South was segregationist; its many subsystems were equally homogeneous on other values as well. Governors and other state officials reflected in their resistance a regional public clearly of a similar mind. Federal district judges, creatures of their regional culture but also part of the judicial subsystem they were sworn to support, were torn different ways. Those least tied to the dominant culture were most supportive of the Court; consequently, authoritative actions of the Southern judiciary ranged from constant support of *Brown I* and *II* to evasion or outright refusal of support. The resistance set by many of these authoritative figures in the Deep South was mirrored by that of the region's schoolmen, police, lawyers, clergy, and businessmen.

The instruments of resistance clearly demonstrated the ingenuity of Americans in protecting their individualism. At one end of the continuum of resistance was a stark record of outright violence. In the four years of 1955-58 alone, observers recorded at least 225 acts of violence against private liberties and public peace: six Negroes were killed, twenty-nine persons shot (eighteen Negro), forty-four beaten, five stabbed; homes were bombed (thirty), burned (eight), shot into (fifteen), and stoned (seven); and schools and churches were bombed or burned. At the other end was the instrument of the statute, rich in variety but single in purpose —to maintain school segregation. Table 13-1 encapsulates what was a broad and deep defensive reaction in this form.

Many local laws provided alternative means of keeping the races separate but on ostensibly nonracial grounds. Thus, pupil placement laws created complicated nonracial criteria by which school boards assigned students, with the outcome that separation was still maintained. Some states provided for the closing of schools threatened with desegregation, although this tactic was used sparingly. Too, school funds could be withheld if desegregation threatened, and private schools could be established with state monies. Further, the NAACP was attacked by laws designed to hinder its effectiveness as the agent most responsible for bringing litigation. All of these defensive statutes in their time collapsed under court orders, which called them evasions of the purpose of *Brown I* and *II*. But for at least a decade in the Deep South, although less in the surrounding states, they were major barriers against transforming the Court't output into any new outcome.

This response was echoed, if not stimulated, by the region's spokesmen in Congress. Their most publicized effort was a 1956 "Declaration of Constitutional Principles," quickly labeled the "Southern Manifesto." This accused the Court of abusing its power, of usurping the power of Congress, and of encroaching upon the rights of states to control education as they judged best. It commended "those states which have declared the intention to resist enforced integration by any lawful means," a clear signal for mobilizing Southern resistance to the law. Most Southern congressmen signed it; of those who did not, two were defeated and one almost lost.

Table 13-1

Major Legislation on School Desegregation in 17 Southern and Border States, Plus District of Columbia [a]

Legislation	Ala.	Ark.	Del.	D.C.[b]	Fla.	Ga.	Ky.	La.	Md.	Miss.	Mo.	N.C.	Okla.	S.C.	Tenn.	Tex.	Va.	W. Va.
Anti-NAACP/Barratry	X	X			X	X		X		X				X	X	X	X	
Closure of Schools Permitted	X	X			X	X		X		X		X		X	X	X	X	
Compulsory Attendance Amended or Repealed	X				X	X		X		X		X		X		X	X	
Emergency Powers to Officials	X	X			X	X		X		X				X		X	X	
Freedom of Choice—Seg./Deseg.	X	X	X	X			X		X		X	X	X		c	X		X
Human Rights Commissions			X	X											c			
Interposition/Protest	X	X			X	X		X		X				X	X	X	X	
Legal Defense Authorized	X	X			X	X		X		X		X		X	X	X	X	
Limitations of Federal Powers Proposed	X				X	X		X		X				X				
Private Schools: Authorized/Encouraged	X	X			X	X		X		X				X	X		X	
Property Sold/Leased to	X	X			X	X		X		X		X		X	X	X	X	
Pupil Assignment	X				X			X	X	X	X	X		X	X		X	X
Racial Designations: Removed / Required	X				X			X		X	X	X		X	X		X	X
Scholarships Out-of-State	X	X	X		X	X	X	X				X	X	X	X	X	X	X
Segregation by Sex	X	c			X			X		X		X		X	X	X	X	
Segregation Committees	X				X	X		X		X				X		c	X	
Sovereignty Commissions	X	X				X		X		X							X	
State Constitutional Provision for Public Schools Removed	X									X				X				
Teachers: Tenure/Removal Protected in Private School	X	X			X		X	X			X		X				X	
Tuition Grants to Schools/Students	X	X			X	X		X		X	X	X	X				X	
Withheld Aid to Deseg. Schools	X					X		X						X	X	X	X	

Source: Southern Education Reporting Service, in Reed Sarratt, *The Ordeal of Desegregation: The First Decade* (New York: Harper & Row, 1966), 363.

[a] The table indicates types of legislation passed, not the number. One bill often included several features; several bills might duplicate each other.
[b] D.C. Board of Commissioners.
[c] Appointed without legislation.

But these national regional spokesmen had more than words at their disposal. They used the considerable power that has regularly accrued to their tenure in Congress to block any assistance for the Court and to use investigating committees to denigrate the total effort. As an example of the last, the District of Columbia school system was presented as a particular chamber of horrors; Southern congressmen received and magnified every complaint they could find in the very schools they themselves were responsible for. Further, the greatest number of bills ever introduced in our history to curb the Court's powers came in 1955-57. Efforts in 1957 and 1960 to authorize the attorney general to bring desegregation suits were blocked, leaving it to Negro parents and the NAACP to shoulder the entire burden, as they had for many decades. Later, President Kennedy's 1963 civil-rights bill was being stymied by Southern opposition when he was assassinated. But thereafter, although Southern Senators fought grimly, their cause became lost in the popular reaction to Kennedy's death and the national publicity occasioned by protests in the South itself.

Variations in Outcomes

Thus, from the poorest rural school in Mississippi to the United States Senate, a whole battery of devices was aimed at delaying implementation of *Brown I* and *II*. The Deep South could find an encouraging analogue in the North's efforts at control that had failed after the Civil War. The weapons of delay and obstruction that had served the Confederate Army so well, and that had also borne fruit in the Reconstruction, were quickly and effectively used. Yet noncompliance varied according to subregional culture, with the result that Mississippi was not typical.

We may see these Southern reactions along a range of compliance, recognizing that a given district might skip many of the following:

1. *Voluntary noncompliance,* i.e., close the schools entirely rather than comply, e.g., Prince Edward County, Va.; although many Southern states passed such laws, closure was rare.
2. *Involuntary minimal compliance*
   a. Refuse voluntary compliance and ignore threat of litigation, e.g., Miss.
   b. Notice *Brown I* and *II* only when Negroes bring suit.
   c. Defend suit by supporting state over national law ("interposition" was popular for a time) or by denying the legitimacy of the Court to rule in the matter.
   d. Appeal all adverse decisions and otherwise put off change by recourse to every delay built into legal procedure.

e. When higher court upholds Negro claim, adopt minimal adjustment to his claim by
   (1) granting claim only to specific Negro litigant and not to class of segregated Negroes.
   (2) interposing alternative methods of student placement (e.g., pupil placement, freedom of choice, gerrymandering) that desegregate only a few.
3. *Involuntary token compliance,* i.e., steps 2a-2c but desegregate after first adverse decision; yet use alternative that desegregates the least.
4. *Involuntary moderate compliance,* i.e., same as 3 but made wider plan for desegregation without, however, effecting it on a compulsory basis.
5. *Voluntary minimal compliance,* i.e., move before threat of litigation, with compliance only minimal.
6. *Voluntary compliance,* i.e., providing full compliance without threat of litigation.

We cannot know how Southern districts distributed themselves across these feedback responses, but we can summarize the possibilities. In Figure 13-1 we find eight broad categories along the two dimensions of the proportion of students desegregated and of the willingness to comply in the district. In general, Deep South districts were in the upper left cells, those in the immediate Border States in the "involuntary" or "voluntary moderate" cell, and those farthest from Mississippi in the "voluntary maximum" cell.

Certainly on a state-by-state basis we can see this propinquity factor operating. In Table 13-2, the states are distinguished subregionally and by their proportion of desegregation in districts and students. This dramatic differential in compliance ranges from Mississippi's stance of "Never!" to

Percent of students desegregated	Involuntary	Voluntary
None	Mississippi Deep South districts	
Minimum	Token districts	
Moderate	Border districts	
Maximum		Districts farthest from Mississippi

Figure 13-1.

Typology of Southern School District Compliance with *Brown* Decision: Willingness to Comply.

Table 13-2

Status of Southern School Desegregation, 1963-64

Subregion and states	Districts desegregated [a]	Negroes in desegregated schools
Border	92.4%	54.8%
Delaware	100.0	56.5
District of Columbia	100.0	83.8
Kentucky	98.6	54.4
Maryland	100.0	47.8
Missouri	95.6	42.1
Oklahoma	81.7	28.0
West Virginia	100.0	58.2
Token tier	26.5	2.26
Arkansas	5.7	.33
Florida	23.9	1.53
North Carolina	23.4	.54
Tennessee	31.5	2.72
Texas	29.3	5.52
Virginia	43.0	1.63
Deep South	1.77	.13
Alabama	3.51	.007
Georgia	2.21	.052
Louisiana	3.00	.602
Mississippi	.00	.000
South Carolina	.92	.003
Total region	37.3	9.3

Source: Adapted from Staff Report, *Public Education* (Washington, D.C.: Government Printing Office, 1964), 287-92.
[a] Only for districts containing both races.

the District of Columbia's "Now!" After a decade of effort at judicial enforcement, 1 of 2 black students in the upper South attended a desegregated school, but only 1 in 45 in the middle South and a microscopic 1 in 750 in the Deep South did so. For the whole region, these efforts of a decade found only a little better than 1 in 3 districts desegregated; only 1 in 11 black students attended desegregated schools.

The pace of desegregation differs subregionally, as the Border States moved quickly, particularly in urban schools. Here, between *Brown I* and *II,* 156 districts desegregated and a year later 70 percent had complied; in five years about 45 percent of the Negro students were in desegregated schools. In the Token Tier of states, all began desegregation in the first five years and, except for Virginia, did so voluntarily. But the pace was slow and faltering, accompanied by massive resistance in Virginia, including closing down one county's schools, and by the governor's armed refusal in Arkansas. The somewhat faster pace of Texas and its large weight in numbers makes the subregion's total rate of compliance artificially large.

In the Deep South, almost nothing changed in response to this judicial policy output. The minimal compliance seen in Table 13-2 is actually somewhat elevated because of the unusually large number of black students desegregated in Louisiana (1814). More normal for the heart of the Old Confederacy was Alabama with twenty-one students, South Carolina with nine, and Mississippi with its rigid zero. By the end of this era, only 11 of the 620 districts in the subregion had even begun desegregation, and all but two of these (both in Georgia) did so only under a direct court order.

Judicial and Public Response to Resistive Feedback

As these differential outcomes developed, the Supreme Court was silent. In the face of this civil disobedience, what it did not say is as important as what it did say. While a national storm began building around its calm chambers, the Court offered no defense or detailed explanation of the ideal it had proclaimed. Discussion ensued all over the nation, as Southern resistance was met increasingly by civil-rights protests, and both were fastened in the spotlight of national news media. Litigation provoked discussion among whites who had never considered, and blacks who had never raised, the possibility that segregation violated a basic value in the American creed.

But the Court itself issued few opinions on the feedback of resistance. For a decade it mostly restrained itself to *per curiam* decisions tersely upholding without opinion the lower court enforcement of the *Brown* decrees. Between 1955 and 1958 it did not discuss desegregation at all, simply declining to review such cases. The Court broke its silence in 1958 only for the sensational Constitutional crisis surrounding the Little Rock case. Here it took the chance to reaffirm the principle of *Brown I* and *II* and to assert its continuing unanimity in the matter. But it said very little directly about the details of the segregation plan for Little Rock. For the next five years the Court resumed its silence, merely declining to review Southern challenges, whether brought by whites or blacks. It next broke that silence in 1963 in an opinion that struck down a blatant evasion scheme, while powerfully complaining about delay nine years after *Brown I*.

This decade of silent Court reaction can be seen as part of the procrastination strategy mentioned earlier, giving the political context of the environment the time to reshape itself to support the Court-endorsed social norm. By not getting involved with details of numerous plans in diverse communities, the Court may have diverted some of the lightning then flashing about the Southern countryside. Further, by affirming only occasionally, unanimously, and on the level of fundamental principle, it served as a teacher of norms to the public beyond the South.

Whether because of or despite this strategy, as the first decade of its use ended the Court was supported in the *Brown* decision by at least a majority of Americans and by almost three-quarters of non-Southerners, as seen in the national polls of Table 13-3. The turbulent events of Little Rock in September, 1957, were associated with some reduction in support; Southern support, particularly by whites, remained low and stable. But whites outside the South and blacks inside it provided support that began and remained high.

However, views of the *Court* are not the same thing as views on the

Table 13-3

Percent Approving of Supreme Court Decision on School Desegregation

	National	Non-South	South	White: South	Negro: South
1954	54	64	24	—	—
1955	56	68	20	—	—
1956	57	71	22	16	53
1957: January	63	74	27	—	—
1957: October	59	—	23	15 [a]	69 [a]
1959	59	72	22	—	—
1961	62	—	24	—	—

Source: Polls reported in Hazel G. Erskine, "The Polls: Race Relations," *Public Opinion Quarterly*, 26 (1962), 140. Reprinted by permission.
[a] November, 1957, polls.

principle for which that body acted, namely, that students of both races should go to school together. We could expect strong support of this by blacks, but it is more important to know the effect on white attitudes if there is any substance to the concept of the socialization function of the Court. Figure 13-2 shows evidence consonant with the concept, as measured by poll responses of white Americans to the question of whether races should attend schools together.

Whites in both North and South reflect a changing national view from 1942, when not even one-third of all whites favored school desegregation, to 1963, when almost two-thirds did. Among Northern whites, the shift was from 2 in 5 to almost 2 in 3 and finally to almost 3 in 4. Even Southern whites showed some effects; in 1942, 1 in 50 approved but two decades later about 1 in 3 did. By 1963, the whole nation stood where only Northern whites had stood seven years earlier, and the Southern whites stood in 1963 where the nation had stood in 1942. This is clearly a shift

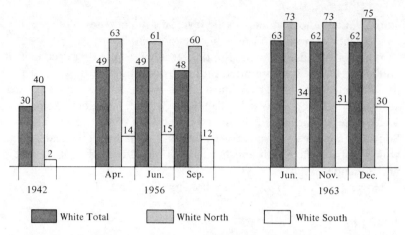

Source: Paul B. Sheatsley, "White Attitudes Toward the Negro," *Daedalus,* 95 (1966), 219. Reprinted by permission of *Daedalus,* Journal of the American Academy of Arts and Sciences, Boston, Massachusetts, Winter 1966, The Negro American—2.

Figure 13-2. Percentage Agreement That Black and White Children Should Attend School Together.

of no small proportions, much of it, particularly in the South, rather sizable in the years after *Brown I* and *II.* Southerners might reject the Court's decision, but many *were* accepting its normative message.

The exact role played by the Court in this transformation is not clear, of course. Other events were operating in the environment that had some influence in this direction. The numbers of Americans educated has changed since 1942, a fact having direct bearing on increasing tolerance. Americans were moving about inside their nation in great numbers after World War II, being exposed to new ideas and closer racial contact. The characteristics of a community's population and political system are other factors that could affect the degree and rate of desegregation. Dye found that by 1960 cities both North and South differed regularly in the socio-economic and political factors associated with segregation, although the proportion of black students everywhere was directly related to this practice.

Yet, as potential explanations of these changes there were also the publicized events of this decade that centered around what the *Brown* cases had begun: highly visible conflict in schools in Prince Edward County; Clinton, Tenn.; Little Rock; and Oxford, Miss.; national legislation on civil rights in 1957 and 1960; sit-ins, "freedom rides," and a March on Washington, etc. And at all these places were the national media, transmitting to the nation—and to the South—not merely what was transpiring but how it fit into a new consciousness about black rights.

In little of this did the hand of the Court appear directly, but in all of it was the indirect influence of the forces it had set in motion by the *Brown* decisions. At least the resistant Southerners had no doubt that the Court was the *bête noire*. That body figured large in its total condemnation of all the change in process; a highly popular book in the region described the evils that flowed from the *Black Monday* when the Court had issued *Brown I*.

Systems Applications to the 1964 Civil Rights Act

Conversion and Output

It was against such Southern obstructionism that the Civil Rights Act of 1964 was to move. The year before its passage was the most dramatic in the history of this country's efforts to realize the value of equality for its black citizens. The conversion process that led to the 1964 Act transpired in a thunderstorm of sensational events in the streets of obscure Southern towns, in Dallas, in the offices of the White House, and in the chambers of Congress—all fed continuously to an American public generally supportive of the change. An enormous coalition of libertarian interest groups was linked directly with executive and legislative cohorts to succeed finally in overriding Southern bastions of congressional power. In this moral and political struggle, an enormous change occurred in the stance of the federal government vis-à-vis American—and particularly Southern—blacks. Despite setbacks and hesitancies of political authorities since then and in the future, the position of that minority will never again be what it had been. What it will be, however, is a story not yet written.

The core of the 1964 Act for our purposes appears in Title VI:

> No person in the United States shall, on the ground of race, color, or national origin, be excluded from participation in, be denied the benefits of, or be subjected to discrimination under any program or activity receiving Federal financial assistance.

By this wording, the cutoff of federal funds suddenly became a weapon against long-stalled school desegregation. It was augmented by the authorization of federal enforcement power, both in the Health, Education, and Welfare and the Justice Departments. Through its Office of Civil Rights, HEW administered the cutoff program, and Justice, through its Civil Rights Division, initiated litigation against discriminating school districts. The Court itself suddenly became more active with more frequent and sweeping opinions.

Against this battery of new forces, Southern schoolmen's power was reduced considerably, but they still retained large resources of delay and evasion. Unlike the ESEA output reviewed earlier, there was *no* state enforcement of a federal policy in desegregation matters in the Deep South. Washington's enforcement efforts were in the main made directly against local districts. What might seem an uneven contest was equalized because the resources of the state governments reinforced local district noncompliance. Under ESEA, the states wanted to control the subsidy, sometimes in keeping with Washington's guidelines, sometimes—perhaps often—in accordance with state wishes, and sometimes as local districts wished. But here, states wanted nothing to do with desegregation—unless it was to prevent enforcement of the law. In that difference lies an essential distinction between subsidy and regulatory policies.

Feedback in the Johnson Years

A brief review of these contending elements will demonstrate how their interactions advanced desegregation farther than opponents deemed desirable but less than supporters hoped. The feedback to this law was influenced by several conflicting strains in the enforcement process. As a rough measure of these strains, we can place Southern segregationists at one extreme fighting off any change, the Supreme Court and civil-rights groups pushing at the other extreme for full and prompt compliance, and the federal administrative agencies working somewhere in the center of these opposing pressures. The center's location fluctuated with the pressures of Southern congressmen to block or attenuate any federal enforcement, with the will of presidential enforcement, and with the courts' changing opinions on acceptable desegregation plans. By 1970, this push-pull process had accomplished far more desegregation in the Deep South than seemed possible a few years earlier. But it had also brought into play forms of resistance not evident earlier, particularly in the rural South and urban North.

The pivotal position of the administrative enforcers is quite clear. From the first days when the 1964 Act was handed to HEW, its agents (at first law professors travelling to Washington) moved into a complex matrix of local pressures transmitted through powerful congressmen and modulated by their own uncertainties about how to proceed. They had to impose guidelines for administering these provisions upon a mosaic of school systems for which no single formula made sense. The first guidelines were delayed for almost a year and were revised in successive years, a mark of the difficulty of administering this school complex.

From 1965 on, these guidelines concentrated greater weight upon the

Southern segregationists when the fund cutoff penalty came to have significant meaning with passage of ESEA. Southerners had not fought the cutoff provision very hard when the 1964 Act was being shaped, as they were more concerned with public accommodations provisions. Federal monies, not very extensive before 1965, thereafter reached enormous proportions. To a Southern educational system already well below national levels, ESEA money meant the possibility of quantum jumps in educational quality—and particularly for black students. The threat, in short, became very large and very real, so that Southern efforts were moved by a concern not only to evade desegregation but to do so without losing money. On the other hand, HEW was given a statute with undeniable national majority support that could threaten cutoffs of funds sorely needed, and, under Lyndon Johnson, the pressure of a president earnestly supporting Southern desegregation. In the first years after 1965, HEW moved quickly into hundreds of school districts with effects we will shortly note.

In that movement, the Supreme Court played an increasingly demanding role. Despite a silence broken only rarely in the previous decade, it handed down three important school decisions in the 1965 term; in one, *Rogers vs. Paul,* it treated the details of a district desegregation plan, ordering prompt admission of black children to a high school. At the district and particularly appellate court levels, decisions increasingly overturned desegregation plans on the grounds that they were evasions. Whereas these courts earlier had accepted pupil placement and "freedom of choice" plans because they were not evasions on their face, in the late 1960s they repeatedly found them invalid because the result had only been to continue segregation.

The justices were quite consistent about several points. First, the elimination of racial schools was the guiding star. In the *Jefferson County* case, Appellate Judge Minor Wisdom put quite clearly the purpose of the law and of any plan evaluated under it; it was to "bring about an integrated, unitary school system in which there are no Negro schools and no white schools—just schools." The second consistency was that the judges had little willingness to condone delay any longer. In this same case, Wisdom expressed such judicial exasperation; "The clock has ticked the last tick for tokenism and delay in the name of deliberate speed."

The end of the Southern delay engendered by *Brown II* may have come in the Supreme Court's terse, two-page opinion in the *Holmes County* decision of October, 1969. Continued segregation "is no longer permissible," it said, and "the obligation of every school district is to terminate dual school systems at once and to operate now and hereafter only unitary schools." They must "begin immediately to operate as unitary school systems." Moreover, any further effort at litigation over desegregation is foreclosed until that unitary condition is achieved. Thus, the kind of decree that many had called for fifteen years earlier now emerged, and if compliance be merely a matter of the proper wording of a judicial decree, the job should be done.

The joining of HEW to the Supreme Court in the enforcement of school desegregation shaped the role of that agency, for in general, the judiciary led it in standards of the permissible and the expected. The justices' standards set general policy guidelines—sometimes by denying the suitability of a specific desegregation plan—that were difficult for the agency to evade. Moreover, this judicial pressure provided national administrators with a shield against Southern congressional pressures to move slowly—if at all. With the Johnson and Court pressure to move quickly, the HEW and Justice Departments were able to fend off Southern pressures. But if desegregation pressure from either of those sources faltered, the Southern power in Congress would be much harder to hold in check.

Feedback in the Nixon Years

That pivotal position of HEW and Justice was illuminated by the coming to office of Richard M. Nixon. The yearning to build the Republican party's strength in the South, which we earlier noted had affected Eisenhower's stance on civil rights in the 1950s, came to the fore again. Southerners felt they had received signals from Nixon as candidate in the 1968 campaign that the pace of desegregation would be slowed if not stopped. And in the first year of his administration, they felt they had received signals to that effect from Nixon as president. For over a year, his top officials suggested indirectly that a reconsideration was under way on the question of pace.

More direct actions seemed to validate the reality of this shift. Soon upon entering office, Nixon called for a delay in fund cutoffs for a few schools; when the schools failed to meet guidelines, however, the cutoffs were reimposed in all but the one case that had met them. But thereafter fund cutoffs almost disappeared as an enforcement technique. In the fall of 1969, the Justice Department's top officials counseled delay in enforcing stricter plans in thirty-one Mississippi districts. This occasioned a splash of publicity over the government's opposing the NAACP for the first time in school litigation, over the Civil Rights Division lawyers' rebellion against the attorney general's reluctance, and over the eventual firing of the division director.

President Nixon finally laid down his desegregation policy in March, 1970. He denounced racial segregation in schools and their facilities as this practice existed in the South, but declared that Northern segregation, based on *de facto* circumstances of housing patterns, was to be treated differently. Although *de jure* segregation was to be eliminated, it required "an area of flexibility—a 'rule of reason'. . . in which school boards, acting in good faith, can formulate plans of desegregation which best suit the needs of their own localities." On the other hand, *de facto* segregation "is undesirable but is not generally held to violate the Constitution." He had strong reservations about past school policy "which demands too much of our schools," for "there are limits to the amount of government coercion that can reasonably be used." An example of a policy that exceeded this limit was school busing, which he firmly opposed.

This policy statement gave desegregationists far less than they had known under Johnson, and was also probably less than Southerners had hoped for. Yet it did fit a highly differentiated school system, suggesting that different causes for the same effect require different methods for changing the effect. It did affirm, as Eisenhower never had, the moral correctness of the Court's decisions about the unconstitutionality of segregation. It did agree that segregation, when *de jure,* must be "eliminated totally." This was some cheer for desegregationists. But it also gave prime weight in making such changes to local school boards' judgments; it asserted the primacy of the neighborhood school as the basis of our educational system; it announced that if both kinds of segregation existed only the *de jure* need be remedied, and it cautioned that although Washington would provide federal advice if needed, it was not to go beyond "requirements of law" in imposing its judgment on local schools. All these items contained equal good cheer for segregationists.

Yet the policy shared one element of all compromises—it did not really make everyone happy. Southern segregationists felt misled, although as we shall see, they did enjoy some slackening of the pace set in the Johnson years. Desegregationists in the North and South felt deeply hindered, although as we shall see, the enforcement did not stop. Possibly the group most pleased were Northern segregationists, who felt relief that the enforcement power was not to be turned in their direction in any meaningful way. Nixon's displeasure at school busing had most meaning in their region, as so little of this involved the South.

The criticism from desegregationists was extensive and bitter. The Southern Regional Council illustrated private group counter-pressures in its itemized condemnation of post-1968 "federal retreat" and "fourteen years of failure." The United States Commission on Civil Rights illustrated governmental pressures by its critical surveys of each stage of the desegregation after the 1964 law. Its 1966-67 survey could report "results . . . both heartening and discouraging." The report in September, 1969, however, was a thorough-going attack on the Nixon policy for employing a "numbers game" of statistics seeking to prove that the administration was enforcing desegregation. Finding Southern resistance still extensive, it concluded that without strong law enforcement nothing would change. State and local officials were still recalcitrant and evasive. Their wide use of "freedom of choice" plans put the burden on black families to initiate desegregation instead of requiring affirmative action by school officials themselves.

Enforcement Outcomes: Local

The value of the 1964 Act, with its emphasis upon federal administrative rather than private individual power, seems obvious if judged by the outcome of enforcement. Thus, the microscopic desegregation recorded in Table 13-2 for the Deep South in the 1963-64 school year, where only private action was available, had grown considerably by 1968-69 under the federal thrust. In percentage terms, the later desegregation rates were: Alabama 7.4, Georgia 14.2, Louisiana 8.8, Mississippi (where none had existed) 7.1, North Carolina 27.8, South Carolina 14.9, and Virginia 25.7. However, as noted in the Commission on Civil Rights criticisms above, reliance upon litigation instead of administrative enforcement would mean a decrease in desegregated districts. In every Southern state, the use of guidelines had led to more desegregated districts than had the use of litigation; the commission reported that the latter had desegregated only 9.4 percent of the districts, whereas guidelines had desegregated 21.0 percent. With massive documentation, the commission argued that the undermining of administrative enforcement left the action up to a much weaker organ, the local courts, whose biases and ineffective orders had been clearly demonstrated in the decade after *Brown II*.

Even if we grant much of this criticism, it does not follow that Southern desegregation had stopped. In states of the Confederacy, the proportion of black *students* in formerly all-white schools (the reverse is a rarity) had been less than 1 percent in 1962-63 and a year later just past 1 percent. By 1964-65 it had doubled to 2.25 percent, but a year later—the first full year of Title VI—it reached 6 percent. In 1966-67 there was a relatively great increase to 17 percent, a year later to over 20 percent, and in 1969-70 the figure was estimated at 40 percent. The figures for school *districts* desegregated have always been higher; HEW reported more than 97 percent in the fall of 1970. Here, though, "desegregation" might mean for any one district that only several blacks were in white schools.

In the Nixon years, these figures continued to grow, although the creation of private schools to drain off the bitterest segregationists makes such data uncertain. Too, despite the administration's reluctance to push stronger desegregation in 31 Mississippi school districts, those districts complied with court orders in early 1970 with an ease that surprised the press—and possibly Mississippians themselves. Further, the first reactions of both races at the change was relief that it had not hurt as much as feared. Press reports and more careful opinion surveys found extensive accommodation to new roles by parents, students, and faculty of both races. However, not all accommodated, for many whites rushed off to hastily devised private schools. But their financial support was too limited for them to survive for long, and efforts at state subsidy were nullified by federal court decisions in May, 1970.

At a pace once believed impossible by friend and foe alike, then, Southern school districts were moving into a desegregated stance. They had a distance yet to go to achieve the Court goal of a unitary school system. While complaining bitterly at the successful attack on cherished values, they were, nevertheless, moving. In the process, not only behavior but also attitudes changed. By mid-1969, almost one-half of white Southern parents would not object to sending their children to a school where half were black; 78 percent would not object if there were just a "few" blacks. However, six years earlier 61 percent had *opposed* having their children in school with that "few," and 78 percent opposed if the schools were half black.

Outside the South appeared other signs of popular support of the Court's socialization efforts. By mid-1970, only 15 percent of Americans reported favoring *de jure* segregation, although 61 percent supported the *de facto* kind. Polled on their support of the Court order in early 1970 requiring that districts in Mississippi and Tennessee desegregate at once, although 40 percent of a national sample disapproved, 48 percent approved; 12 percent were unsure. But wide regional and status variations existed in this approval, which enlisted only 8 percent among whites in the Deep South. Higher-status whites gave majority support; lower-status whites gave majority opposition. But by the end of 1970, Southern attitudes were in the midst of abrupt change. Whether because desegregation has not been as bad as feared, or because whites were still evading it in classrooms, they were more nearly divided on the question of desegregation without further delay. A 42-43 percent split of approval-disapproval of a Supreme Court decision to this effect reflected this shift.

Whether viewed in terms of the participants in, or observers of, the federal action, by 1970 a major reversal in American opinion had transpired—at least as it applied to one form of segregation. As Orfield noted of the efforts by HEW to apply its guidelines.

It has been a strange sort of revolution. There has been only isolated violence, and few people outside the South knew anything significant was happening. There have been no manifestoes, but only dry bureaucratic documents. Instead of charismatic figures, the leaders have been a small group of civil servants.[a]

Enforcement Outcomes: National

But historic change also took place both in the practices of federalism and in a new priority to old values. Thus, the federal fund-cutoff provision was a departure from traditional intergovernmental relations. Historically, we have rejected national controls for their frustration of our individualistic localism. Enforcing fund-cutoff provisions in the past have not worked because of the political backlash for federal officials who tried it. That is, national cutoffs were regularly followed by political attacks on "federal bureaucrats," attacks that could weaken support for the program's financing in later years and weaken local cooperation in other programs. Active enforcement of Title VI, therefore, was a major change in American federalism. The negative feedback from cutoffs, which led to President Nixon's drastic reduction—if not cessation—in use of this instrument, illustrates the strength of the political tradition traced here. Another president might have ignored this feedback, but, after all, it had played some part in putting him into office in the first place.

Another historic shift occasioned by Title VI and these Court decisions was to place Washington squarely in the conversion processes of local education. Local control of schooling, as noted earlier, has been part of the foundation of American public policy. The federal government had been involved locally in the past, as we have noted, but all this was supportive of local education, not regulative. Title VI, however, was clearly supportive of another norm—equality—which sharply confronted local norms of white supremacy. Obviously, law supportive of one group and its norms is seen as regulative by another.

The Court has been quite clear about which norm it chose, but other national political authorities were divided. President Eisenhower never endorsed the Court's norm or sought statutes to implement it; Kennedy made a few more efforts, although without securing a statute. As we have seen, the efforts of Johnson and Nixon produced quite different paces of enforcement. Even with the backing of the 1964 Act, administrative agencies had to reorient themselves to an entirely new set of values. For all its century-long history, the United States Office of Education had been an instrument of *local* education forces, serving them primarily in a sup-

---

[a] Gary Orfield, *The Reconstruction of Southern Education,* copyright © 1969 by John Wiley & Sons, Inc. Reprinted by permission.

portive capacity. But under Title VI, as Orfield observed, it "was caught in a conflict between equality and localism [and was] expected to force local officials to recognize the rights of Negro children but do nothing else to threaten the tradition of local dominance." The cooperative methods of earlier supportive policies achieved nothing in the Deep South, of course; only the threat of cutoff moved these districts. In the process, the feedback from enforcement of Title VI, as well as of ESEA, marked drastic changes in that "tradition of local dominance." But behind all this was the pressure of the Court.

The Judiciary in the Political System

We return to the singular role of the Court in this policy process. In Easton's terms, it sought a *regime change,* an alteration of the basic norms or principles by which the political system operates. The value of equality had existed for some time in the American creed but without effective meaning in the lives of black, Southern citizens. From *Brown I* and *II* onward, however, the Court worked to change that condition, thereby revitalizing a norm for this minority. Such legitimization was conducted under a strategy of procrastination, possibly for fear of undermining its authority in this and other cases. As Krislov has noted,

> In stressing the continuity of its moral authority even at the risk of foregoing a victory, the Court follows the pattern of other institutions like the Catholic Church, which instills respect through its moral standing rather than through the imposition of sanctions. The Court, like the Church, has not sought to challenge and test the limits of its power, preferring to display the impression of power.[b]

Has the Supreme Court's "moral authority" in the political system been damaged by its decisions on civil rights matters over the last two decades? It seems unlikely. We have noted previously the popular support of Court decisions and the even greater support of their specific norms. From a national survey by Murphy and Tanenhaus in 1964 and 1966, it is clear that such support is highly differentiated by the kind of policy in view. More important, many if not most Americans know little of the Court's work and constitutional role; little better than 1 in 4 are so knowledgeable, and these are generally well-educated and politically attentive Americans.

If we distinguish between specific and diffuse support for the Court (that is, popular judgment on its specific issue outputs or on its general

---

[b] Samuel Krislow, *The Supreme Court in the Political Process.* Copyright © 1965 by The Free Press, a Division of the Macmillan Company.

impartiality and competence), as we see in Table 13-4 there seems to exist more diffuse than specific support. That is, many persons critical of specific Court actions still support the Court in its institutional capacity; 9.6 percent gave strong to moderate specific support but 37 percent were in that range on diffuse support. There was some congruity, however, as those positive on one kind of support were also positive on the other, and those negative clustered similarly. The boxed figures of 69 percent and 42 percent show the reinforcing influence of the two classes of support. Yet even many of those negative because of some specific Court decision did continue to render diffuse support.

Finally and most evident in Table 13-4, large numbers of citizens were unclassifiable because they knew little about specific Court outputs (53.8 percent); even at the more generalized level of diffuse support, 29.4 percent had no opinion about the Court's role. Indeed, if we ask what proportion perceives the Court at all, knows its proper task, and has judgments about its specific and general activity, almost 3 in 4 citizens are *excluded*. Of these knowledgeable opinion holders remaining, most are positive in diffuse support, but they represent only about 1 in 8 of all Americans.

The preceding suggests that the Court, as it interacted with the federal political system in these years, did not cause dissolution of its support, although we know little about what level of support it enjoyed before 1954. Public acceptance of Southern school desegregation increased, even among Southern whites, over these years. Public evaluation of the Court in this process is vague because so few are aware of what the Court does in general or in specific. Yet among those with knowledge and opinions, support outweighed opposition, particularly among those most active in the conversion process. However, such data do not tell us much about the success of the strategy of procrastination. Obviously, we have no alternative strategy whose effectiveness in the social environment we can judge. Certainly national opinion, an invaluable ally in a democracy, was not as supportive of desegregation in 1954 as it was to become later, suggesting it might not have adapted as easily if a quicker strategy had been employed. It seems certain that enforcement of the 1964 Act began in a climate of opinion quite supportive because of events traceable to *Brown I* and *II*.

One might better judge the efficacy of this strategy by asking what forces the Court *could* have rallied to its side in 1954 if it had called for prompt desegregation. Congress, particularly in its bastions manned by powerful Southern chairmen, was of little help. Not for three years after *Brown I* could Congress manage a civil rights law, and at that it was a weak effort that did nothing for school desegregation. President Eisenhower was distinctly unsympathetic to the Court's norm, although he would defend the institution if it faced outright disobedience, as in Little

Table 13-4

Specific vs. Diffuse Support of the Supreme Court by Percentages, 1966 [a]

Specific support	Diffuse support						Total sample
	Strong pos.	Mod. pos.	Pro/Con	Mod. neg.	Strong neg.	Unclassifiable	
Strong positive	69	15	12	—	—	4	2.6 = 100%
Moderate positive	56	13	13	4	3	11	7.0
Pro/Con (divided)	34	18	28	8	10	4	5.0
Moderate negative	18	16	19	20	17	9	19.2
Strong negative	12	13	11	18	42	4	12.5
Unclassifiable	14	19	8	9	2	49	53.8
Total sample	19.9	17.1	11.9	11.4	10.3	29.4	= 100.0%

Source: Walter F. Murphy and Joseph Tanenhaus "Mapping of Some Prerequisites for Court Legitimation of Regime Changes," *Law and Society Review*, 11 (1968), recalculated from data in Table 9, 377.
[a] Figures within the lines are to be read along the rows, each row totaling 100 percent. Figures outside the lines represent the proportion of that row or column in the total sample of 1291 persons.

Rock. The lower federal courts in the region most affected were, in some cases, downright hostile to the *Brown* decision; the enforcement difficulties these judges could create contributed to a null effect in the Deep South for a decade. Political parties could not coalesce on the matter, as each had some interest in either supporting or opposing Eisenhower or in attracting Southern voters. In short, it is difficult to see how greater and speedier compliance could have been achieved by alternative strategies, given this lineup of negative or neutral forces in the political system.

The dimensions of the system interactions described in this chapter suggest many of the political aspects of the judiciary as an authoritative allocator of values and resources. Within its own political system, the Supreme Court used numerous methods to keep lower court resources in line with its opinions. In its relationship to other political authorities, the Court has insisted without deviation upon a normative goal, imposing on presidency, agencies, and legislature an unceasing pressure. Indeed, after 1964, HEW's work was directly tied to implementing plans that the Court would accept. In its relationship to the political subsystems of state governments, the Court has permitted delay in implementation without altering its objective; the delay suggests a sensitive awareness of the limits of its own resources. In its relationship to thousands of school districts, each a mini-political system, the Court's willingness to accept delay only encouraged delay, of course. But it also helped build the massive details of segregation that could be used to sensitize public and lawmakers in the future.

In this sense, a strategy is a resource as much as available armament or capital. The Court's strategy had to fit conditions of 1954-55. At that time, it lacked physical resources, it was confronted by hostile or indifferent elements of the larger political system reflecting the social environment, and yet it was seized by a desire for a change in the regime's effective norms. The Court could only borrow on its legitimizing resource and expend it through a procrastinating strategy until the vague national majority jelled and other elements in the political system fell in line. The Court does not need to use procrastination, however, on every regime change. In the case of reapportionment, the impact was almost invisible to the wide public, although the Court itself had instruments for achieving effective compliance. But in the case of Southern school desegregation, the Court's feedback channels were clogged by white Southerners, who felt deeply on the matter and who had powerful resources of delay and obstructionism. Thus the political conditions in the environment necessitated distinctive judicial responses, another sign of the political quality of the judiciary.

Finally, although this chapter examines the role of the Court's political impact upon schooling, we must not fail to note that *on its own* the Court has been ineffective in imposing a uniform norm upon a pluralistic school system. In Southern desegregation, the data show such a slow Deep South response to *Brown I* and *II* that full compliance would have required another century. Not until a statute backed by a willing Congress, energetic enforcers, and a supportive public came into being did much happen, and even now that region is still resisting. As the nation turns its face north to deal with desegregation there, we can see clear signs of firm resistance to ending *de facto* segregation, particularly if it requires busing. Congress and the presidency (under both Johnson and Nixon) have assumed the same reluctance stance they held in the same period after *Brown I* and *II*. Further, in school prayer and Bible-reading decisions, the Court has been ineffective except in those localities where political forces existed to implement them. Where they did not exist, little has changed.

Nor can the Court do everything, even with supportive inputs. We are just beginning to learn that desegregation—an administrative, physical act—is not the same as integration—the emotional and spiritual belief of men. Intervening between these two conditions are group resistance, popular ignorance, communication failures, information overloads, and other dysfunctional aspects of social disorganization. In the sequential process from segregation to integration many facets of social life must be combined to achieve any results. Even with a Court mandate, much must be done to move people. Judicial action can be immensely supportive for desegregationists, of course, but its major function—and we do not belittle it—is to initiate social change. That does not bring total or quick acceptance, provide all resources for the resourceless, teach how to resolve conflict or live with ambiguity, or develop other accommodative skills. Other persons and events must perform these tasks.

In this regard, then, the Court is in the position of Glendower in *Henry IV:* "I can call spirits from the vasty deep."

Hotspur responds, "Why so can I, or so can any man, but will they come when you do call for them?"

But it is also obvious that the Court's call on school segregation did evoke spirits. Possibly the simplest way of gauging the consequences for the Southern school system of the political system of the judiciary is to answer the queries: What if there had never been *Brown vs. Board of Education of Topeka*? What would be the condition of school desegregation in the South today? Both friend and foe of the Court would have to agree that little would be changed. That recognition marks the significant potential of the Court for affecting the educational system. Even on its own, it can at least create a national dialogue about regime norms.

In this way, the unthinkable of yesterday becomes the convention of today. Creating this flexibility of mind is a function that the Court and good teachers share.

**Part VI
National School Systems in a
Comparative Framework**

Introduction to Part VI

National School Systems in a Comparative Framework

In a tradition reaching back 2500 years to Aristotle's *Politics,* political science has sought understanding of the polity through comparisons of political systems. Nor is the comparative study of *education* systems of contemporary origin, as historians can trace this analytic method to other cultures and other eras. But this inquiry has in recent years dealt very little with the significance for school policy and administration of the effects of differing political systems, just as political science has dealt little with education at all. In the two following selections, we see the difference that results when political analysis is applied to the context in which education arises and is conducted, instead of focusing only upon the latter in isolation from the political system. If, as the previous section demonstrated, there can be considerable variation in policy effects within a nation-state even when possessed of a common culture and history, then we should expect even more when we compare nation-states with their diverse cultures.

Paul Peterson finds contrasts in the English and American schooling systems that are traceable to different sociological and institutional factors; these, in turn, create differences in the stances of political parties on education policy. Nevertheless, recent events are making the two systems more alike. This contribution illustrates the utility of the traditional method of comparative government analysis; with its roots in Aristotle, this study links political systems and their policies to their institutional and class features. This selection has an especially rich set of footnotes for those interested in exploring this further.

A newer methodology is illustrated in the selection by David Cameron and Richard Hofferbert. Here, the emphasis is upon quantitative methods of macro-analysis, utilizing numerous systems for comparison, and distinguishing between features of the social, economic, and political subsystems of all nations. This study of 18 European and North American nations finds that there is little inter-nation difference in education finance outcomes associated with the presence or absence of federal vs. non-federal systems. However, intra-nation differences in policy do reflect similar differences in industrialization and integration, with exceptions.

14

The Politics of Educational Reform in England and the United States
Paul E. Peterson *

Historically, the politics of educational reform in Britain and the United States differed both in the character of the reformer's objectives and in the political strategies that they followed.[a] In Britain reformers sought, above all, to democratize the educational system, while American reformers focused more on "modernizing" educational practices. British reformers sought to use the Labor party as the major political mechanism for achieving their objectives, while reformers in the United States developed a non-party, indeed, an anti-party, movement to promote their cause. The sources of these differences lay, first of all, in the greater significance of class differences for both British education and politics, and, secondly, in the quite different structures for governing education which have evolved in the two countries. Some of these historical differences have begun to wane in recent years, however, as the politics of education in the United States show some signs of taking on a more "British" character. At least this is what is suggested by a review of the literature on the politics of education in Britain and the United States.

Educational Reform Politics in Britain

British reformers historically have been concerned with democratizing educational opportunity by seeking to provide equal educational opportunities for children of all social groups. They criticized the Education Act of 1902 for the limits it placed on the rapidly expanding elementary school

Reprinted with permission of the publisher from Paul E. Peterson, "The Politics of Educational Reform in England and the United States," *Comparative Education Review*, 17/2 (June 1973), pp. 160-179. See the original article for footnotes omitted here.

* University of Chicago

a This analysis is dependent in part on research the author has done on the politics of comprehensive education in Great Britain and on school politics in Chicago. This research has been supported by the Danforth Foundation, a North Atlantic Treaty Organization Postdoctoral Fellowship, and a grant from the Division of the Social Sciences at the University of Chicago. This is a revised version of a paper delivered at the 1972 Annual Meeting of the American Political Science Association, Washington Hilton Hotel, Washington, D.C., September 5-9, 1972.

system, extended the "free place" arrangement during the inter-war years, provided for free, universal, compulsory secondary education in the Education Act of 1944, and have fought for the comprehensive school in the post-war period. Educational politics have been class politics, and reformers have sought to introduce educational changes that would improve the opportunities of the working class. The pattern became evident shortly after the passage of the Education Act of 1902.

This Act, passed by a Conservative government, had great implications for the future governance and administration of British education, and we shall discuss some of its most important features below. But the Conservative government that passed the legislation hardly intended to make significant changes in the educational opportunity structure. Conservatives instead wanted both to prevent Liberal-dominated school boards from continuing to build many additional state schools and to bolster the faltering position of church-related voluntary grammar schools, which had previously been the foundation, such as it was, of the British educational system. Indeed, the battle between Liberals and Conservatives was as much a conflict between church and chapel as anything else.

If much of the conflict was over religious issues, the legislation significantly affected class relationships by sharply distinguishing between elementary and secondary education. Elementary education provided free schooling for children of the working class masses up to the age of thirteen, though more able children continued on to the age of fifteen. Secondary education catered to the needs of children of middle class, fee-paying parents at least to the age of sixteen and often for two years beyond that. In contrast to the elementary schools, secondary schools offered an educational program that prepared students for the university or for a position among the country's managerial and professional elite.

In 1908 the Board of Education, now under Liberal Party direction, recognized the need for linking the elementary and secondary educational systems.[b] It therefore instituted a system of "free places" in secondary schools for pupils who passed a qualifying examination taken at the age of 11+. Since the state contributed to the maintenance of these voluntary schools, it could require that schools provide a specific percentage of "free places." Over the next three decades the percentage of these "free places" increased from 25 percent to 57 percent, as the Government responded both to working class demands for more educational opportunity and

[b] Throughout this paper we will use various names for the Central Department responsible for administering the educational service. The Education Act of 1902 established the Board of Education; the Education Act of 1944 created a Ministry of Education with considerably more authority vis a vis local educational authorities; in the 1950s, this was renamed the Department of Education and Science, and we refer to it in this paper as the Department of Education.

secondary school demands for more extensive state financing. Yet the change in the class composition of secondary schools did not democratize educational opportunities as much as these percentages suggest. Children of middle class families constituted a substantial portion of those who passed the qualifying examination. Indeed, the probability that the child of a middle class family would win a "free place" was six times as great as for working class children.

Throughout this period the Labor party never commanded a clear majority in Parliament. But in 1922 it adopted a democratizing program of "Secondary Education for All" from which it did not waver until its essentials were secured in the Education Act of 1944. Following R. H. Tawney, the Socialist party's greatest educational reformer, it called for free, compulsory, secondary education for all children through the age of sixteen. Elementary education, rather than being a separate educational structure for the children of the poor, was to become a system of education for all young children prior to the age of twelve. At that time all children would transfer to the secondary educational system, which would provide a range of courses suitable to the various abilities pupils exhibited.

The conflicts between the parties during this period can scarcely be exaggerated. As late as 1933, the Conservative Parliamentary Secretary to the Board responded to Labor demands by arguing that "to throw secondary education open to all and sundry would very likely be the reverse of an educational advance and might easily be an educational regression; we might easily turn the nation into something like an educational soup-kitchen." And party policies reflected these ideological differences. The Labor Governments, during the short periods they were in power, constantly strove to increase educational expenditures, increase the number of "free places" in secondary schools, reorganize educational structures so as to facilitate the introduction of a universal secondary system, and, in general, promote the democratization of educational opportunity. Conservative governments, when restored to power, did precisely the opposite. Pointing with alarm at the financial crises that plagued Britain throughout the inter-war period, Conservatives called for major cuts in educational expenditures. These, in turn, inevitably slowed the process of merging the two educational systems.

If in general party conflict was eased by the unifying impact of World War II, this was nowhere more evident than in the area of education. Before the end of the war the National Government passed the Education Act of 1944, another landmark piece of legislation which still provides the basic governing structure for British elementary and secondary education. This Act implemented virtually all the major policies that the Labor party had agitated for during the inter-war period. Secondary education became free, universal and compulsory up to the age of sixteen, and elementary education designated the schooling children took prior to the age of twelve.

But this truce in party conflict over education was broken in the post-war period by the debate over the character of the new structures that provided universal secondary education. The Education Act itself was not very specific in this regard (probably intentionally so). At one point it called for a "comprehensive" development plan, but it also stated that each child should receive education "suitable to his age, ability and aptitude." The question of the character of the school through which this education should be provided remained open.

On one side, most Conservatives, and, in the early post-war years, even Labor Ministers of Education preferred a bipartite secondary educational structure that in fact became the dominant post-war pattern. The old voluntary secondary schools continued to be known as secondary grammar schools, and they continued to offer a basically academic course of study preparing students for examinations leading to the university. The old elementary schools for older children were renamed secondary *modern* schools, and they provided more general educational courses that did not take academic examinations as the focus for their study. Although both types of schools were expected—at least in theory—to recruit equally qualified teachers, pay the same salaries and have equal status, they offered significantly different types of educational experiences, each aiming at a limited range of abilities. Students were assigned to grammar or modern schools according to their level of performance on an examination given at the age of eleven (the so-called 11+ examination), which thus became the post-war equivalent of the old qualifying examination.

On the other side, educational reformers argued that the distinctions between grammar and modern schools maintained much of the stratified pre-war educational system. They noted that middle class children were much more likely to "pass" the 11+ examination than were working class children. And whatever the rhetoric of equal status between grammar and modern schools, the prestige of the latter was inevitably affected by the fact that it did not provide the education necessary for university entrance or for higher status occupations. Reformers thus insisted that further democratization could be achieved through the establishment of comprehensive schools that included both grammar and modern educational components, which would serve all secondary children in the community. With the establishment of comprehensive schools along the lines of the ideal American neighborhood school, the invidious distinctions between grammar and modern school children would no longer be made.

Once again, democratizing reformers organized their efforts around the Labor party. Even while the Atlee Government was in office, Labor party left-wingers secured party conference support for the comprehensive idea.

After it left office, comprehensive education became a major campaign cry of the Labor party—at least in part because it was a popular reform among parents who themselves had failed to pass qualifying or 11+ examinations. Many Labor-controlled local educational authorities (LEAs) began developing comprehensive plans, which, however, were usually rejected by the Conservative-controlled Ministry of Education. Finally, when the Wilson Government came to power in 1964, one of its early acts was to issue a government circular asking local authorities to submit plans for establishing local education on a comprehensive basis. And the pattern of response by LEAs clearly followed partisan lines, as Socialist-controlled communities developed comprehensive plans much more quickly than did Conservative ones. Indeed, many Conservative-controlled authorities were so recalcitrant that they managed to avoid "going comprehensive" throughout the period of the Wilson government. When the Tories returned in 1972, virtually their first official act was to withdraw the Labor government's request for comprehensive plans. The whole conflict over this major reform issue illustrates well the partisan character of reform efforts to democratize Britain's educational system.

Educational Reform Politics in the United States

Partisan controversy is far less evident in the politics of education in the United States. The one national issue that generated almost as much conflict as has the comprehensive school issue in Britain was federal aid to education. To some extent, this issue involved partisan conflict. Throughout the post-war period federal aid was supported by Democratic Presidents and at critical points was opposed by President Eisenhower and Republican leaders on Capitol Hill. The issue was particularly contentious within the House Committee on Labor and Education, where conservative Republicans and liberal Democrats regularly fought a bitter ideological battle over federal control of schools. On the other hand, not even this issue clearly and completely divided the parties in the same way conflicts over secondary education did in Great Britain. Not only did Southern Democrats regularly oppose federal aid to education, but even many liberal Catholic Democrats were hesitant about aiding public schools when parochial schools were in critical financial condition. Moreover, many Republicans supported federal aid to education. It had strong Republican backing in the Senate, where it hardly became a partisan issue. At times Eisenhower supported federal aid, and the differences on the issue between Nixon and Kennedy in the 1960 presidential election were at best marginal. The prolonged stalemate over federal aid to education cannot be attributed simply to conservative Republican opposition; more important were the race and religious issues with which it was inevitably intertwined.

State aid to education has not clearly been a partisan issue either. In contrast to the partisan response of localities to the comprehensive school issue in Britain, variations in educational expenditures among states in this country are in no significant way associated with the strength of the Democratic party within the state. Nor have case studies of the state politics of education revealed a pattern of strong party conflict such that the Democratic party regularly promotes state aid in the face of Republican opposition. This pattern has emerged at times, as for example in Michigan and California, where parties generally collide over issues in an ideological manner. But the low pressure politics that Masters and Salisbury found in Missouri, where consensus is sought among influential legislative leaders, seems to be the more typical pattern.

This pattern of political conflict was consistent with the objectives of educational reformers in the United States. In contrast to their counterparts in Britain, reformers have been interested not so much in democratizing educational opportunities as developing widespread support for an expanding, rationalized educational order. In a word, American reformers have been "modernizers." They were concerned, primarily, with expanding support for public education in a society where Catholic and rural parochialism, not the conservatism of an established elite, placed limits on the growth of the state educational system. They sought to gain support for public education at local, state and even the federal levels. No other consideration—certainly not egalitarian questions—should frustrate the development of an enterprise that was expected to strengthen the social, economic and political well-being of an industrializing society.

Accordingly, educational reformers in the United States focused much of their attention on the amount of federal and state aid allocated to the educational sector. And in the debates over federal aid most of the major issues revolved around matters of little relevance to the nature of the opportunity structure provided by the educational system. Should aid be given for building purposes only? Or teachers' salaries too? Should it include aid to parochial schools? It is true that the implications of the program for school desegregation were hotly debated, but, significantly, the educational reformers fought *against* using the monies to desegregate Southern schools! Little attention was paid to distributing federal funds so as to aid poor states and districts—except by Republicans and conservative Southerners whose states stood to benefit from a redistributive formula. Not until 1965 would this become a central problem in the federal aid issue, a matter we shall consider later.

At the state level, these "modernizing" reformers were once again more concerned about increasing levels of educational expenditure than they were about securing an equalizing distribution of funds among communities. To be sure, Ellwood Cubberly, George Strayer, Robert Haig and other early educational finance reformers called for the establishment of "equalizing" foundation programs by the state legislature. Theoretically, these foundation programs were to determine the *minimum* level of per pupil expenditure that every district would need in order to establish an adequate educational program. If a "reasonable" local property tax rate could not raise sufficient revenue for any given local school district, the foundation program called upon the state to make up the difference. To some degree, then, the foundation program seemed to commit the state to providing at least a minimally adequate educational program for every child within its borders. But note that even in theory some school districts could have more lavish educational programs than the minimum provided for in the foundation program—simply by taxing themselves at a somewhat higher level. And rich districts with a more ample tax base could provide a higher quality program with little, if any, more effort than was necessary to provide even the minimum educational offering in poorer districts. Thus the scheme even in theory was hardly egalitarian—as the reformers themselves well knew. But they apparently were reluctant to propose any more egalitarian scheme for fear that it would limit the growth of the educational sector. They argued that communities that wanted to and could afford to spend more money should have that flexibility. The superior education offered there would stimulate other school districts to higher levels of performance.

In practice foundation programs did not even live up to what equalizing potential they had in theory. Legislators from wealthy districts were reluctant to support a state aid plan that would give nothing to their district, while allocating very large sums elsewhere. As a result, the "reasonable" local tax rate settled upon was typically very low, and the minimum level of expenditures necessary to support an "adequate" foundation program was also usually set very low. These practical compromises severely limited the equalizing potential of foundation programs such that Coons et al. have been able to show that some wealthy districts spend several times per pupil what is spent in poorer districts. Significantly, this contrasts with a far more equal pattern of expenditures among local educational authorities in Britain, where a complex, but strongly equalizing system of financial aid has been devised by the Department of Education.

If these modernizing reformers were willing to sacrifice egalitarian objectives on the altar of educational expansion, they worked to modernize the schools in other ways as well. They promoted the rationalization of the educational enterprise, emphasizing the principles of universalism and achievement in the administration of schools. They argued that schools should be separated from the machine politics so prevalent in American cities at the turn of the century. Recruitment of principals, custodians and secretaries on the basis of their associations with party followers was roundly criticized, as were school contracts with businessmen associated with party organizations. In order to remedy such practices, superintendents trained in the field of educational administration and well-indoctrinated in professional norms were to assume responsibility for every phase of the educational enterprise. Teachers were asked to undergo a rather specific set of training experiences before being admitted to the profession, and in many big cities they had to pass a qualifying examination before being hired. Promotions within the organization came to be determined largely by performance on examinations. Textbooks, crayons, paper and teachers were to be allocated among schools in big cities according to formulas based on the number of students enrolled in each school. Universalism and achievement norms were first vigorously promoted and later slavishly followed.

Eliminating the pernicious influences of rascal entrepreneurs and politicians may have been all to the good. The inculcation of a sense of professionalism among school administrators very likely contributed to their "esprit de corps." Better management practices were undoubtedly introduced. But these questions hardly came to grips with the lower achievements of children in less prosperous parts of the city. Indeed, all the formulas devised by administrators committed to universalistic norms did not prevent disproportionate financing of middle class schools—even within a single school district.

This is not to say that reformers were simply conservative businessmen interested in economizing on education. On the contrary, many of the staunchest Progressive reformers resisted business efforts to focus vocational education heavily on occupational skills needed immediately by local industry. Reformers also continually sought to introduce new techniques and provide a broader range of teachers and other skilled personnel, so that educational costs usually rose when their influence was greatest. Even so, all these reform commitments were to a modernized educational system, one as modern as the industrializing society in which it was growing. In order to accommodate the new industrial order, it needed to expand, to adopt modern business methods, and to experiment with new technologies. None of these reforms necessarily required further democratization of the American educational system.

Not surprisingly, progressive reformers could thus easily attract the enthusiasm of intelligent and forward-looking members of the middle class. In contrast to reform dependence on the Labor party in Britain, reformers in the United States were typically antagonistic to both political parties. They wished for politics to be taken out of education rather than to use the party organizations as a mechanism for achieving their social goals. In fact reformers had greater success in the educational arena than almost anywhere else, for many ordinary citizens agreed that children were too innocent to be victims of political intrigues. Moreover, Catholics usually conceded that reform-minded Protestants had a greater stake in the public schools than they had. As a result, the Protestant and Jewish middle class, organized in PTAs, Public Education Associations, Citizens Schools Committees and other such reform organizations became the socio-political base for educational reform.

Differences in Reform Politics: A Cultural Explanation

The less emphasis on egalitarian questions, the rejection of party as a reform vehicle, and the solidly middle class base of the educational reform movement in the United States contrasts sharply with the pattern evident in Britain. These differences can be explained by two general lines of interpretation. The first, more cultural interpretation, stresses the differing impact of the social structure in the two societies on their political culture; the second emphasizes the differing historical developments of the two countries' educational institutions. Although each is not quite satisfactory by itself, together they seem to account for much of the differing patterns of educational reform politics.

Perhaps the most obvious explanation focuses on the far greater significance of class relationships for social and political life in Great Britain. As Louis Hartz has argued, the lack of an aristocratic tradition in the United States precluded the class sensitivities and antagonisms necessary to breed a socialist movement, leaving America an almost uniformly middle class, bourgeois society. In Britain, on the other hand, the traditions of a medieval past were modified only slowly—at least until the upheavals that flowed from two world wars. Accordingly, the British system of secondary education reflected and reinforced class awareness in British society. Fine but precise social distinctions were made among the great variety of schools included within its educational system. At the top of the heap were the *Clarendon schools,* the ten most exclusive Public Schools in Britain. They were the leading schools in the Headmasters Conference, which included some four-hundred day and boarding schools, most of which could legitimately regard themselves as *Public Schools,* though some very good grammar schools also had headmasters who were part of the Conference. Next came a number of the less financially secure, but still respectable private schools, which had become *direct grant* schools with the passage of the Education Act of 1944; these schools received a state subsidy in return for taking a select number of children, usually the highest performers on the 11+ examination, from the state elementary schools. As a sign of their status, these direct grant schools continued to be governed by a private board of directors. As a group, the voluntary-controlled grammar schools ranked next in the hierarchy. Originally, many were controlled either by the National Society for Promoting the Education of the Poor in the Principles of the Established Church or the British and Foreign School Society. They received virtually all their maintenance assistance from the state, but the buildings themselves remained the property of one or another of the Societies, who appointed a majority of the school's board of governors. Voluntary-aided schools were formerly private schools that were now controlled by local educational authorities, though they could still pride themselves on the fact that one-third of their governing board were still independently selected. Ordinary grammar schools were next in status, then technical schools, and finally the secondary modern schools, which themselves were distinguished according to whether they had been old central schools, were developing their own ordinary level courses, were separate from the elementary school plant, and so on.

British secondary education, therefore, was not simply a bipartite arrangement. Rather, almost every school in each community had a specific position in the educational hierarchy. In any but the very largest cities, every grammar school could be assigned its own particular position according to its past traditions and presumed educational accomplishments. Because the Education Act of 1944 allowed parents their choice of school to as great an extent as possible, concerned parents would attempt not only to send their children to grammar school but to the best possible grammar school. The prestige of the very best schools was thus perpetuated by the quality of the students which they could attract.

The post-war British educational system may in fact have *appeared* less egalitarian than it in fact was. While concrete physical structures continually reminded parents and children of the hierarchical structure of the educational system, the extent to which it discriminated against working class children was much more difficult to establish. To be sure, the Public Schools remained fee-paying institutions. But many of England's finest direct grant and grammar schools provided opportunities for an advanced academic education to those working class children who excelled on the 11+ examination. Indeed, this examination, together with primary school teachers recommendations, enabled local authorities to assign students according to achievement criteria that proved capable of predicting future performance in secondary school with considerable accuracy. Moreover, the financing of the state sector of education, though far from perfectly egalitarian, provided fairly uniform revenues per pupil for local educational authorities throughout the country.

The reverse was true in the United States, where appearances were more egalitarian than the actual functioning of the educational system. The American high school was comprehensive *in appearance* in that it catered to the educational needs of all students living in the community. Certainly this softened the rigidities of the class structure in small town and rural communities, where one school did in fact serve the entire community. But with the growth of cities and eventually great metropolitan centers, the class and racially segregated residential patterns inevitably created great distinctions among "comprehensive" neighborhood schools. Moreover, the differentials in the social and intellectual compositions of the student population were accentuated by financial differentials.

Yet these developments occurred without any obvious, explicit political decisions and without any formal recognition of status distinctions. Accrediting institutions continued to recognize the degrees of even the poorest of inner city high schools. And in contrast to Britain, universities relied more on aptitude tests than on the quality of the high school in determining whom should be admitted to further education. Although the class biases of the American educational system had hardly been eliminated, the image it presented to the public was far less hierarchical than the images presented by the British system. As a result, educational reform did not take the same democratizing focus.

If educational structures clearly symbolized class rigidities in Britain, party structures facilitated efforts to democratize the system. A self-consciously working class party, dominated by both the financial and organizational power of the trade union movement, drew its support almost exclusively from the working classes of Britain. The differences in the party orientations of white and blue collar workers in Britain were two to three times as great as the party orientations of these two broad occupational groups in the United States, where parties reflected regional, religious, racial and ethnic loyalties as much as class identifications and awareness. At the same time, the Labor party's socialist commitments focused its attention on broad-scale reform of nearly every area of social life, including the nationalization of industry, the establishment of a national health service, and the provision of more egalitarian educational opportunities.

In the United States, the Democratic party, even though it became identified with the labor movement, developed few such broad-scale commitments. It is true that the AFL-CIO pressed the Democratic party to oppose narrowly defined vocational education and to support federal aid to education. But at the local level Democratic parties saw the educational system as a source of patronage for its ethnic coalition instead of a mechanism for reconstructing social opportunities. Both leaders and followers lacked the class awareness and self-consciousness to attack educational inequity—particularly when that inequity was obscured by the widespread commitment to the common neighborhood school. Thus educational reform came to be an anti-party movement concerned about modernizing education rather than a party movement that would democratize the system.

This cultural explanation is compelling, and for some it may provide by itself an adequate explanation of the differences in educational reform movements in the two countries. However, to argue that the closer partisan ties of the reformers in Britain are due to the greater class consciousness in that country requires a great deal of specification before it can be entirely convincing. Although a society's political culture shapes the outer boundaries of a range of political behavior it is doubtful that it determines any single outcome. In any case, such a conclusion should not be reached until other more proximate institutional factors that might have affected the politics of educational reform are considered.

Reform Politics: An Institutional Explanation

The institutional features of the educational systems in the two countries that seem to have had their own quite independent effect on reform movements are: (1) the greater centralization of authority in Britain; (2) the historical legacy of headmaster autonomy that Britain enjoyed from the days of Matthew Arnold; (3) the closer formal linkage between educational and other local governmental structures in Britain; and (4) the financing of education through local bond and tax referenda in the United States. Each of these factors deserves separate consideration.

Centralization or Decentralization

Ever since the Education Act of 1902, the British educational system has been far more centrally directed than the American. The differences continued to grow throughout the twentieth century until the Education Act of 1944 provided for a Ministry of Education, which in contrast to the United States' weak, resourceless and ineffectual Office of Education, controlled the dispersal of funds among local educational authorities, determined the pattern of new building construction, indirectly but decisively shaped teacher salaries throughout the country, and regulated a host of other local educational activities. In contrast to the small staff housed in the U.S. Office of Education, the Ministry profited from detailed, informed reports on local authorities written by Her Majesty's Inspectors, an elite cadre of experienced educational professionals.

Because of this high degree of centralization, uniform and equitable standards—or at least some approximation thereof—have been established throughout England and Wales. Thus, uniform teacher salaries are negotiated, except for special cost of living modifications allowed for the London area. And in order to pay for uniform teacher salaries, grants to local authorities compensate for differences in local property values. Moreover, with new construction determined by decisions within the Department of Education, uniform criteria are applied to all authorities equally. Special luxuries can not be allowed in some areas unless they are approved generally. In the United States, on the other hand, local control has meant great variety in local teachers salaries, building standards, educational programs and, of course, overall educational costs.

Centralization has had political as well as policy consequences. With so much power concentrated in the hands of the Central Department, reformers could have an enormous impact on the character of British education simply by capturing control of that Department. Without such control their accomplishments would necessarily be marginal. The obvious institution through which such control could be obtained was Britain's change-oriented political party. Yet in order to capture the enthusiasm of the Labor party, educational reform had to be cast in ways consistent with its socialist principles. As a result, British reformers had to be more concerned with democratizing than rationalizing the educational system.

In the United States, on the other hand, little could be expected of the federal government in terms of educational change. Until the Johnson Administration, even the proposals for federal aid to education were hedged with so many restrictions (so as to avoid federal control) that federal aid would not have substantially increased the power of the Office of Education. Instead, change had to be promoted and guided through thousands of local communities. Inasmuch as local board members were usually elected on a non-partisan ballot, reform identification with any political party would have seriously hampered its efforts. Reformers thus worked primarily through the educational profession itself, whose interests were consistent with efforts to promote efficient administration, modernized curriculum, and higher levels of educational support. When these efforts required entrance into the political arena, non-partisan or bi-partisan efforts were usually the norm.

Professional autonomy

If centralization focused the efforts of British reformers in a partisan, egalitarian direction, the long tradition of professional autonomy for educational administrators shifted British reform attention away from modernizing concerns. Overwhelming authority has been conceded a school's headmaster—both within the school and vis-a-vis higher administrative officials. Following the Public School traditions, headmasters in state schools cannot be removed from their post without "good cause." They have great discretion over the recruitment of teachers within their schools, the internal organization of the school, and its curricular materials. To be sure, the head's actions are influenced by the decisions of the LEA's central office, by the reports of Her Majesty's Inspectors, and perhaps even by the comments of his lay board of governors. But the influence of the head-master of a prestigious school often approaches and sometimes surpasses that of the Chief Education Officer for the LEA. He is hardly at the bottom of a bureaucratic hierarchy, as principals in large American cities often tend to be.

Headmasters had this prestige and power from the beginning of the de-velopment of the state system of education. Since they did not need to win respectability, there was no need in Britain for a strong emphasis on edu-cational administration as a profession. A first in Classics at Oxford was as good evidence of a headmaster's ability in Britain as an Ed.D. degree was of a superintendent's capacities in the United States. With virtually no interest in a profession of educational administrators, British educationists did not need to develop a body of specialized knowledge, a science of ad-ministration, in order to legitimize their profession. Britain thus lacked what in the United States was a powerful incentive for emphasizing the "modernization" of the educational enterprise.

Local Councils vs. Schools Boards

Thirdly the very organization of LEAs facilitated the entry of partisan politics into the educational sphere in Britain. As established by the Edu-cation Act of 1902, control of education in rural England and Wales is vested in the county council; in urban areas the county borough council is the governing entity. Generically, they are known as Local Education Authorities. LEA councils must appoint an education committee, which consists of members of the council as well as a number of co-opted mem-bers who are expected to be chosen for their interest and expertise in education. But all decisions of the education committee have to be ap-proved by the council as a whole. Financial decisions, in particular, are usually reviewed by other local officials before being approved by the council. Thus, a strong, centralizing leadership within the council can co-ordinate educational policy with that of other services. The contrast with educational structures in the United States could hardly be greater. Here separate school boards are elected on what is usually a non-partisan ballot. It is not unusual for the school board to have almost no relationship with other municipal governing structures. In many cases, school boards are financially independent as well, having the power to raise the monies necessary to run the schools.

The legal separation of school boards from other municipal governing structures limits the role that political parties will play in educational politics. In Britain, where structures are integrated, control of local government by one party or the other insures that school government will be in the same partisan hands. In the United States, on the other hand, the school board can be captured either by the opposition party, or more likely, a non-partisan group. Indeed, in some big cities, it seems that politicians and reform-minded civic elites reach an accommodation or agree upon a division of labor such that the civic elite takes the responsibility for organizing the school board while the party regulars are allowed control over the administration of other city departments. The separate jurisdictions of schools and city governments fosters such a division of labor.

Taxing policies

Finally, bond and tax referenda in the United States open up the politics of education to a broader range of political forces than is possible at the local level in Great Britain. Whereas in Britain one can control educational policy only by working through the dominant political party in the community, in the United States groups can seek to influence boards of education by threatening to attack tax and bond proposals. In all communities citizens resist tax increases. Older people who no longer have children in school, Catholics who send their children to parochial schools, and homeowners who must bear the brunt of any property tax increase all have strong interest in voting down a tax increase. Even a weak anti-school bond campaign can frequently bring about its defeat. As a result, school boards in the United States have to be sensitive to any organized community group. This may be done imperfectly, and the co-optation of outside forces may sometimes be more nominal than involve any actual power-sharing. Yet pressures to respond to outside forces are much stronger in this country than in Britain, where the county borough council both levies its tax rate without a referendum and receives substantial assistance from the Department of Education and Science. As a result, a small, non-partisan reform group can more easily influence local decision-making in the United States than in Great Britain.

In sum, a variety of institutional factors have reinforced the pattern of partisan support for democratizing reforms in Britain as compared to the United States. The greater centralization of authority in Britain requires massive political power in order to have a substantial impact on the educational system. Only political parties have been able to build such a potent power base. The prestige and power of a key component of the administrative staff—the headmaster—has limited the support British reformers could secure for any efforts at administrative modernization. The closer ties between school and other municipal government activities has brought the former within the orbit of the political party dominant in local politics generally. And the capacity of local decision-makers to make financial decisions without obtaining explicit voter approval has freed them from other group pressures, further strengthening the party as the key link between the government and the citizenry.

In the United States these factors have worked in the opposite direction. Decentralization has made parties an ineffective vehicle for widespread educational change; the need to defend school administration from partisan interference has encouraged an emphasis on educational administration as a profession, the separation of educational from other local government structures has made it more difficult for parties to dominate boards of education, and tax and bond referenda force boards to be responsive to a variety of organized groups in the community.

If the British political culture has encouraged a more partisan focus on more democratic reforms than has the United States' political culture, the institutional structures affecting educational policy-making have only reinforced these patterns. On the other hand, it is doubtful that the degree of centralization, the degree of separation of educational from other municipal structures, the autonomy of professionals, or the taxing powers of LEAs would have so clearly differentiated the politics of educational reform unless the political culture already predisposed political participants to act in the differing ways we have described. Given the qualitative nature of our data, it is difficult to be more precise, but perhaps an examination of recent changes in the politics of educational reform in the United States will shed further light on the relative importance of cultural and institutional factors.

The Changing Politics of Educational Reform

In recent years, changes in the politics of educational reform in the United States have been so substantial that the British pattern is becoming more evident in this country as well. The inegalitarian features of the American educational system have recently been attacked more directly and forthrightly than at any point in the twentieth century. In this regard, the passage of the Elementary and Secondary Education Act of 1965 was of the greatest political significance, for it took as its basis for distributing federal aid the number of children from low income families living in a school district.

Admittedly, the formula was chosen in part because it would concentrate federal aid in both urban cities of the North and the poor Southern states, two key components of the Democratic coalition in Congress. And since local educational resources are a function of the assessed valuation of a district, not the number of poor families within it, this formula, too, was not a direct attempt to equalize educational resources among school districts. But its stated emphasis on compensatory education for the poor focused attention on inequalities in education in an important, new way. Even more recently, inequalities in educational expenditures among districts within states have been challenged in several court suits, and two of them have succeeded—at least in lower federal court decisions. At the same time educational research has begun to focus on the social and educational factors that lead to differential educational performances of class and racial groups. In general, the new educational reform effort has focused, admittedly without much success, on the mechanisms by which such differences can be moderated by institutional changes.

These changes in the politics of education have been due in large part to the increased saliency of the racial conflicts in American society, which have become at least as intense as the class conflicts in Britain during the inter-war period. The rising social and political aspirations of black Americans directed public attention to the differences between its democratic ideals and educational practices. The 1954 *Brown* decision at once made manifest the racial cleavage in American society and focused attention on the social significance of educational institutions. Whether the conflict has been about implementing this court decision, *de facto* segregation, busing, compensatory education or community control of schools, middle class reformers have been joined (and at times led) by racial groups articulating the aspirations of low income blacks. Indeed, it was just this set of forces that produced the Civil Rights Act of 1964 and the war on poverty, both of which were obvious precursors of the Elementary and Secondary Education Act of 1965. Clearly, without these new socio-political forces, federal aid to education would never have taken the form it did.

Since then, the debate over education, at least at the federal level, has become increasingly partisan in tone. Republicans under the Nixon Administration have sought to limit federal expenditures on education, while the Democrats have sought to expand them. Republicans have sought to limit racial reform in education, while northern Democrats have generally opposed these efforts. To be sure, the two parties are not cohesive, disciplined, programmatic parties to the extent that British parties are. But it is unlikely that a bipartisan approach to education reform, such as was almost worked out in the Eisenhower years, is possible in the near future.

If educational reform in the United States has taken a democratizing direction, it has also simultaneously turned against the educational professionals who were once the promoters of reform themselves. The bureaucratization of educational systems has been taken by reformers as a major impediment to educational progress. The power of professionals, once only the concern of right-wing groups, is now the object of concern among left and right alike. Community control, tuition voucher plans and free schools are all alternatives that have been proposed to weaken the autonomy educational professionals have enjoyed in the past.

These are significant changes in the politics of education in the United States, but they should not be taken as signs that the British model will become dominant here. In the first place, race conflict cannot be quite the equivalent of class conflict, especially when the subordinate racial group is only about ten percent of the population. The support of this group does not provide a broad enough political base to build a broad partisan movement. Pressure group tactics and *ad hoc* alliances, however inadequate, must serve as the only substitutes available. Secondly, the institutional differences between the two countries remain. To be sure, greater centralization of financing may occur, particularly if teacher unions continue to gain in strength, and court suits to equalize financing are successful. The property tax may disappear, and with it will go the citizen participation that surrounds tax and bond referenda. The increasing capacities of the Office of Education may eventually make that institution a potent shaper of educational policy. Yet the traditions of local control run deep, are supported by a decentralized party system, by the federal arrangements written into the Constitution, and by the separation of school boards from other municipal agencies. As long as these decentralized, fragmented institutions remain, educational reform efforts are likely to lack the same centralized, focused character that is typical of the partisan politics of educational reform in Britain.

15

The Impact of Federalism on Education Finance: A Comparative Analysis

David R. Cameron and Richard I. Hofferbert *

Making policy involves the distribution of social resources among arenas of public concern. Thus, policies are frequently evaluated in terms of their distributional effects—what policy arenas and which policy advocates receive a relative advantage in the allocation of outputs? That is, who gains at whose expense in the policy process?

It is not by chance that students of public authority who are concerned with patterns of distribution very often study education policy. Education policy lies at the crossroads of the economy and the polity. The education policy process involves interaction of class, religion, ethnic and linguistic conflicts. No other arena of social policy more accurately reflects patterns of social distribution which have cumulated through past resolution of these conflicts in favor of particular groups. And because educational outcomes structure the allocation of values within a society not only for the immediate period but also for future generations, no other arena of policy has been more politicized by those advocating or opposing fundamental social reform. Rokkan, for example, has ably demonstrated that the conflicts between center and periphery which emerged at critical junctures in the process of nation-building in Europe were politicized in jurisdictional disputes over the control of education.

Wherever support for education has become a politically contested issue there has been continuing experimentation and dispute over the format of public responsibility. In particular, those who perceive distributional inequities in educational systems often advocate centralization of financial responsibility. Thus, for example, much of the recent discussion about educational finance in the United States has advocated an assumption of greater financial responsibility by the American states and/or the federal

The research reported here has been supported by a grant from the National Science Foundation (GS 38031) for the study of education finance in Canada, the Federal Republic of Germany, Switzerland, and the United States. We wish to acknowledge the aid provided by the Inter-university Consortium for Political Research in this research. We are also grateful to Stefanie H. Cameron of the University of Michigan and Stephen Schechter of the Center for the Study of Federalism for several important suggestions. Reprinted from the *European Journal of Political Research*, 2, 1974, pp. 225-258, with permission of Elsevier Scientific Publishing Company, Amsterdam.

* Center for Political Studies, University of Michigan

285

government. Centralization, it is argued, may reduce the extent to which education spending mirrors territorial disparities in social resources. On the other hand, advocates of decentralization may argue that centralization does not result in any measurable improvement of disparities and may only increase the bureaucratic overload of a society and its policy-making apparatus. Although advocacy of greater or lesser centralization usually rests upon values placed on fundamental aspects of cultural pluralism, positions are often taken or rationalized in terms of assumed implications for substantive policy. The growing attraction of decentralization and the related concept of regional autonomy is amply demonstrated by the serious proposals for, and, occasionally, implementation of fundamental reforms in such formally unitary systems as Britain, Belgium, France, Italy, and Sweden. To the extent that this attraction with decentralization takes on institutional reality, it is plausible that the distributional consequences in the field of education—one of the largest arenas of domestic policy—will change.

In the face of contemporary patterns of flux in intergovernmental relations within advanced industrial nations an inquiry into the distributional consequences of these relations has more than heuristic value. In particular, it is useful to assess patterns of resource allocation to education within and across a set of nations which display wide variations in their degree of centralization. In so doing, we shall attempt to provide answers for the following questions: Is the structure of intergovernmental relations systematically associated with the allocation of resources across and within nations? Do nations which are more centralized spend more, both in absolute terms and relative to their resource base, than decentralized nations? And, more importantly, do nations which are more centralized distribute funds for education more evenly than decentralized systems? Does centralization affect policies of equalization of within-nation disparities in resources? Do unitary systems, in fact, go so far as to carry out a system-wide redistribution of resources from the wealthy to the poor—from, to use Rokkan's terms, the center to the peripheries?

Previous Research Base

In recent years, comparative research has begun to suggest the probable significance for public policy of the structure of intergovernmental relations of a nation. This contrasts with the pattern of explanation which emerged from the first comparative and empirical studies of public policy variations in the American states. In these early studies, the importance of a wide set of political variables for explaining public policy was questioned. Instead, it was sometimes suggested, differences in policy were more closely associated with variations in the socioeconomic resource base and, in particular, with levels of wealth of the states than with any measurable aspects of their governmental or political structures.

As the technology and domain of inquiry expanded, however, initial conclusions about the importance of socioeconomic variables, relative to political variables were refined, elaborated, and in some cases, rejected. For example, it has been found that policy outputs across several arenas tended to cluster together, and some of these clusters—in particular, one composed of welfare and education policy outputs—are as closely associated with political attributes as they are with measures of socioeconomic structure.

The suggestion that certain elements of the states' political structure are as important as those of the socioeconomic environment has been supported by several studies. Walker, for example, found that the propensity of American states to adopt new programs in a variety of fields was in part dependent on the degree of equity in the apportionment of representation. Cowart found that indicators of the electoral process were more closely associated with expenditures in a new program area—the Anti-Poverty Program—than were various indicators of socioeconomic environment. Similarly, Boaden found, in an analysis of English county boroughs, that partisan control of municipal councils was significantly related to education policy outputs.

Only with recent development of comparative subnational research has the term "political variables" come to include a specification of the structure of intergovernmental relations. Yet, in spite of the underdeveloped nature of theory in this field, various studies have suggested that the pattern of intergovernmental relations may be of critical importance for policy, since it establishes the framework within which all other variables —political and socioeconomic—operate. This conclusion emerges from three modestly different analytical settings: comparative urban research, single-country subnational studies, and some cross-national research.

Several comparative urban studies have concluded that one must examine the relation of localities to higher levels of government in order to understand patterns of urban policy. Kesselman, for example, sketches a system of interaction by which urban policy makers are constrained by officials at other levels of government. More importantly for our purposes here, this system of interaction is defined to a large extent by the manner in which financial responsibility is allocated among levels of government. Thus the variations across nations in, for example, the degree of centralization, may explain why urban policies vary comparatively. This is one of the conclusions which emerges from Anton and Williams' comparative study of housing policy in Stockholm and London. They suggest that differences in residential class segregation in the two cities may be a function of Stockholm's greater centralization in housing policy making.

This theme has been stated most forcefully by Jacob, Teune and their colleagues in their study of community activism in America, India, Yugo-slavia, and Poland. The authors concluded that the explanation of community activism was system specific rather than universal, largely because structures of national/local responsibility dominated the character of the explanatory variables. That is, national policies, such as the allocation of most funding responsibility for education to the American localities or the emphasis placed on the development of the new western territories by the Polish government, determined the relationships within each nation among the local level sociopolitical and policy variables.

The general conclusion to be drawn from these comparative urban studies is that policy outputs at one level of government are critically influenced by the structure of relations among several levels of government. Variation in urban policy outputs across several nations is a result of the differences among them in the structure of intergovernmental relations.

Several studies in single nations have drawn conclusions similar to those emerging from comparative urban research. A recent study by Simeon of federal-provincial relations in Canada addresses the question: "What are the consequences of federal structures and institutions for the processes of policy-making?" Simeon concludes his analysis of Canada's peculiar form of executive federalism, to use Smiley's term, with the suggestion that this form of intergovernmental relations produces patterns of policy that differ from those which would occur in either a more centralized system or a federal system with little coordination across levels of government.

The significance of intergovernmental relations has emerged from another single nation study of policy making in a federal system. We have analyzed patterns of change over time in education policy in the American states and have found that the strongest determinant of progressive policy change was a measure of the increase in the share of financial responsibility carried by the states rather than the localities. The fact that the analysis was longitudinal, treating degree of change as the dependent variable, considerably strengthens the validity of the causal inferences relating intergovernmental relations and public policy.

A third type of study—that conducted with nations as units—has also affirmed the significance of intergovernmental relations and, in particular, the impact of centralization on educational policy. Pryor has considered the extent to which centralization, viewed as a systemic attribute setting the background for the policy process, affects various public consumption expenditures. He found that the proportion of national wealth devoted to education was greater in a set of seven centralized systems, and that centralization was in fact the only significant determinant of variations across the nations in the proportion. On the other hand, Pryor found that total allocations to education did not seem to vary between the centralized and non-centralized systems. While shortcomings in Pryor's analysis make these conclusions speculative at best, the mode of research is innovative and is particularly useful for assessing the impact of intergovernmental relations. As we shall suggest, however, it is necessary to combine Pryor's type of analysis between dichotomized sets of nations with the approach of those concentrating on within-nation patterns by means of urban and subnational data.

Hypotheses

The existing research base, summarized in the preceding section, provides a provocative point of departure for our research. The core message is that the patterns of allocation of public resources, for example, funds for education, may be critically affected by the structure of relations among levels of government. More particularly, the distributional consequences of education policy may systematically differ across sets of nations as a function of variance in intergovernmental structures. The impact of these structures on public policy may be neither nation-specific nor comparable across all nations. Instead, distributions of resources to education may be comparable within a set of systems, e.g., decentralized systems, and yet markedly different from those in systems with a different structure of intergovernmental relations. Whereas Jacob, Teune and their colleagues were forced by their findings to abjure cross-national generalizations, it may be possible, by maximizing variance on one promising facet of several systems, to move a step beyond system-specific conclusions.

The surest means of assessing the impact of different structures of intergovernmental relations is by maximizing the variance on this systematic property across the set of nations under investigation. We do this by contrasting the patterns of resource distribution in certain centralized systems with those found in a particular sub-set of decentralized systems—federal nations. The choice of constitutionally defined federal systems highlights a key distinction—that the important difference in intergovernmental relations is not simply that between *de facto* centralized and decentralization but that between unitary and federal systems of government. Two federal (or unitary) systems may manifest different degrees of allocation of financial responsibility to the central government and yet the two may not differ in any measurable way in the structure of intergovernmental relations (e.g., Austria and Switzerland as seen in Table 15-1). On the other hand two systems, one of which is unitary and the other federal, may have very different structures of intergovernmental relations in spite of comparable levels of fiscal centralization (e.g., Norway and Austria).

Federalism differs from unitary systems in the reservation of certain specified or implied public policy responsibilities to authorities within intermediary subnational governments. The decentralization of policy making characteristics of federal systems recognizes internal diversity in the sociopolitical composition of territorial jurisdictions and the right of these jurisdictions to use their resources in different ways. The nature of federal systems thus insures considerable variation in policy performance among subnational units. In fact, the opportunity for such variation is part of the inherent constitutional logic of this system of government.

Public education in federal systems has, perhaps more than any other policy, been the preserve of subnational governments (which have frequently chosen to pass much of the financial responsibility on to municipalities). In contrast to the implied, and occasionally explicit, limits in federations on the central government's educational role, the growth of public policy authority of the national government in unitary systems has more often than not been fought out precisely in the arena of education. Thus while subnational and local dominance characterizes education policy in federal systems, national government dominance generally characterizes unitary nations' education policy. As may be seen in Table 15-1, the constitutionally federal systems—Austria, Canada, Germany, Switzerland, and the United States—are generally characterized by a much lower central fiscal role than the unitary systems. There are notable exceptions, however, and we shall consider these later in our analysis.

Since differences in the structure of intergovernmental relations between federal and unitary systems seem to be clear in the field of education policy, we hypothesize that the distributional consequences for public policy are markedly different in these two types of systems. This is the

Table 15-1

Percent of Total Educational Expenses, 1965, from Central Government in Eighteen Nations

Nation	% Central Government	Nation	% Central Government
Federal Republic		Denmark	66
of Germany	3	Sweden	67
Switzerland	9	Finland	67
Canada	10	Netherlands	81
United States	12	Belgium	81
Norway	50	Italy	81
United Kingdom	57	France	83
Austria	59	Portugal	90
Luxembourg	61	Ireland	91
Spain	63		

Source: The education data were obtained from World Survey of Education, *Vol. V: Educational Policy, Legislation, and Administration* (Paris: UNESCO, 1971).

fundamental hypothesis underlying our analysis. We shall seek confirmation by testing a series of derivative hypotheses about the nature of the difference between education policy outputs in federal and non-federal systems. In so doing we shall be able to provide at least a partial answer to the following question: What differences for public policy does federalism make?

One of the most important aspects of education policy, and one which might vary in federal and non-federal systems, involves the aggregate size of funds allocated to this policy area, relative to the resource base of the nation. There is a widespread view that more of a nation's wealth is allocated to education in centralized than in decentralized systems. Pryor suggests several reasons why this should be so. In centralized systems, he argues, there is greater hierarchic control and unity of budgetary organs, greater comparability of budgets and thus greater policy emulation across nations, thereby heightening the capacity to concentrate resources in such fundamental policy areas as education. In discussing the relation of increasing affluence and centralization Peacock and Wiseman infer that greater centralization will result in greater allocations of funds for the following reasons: centralization is both a product and cause of the development of uniform standards of policy; it enables government to overcome problems which transcend or are external to local governments; and it allows a greater reliance on more efficient, i.e., wealth elastic, revenue systems. In addition, Heidenheimer has suggested that the very nature of decision making in a federal system—the myriad of decision makers and policy making institutions—contributes to the fragmentation of effort by national advocacy groups and the entrenchment at the subnational level of forces which resist reform. In contrast, centralization tends to produce an integration of academic and bureaucratic experts, advocacy groups, and national policy makers. Finally, one might assume that a relatively large central government role reflects a broad national consensus in support of the policy—a carry-over from the nineteenth century struggle for national integration which prompted the assertion of central government responsibility for education in the first place. Thus we hypothesize that:

H_1: The greater the central government's financial responsibility for education the greater the funds expended on education in the total system, relative to the resource base of the system.

As noted earlier and illustrated in Table 15-1, however, fiscal decentralization and constitutional federalism are not necessarily identical. The relative decentralization of England and Norway, compared to the other constitutionally unitary systems, and the centralization of the Austrian federation are the most notable deviators. One may argue that, irrespective of the level of government doing the spending, that the formal autonomy of multiple decision points implicit in federalism will have an overall conservative effect upon aggregate educational spending. Therefore, it is reasonable to test a sub-hypothesis of the first proposition, namely:

H_{1a}: Federal systems allocate less to education, relative to their resource base, than do unitary systems.

Although the question of the impact of federal and unitary structures of government on the level of education spending of whole nations is interesting, this is only one aspect of the distribution question. A more important aspect, and one which lies at the heart of the problem of distributional inequities, involves the patterns of allocation within nations. There are, of course, many standards by which the equity of distribution might be measured. One of the most meaningful, although certainly not the only standard, is the pattern of variation in the allocation of funds for education among the territorial jurisdictions within each nation. Since the distinction between federal and unitary systems involves the question of territorial jurisdictions, it is plausible that within-nation variation in outputs may be strongly related to differences in the structure of intergovernmental relations.

Federalism insures considerable variation in policy performance among the subnational units. Not only are there multiple layers of authority and numerous decision points, but decision makers at the subnational level have substantial autonomy. The effect of multiple levels and units of decision making, each characterized by a degree of autonomy, is likely to be the perpetuation of policy diversity in federal systems. The overall effect would be wide territorial variation in the total funds allocated to education. In contrast, the presence of a strong central role in funding education reduces the multiplicity of decision points. Centralization should encourage, in contrast to the situation in federal systems, uniformity and equalization of outputs across the nation. Thus we hypothesize that:

H_2: Unitary systems manifest less relative variation than do federal systems in educational expenditures across the nation's subnational jurisdictions.

The structure of intergovernmental relations may affect not only the magnitude of intranational variation in spending, but also the extent to which this variation is socioeconomically constrained. Federalism may result in a pattern of allocation which is, in terms of the entire system, constrained by variation in resource bases across the subnational decision units. It is common for subnational (e.g., state, province, canton) decision makers in a federal system to implement partial equalization programs to compensate for resource disparities of municipalities or local subdivisions within their jurisdiction. Subnational governments usually attempt to reduce variations across localities in total allocations to education. Furthermore, federal governments sometimes attempt to reduce variations across the subnational units. However, national government in most federal systems is responsible for only a small portion of all funds allocated, their equalization programs are partial at best, and much of their funding is allocated on a strict per capita basis quite irrespective of within-nation disparities in resource bases. Thus public policy outputs may, with only slight adjustments, mirror existing disparities within a nation in, for example, levels of wealth. In contrast, nations with major funding from central governments, granting little autonomy to intermediate levels, may produce policy outputs which are less constrained by intranational resource variations. That is, internal variations in policy outputs which do occur across territorial units of unitary systems may be less closely associated with internal variations in socioeconomic structure and, in particular, levels of wealth, than is the case in federal systems. As a result, the policy process in non-federal systems may effect a more territorially equitable distribution of allocations, thereby equalizing intranational disparities in social resource base. Accordingly we hypothesize that:

H$_3$: Variations in educational expenditure within non-federal systems are less closely associated with subnational disparities in socioeconomic resource base than in federal systems.

These hypotheses preface our consideration of the impact of federalism or non-federalism on the distribution of educational funds within nations. As was suggested earlier, one important facet of the distribution pattern is whether certain areas benefit at the expense of other areas in the allocation of education funds. If the structure of intergovernmental relations, and more precisely the distinction between federal and unitary systems, is related systematically to public policy, then surely the patterns of relative advantage should differ in the two systems. We need to see to what degree federalism results in an advantage, in terms of cumulative spending by all levels of government, for the richer areas of a nation. Is total spending higher in industrial than in agrarian areas? To what degree is education spending higher in the more commercialized, tertiary-dominated urban centers of a nation? If either type of governmental system results in a relative advantage to the urban industrial and/or wealthy commercial centers then the impact of policy is to mirror social disparities and to perpetuate the inequalities of treatment in a system. That is, less would be allocated for each student's education in the non-industrial and non-commercial peripheries than would be in their opposites, thereby discriminating according to residential location. On the other hand, systems in which total educational allocations are distributed in relatively equal amounts among the socioeconomically disadvantaged and the wealthier areas tend, by this equalization, to compensate for territorially based social disparities.

Finally, the impact of public policy may be not only to *equalize* distributions but to effect a system-wide *redistribution* of social resources. That is, education allocations in one or both types of systems may give a relative *advantage* to the most socioeconomically deprived areas of a nation.

If it is true, as the previous hypotheses suggest, that federalism results in a system of expenditures which is to a considerable extent constrained by social resource disparities across the subnational units, then we expect policy outputs to favor the most advantaged areas in federal systems. Both the industrial and the commercial centers, and in particular the wealthiest areas, will receive relatively larger allocations. In contrast, in unitary systems, where outputs are hypothesized to be less constrained by areal disparities in social resources, the impact of policy would be to equalize distributions, and possibly to redistribute resources from the wealthiest areas to the poorer, non-industrial, non-commercial and rural areas. Thus we hypothesize that:

H$_4$: Unitary systems tend to compensate for disparities in socioeconomic resource base by effecting redistribution of resources to the non-industrial, non-commercial, and poorest areas. In contrast, allocations in federal systems are non-equalizing and tend to mirror these disparities.

Findings

Federalism and Education Allocations Across Nations

The first major hypothesis suggests that nations in which financial responsibility for education is relatively centralized will allocate more of available social resources to education than will decentralized systems. In order to test this proposition, nation-level data for the eighteen countries of western Europe and North America have been analyzed. Most of these nations are, by world standards, relatively wealthy and industrialized. By limiting our analysis to this subset and by treating the level of expenditures relative to the level of national income as the dependent variable, we have attempted to control for the overwhelming relation between levels of expenditure and levels of wealth which has been reported by most cross-national studies.

In Table 15-2, the correlations are presented for these eighteen nations among attributes of their systems of education finance and the proportion of national income devoted to education. H_1 is clearly rejected. Nations with a relatively large central government role in education funding devote less of their national wealth than do those nations in which subnational and local governments have predominant financial responsibility. The relation between central government role and the dependent variable is certainly not overwhelming. Yet the fact that the relationship between these two variables is slight at best, and in fact in the contrary direction (i.e.,

Table 15-2

Correlation of Educational Spending as Percent of National Income with Scope of Levels of Government, 1965

Percent of all education funds from:	% National Income Spent on Education 1965
Central government	−.17
Subnational and Local governments	.26
Subnational	−.01
Local	.54

a negative sign) clearly suggests that the type of financing system may, in terms of national allocations, have no significant policy impact. To the contrary, the most significant attribute of the funding system is the role of localities. This role, it should be noted, is obviously large in federal systems. However, certain unitary systems such as those of Britain and Scandinavia assign as much responsibility to the localities as do federal systems.

In order to test the subordinate hypothesis, H_{1a}, which asserts that constitutionally federal systems in particular tend to allocate less of their national resources to education than unitary systems (which is not, we have noted, the same as testing the impact of mere fiscal centralization), we created an index of policy effort relative to level of centralization. By regressing the proportion of national wealth devoted to education upon the proportion of funds deriving from the central government, the effect of fiscal centralization is held constant. If the hypothesis is true, the residuals from this regression—which, when standardized, compose the index— should cluster the federal nations together. In particular, the residuals for the federal systems should form a distinct group at the negative pole of the index. This would confirm the suggestion that these systems are, in comparison with unitary systems of government, relative under-achievers in terms of total distributions of national wealth to education.

Table 15-3 presents the effort/centralization index. There is some confirmation of the hypothesis, although it is not primarily the federal systems but rather those of the Iberian peninsula which are the major under-achievers. The European federal systems—Germany, Switzerland, and Austria—do cluster together and allocate considerably less to education than do most of the nations of northern Europe. On the other hand, federal systems do not all behave alike. In particular, those of North America differ from those of Europe in their allocations to education. In fact, if one were to exclude Spain and Portugal, Canada and Germany—two decidedly "federal" systems—compose the two poles of the index.

The difference between Canada and Germany suggests that both, but Canada in particular, may be deviant cases. Why is it that Canada out-performs not only other federal systems but all the unitary systems of Europe—in marked contrast to Germany's performance? The data in

Table 15-3

Index of Education Effort Relative to Degree of Centralization of Education Finance [a]

	Index of Effort/Centralization Ratio
Canada [b]	1.27
Netherlands	1.17
Finland	0.98
Denmark	0.97
Sweden	0.92
Italy	0.56
Norway	0.38
Luxembourg	0.38
United Kingdom	0.36
United States [b]	0.15
Ireland	−0.12
Belgium	−0.17
France	−0.44
Austria [b]	−0.53
Switzerland [b]	−0.70
Germany [b]	−1.13
Portugal	−1.92
Spain	−2.13

[a] Effort is measured by taking percent of national income allocated to education. Index is obtained by regressing Effort on percent of education revenues deriving from central government.
[b] Constitutionally federal systems.

Table 15-4 suggest several explanations for the contrast between Canada and Germany. Education consumes twice as large a portion of total governmental budgets in Canada. It would appear that a major reason involves the much greater development of higher education in Canada. Any explanation must be somewhat speculative, but it seems that some of the differences in policy may flow from Canada's relatively greater flexibility in financing education.

The two systems differ markedly in the extent to which non-central, and in particular provincial and Länder, governments changed their scope of financial responsibility in a five year period in the mid-1960s. In Canada the provinces have moved into the field of education as part of a broader assertion of provincial responsibility. In Germany, however, the scope of financial authority has remained inflexible. Municipalities continued in the middle 1960s to have no share in funding higher education while that of the Länder has dropped. The greater financial flexibility of Canadian federalism, as manifested by its ability to respond to increased demand for higher education in the 1960s, may be a product of the greater institutionalization of intergovernmental coordination. In contrast to Germany, where a Bund-Länder Commission for Education Planning came into effect only in 1970, Canada has had throughout the last decade a form of intergovernmental coordination in the Federal-Provincial Conference. Through this latter body, a system of revenue sharing has been created, based largely on wealth-elastic categories such as personal and corporate income. Flexibility, in the sense of adjusting the funding shares of the various levels

Table 15-4

A Comparison of Attitudes of the German and Canadian Education Systems

	Canada	Germany
Percent of government expenditures for public education, 1965	23.6	10.9
Percent of the population age 20-24 in higher education	30.1	11.3
Change 1963-1968 in non-central government percentage in funding higher education	+7.6	−3.5
Change 1963-1968 in province/land percentage in funding higher education	+19.8	−3.5

Source: Data from OECD, *Reviews of National Policies for Education: Germany* (Paris: OECD, 1972), p. 132; and *Education Statistics: A Review from 1960-61 to 1970-71* (Ottawa: Statistics Canada, 1973), pp. 178, 493-495, 500, 502.

of government, is assured by the quinquennial re-negotiations provided by the Fiscal Agreements Act. Of major importance, from the view of the large allocation of education funds relative to national income, is that these negotiated arrangements have contained sophisticated systems of equalization grants from the federal government to the provinces, particularly to Quebec and the Atlantic Provinces. The institutionalization in Canada of a system of intergovernmental coordination which provided revenue sharing to aid poorer Provinces and periodic adjustment of funding responsibilities stands in marked contrast to the situation in Germany. In the latter, systems of intergovernmental equalization, renegotiation, and adjustment of financial shares remain largely non-existent.

Federalism and Education Allocations Within Nations

Questions of the magnitude of aggregate national education funding are interesting. However, the thrust of debate over the impact of structures of intergovernmental relations (and in particular the differences between federal and unitary systems) is aimed at patterns of distribution within nations. Our second hypothesis suggested that there is less variation in education expenditures across the territorial units of a unitary system than among those of a federal system. In order to test this and subsequent hypotheses, patterns of within-nation variation have been examined in four federal systems (Canada, Germany, Switzerland, and the United States) and compared with those in four unitary systems (England, the Netherlands, Norway, and Sweden). Austria was excluded from the analysis on the grounds that the large central share (59 percent) and lack of legislative and policy making autonomy in the field of education make it an atypical federal system, at least in this policy area. The choice of the four non-federal systems was somewhat more complex.[a] Table 15-5 presents various data on the financial aspects of education in the four non-federal and four federal systems considered here.

If our second hypothesis is valid, the non-federal systems should have

---

[a] We have used data on expenditures per pupil except for Switzerland, Norway and Sweden where pupil data were unavailable and per capita data were substituted. Except for Sweden and the Netherlands, where 1965 data are used, the time point is 1966. We wish to express our gratitude to several individuals who supplied subnational data in the non-federal systems: M. F. Stonefrost of the Institute of Municipal Treasurers and Accountants in England, Terje Sande of the University of Bergen, Margareta Askeland of the Statistiska Centralbyrån in Sweden, and J. Ch. W. Verstege of the Central Bureau voor de Statistiek in the Netherlands.

The subnational units are as follows: 50 American states, 10 German Länder, 10 Canadian provinces, 25 Swiss cantons, 20 Norwegian fylker, 25 Swedish län, 11 Dutch provinces, and 45 English geographic counties.

Table 15-5

Percent of Total Education Expenditures by Source, 1965

	Central	Subnational	Local and Private	% National Income, Education 1965
Non-Federal				
England	57	0	43	6.4
Netherlands	81	0	19	7.6
Norway	50	2	48	6.5
Sweden	67	2	31	7.3
Federal				
Canada	10	46	44	8.5
Germany	3	68	29	4.3
Switzerland	9	47	44	5.0
United States	12	29	59	6.5

Source: The education data were obtained from World Survey of Education, *Vol. V: Educational Policy, Legislation, and Administration* (Paris: UNESCO, 1971).

considerably lower degrees of intranational variation in educational expenditures per pupil than the federal systems. In order to test this, coefficients of relative variation ([standard deviation/mean] × 100) have been computed for total education spending per pupil in the subnational units of the eight nations. The results, in Table 15-6, suggest that, although there are some exceptions to the rule, federal systems display considerable intranational variation in total funds allocated to education. Conversely, unitary systems and, perhaps surprisingly, particularly that form in existence outside Scandinavia, seem to moderate their inter-regional disparities. Thus the second hypothesis is confirmed.

In order to test the third and fourth hypotheses, relating to the structure of intergovernmental relations and the degree and patterns of socioeconomic constraint of education policy, it is necessary to develop measures of within-nation variations in resource base. These measures must be parsimonious and cross-nationally comparable and yet also reflect unique constellations of social differentiation likely to constitute political cleavages in each system. That is, they must be equivalent while still accommodating unique system-specific features associated with racial, religious, ethnic, and linguistic variations in the nations.

In order to develop measures which are both cross-nationally equivalent and yet system sensitive, a multidimensional perspective of social structure has been utilized. By means of factor analysis of a set of socioeconomic and cultural attributes of subnational units in several nations, Hofferbert, et al. have derived two independent indices of social structural variation.

Table 15-6

The Intra-National Variation in Educational Expenditures per Pupil, 1965-66

	Coefficient of Relative Variation [a]
Non-Federal Systems	
England	7.4
Netherlands	5.2
Norway	11.9
Sweden	16.9
Federal Systems	
Canada	29.0
Germany	15.6
Switzerland	26.8
United States	20.3

[a] $\dfrac{\text{Standard deviation}}{\text{mean}} \times 100$

One, labeled industrialization, traced the differences among the units in the extent of secondary sector employment and production, and, conversely, the differences in the size and degree of reliance on primary sector activity. The second dimension, presently labeled integration, is more complex in so far as it is independent of the measure of primary-secondary differentiation. This second dimension does nevertheless trace an important pattern of variation, although it is one generally ignored by many development theorists. It traces the difference across subnational units in the attributes of the most "modern" sectors of society—in this day and age, measures which are often associated with post-industrial society: tertiary sector dominance, commercialization (including commercialized agriculture), higher education, employment in the professions, media diffusion, and personal affluence. What makes the integration dimension particularly interesting, however, is the juxtaposition of the variation across a nation in these modern and post-industrial attributes upon a variation based on the ethnic, linguistic and religious cleavages of a society. It is precisely those areas of least tertiary sector development, and least commercialization and affluence, which have often contained relatively large groups of individuals who by their language, religion or their ethnicity constitute national minorities. And as a result it has been these areas which have most often been the site of confrontations against secularization and commercialization, and which have manifested regional defenses against what Rokkan has termed the "central nation-building culture."

The essential utility of the two-dimensional indexing of social structure is the ability to move to a more sophisticated conception of "modernity" or "development" than is customary in much comparative research. The factory/farm distinction can thus be viewed separately from the conceptually richer and more distinct index of post-industrial/traditional or center/periphery dimension which we have here and elsewhere labeled "integration." Integration—in the sense of a national network of interaction between remote actors and relative strangers—is not necessarily or historically dependent upon industrialization. The advantage of the factor analytic technique (as revealed in Appendix 15A) is its ability to approximate cross-national comparability despite variations in measurement accuracy of specific indicators.

Appendix 15A presents the factor structures for the dimensions of industrialization and integration. By comparing the composition of these dimensions one can determine the extent to which they represent cross-nationally equivalent patterns of within-nation variation. The most highly loaded variables on the industrialization dimension are ones which trace the occupational and sectoral attributes associated with manufacturing or industry, urban work force, size of firm, etc. Wealth tends to be related to this dimension, but only moderately so. The non-industrial areas tend, not surprisingly, to be those with the most predominant primary sectors (although not necessarily agrarian, as the Norwegian case suggests).

It is more difficult to assess the cross-national comparability of the integration dimension, precisely because it does contain the complex juxtaposition of "traditional" and "modern" aspects of society. However, one notes certain features common to all. The highest loaded variables are associated with affluence: commercialization either in the sense of occupation, as in the case of the Netherlands, Norway, Sweden, and Switzerland, or in the sense of exchange, as in the case in the United States (retail and farm sales) and Canada (farm sales); professionalization, as is the case with the loading of doctors per thousand in several nations; and, where available, education, particularly higher education. Recalling Bell's emphasis on the importance of the role of services and the production of knowledge in post-industrial society, it seems clear that this dimension traces within these nations, a phenomenon which has heretofore been treated solely in terms of whole nations.

We continue to label the dimension "integration," however, in recognition of the particular salience of those system-specific cleavages which distinguish areas in terms of those attributes discussed in the preceding paragraph. The culture features of integration are ethnicity in Canada and the United States, language in Switzerland, Canada and Norway, and religion in Canada, Switzerland, Germany, Norway, Sweden and the Netherlands. It should be noted that the salient cleavage in terms of integration in the Netherlands is that of no religion versus Catholicism and orthodox Calvinism rather than Protestantism versus Catholicism. One should also note that, of the attributes of non-integrated areas, religion seems to be the most cross-nationally prevalent (although the other bases of differentiation may be more liable to produce internal conflict) and that, not surprisingly, federal systems (and in particular Canada) tend to contain a complex multiplicity of these features of cultural pluralism.

The factor scores obtained for each of the subnational units on these dimensions seem intuitively plausible. For example, industrialization for Norway contrasts the fylker of Ostfold, Oslo, Buskerud, Vestfold and Telemark from the fishing-dominant areas in the north. Integration contrasts Oslo and Bergen with the fylker of Oppland, Hordaland, Søgn og Fjordane, and Nord Trøndelag. Those for Switzerland contrast, on industrialization, the cantons of Solothurn and Schaffhausen with Valais and Ticino while integration contrasts Zurich, Geneve, Basel-Stadt and Vaud with Uri, Schwyz, Obwald and Appenzell Inner Rhoden. Industrialization for England contrasts Staffordshire, Warwickshire and Yorkshire West Riding with Cornwall, Lincoln and Shropshire, while integration contrasts London, Surrey, Sussex, Oxfordshire and Berkshire with Durham and Northumberland in the north, and the rural west. And the dimensions for the Netherlands contrast the heavily industrial (and Catholic) provinces of Noord-Brabant and Limburg with the rural provinces of Zeeland and Friesland. Integration contrasts Noord-holland, Zuid-holland, and, to a lesser extent, Utrecht with the rest of the country.

The factor scores for these two dimensions allow a parsimonious but comparable measurement of variations in resource base within each nation. Thus by investigating the intranational relationships of the scores on these dimensions and total educational expenditures per pupil it is possible to test the third and fourth hypotheses.

According to the third hypothesis, variations in educational expenditures in federal systems are much more constrained by variations in resource base than are those in non-federal systems. A relatively simple way of testing this proposition, once one has appropriate measures, is to compare the coefficients of determination (R^2) obtained for each nation with the expenditures per pupil predicted by the two social structural dimensions. If educational expenditures in non-federal systems are territorially non-discriminatory this should be manifested in markedly lower coefficients than those found in federal systems. This seems to be the message of Table 15-7, bearing out the third hypothesis. There are, however, some important differences among the non-federal systems. In particular, Norway and Sweden display a lower degree of constraint than does the Netherlands. However, as will be seen shortly this simple measure masks as much as it suggests.

These differences between federal and non-federal systems in the degree of intranational variation and socioeconomic constraint are surely im-

Table 15-7

Coefficients of Determination for Intra-National Variations in Educational Expenditures per Pupil, 1965-66 [a]

	Coefficient of Determination
Non-Federal Systems	
England	31
Netherlands	73
Norway	22
Sweden	17
Federal Systems	
Canada	69
Germany	69
Switzerland	80
United States	58

[a] Percent of the variance explained by industrialization and integration.

portant. Nevertheless, the critical question from the perspective of the impact of policy on the equity of distribution involves the patterns of relative advantage in the two types of systems. The fourth hypothesis suggested that distribution in non-federal systems compensates poorer areas for disparities in resource base, while distributions in federal systems tend to mirror, and thus perpetuate, these disparities. Hypothesis four can be tested by investigating the relation between the total per pupil education expenditures and the two socioeconomic dimensions.

If it is true that non-federal systems compensate for resource disparities one would expect to find the relationship between expenditures and these dimensions to be moderate. In contrast the relationships, especially that involving the integration dimension, should be strong and positive in federal systems. This is indeed the general message of Table 15-8. Non-federal systems may effect either an equalization of allocations—possibly reflected in near-zero relationships—or even a system-wide redistribution of funds—reflected in negative relationships between the dimensions and the dependent variable, indicative of greatest expenditure levels in the least advantaged areas. Regardless of which pattern is found in the non-federal systems, it is critical to our fundamental hypothesis regarding the consequentiality of intergovernmental relations that the relationships of the dimensions to the spending variable are comparable for each system of government and that the two patterns of distribution advantage are distinctive.

Table 15-8 presents the simple correlations between the two dimensions

Table 15-8

Correlations of Industrialization and Integration with
Total Educational Expenditures Per Pupil, 1965-66 ᵃ

	Industrialization	Integration
Non-Federal Systems		
England	−.13	.54
Netherlands	−.85	−.04
Norway	−.46	−.07
Sweden	−.41	−.02
Federal Systems		
Canada	.39	.74
Germany	−.41	.73
Switzerland	.22	.87
United States	.23	.73

ᵃ Pearsonian product-moment correlations.

of industrialization and integration and the spending variable in each of the eight nations. These data confirm the fourth hypothesis. They provide strong evidence that the patterns of distribution differ systematically according to the structure of intergovernmental relations. In particular, three of the four federal systems effect a distributional advantage for those areas which are industrialized. More important, in view of its closer association with wealth, is the very strong positive relationship between integration and spending (the range in the coefficients is from 0.73 to 0.87). Quite clearly, federal systems in their distributions in this policy area tend to mirror and thus perpetuate the wealth-related disparities of the nation. In spite of the variability in proportion of wealth devoted to education found in Table 15-2, all four nations reflect a nearly identical pattern of relationship in this, the fiscally most important domestic policy area in these systems.

The non-federal systems, on the other hand, differ significantly from the federal pattern. And with the exception of England, all three non-federal systems display a similar pattern of distribution. The impact of public policy in these systems is, in distribution terms, to equalize the within-nation disparities associated with integration. While the federal systems perpetuate the disparities and the inequalities which are the inheritance of the historic patterns of social cleavage and wealth, non-federal systems tend to compensate for these disparities. And one also finds that again with the exception of England the three non-federal nations effect a system-wide distribution to the least industrialized areas—the fishing dominant north in Norway, the timber and agrarian north of Sweden, and heavily Protestant north of the Netherlands. The comparable patterns of distribution in these three non-federal systems—the equalization of integration-related disparities and the redistribution in favor of the non-industrial areas—seem to suggest that the most conscious criterion of compensation involves differential levels of industrialization. This may reflect institutionalization in the party system and the policy arena of advocacy groups—such as primary sector based unions and trade associations.

There is, in the comparability of the patterns of distribution of Sweden, Norway, and the Netherlands an intriguing phenomenon. Since the pattern of distribution in these nations is not socioeconomically constrained in the manner common to the federal systems, it is particularly interesting to note the similarity in this pattern, and especially the nearly identical correlates displayed by the two Scandinavian systems. It has often been suggested that nations may emulate their neighbors by borrowing policy program innovations. However, the equally interesting question of whether nations "borrow" the criteria by which public policy effects a redistribution or equalization of regional disparities has seldom if ever been addressed. And yet these data clearly imply the presence of similar criteria.

In the discussion of the three non-federal systems, England has thus far been excluded. This nation represents for the non-federal systems something of a deviant case just as Canada did for the federal systems in the cross-national analysis. When one considers the pattern of distribution, and particularly the pattern vis-a-vis the wealth-related integration dimension it seems that England behaves in a sense more as a federal than a non-federal system (a finding which we suspect would be even more noticeable if the analysis had included Scotland and Wales). While central government grants to the Local Education Authorities—the administrative counties and county boroughs which together form the geographic counties—do manifest the non-federal pattern of giving a relative advantage to the least industrialized areas ($r = -.40$), it is also true that the total allocations tend to be greatest in the most integrated areas, i.e., in London, Surrey, East Sussex and Hertfordshire.

In one sense, this finding should not be surprising. While England lacks a meaningful intermediate policy-making jurisdiction comparable to that found in federal systems, there is nevertheless a myriad of decision points —including not only boroughs and counties but also excepted districts and divisional executives—and the net effect when combined with the tradition of strong local government has been to fragment decision-making authority in a manner quite distinct from the other three non-federal systems. England's rather unique, semi-federal pattern of distribution also reflects the important changes made in the 1958 Local Government Act. In this act, the previous system of central government grant aid was changed from a percentage equalization to a general grant system. The new system weighted local need by the age and number of children but it did not include, as the former system had, an equalization of the variation in local property values. The system was improved somewhat in the Local Government Act of 1966 which replaced the general grants by rate support grants. That is, the new formula for aid to the LEAs included a partial equalization of the differences in yield which occurred with identical rates. Nevertheless, because equalization is pegged to average rather than peak tax yields, there is equalization only up to the national average and "above average authorities in terms of resources still do exceptionally favorably.

Conclusion

Drawing on the implications suggested by several recent studies in comparative public policy analysis, we have attempted to determine the impact of federalism on the equity of distributions of education policy outputs. The fundamental hypothesis underlying this analysis has been that the structure of intergovernmental relations systematically affects the pattern of distribution. Several subsidiary hypotheses were tested in order to discover whether this structure, and in particular the distinction between federalism and non-federalism, affects public policy. The hypothesis was not confirmed in the cross-national analysis where, among a set of eighteen nations, the structure of intergovernmental relations was only weakly related to proportions of national wealth devoted to education. In the within-nation comparisons, based on four federal and four unitary systems, however, the hypothesized distinctions did appear. The structure of intergovernmental relations does indeed exert a strong contextual effect on the policy process. Unitary systems manifest considerably less internal variation and socioeconomic constraint on expenditures for education that do the federal systems. Most importantly, the non-federal systems compensate for the inherent disparities in resource base within the nations. They tend to equalize the wealth-related disparities associated with a dimension of sociopolitical integration while redistributing resources to the least industrialized areas. Federal systems on the other hand tend in their educational allocations to mirror and thus perpetuate the wealth-related intranational disparities. Traditional, poor, non-integrated areas—those with the greatest concentrations of religious, linguistic, and ethnic particularities—are left to their own devices. They "take advantage" of their policy autonomy by providing relatively less fiscal support for education than is available to their counterparts in the unitary nations.

The most important deviations from the systematic relation of structure of intergovernmental relations to distribution pattern are the relatively high proportion of national wealth devoted to education in Canada and the relative lack of equalization of wealth-related intranational disparities in England. The causes of both deviations can be traced to periodically negotiated legislation which alters existing patterns of intergovernmental systems of revenue sharing.

Although we find that the pattern of distribution systematically differs in the two types of systems, we have only begun to suggest why this may be so. It seems clear that one possible area of fruitful policy research will be an investigation of the criteria for equalization and redistribution within nations as well as an examination of the processes by which nations borrow and emulate these distributional criteria.

We can conclude by returning briefly to a consideration of contemporary changes in patterns of intergovernmental relations and, in particular, to the growing attraction of decentralization and quasi-federalization. It seems clear that a trade-off may be involved between the degree of local and subnational control and regional autonomy on one hand and the degree of equity in policy distributions on the other. Whatever the appeals of decentralization it seems obvious from the analysis presented here that a fundamental change in intergovernmental relations toward federalism may in fact exacerbate rather than alleviate intranational disparities in socioeconomic resources.

Appendix 15A

Factor Structures for Dimensions of Industrialization and Integration: Four Non-Federal and Four Federal Nations

Netherlands

Industrialization		Integration	
% economically active in manufacturing, '60	.89	% economically active, commerce and finance	.96
% pop. Catholic, '60	.84	Doctors/000 pop.	.85
Employees/firm, manufacturing '60	.74	Density	.84
Net migration/000 pop., '58, 1958-71	.67	% pop. no religion	.71
Average family income, '62	.62	University students/000 pop.	.70
% pop. in municipalities over 20,000, '62	.61	% pop. in municipalities over 20,000	.63
Density, '62	.44	Average family income	.59
University students/000 pop., '71	.09	% pop. Protestant	.01
Doctors/000 pop., '62	.02	Average size of farms	−.08
% economically active in commerce and finance, '60	−.17	Net migration, 1958-71	−.08
% pop. scattered (verspreide), '60	−.39	Employees/firm, manufacturing	−.29
% pop. no religion, '60	−.39	% pop. Catholic	−.30
% economically active, agriculture, '60	−.77	% economically active, manufacturing	−.47
% pop. Protestant, '60	−.85	% economically active, agriculture	−.60
Average size of farms, '59	−.86	% pop. scattered (verspreide)	−.70

England

Industrialization		Integration	
% active pop. in manufacturing, '61	.90	% pop., university educated	.82
% active pop., skilled workers, '61	.79	% active pop., employees	.64
Income/capita, '61	.55	% active pop., self-employed	.62
% active pop., employees, '61	.36	Income/capita	.53
Televisions/000 pop., '61	.16	% active pop., own-account workers	.52
% active pop. in utilities and transportation, '61	.11	Annual natural pop. increase 1951-61	.07
% farms over 1,000 acres, '64	.05	% active pop. in utilities and transportation	.06
Annual natural pop. increase, 1951-61	−.07	% active pop., manufacturing	−.07
% pop., university educated, '61	−.28	Televisions/000 pop.	−.23
% pop., born in Britain, '61	−.28	% active pop., agriculture workers	−.26
% active pop., own-account workers '61	−.41	% active pop., agriculture	−.28
% increase pop. via migration 1951-61	−.45	% farms over 1,000 acres	−.28
% active pop., self-employed, '61	−.60	% active pop., skilled workers	−.35
% active pop., agricultural workers, '61	−.71	% increase pop. via migration	−.37
% active pop., agriculture, '61	−.77	% pop., born in Britain	−.39

309

Appendix 15A (cont.)

Sweden

Industrialization		Integration	
% economically active in manufacturing, '65	.89	% economically active in commerce	.96
% economically active in secondary sector, '65	.88	Personal income/family	.95
% pop. 65, foreign immigrants, 1961-69	.68	% pop. in localities over 10,000	.93
Net migration/100 pop., '65, 1961-70	.65	% pop. 15-19 in gymnasier	.71
% pop. in localities over 10,000, '65	.23	% pop., foreign immigrants	.50
Personal income/family, '65	.11	Net migration	.37
% pop. attending Church, '64	—.02	% economically active in mining	—.06
% economically active in commerce, '65	—.08	% farms under 10 hectares	—.06
Value of forest lands & forests/capita, '66	—.17	% economically active in manufacturing	—.17
% pop. 15-19 in gymnasier, '67	—.31	% economically active in secondary sector	—.21
% pop. in sparsely populated areas, '65	—.43	% farm land, wholly owned	—.44
% economically active, mining, '65	—.45	% pop. attending Church	—.58
% economically active, agriculture and forestry, '65	—.45	Value of forests & forest lands/capita	—.69
% arable farm land, wholly owned, '66	—.52	% economically active in agriculture and forestry	—.79
% farms under 10 hectares, '66	—.65	% pop. in sparsely populated areas	—.83

Norway

Industrialization		Integration	
% economically active, manufacturing, '60	.84	% economically active in commerce	.82
% manufacturing employees in firms over 6, '60	.76	% pop. in densely populated communes over 2,000	.80
Employees/manufacturing firm, '69	.72	Doctors/000 pop.	.76
Personal income/taxpayer, '60	.63	Income/taxpayer	.72
% men 20-24 finished secondary education, '60	.62	% men 20-24 finished secondary education	.61
% pop. in densely populated areas over 2,000, '60	.53	% manufacturing employees in firms over 6	.47
Doctors/000 pop., '60	.38	Employees/manufacturing firm	.44
% economically active in commerce, '60	.32	% economically active, manufacturing	.16
% pop. members teetotalers organizations, '60	.07	% economically active, fishing	—.01
% primary pupils in schools using Nynorsk, '60	.04	% pop. in fishing dominated sparsely populated communes	—.08
% economically active, agriculture and forestry, '60	—.21	% primary pupils in schools using Nynorsk	—.77
% pop. church goers, '56	—.37	% pop. in teetotalers organization	—.79
% pop. in sparsely populated communes, '65	—.52	% pop. Church goers	—.79
% pop. in fishing-dominated sparsely populated communes, '65	—.84	% pop. in sparsely populated communes	—.81
% economically active, fishing, '60	—.87	% economically active, agriculture and forestry	—.87

Appendix 15A (cont.)

Switzerland

Industrialization		Integration	
% pop., industry & trades, '60	.96	% pop., commerce & finance	.94
% pop., factory workers, '60	.94	% taxpayers earning over 20,000 Fr.	.92
Workers/factory, '60	.69	% pop. in towns over 10,000	.91
% taxpayers earning over 20,000 Fr., '60	.21	Doctors/000 pop.	.90
		Certificats de maturite/000 pop.	.66
% pop. in towns over 10,000, '60	.19	Density	.60
Density, '60	.00	% pop. French speakers	.45
% pop., commerce & finance, '60	−.08	% pop. Italian speakers	.10
Certificats de maturita/000 pop., '64	−.10	% pop. factory workers	.08
Doctors/000 pop., '61	−.22	Workers/factory	.06
% pop. Italian speakers, '60	−.23	% pop. in industry and trades	.03
% farms under 10 hectares, '55	−.24	% farms under 10 hectares	−.46
% pop. French speakers, '60	−.35	% pop. born in same canton	−.53
% pop. Catholics, '60	−.50	% pop. Catholics	−.54
% pop., agriculture, '60	−.50	% pop., agriculture	−.77
% pop. born in same canton, '60	−.66		

Germany

Industrialization		Integration	
% economically active, manufacturing, '61	.89	% pop. in communities over 10,000	.97
% economically active, workers, '61	.88	Gross domestic product/capita	.93
Workers/manufacturing firm, '61	.84	% economically active in finance	.90
% Catholic, '61	.66	% economically active civil servants and white collar employees	.86
% economically active, civil servants and white collar employees, '61	.06	Doctors/000 pop.	.70
		Workers/manufacturing firm	.49
% pop. in communities over 10,000	−.03	% economically active, workers	−.09
Gross domestic product/capita	−.11	% pop. refugees	−.17
% economically active in primary sector, '61	−.30	% economically active in manufacturing	−.23
% economically active, banking, finance and public administration, '61	−.36	% pop. Catholic	−.56
% gross domestic product from agriculture, '60	−.46	% economically active in agriculture	−.84
Doctors/000 pop., '61	−.49	% economically active in primary sector	−.91
% pop. refugees, '61	−.66		

Appendix 15A (cont.)

United States			
Industrialization		Integration	
Value added/capita, manufacturing	.92	% population over 25, college graduates	.81
% Employed persons, manufacturing	.88	% employed persons, professions	.80
Density	.78	Income/capita	.80
% Urban	.64	Retail trades sales/capita	.77
% Population, foreign white stock	.47	% farms with products over $40,000	.76
% Employed persons, finance and insurance	.45	% employed persons, finance and insurance	.69
Newspaper circulation, copies/1,000	.44	% urban	.62
Income/capita	.43	Acreage/farm	.58
Retail trade sales/capita, '58	.13	% population, foreign white stock	.56
% employed persons, professions	.10	Newspaper circulation, copies/1,000	.34
% population over 25, college graduates	.09	Density	.14
		Value added/capita, manufacturing	−.02
% population, black	.03	% employed persons, manufacturing	−.26
% farms with products over $40,000	−.17		
Acreage/farm, '59	−.59	% employed persons, agriculture	−.34
% employed persons, agriculture	−.66	% population, black	−.62

Canada			
Industrialization		Integration	
% labor force over 15 in manufacturing, construction and mining, '61	.96	% commercial farms with sales over $10,000	.92
Value added/capita, manufacturing, '61	.91	% population 19-24 attending university	.89
Employees/manufacturing firm, '61	.90	% non-British and French stock	.88
% population in urban areas over 10,000, '61	.85	% population 1961, immigrants 1946-61	.76
% labor force over 15 in tertiary sector (services, commerce, and finance), '61	.74	Average earnings, males in labor force	.74
Net interprovincial migration, 1956-61	.62	% labor force in public administration	.48
Average earnings, males in the labor force, '61	.62	% population in urban areas over 10,000	.42
% population 1961, immigrants 1946-61	.61	% labor force in tertiary sector	.40
% population, French, '61	.47	Net interprovincial migration, 1946-61	.36
% commercial farms with sales over $10,000, '61	.29	Value added/capita, manufacturing	.26
% labor force over 15 in federal, provincial, & local administration, '61	.17	% labor force over 15 in primary sector (farming, logging, fishing)	.11
% population 19-24, attending university, '61	.10	Employees/firm	.01
% population, non-British or French stock, '61	−.12	% population, British	−.11
% population, British, '61	−.39	% labor force over 15 in manufacturing, construction & mining	−.17
% labor force over 15, farming, logging and fishing, '61	−.87	% population, French	−.64

**Part VII
Political Supports: The Socialization
of the Young**

Introduction to Part VII

Political Socialization

One of the major results of conceptualizing the school as a political system is an understanding of what it is doing with the children in shaping their political attitudes. The interaction of the young with the political system is not a new concept, of course, for to the Greeks, all of what we term "subsystems" interacted to produce the polity, and all these in turn are what created the citizen. Separation of state and church or of state and schools were inconceivable in their outlook. Much subsequent political philosophy has concerned itself with the state's role in socializing the young to right values. While, as noted in the introduction, political science in the last half-century or more had turned away from interest in the schools and the young as items of scholarly inquiry, there is one field in which it has returned in force in recent years. That is the subject of political socialization, which seeks an understanding of the formation of the child's attitudes and knowledge about the political system and his role within it. Heavily cross-referenced to the field of psychology, especially learning theory, this focus has produced a very extensive literature in a remarkably short time.

The decision to choose from that literature was consequently very difficult and was resolved by combining several utilities in a single piece. These were satisfied by the work of Sarah Liebschutz and Richard Niemi which follows, for it provides an analysis of the existing literature's main findings about political socialization processes, as well as demonstrating instructive analytical methods. This study, involving almost 900 children in 1969, tests alternative developmental models of attitude change among black and white students, in order to test the effect of a special curriculum and of the teacher's race. The development of the students of both races is found to be parallel, the curriculum (but not the teacher's race) is associated with improved self-images of the children, and the curriculum seems to create more realistic attitudes about political authorities, although fading with time. Like much research of this kind, this study finds the school to have only limited influence in shaping the total cognitive and affective maps of the child's political world.

This study of the young is an appropriate place to finish this exploration of the ties between the political system and the school and of the political aspects of the schools themselves. It is, after all, what these schools do to the children in shaping these political maps that contributes in some part, to how these children as adults will later interact with their schools in a political fashion. Much other work is currently underway on this and all other subjects upon which previous contributions have touched. Much of it is motivated by the awareness of the increasing politicization of school policy, which for so long has remained very much in the province of the school board member and professional alone. The calls by different constituencies which became numerous and insistent during the 1960s—remove discrimination, equalize educational resources, provide teachers with power to deal with political authorities, protect students from abuses of these authorities, return more direct control over policy services to the hands of parents in the neighborhood—all contribute to an increasingly turbulent political atmosphere in which the polity of the school operates.

16

Political Attitudes among Black Children

Sarah F. Liebschutz * and Richard G. Niemi †

The recent surge of interest in political socialization, resulting in a growing body of empirical research on urban schoolchildren, has concentrated mainly on mapping developmental attitudinal patterns of white children. Recent studies have reported interesting and suggestive contrasts in the developmental patterns of black and white schoolchildren. Yet the studies done so far have been both fragmentary and contradictory, impelling further evidence and interpretation.

Unlike the major study of whites, no study of young blacks has questioned children as early as the second grade. Moreover, previous studies of blacks have typically skipped every other grade in gathering data or have combined two or more grades into one category at the analysis stage. These facts are more important than they might seem to be, since to determine the magnitude, scope, and timing of any possible divergencies, between black and white children complete data are needed. We have thus included second graders in our study and have analyzed data for each grade from second to eighth.

We also attempt to assess the impact of a curriculum in the lower grades which is designed explicitly to promote and strengthen the self-concept of culturally disadvantaged children. Evidence that blacks at the high school level are particularly affected by explicit teaching of civics suggests that blacks are also affected by teaching at the elementary level, particularly under a curriculum designed specifically for them.

In addition, we explore the suggestion that black teachers in positions of authority and as respected goal models heighten the self-respect and self-confidence of the developing young black child.

We obtained the data for this study in a June 1969 survey of 886 second through eighth grade children in selected classes of five schools in the Rochester City School System, New York. Three of the schools are inner-city, largely black, elementary schools; one is an elementary school

---

Reprinted with permission of the publisher from Richard G. Niemi and Associates, *The Politics of Future Citizens* (San Francisco: Jossey-Bass, 1974), chapter 5. See original for footnotes omitted here.

* State University of New York at Brockport

† University of Rochester

bordering the inner city with about equal numbers of black and white children. An inner-city, largely black, high school provides the seventh and eighth grade respondents. During the regular social studies periods questionnaires were circulated. Length of questionnaires vary: the shortest for the second graders and the longest for children in grades five through eight. Each questionnaire took about twenty-five minutes to administer.

The test instruments were administered by black college students, who, we hoped, would cause the children less inhibition in expressing attitudes than if white administrators were used. The questionnaire was developed to allow for direct comparison of data with those obtained in earlier studies of white children. A pretest, however, showed that the questionnaire had to be considerably simplified and shortened for our sample.

To eliminate any cultural distinctiveness that might confuse the comparison of black and white children, we excluded Spanish surname (Puerto Rican) respondents, who comprised 4 percent of the sample. Black children are 76 percent of the sample; the rest are white. Judging by fourth through eighth graders' reports of their father's, stepfather's, or mother's occupation, 52 percent of the sample is of low socioeconomic status (unemployed or unskilled labor), 34 percent is of medium status (skilled labor, clerical, sales); and 14 percent is of high status (professional and managerial).

Attitude Development

White children's orientations toward political authority figures, especially the President and policemen, are relatively well documented. At least until recently, youngsters regarded these political authority figures as benevolent, knowledgeable, powerful, competent, and responsive. The intensity of these idealistic attitudes is modified by the end of elementary school, but the disposition of children still remains highly favorable toward both the President and policemen.

Greenberg, examining levels of support for the President, the policeman, and "the government," suggests that children who have very similar orientations in the lower grades diverge as they grow older. Greenberg's divergence theory, however, is anything but conclusive, and other researchers show no real substantiation for a predictable divergence. While we make no pretense that present data are definitive, we claim a more accurate description of young blacks' nascent political attitudes, because our survey covers the elementary grades more completely than previous surveys and the items are presented separately, which avoids the problem of basing conclusions on one or two figures. While this procedure also opens up the possibility of conflicting, inconclusive patterns, some reasonable conclusions can be drawn. Finally, we draw on questions about the President, policemen, the fairness of laws, and political efficacy (and questions on "the government" to a lesser extent) in order to overcome possible biases due to the particular items chosen.

Our study examines children's evaluation of both personal and role performance attributes of the President and policemen as other studies have done. Ten statements on the questionnaire concern the coercive ability, knowledge, and magnitude of decisions—role performance—and the helpfulness and personal attractiveness—personal qualities—of the President and policemen. The items are as follows: Do you think the policeman (President) can make people do what he wants? Do you think the policeman (President) knows more than most people? Do you think the policeman (President) would want to help you if you needed it? Is the policeman (President) your favorite? The answers are: (1) YES, strongly agree; (2) yes, moderately agree; (3) don't know, no opinion; (4) no, moderately disagree; (5) NO, strongly disagree. Mean responses of the children by race and grade level are presented for each of the ten items in Figure 16-1, *a* through *j*. In calculating the means, don't-know responses were *not* excluded, so that possible scores range from one to five. (Figures 16-1a through 16-1j show only the mean range that applies.) Eliminating the don't-know responses obviously changes the mean scores, but not enough to make a significant difference in the overall patterns. Figure 16-1 shows that even in the early grades blacks often have more negative attitudes than whites do. In the second grade the differences between blacks' and whites' attitudes are about evenly split. Blacks have more slightly positive views of the President in four of the five comparisons, and whites have more positive views of the policeman in the same ratio. By the third grade, where Greenberg found no difference, blacks uniformly have more negative attitudes. This pattern of more negative attitudes by black children is maintained quite consistently throughout the remaining grades. In the next section we note that because of a special curriculum some of the black children had more realistic attitudes than might normally be found among second and third graders. However, the use of only the students not in this curriculum (Figure 4) would leave our conclusion unchanged.

We do not wish to overexaggerate the differences found, especially at the second grade level. If our sample had contained more middle-class whites, whom Hess and Torney found to have more realistic views, blacks' and whites' attitudes may have been similar throughout all the grades. It is significant that black youngsters in second grade seem to view the President even more highly than whites and that their feelings about policemen are so similar to those of whites. But the important point here is that black children begin to develop more negative attitudes at an earlier

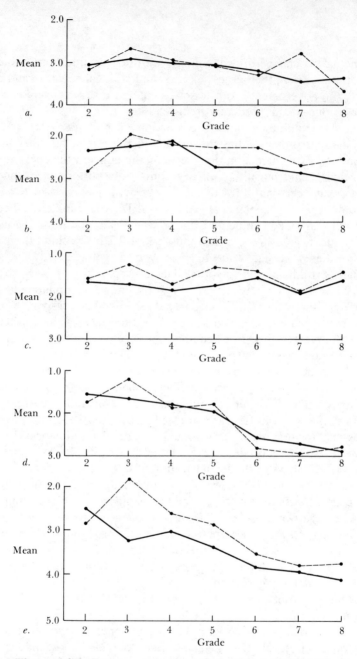

Figure 16-1. Responses to Questions about the President and Policemen. Solid line indicates blacks; dashed line indicates whites. *a*. President's coercive ability. *b*. President's knowledge. *c*. President makes big decisions. *d*. President's helpfulness. *e*. President your favorite. *f*. Policeman's coercive ability. *g*. Policeman's knowledge.

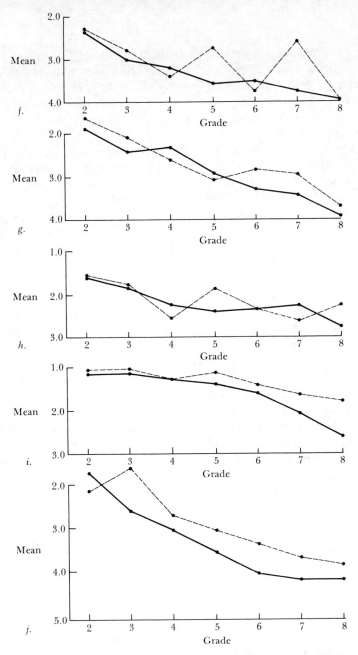

h. Policeman makes big decisions. *i.* Policeman's helpfulness. *j.* Policeman your favorite. Numbers of cases (these vary slightly between graphs because of missing data): blacks—110, 126, 93, 110, 105, 76, 41; whites—23, 21, 25, 23, 22, 13, 35.

age than whites do. Any efforts to build on youngsters' benevolent views must begin very early to be successful with black as well as white children. Conceivably this could be done in imaginative ways (for both blacks and whites) by using children's positive views as a basis for introducing them to notions of participation and governmental responsiveness (and unresponsiveness).

Our findings also indicate that the pattern of attitudes follow roughly parallel rather than divergent courses. There are some fluctuations, especially among whites where there are fewer cases; and there are some "reversals," where blacks have more positive views than whites. The predominant pattern, however, seems to show roughly parallel development. Blacks typically fall below whites on the curves, but not increasingly so. Even allowing for a generous infusion of error into the response curves, only *b, i,* and perhaps *j* of Figure 16-1 suggest divergent paths. Hence we conclude that the basic developmental pattern of black and white attitudes toward policemen and the President is parallel rather than divergent.

Additional corroborating evidence is found in black and white youngsters' views toward laws, the outputs of the political system. Analysis, by race and grade, of responses to the item "all laws are fair" again demonstrates differential, basically parallel, affect by black and white children (see Figure 16-2). Even as early as second grade, young children seem to be aware of the impact of laws on them, and attitudes erode at later grade levels, similarly in both racial groups.

Interestingly, Rochester students, both black and white, less often saw all laws as fair than did the white students in the "Chicago" study. On this question the format in both studies was the same, so that a direct comparison is possible. Since Hess and Torney excluded don't-know responses before calculating mean scores, we did likewise to arrive at the comparison in Table 16-1.

In all grades except third, Rochester whites responded more negatively than did those in the "Chicago" study, and blacks' views were even more negative. The contrast is especially sharp at seventh and eighth grade levels.

The explanation for this contrast is not obvious. Comparison of our figures with those of Hess and Torney indicates that the differences are not due to social class differences. The roughly eight years intervening between the two studies or the fact that the Rochester students are in largely black schools might account for the contrast. In either case, however, children appear to be more sensitive to the outside environment than we have given them credit for. Even in second grade, children's race affects their perceptions of laws. And the pattern of attitude development supports the concept of parallel rather than divergent development.

The development of political efficacy offers a stark contrast to the

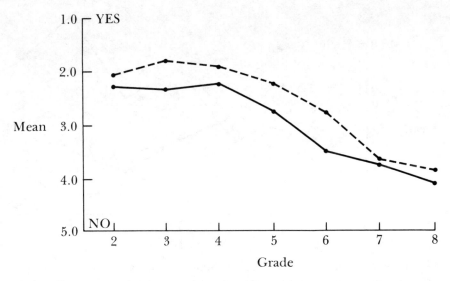

Figure 16-2. Responses to "All Laws Are Fair." Solid line indicates blacks; dashed line indicates whites. Numbers of cases are the same as in Figure 16-1.

preceding results. Our measure of efficacy is a five-item index ranging from one to sixteen: (1) My family doesn't have any say about what the government does; (2) Citizens don't have a chance to say what they think about running the government; (3) What happens in the government will happen no matter what people do. It is like the weather, there is nothing people can do about it; (4) There are some big powerful men in the government who are running the whole thing and they do not care about us ordinary people; and (5) I don't think people in the government care much what people like my family think.

Figure 16-3 shows that the responses to the political efficacy statements

Table 16-1

Comparison of "Chicago" and Rochester Studies

Grades:	2	3	4	5	6	7	8
"Chicago" study	1.40	1.50	1.54	1.76	1.92	2.14	2.38
Rochester whites	1.67	1.41	1.71	1.90	2.28	3.00	3.06
Rochester blacks	1.93	1.92	1.86	2.24	2.89	3.12	3.30

Source of "Chicago" study: Robert D. Hess and Judith V. Torney, *The Development of Political Attitudes in Children* (Chicago: Aldine Publishing Co., 1967), p. 53.

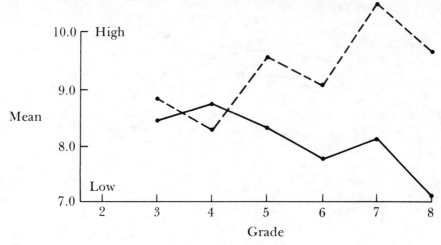

Figure 16-3. Political Efficacy Scale. Solid line indicates blacks; dashed line indicates whites. Numbers of cases are the same as in Figure 16-1.

offer an instance in which a divergent model seems appropriate. (Efficacy questions were not asked of second graders.) In the third and fourth grades black and white children are not clearly different, but from fifth grade on, blacks become increasingly less efficacious than whites. Blacks, it would seem, become especially aware of the difficulties they will encounter in altering the political world, even though their views of the benevolence of political authority decline no faster than those of whites.

As one last comparison between blacks and whites we calculated mean responses on "the government's" knowledge, making of big decisions, helpfulness, and fallibility. (This was done only for fifth through eighth graders.) This set of items resulted in unstable results. If this were true only for whites, whose numbers are small, we could perhaps attribute it to sampling error, but the response instability is just as characteristic of the blacks' answers. We do not know why such fluctuations occurred so differently from the patterns found in the "Chicago" study. But we must conclude that these data lend little support to either a parallel or a divergent development model.

Overall, then, our data for the President, the policeman, and the fairness of laws support a model in which differences between blacks' and whites' attitudes appear early and develop in more or less parallel fashion. Political efficacy follows a divergent path, with whites becoming increasingly convinced that they can be influential in politics and blacks increasingly convinced of the opposite. Attitudes for the government seem to be in a state of flux for both races.

Thus, rather than supporting a single model of attitude development, our results suggest that models differ according to the types of clusters of ideas, with the parallel model being most appropriate for the trend toward realism in children's views of political authority figures. It is important that only in children's feelings of political efficacy does a divergent model adequately describe the results. The importance of this finding may be not that blacks view political authority as less benevolent than whites—for these views develop in concert with, if to a stronger degree, than those of whites—but that blacks increasingly see the government as unresponsive to them. Perhaps this trend can be reversed by increasing opportunities for political participation by blacks and, at a programatic level, perhaps by increasing efforts to show both black and white youths how to effectively take part in the political world.

Curriculum Effect

We now direct our attention to the possible effects on student attitudes of a specially designed curriculum for the early grades. Such an analysis seems appropriate to test whether blacks may be particularly affected by school material and whether a new curriculum designed for the very early grades might alter young children's views before they became firmly fixed. Our discovery of differences as early as the second grade cautions us that reality may already have been fully enough grasped that the curriculum could not completely erase the black children's trend toward negative feelings.

The focus of our attention is a curriculum known as "Project Beacon," a program directed toward improvement of the self-concept of disadvantaged children in their regular classrooms. While the ultimate goal of Project Beacon is to upgrade academic achievement in the primary grades of elementary school, its focus on improving the concept of self would seem to have implications for children's attitudes toward the political system. We compare the relative political efficacy scores and attitudes toward political authority figures and laws of those who have participated in Project Beacon and those who have not.

Project Beacon was developed by a team of guidance, curriculum, and teaching personnel of the Rochester City School District in response to a 1961 directive from the New York State Education Department to "demonstrate practical solutions to the problems of educating [culturally] disadvantaged pupils." Since 1964, Project Beacon has operated with pupils in kindergarten through grade three of five elementary schools that are located in low-income, low-middle-income, largely black, inner-city neighborhoods of Rochester. Project Beacon attempts to improve the self-concept of children from these areas by utilizing such techniques as photography, tape-recording, role-playing; by visiting parents and inviting them to volunteer to participate in the classroom, by emphasizing black historical and cultural materials; and by holding teacher orientation and sensitivity workshops.

While we did not directly measure levels of self-esteem among our respondents, an independent study confirmed the effectiveness of this curriculum in improving self-concept. That study, conducted during the same period as ours and including the same children from which our Beacon sample was drawn, reported that fourth graders who had been in Project Beacon from kindergarten through third grade scored higher on the California Test of Personality and exhibited more positive social and work habits than a matched sample of children who did not participate in Project Beacon. The California Test of Personality consists of self-adjustment (feelings of personal security) and social adjustment (feeling of social security) components.

Since the concept of the self (usually called *personal efficacy* or *effectiveness* in political science literature) has been shown to relate to political efficacy and some aspects of political participation, we have a unique opportunity to see whether a concerted effort to upgrade the black child's conception of the self also has effects on his developing political views. Although our initial concern is with second and third grade black students in Project Beacon and others in their schools who are not in Project Beacon, we also include students who were in Project Beacon classes during kindergarten through third grade but are now in a later year in school, comparing them with students in their grades who did not participate in Project Beacon. These students give us a chance to make an initial judgment on whether the effects of Project Beacon are temporary or more long lasting.

We begin by looking at the same personal and role performance attributes of the President and policemen that we considered earlier. Figure 16-4, *a* through *j,* graphically depict the mean responses for present and past Project Beacon blacks and those not in Project Beacon. Looking initially at the second graders, we find that mean responses of Project Beacon children are more negative for eight of the ten items than those of their counterparts who are or were not in Project Beacon. In several instances the differences are fairly large, indicating that Project Beacon children are considerably less idealistic about these two political authority figures. Their assessments of role performance characteristics are particularly noteworthy, as the Project Beacon second graders ascribe substantially less coercive ability and knowledge to the policeman than other second graders do. In addition both personal characteristics of the policeman are judged less favorably, suggesting that young Project Beacon students more accurately reflect the generally negative attitudes of black adults toward local law authorities.

For third graders, our analysis again suggests that the Project Beacon curriculum tempers idealism toward authority figures. For four of the five items regarding each the policeman and the President, Project Beacon children's mean responses are more reflective of adult attitudes than those of the other third graders. Again, the more realistic responses are concentrated on role performance characteristics. (Here we note as a more realistic attitude the attribution of greater decision-making prowess to the President, a trend also found in the "Chicago" study.) In addition, the third-grade Project Beacon child sees both the President and the policeman as having less coercive power and less knowledge.

The students' judgment of the fairness of laws is shown in Figure 16-5. The greater realism toward political authority figures among second and third grade Project Beacon students is also evident in their responses to this item. Among children at both grade levels, more negative perceptions are made by black Project Beacon youngsters, than by the others, about the fairness of laws.

Greater realism by Project Beacon students concerning political authority figures and laws may well derive from a more positive concept of the self. The political efficacy scores of Project Beacon children also seem to support this relationship. As seen in Figure 16-6, the mean efficacy scores for Project Beacon third graders are higher than for third graders without the special curriculum.

An examination of responses by third graders to the individual items on the efficacy scale indicates that those items which seem to tap a sense of internal self-confidence (whether family or citizens have a say in government) elicit higher mean scores from the Project Beacon children, while those which tap a sense of confidence in external response (what the government will do for people) elicit lower means scores, in comparison with third graders not in Project Beacon. Hence, political efficacy, especially in the dimension relating to internal control, does appear to be related to personal efficacy. Moreover these findings of lower levels of confidence in the responses of authority figures would seem to be consistent with our earlier findings of less idealism among Project Beacon children.

Overall then, our examination of political efficacy, as well as the analysis of attitudes, supports the proposition that curriculum can affect the socialization of minority group elementary schoolchildren's attitudes toward authority. In Project Beacon, an upgrading of the black child's self-concept appears to result in less idealism toward political figures and laws, coupled with an increased sense of self-confidence as a citizen. In the

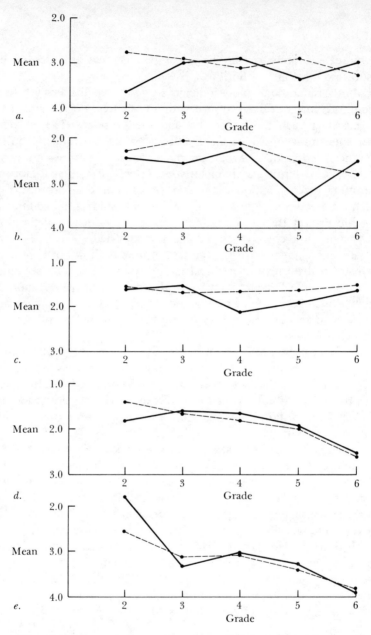

Figure 16-4. Responses to Questions about the President and Policemen. Solid line indicates those in Project Beacon; dashed line indicates those not in Project Beacon. *a.* President's coercive ability. *b.* President's knowledge. *c.* President makes big decisions. *d.* President's helpfulness. *e.* President your favorite. *f.* Policeman's coercive ability. *g.* Policeman's knowledge. *h.* Policeman makes big decisions. *i.* Policeman's

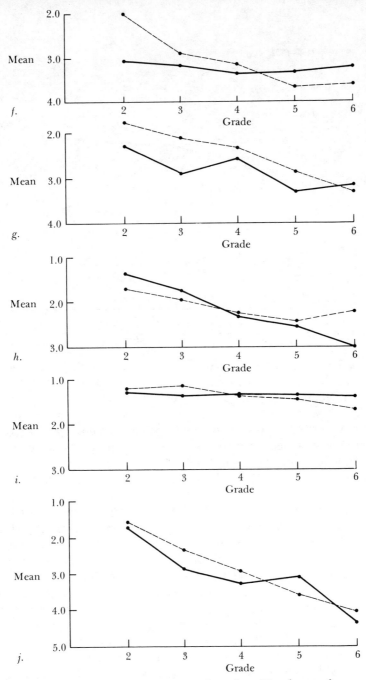

helpfulness. *j.* Policeman your favorite. Numbers of cases (these vary slightly between graphs because of missing data): Project Beacon children—36, 50, 26, 26, 20; children not in Project Beacon—74, 76, 67, 84, 85.

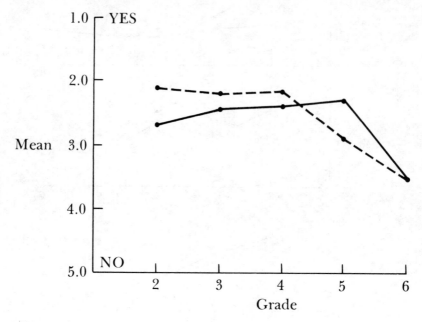

Figure 16-5. Responses to "All Laws Are Fair." Solid line indicates those in Project Beacon; dashed line indicates those not in Project Beacon. Numbers of cases are the same as in Figure 16-4.

broader context of relative socialization patterns of black and white children, it appears that Project Beacon intensifies the negative trend of the parallel model with respect to political authority figures but retards or diminishes it with regard to the internal control dimension of political efficacy.

We now consider whether these effects of Project Beacon last beyond direct exposure to the curriculum. To do this, we examine the attitudes of black fourth, fifth, and sixth grade respondents who were in Project Beacon classes during kindergarten through third grade, in comparison with those who were not. Figure 16-4 shows that Project Beacon fourth graders express diminishing realism toward political authority figures. In only one instance (*h*) do former Project Beacon students become more realistic than other students, whereas they become less realistic in four cases (*a, c, e, i*). Where they remain more realistic than students who have not been in Project Beacon, the differences are reduced (*b, g, j.*) In the remaining cases, as well as in perceptions of laws (Figure 16-5), no change is observed in which group is more realistic.

The attitudes of former Project Beacon fifth and sixth graders, in comparison with their peers, seem to reinforce the trend in attitudes toward political authority and laws which we notice starting with fourth graders.

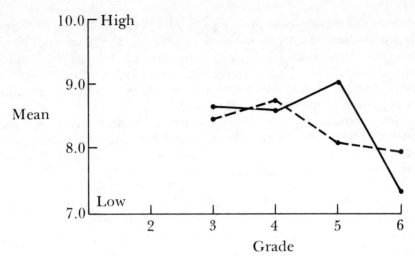

Figure 16-6. Political Efficacy Scale. Solid line indicates those in Project Beacon; dashed line indicates those not in Project Beacon. Numbers of cases are the same as in Figure 16-4.

Fourth grade appears to mark the beginning of a reversal in the trend toward realism by Project Beacon students. At the fourth grade level former Project Beacon students were more realistic on exactly half of the ten items about authority figures (*b, f, g, h, j*), as well as in their view of laws. Among fifth grade respondents we observe more realistic attitudes among former Project Beacon students on only four of the eleven items, counting the laws (*a, b, g, h*). By sixth grade this tendency is strengthened, as former Project Beacon students are more realistic on only three items (*e, h, j*).

The responses of sixth grade former Project Beacon children toward the policeman are particularly interesting, for they indicate that while the policeman is not regarded as a personal favorite of the child, his coercive ability and his knowledge are regarded with respect. These attitudes toward the policeman stand in sharp contrast to those of the other fifth and sixth graders and of black children in later grades. Since we do not have data to examine the effects of Project Beacon beyond the sixth grade, we cannot project with confidence whether positive attitudes would continue to grow toward political authority figures among former Project Beacon students.

Our data on political efficacy of fourth through sixth graders (Figure 16-6) makes us cautious about assuming that Project Beacon has long-term effects on political attitudes. The political efficacy levels of former Project Beacon students are lower at fourth and sixth grade than those of students not previously in the program. And although fifth grade former Project Beacon students show a high political efficacy score, both of the items that tap internal confidence are lower both for fifth and sixth graders who were in Project Beacon. Hence, the goal of improved self-concept of the disadvantaged child does not seem to have a consistent long-term effect of engendering improved political efficacy.

Direct exposure to the Project Beacon curriculum seems to induce realism about political authority figures and laws and a heightened sense of political efficacy among children. But almost immediately afterward, the realities of being a black citizen in a political system dominated by whites seem to impair the sense of political effectiveness found among children during their direct participation in the curriculum. On the other hand, as efficacy declines, idealism about authority figures increases. We return to these seemingly conflicting developments—that as idealism increases efficacy declines, and vice versa—in the conclusion.

Effect of Teacher's Race

The teacher's race might be expected to cause children to be more, or less, realistic and politically efficacious. Black teachers' attitudes might be more realistic or cynical than white teachers' attitudes. (Our sample of black teachers suggests this is so, although our data is not complete enough to be conclusive.) Thus to the extent that teachers' attitudes are expressed in class and influence students' views, it seems likely that children with black teachers would have more realistic attitudes than children in the same grade but with white teachers.

In addition to expressed attitudes, the race of the teacher may have an impact in terms of example. It may be important for young black children to have black teachers (as well as adults in other capacities) to serve as examples of goals to which they can aspire. The black child's self-esteem or ego strength may then increase, and spill over into political attitudes, increasing political efficacy in particular.

To test this hypothesis, we made comparisons between 122 black children with six black teachers versus 403 black students with twenty-one white teachers in the second, third, fourth, sixth, and seventh grades. The remaining grades have no black teachers. The results (not shown) indicate no consistent pattern throughout all the grades. In grades two through four, children with black teachers have, if anything, more naive or benevolent attitudes toward political authority figures and about laws than do students with white teachers. These attitudes shift somewhere between fourth and sixth grades, and by the sixth and seventh grades, children with black teachers are somewhat more realistic; but even then the difference is not very large. Thus, having a black teacher in the early grades does not in itself alter the typically benevolent views of young children. By sixth grade, the significance of the teacher's race may be beginning to make itself felt, but if so, it is only a weak tendency in our data.

Political efficacy levels differ from attitude development only to the extent that the teacher's race may have an impact slightly earlier. Third graders with black teachers were more efficacious—by a wide margin— than those with white teachers. But the decline of efficacy is particularly steep among subsequent grades with black teachers; fourth, sixth, and seventh graders with black teachers have consistently lower levels of efficacy than those with white teachers.

Overall, it seems as if the teacher's race is not an important factor in the development of political attitudes in the earliest grades. The instructor's race may be critical in other respects and may help determine political attitudes in later grades. But in the elementary school years, and especially the early grades, the race of the teacher seems not to detract from the relatively benign views of authority figures, of laws, and of the efficacy of political activity.

Conclusion

Perhaps the most important finding of our study is that the Project Beacon curriculum affects black students' feelings of political efficacy—but only while they are in these special classes. This suggests that specially designed long-term curricula, coupled with real changes in the political system allowing for and encouraging greater participation by blacks, might create more positive feelings of effectiveness on the part of minority group children. This suggestion supports the recommendation of long-term programs in an evaluation of the Head Start program which concluded that short-term projects—especially summer programs—had no lasting effects on children.

But Project Beacon did not create artificially benign, naive views of authority in children—they saw authority more realistically and perceived more accurately the frequent unfairness of laws. Ironically, then, our results suggest that a curriculum can have a noteworthy effect on minority group children but that it does so by instilling in them a more realistic, and not necessarily more positive, appraisal of the American political system. We conclude that those who best understand the nature of the American political system can most effectively participate in altering it.

About the Editor

Frederick M. Wirt has combined scholarship and consultation in the study of school politics, particularly desegregation. He is a Rand Corporation consultant on desegregation and Professor of Political Science at the University of Illinois at Champaign-Urbana. He has also been director of the Institute for Desegregation Problems at the University of California, Berkeley, and director of the Policy Sciences graduate program at the University of Maryland, Baltimore County. Professor Wirt's writings on school politics include: *Politics of Southern Equality; Power in the City;* and (with coauthors) *Northern School Desegregation* and *The Political Web of American Schools*. He is also the author of "State Politics of Education" in Herbert Jacob and Kenneth Vines, eds., *Politics in the American States* (3d ed.) and a coauthor of *On the City's Rim*. Professor Wirt is the general editor of the Lexington Books Politics of Education Series.